THE BROKEN STAFF

THE
BROKEN STAFF

Judaism through
Christian Eyes

FRANK E. MANUEL

HARVARD UNIVERSITY PRESS
Cambridge, Massachusetts
London, England   1992

24319988
DLC

12-23-92

Library of Congress Cataloging-in-Publication Data
Manuel, Frank Edward.
The broken staff : Judaism through Christian eyes / Frank E. Manuel.
p. cm.
Includes bibliographical references and index.
ISBN 0-674-08370-9 (alk. paper)
1. Judaism (Christian theology)—History of doctrines.
2. Judaism—Relations—Christianity. 3. Christianity and other
religions—Judaism. 4. Hebraists, Christian. I. Title.
BT93.M35 1992
261.2'6'094—dc20

91-28520
CIP

Preface

READERS ACQUAINTED with my other histories might well ask: "Is Saul also among the prophets?" But unrepentant secularist though I am, as I reflect on my past I discern an enduring preoccupation with what William James called the religious propensity of mankind. Whether I was writing on utopian thought in the western world, theories of mythology, shapes of philosophical history, the faith of scientific men of genius, my inquiries always bordered on the many guises and disguises of the religious predicament. In preparing the present work I have drawn into an uneasy relationship my knowledge of the intellectual experience of Western Christendom and the Hebraic studies of my youth.

Parts of this book have been presented orally and in radically different form at the Folger Library in Washington, New York University (the Schweitzer and Leo Gershoy Lectures), Harvard University (a Center for Jewish Studies symposium on the seventeenth century), Tel Aviv University, a Brandeis University faculty seminar in the History of Ideas, and the 1676th Stated Meeting of the American Academy of Arts and Sciences. The address delivered at the Academy was printed in its *Bulletin,* April 1987. An article entitled "Israel in the Enlightenment" appeared in the Winter 1982 issue of *Daedalus.*

For the period since the invention of printing, the collection of Judaica in the Houghton Library, Harvard University, for which a chronological index has been printed (delivering me from the temptation to commit bibliographic redundancy), was my basic resource. The typescript catalogue of the Lee M. Friedman Collection in

Houghton was a point of departure, and this book owes much to that indefatigable gatherer of Christian publications on all aspects of Judaism. In King William III's gift of books to King's Chapel, incorporated into the collection of the Boston Athenaeum, a number of rarities related to my subject have turned up. The Athenaeum has been my working library for more than forty years, and I have come to consider the members of its staff my friends. I first crossed the threshold of Harvard's Widener in 1926; the Andover-Harvard Theological Library is a more recently acquired taste.

I am grateful to the friends and colleagues who have been generous with advice and assistance. Over the years Mordechai Feingold discussed with me many phases of this book, Benjamin Ravid coated his criticisms with wit, Seymour Slive reviewed my selection of illustrations. My former student Gregg Stern kept a vigilant eye out for new literature and saved me from grievous errors of transliteration from Hebrew and Aramaic. Lastly I thank my wife, Fritzie, who, not hampered by false modesty, readily admits that her services have been invaluable.

Frank E. Manuel
Boston

Contents

THE BROKEN STAFF

1

A Gateway to the
City of Books

In his *Pugio fidei adversus mauros et judaeos* (Dagger of the Faith against Moors and Jews; 1278), the Catalan friar Raimundo Martini quoted a reflection he ascribed to Seneca: no plague can be more noxious than an enemy in the household. Martini then drew the analogy further to sustain his mission of conversion: "No enemy of the Christian faith is closer and more unavoidable to us than a Jew." [1] If Martini's dictum were made reciprocal, it could serve as a telling summation of the tragic relationship between Christianity and Judaism. Though Ernest Renan used the term Judeo-Christian to define a sect in the early Church, and the Oxford don Mark Pattison wrote of a Judaico-Christian anthropology, not until the twentieth century did the phrase Judeo-Christian tradition appear with any frequency, and only after World War II did it become popular. Lest we immerse ourselves in ecumenical platitudes, we should reexamine the long history of the spiritual striving of Christianity with its Judaic genetrix. If there exists a cure for Judeophobia, the age-old malady of Christendom, it lies not in the suppression of symptoms but in their exposure to the light.

The history of Christendom's rediscovery of Judaism after an interval of a thousand years, which has continued from the Renaissance down to our own time, was long left in a sort of limbo, neglected by both Christians and Jews. The account of persecutions and the faltering movement toward legal emancipation once served as the major cohesive elements in shaping the chronicle that an early sixteenth-century Jewish historian, Joseph ha-Cohen, called the Vale of Tears. The explosion of Jewish studies in recent decades has allowed for the emergence of a variety of new perspectives. My essay moves away from the traditional history of antisemitism, a narration of the victims' sufferings, to explore a more bookish subject: how triumphant Christendom grappled with the religious and intellectual creations of the Judaism that survived in its midst. Western Christendom, though prolific in the outpouring of diatribes with the generic title *Adversus Judaeos,* never carved out a set of immutable guidelines for its confrontation with Judaism. Should the works in which Judaic beliefs were embodied be burned? Should they be ignored? Should they be tolerated and even consulted for what was to be learned from them? Authoritative Christian opinions emanating from the Church Fathers, popes, and reformers flagrantly contradicted one another. And Christian practice rarely jibed with the thunderous rhetoric of formal doctrinal pronouncements.

This essay deals primarily with the higher culture of Western Christendom—Kiryat Sefer, city of books—as it wrestled with Judaism. Though ideas from folklore and popular superstition, defying the law of gravity, trickled upward into the world of booklearning and colored the most recondite works of Christian theology, political theory, and philology, I make no attempt to reconstruct systematically the judgment and conduct of the great mass of Christian believers. Their simple faith and deeply ingrained hatreds can be recorded, but Judaic learning was beyond their ken. To this day most Christians and most Jews know little about elementary tenets of the others' religion.

Periodization in the history of ideas allows for substantial overlapping of epochs, permitting the emergence of forerunners and the survival of residues long after the main current has been abandoned. The chapters of this book form a chronological continuum from the latter half of the fifteenth century to the present, though there will be occasion for allusion to earlier epochs. There are segments that reveal a dialectical relationship to each other: the Enlightenment denies and contradicts many of the assumptions about Judaism that were broadly accepted north of the Pyrenees in the sixteenth and seventeenth centuries. At this very moment, major Christian denominations and minor sects are engrossed in the problem of finding a plausible redefinition of the theological relations of Christianity and Judaism. The crimes of the Holocaust have marked the question with an urgency hitherto unknown: previous formulas are no longer acceptable either to Christians or to Jews. If my historical reflections contribute to an understanding of the complexities inherent in the ongoing deliberations, this book will have achieved its purpose.

During the Renaissance, literate European Christians, whether or not they ever laid eyes upon a Jew, had strong emotive reactions to Judaism. For any reader of the New Testament, the initial response was revulsion. Matthew (King James version, 27:22–25) had set forth the crime of deicide, in four verses:

> Pilate saith unto them, What shall I do then with Jesus which is called Christ? They all say unto him, Let him be crucified.
>
> And the governor said, Why, what evil hath he done? But they cried out the more, saying, Let him be crucified.
>
> When Pilate saw that he could prevail nothing, but that rather a tumult was made, he took water, and washed his hands before the multitude, saying, I am innocent of the blood of this just person: see ye to it.
>
> Then answered all the people, and said, His blood be on us, and on our children.

In their administrative capacity, European religious and secular authorities enforced laws relating to Jews before their uprooting from most countries of Western Europe in the late Middle Ages, and subsequently, in the sixteenth, seventeenth, and eighteenth centuries, monitored their conduct in the isolated enclaves where Jews came to enjoy special privileges or had slowly infiltrated Christian society without express legal permission. But Judaism was a living presence in the west even where there were no Jews. A flow of books in Hebrew and Aramaic, especially after the invention of printing, was a constant challenge and affront to Christianity. Jewish ideas were bogies that haunted Europe; or, conversely, the same ideas could be adapted as instruments for the instruction of Christians in both civil and religious affairs, though the rabbinic masters might be invisible and the precepts disembodied.

Since the Renaissance, Christian European culture has been omnivorous in the assimilation of alien concepts. In the resurrection of the pagan Greeks and Romans, Christianity adorned itself with dangerous garments, like the cloak Medea wove for Jason's bride. The acquisition of a knowledge of rabbinic Judaism by Christian scholars was no less hazardous, for the followers of the Mosaic law, in Christian eyes direct descendants of the Pharisees, continued to proclaim that Christians worshiped a false God and that the true messiah was yet to come. The mutual antagonism of two prophetic religions occupying the same living space has been attenuated in modern times only since both religions have been reduced to the status of cults tolerating each other as the ancient Greeks and Romans had tolerated the foreign gods in their midst. This is the world in which we live.

From 1480 to the early part of the eighteenth century, a few thousand Europeans outside Spain—members of the clergy and professors in universities—were preoccupied with Hebraic studies in order to strengthen Christianity and become better Christians. They were joined by gentlemen-scholars and a reading public of unknown proportions. With the Enlightenment, the English deists and the radical French philosophes embarked on further researches into Judaism, albeit on a superficial level, but their object was the reverse: to undermine traditional Christianity in all of its sectarian forms. In the Renaissance, the study of the other two cultures of antiquity, the Greek and the Roman, had been preempted for the arsenal of political apologists; yet despite this common usage, there were humanists who made efforts at purely scholarly recovery of ancient texts. By contrast, in the heyday of Christian Hebraism there was little interest in acquiring a knowledge of ancient or rabbinic Judaism for its own sake, as the Renaissance scholar Politian might have investigated a classical author. Before the nineteenth century, objective historical study of Judaism rarely existed in Christendom. Neither Christian Hebraists nor later anti-Christian Christian Hebraists could divorce themselves from the gnawing religious concerns, apologetic or atheistic, that dominated their lives. The umbilical cord that bound Christianity to Judaism was not severed by the legal emancipation of the Jews ushered in by the French Revolution and the formal proclamation of a secular society. Judaism remained alien and threatening in a Christian world even after the widespread acceptance of modern materialism in its many shapes.

The countries of Western Europe and the Americas, each the habitat of a different religious admixture, have been nominally united by a common label that still has some meaning, Christendom. But for a nuanced portrayal of the spiritual relations between church and synagogue during the past five centuries, the doctrinal map has to be subdivided into the denominations and sects that have multiplied profusely since the Reformation, a Babel-like confusion of religious tongues. Though a Christian group might retain the same name for a time, the content of its dogmas and its spirit have been in a constant state of flux. Since the existence of a homogeneous universe of religious discourse in Christianity has become highly questionable, individuation, at least by major denominations, is a prerequisite for an understanding of the Christian judgment of Judaism. The Iberian Catholicism that inspired the celebration of autos-da-fé well into the eighteenth century may have ritual similarities to the Catholicism of the Abbé Grégoire or the Abbé Bergier, who defended Judaism on the eve of the French Revolution, but the contrast in temper is so glaring that the rubric "Catholicism" is hardly an adequate canopy. In knowledge and appreciation of Judaism, there have been only limited conformities among the Protestants—Calvinists, Lutherans, Anglicans, Puritans, Remonstrants, Mennonites, Moravian Brethren, Quakers, Socinians, Methodists, to pass over the two hundred fly-by-night sects that sprouted for a moment and then withered during the English Civil War. The bitter controversies between orthodox Calvinists and Arminians, or Jesuits and Jansenists, were extended to their judgments of Jewish beliefs and rituals. The libertines, deists, free-thinkers, and atheists among the educated classes of the Continent who ventured to speak out in small but increasing numbers cannot be omitted from consideration, for they were all born within the precincts of specific Christian establishments in particular countries, and their apostasy bears the stamp of their national and sectarian origins.

Complications of another order arise when a sect undergoing a transformation—for example, Lutheran orthodoxy when it was swept by the seventeenth-century pietist movement—clings to the mighty verbiage of the old views. The hatred of Jews that Luther instilled into his denomination may have been modified, tempered, but it was not eradicated. Similarly, expressions of Puritan sympathy for Judaism and Jews have at times persuaded historians to ignore the negative theological context within which flattering millenarian prophecies about the calling of the Jews were uttered. Families or clusters of ideas about Judaism, which were formed by the various post-Reformation sects, can be examined with profit and characterized, when they are not ascribed too rigidly to any individual writer; and middle-level generalities about the changes in Christian judgments can be sustained if they are not conceived as straitjackets. The line between full tolerance and mere forbearance of Judaism is difficult to draw; the fuzziness is dictated by the subject. Sectarian divisions turn out to be the most manageable categories of discourse, though national idiosyncrasies intrude to break up the ground plan.

The coverall "Judaism," a term already in use in medieval English and French, is only slightly less fluid than the concept "Christendom." Most Christian sects, with an ahistorical presumption, viewed Judaism as frozen into one mold for all time. For them the religion of ancient Israel was a uniform order of institutions and beliefs enduring unchanged up to modern times. (Rabbinic Jews of course were painfully conscious that, with the destruction of the Temple, the large body of sacrificial law was rendered inoperative.) After the initial Renaissance rediscovery of Judaism, a small minority of learned Christians distinguished among the epochs of Jewish thought and recognized that it had undergone many transformations in its long history. A Christian sect might concentrate on one phase of Judaism, even idealize it, while rejecting vehemently its other expressions. Mosaic law, prophecy, successive ages of rabbinism, the Cabbala, experienced different fortunes in Christendom, each evoking distinctive responses when they were identified as separate entities.

Learned Christians had some awareness that innovations had crept in as one generation of rabbis was succeeded by another in the seminaries of Palestine and Babylon and in subsequent epochs of the diaspora. To explain apparent modifications, Jews often presumed that the ideas and convictions of a later generation of authorities were by definition implicit in the words of an earlier one. This was the more readily understandable to Christian theologians and scholars because it was consonant with the doctrine of types that bound the New and the Old Testaments together. The rule that the posterior opinion cannot contradict the anterior lies close to the heart of the world view of all scriptural religions and the legal systems they have generated, and techniques of exegesis that allow opinions to change in fact but not in theory have been fundamental to both orthodox Christianity and Judaism.

Judaism has been a theological problem among the clergy and

scholars of Christendom for almost two thousand years. Before it became a universal religion, the gospel of Jesus was preached to the inhabitants of Judaea, and the Romans mocked as Rex Judaeorum the man whom they crucified. While Christians were achieving a separate identity as a religious communion with a law and ritual of their own, they were themselves often confounded with Jews in the eyes of the Roman emperors. The nature of the break with the law of Moses has remained hazy over the centuries. In the beginning, attempts of institutional Christianity to distance itself from the Mosaic law gave rise to a rigid codification of Christian doctrine; deviants who retained Judaic ties were denounced as heretics and were vigorously persecuted by the early Church. From the very inception of the Christian era, the connections of the first to the second dispensation have been ambiguous. Clearly the teachings of Christ superseded the Judaic law of the Old Testament and the rabbis and Pharisees mentioned in the New Testament; but it took many centuries to arrive at even a vague description of the intricacies of the residual bond, and the nature of the supersession has never been agreed upon by all Christians. Metaphors—kin, genetrix, elder brothers—have failed to clarify the relationship.

Jewish thought as it appeared to Christians who dealt with it from the Renaissance onward was embodied in an increasing number of printed works and manuscripts, of whose existence they had been unaware for centuries. Christians collected Hebrew and Aramaic texts from all ages, translated them, fought with them as if their ancient authors were living antagonists. Discovery of the true meaning of the Scriptures remained the basic substance of Christian scholarship; but for the learned members of most denominations, whether or not to have recourse to rabbinic interpretations was a grave religious decision, since an excess of "rabbinage" bordered on heresy.

With time, the divergent views of Judaism among Christians were related to many uses of the Hebraic corpus other than biblical exegesis. Christians appealed to Jewish books to justify themselves, their political order, their rituals, and their church organization. They acquired a knowledge of Judaism to better understand their own doctrines and beliefs. At the same time, the more suspicious Christians called to witness hostile Jewish commentaries to raise the specter of a growing Jewish danger to their polity, for these writings were revelations of the malign intentions of the enemy in their midst. Finally, Christians combed the Old Testament and Jewish treatises of all epochs in order to search out arguments that might lead to the conversion of the Jews, the traditional and manifest reason for consorting with heretical Jewish authors and being exposed to the hazards of religious contagion; evidence of the truth of Christianity in Jewish sources was presumed to be especially cogent and persuasive.

The seventeenth and eighteenth centuries were a transitional period for the Jews of Western Europe. Their isolated communities were beginning to be noticed again in Christian states and principalities, but the tangle of religious and legal restrictions that enveloped Judaism had not yet been swept away by the French Revolution. Critical Christian writings about the nature of Judaism are usually associated with dramatic changes in the political, cultural, and economic life of the west that affected in a concrete manner Christian perceptions. The discovery of the New World, the expulsion of the Jews from the Iberian peninsula, the liberation of the Dutch republic, the Thirty Years' War in Germany, the English Civil War, the revocation of the Edict of Nantes, the introduction of the Jew Bill in England, the American Revolution, the triumph of the encyclopedists in France, were political events that profoundly altered Christian attitudes. Judgments of Judaism refashioned during the centuries before the French Revolution had a remarkable tenacity. Their power outlasted new juridical forms and state systems introduced in the nineteenth century, and it has not been wholly dissipated even in our own time.

Images of Judaism cannot be wholly divorced from Christian practice in dealing with Jews in the marketplace. Through the manifold intellectual endeavors of Christians there coursed the turbid waters of ambivalence that had colored Christian relations with Judaism since the days of the Apostles. As Jews became more prominent in tolerated settlements in the west, political and economic questions dwarfed some of the religious concerns, but as a rule they reinforced each other. Still, Christendom's preoccupation with Jewish thought of all ages became far more intense during the seventeenth and eighteenth centuries than the existence of fewer than a million Jews in the world can explain. The number of Jews in Europe outside Poland and the Turkish Empire barely reached half a million, and this small population could not account for the production of thousands of volumes by Christians on Hebraic subjects in Latin and vernacular languages in the early centuries of modern history.

Jewish historiography has sometimes reduced Christian views of Judaism to a few formulas and pigeonholed them with anachronistic abandon as either philosemitic or antisemitic. It is an easy way to debarrass oneself of theological niceties, but the consequence is banal history. Only if one takes cognizance of the Christian worlds in all their different hues and focuses on the question of Jewish thought as something at once strange and very close to Christendom, can relationships emerge in their authentic multiplicity. The variant views of Judaism among the numerous Christian sects and denominations must banish the image of a simple confrontation between church and synagogue. In the seventeenth and eighteenth centuries, the ecclesiastical physiognomy of Christian Europe was stamped with new patterns of complexity; dynastic conflicts became more intricate; and Jews' responses to their own sectarian divisions and to the Christian world around them were often disoriented.

In any effort to appreciate the works of Christian Hebraists, the designations "philosemitism" and "antisemitism" quickly betray their hollowness. Individual writers, with some exceptions, harbor contradictory motives. In a few instances the flagrant antipathy toward Judaism is so violent that it assumes phobic proportions: the rage of Martin Luther in his late works, the dogged accumulation of blood-guilt accusations in Johann Andreas Eisenmenger's *Judaism Uncovered,* the gory fantasies of Voltaire in his perverse exegesis of Old Testament texts. Conversely, there are forthright advocacies of toleration for Judaism in the plays of Gotthold Ephraim Lessing, in the reasoned brief of Christian Wilhelm Dohm on civil disabilities, in the obiter dicta of seventeenth-century scholars like John Selden, and in Isaac Newton's theological manuscripts. But the vast majority of Christian Hebraists and theologians of all sects fall somewhere in between, and their pronouncements are mixed. There was always uneasiness with the Jewish presence. Emotional outbursts against Judaism can be followed in a few pages by appreciations of the rabbinic interpretations of Scripture by Maimonides and Abraham Ibn Ezra. There is something absurd in the spectacle of the Buxtorfs of Basel, whose

Hebraic and Aramaic studies won them world renown, incorporating into their commentaries on the Talmud and the Midrash derisive caricatures of the very works they were interpreting for Christian readers.

The avowed purpose of a Christian writer was often set forth in a dedicatory epistle to his patron. But such formal declarations by no means exhaust the reasons for devoting years of arduous labor to studies less rewarding than Greek and Latin scholarship. Though Christian Hebraists got into trouble for their daring hypotheses on the nature of the Old Testament, there were no Brunos among them (with the possible exception of Michael Servetus in Calvin's Geneva); only Père Richard Simon, the Oratorian of the turn of the seventeenth century who was pursued by Bossuet, could qualify as a quasi-martyr to Hebraic learning. Extravagant conjectures on the nature of the Old Testament were often followed by retractions, such as Isaac de La Peyrère's repudiation of his *Prae-Adamitae* (1655), but Christian Hebraism had no Galileo. By the second half of the eighteenth century, the Oxford professor Robert Lowth's treatment of the Old Testament as Hebrew poetry, without any statement of the theological implications of his views, won him not only wide fame in Europe but the bishopric of London.

A distinction should be drawn between a Christian evaluation of Judaism informed by an authentic knowledge of rabbinic and philosophical texts in which Judaism in its multifarious transformations found expression, and a summary Christian verdict on Judaism delivered ex cathedra in a work with a blatantly polemical bite. The history of Judaic learning among the literate classes and exemplary individuals is intricate enough, but it does not necessarily run parallel with the rendering of Christian judgments. The characterization of these judgments inevitably leads to the question of the intellectual equipment of the judges, particularly to identifying the original Hebraic sources at the disposal of a Christian authority at any given time. The final opinions when formulated in books are traceable and have a history—there is a continuity of old themes and there are abrupt new departures—but the learned information that sustained, or purported to sustain, the judgment is often veiled. We know all too well how frequently scholars bedeck their texts with the erudition of others, a universal vice. The claims of scholarship and the false claims of punditry are inextricably intertwined. The learned Christian Hebraist and the bitter scourge of Judaism are occasionally the same man. And what is the purpose of the scholarly edifice being erected or the authoritative judgment being rendered? Too often an author's learning comes to serve an end that is foreign to his original intent.

The "third culture," the Hebrew, which alongside the Greek and the Latin was once an ornament of the trilingual gentleman-scholar, deserves a more prominent place in the history of western thought than has been accorded to it. The Christian pioneers of Hebraic scholarship in the Renaissance are well known—the Italian Count Giovanni Pico della Mirandola, the Germans Johannes Reuchlin and Sebastian Münster. The giants of the baroque age tower above the multitude—the Buxtorfs of Basel, John Selden and John Lightfoot in England, Père Richard Simon and Dom Augustin Calmet in France, Giulio Bartolocci in Italy, Constantijn L'Empereur van Oppijck and Johannes Coccejus in the Netherlands, the Carpzovs in Germany. But when we inquire about the gross number of those who were merely proficient in Hebraic studies to some degree, as well as the popularizers, we are at a loss to provide reasonable answers. The published curricula of seminaries and universities can be misleading as indicators: academic history overflows with unfulfilled requirements. Key opinion makers on the nature of Judaism such as Voltaire and Herder, even Eisenmenger and Christian Knorr von Rosenroth, Jacques Basnage, and Robert Lowth, often acquired their knowledge at second and third hand.

There have been scholars who sought refuge from the complexity of fathoming and putting in order Christian judgments of Judaism over the last five centuries by transforming the subject into voluminous catalogues of Christian writers on Hebraic topics. These lists are surrounded with an aura of certitude—the authors, titles, and places of publication are usually accurate, though publishers may be disguised, anonymous and pseudonymous works abound, and dates of publication are altered. But the critical historian cannot be appeased by bibliographical plenitude. In a history of the recovery of Judaism in Christendom, it would be good to have a notion of the knowledge of Hebraica that was diffused at any particular period in the long chronicle of relations between the higher cultures of Christianity and Judaism in their many forms. While there are catalogues in which the printed books of Christian Hebraists are recorded, close studies of individual authors that evaluate their use of Hebraic sources are still few. Familiarity with original Hebrew documents was often fudged, and impressions of great learning derived from the side- and foot-notes of erudits are unreliable. There are Christian authors who flaunted their Hebraic knowledge, whereas others, more modest, were not eager to display their learning.

I do not presume to have analyzed the works of all the Christian Hebraists and literary figures who discovered Judaism historically, theologically, and philosophically during the centuries preceding the French Revolution and in the aftermath of liberation. Citations and examples have been kept to a minimum, and I have not quoted the vast literature on technical aspects of many problems—such as the titanic seventeenth-century controversy over the antiquity of vocali-zations and diacritical marks in the Old Testament. In this book, the history of biblical criticism in Western Christendom, the changing economic and social conditions of the Jews and their legal status, and Jewish reactions to Christian doctrine have been underplayed or touched on only peripherally in order to illuminate the main currents in Christendom's recovery of Judaism. The focus is on the Christian host, not on the loved and hated Judaic object.

My aim has been to stake out general lines of development. The choice of exemplars is surely open to question. I have tried to avoid filling the printed page with too many bombastic titles that run on and on in the massive folios of baroque learning. Soundings have been made for an archaeological dig, accompanied by an aerial survey. My notion of the numbers of writers and readers who participated in the Christian recovery of Judaism is frankly impressionistic, though critical monumental bibliographies on all aspects of Judaica in He-brew, Latin, and the vernacular languages, compiled by Johann Bux-torf the Elder, Bartolocci, and Carlo Giuseppe Imbonati in the sev-enteenth century, Johann Christoph Wolf and Augustin Calmet in the eighteenth, Julius Fürst and Moritz Steinschneider in the nineteenth, and encyclopedias in the twentieth, lend plausibility to some of my general estimates. In due time, or at the end of the days, the quanti-fiers will make my casual reflections more precise or dismiss them as far off the mark. About them I feel like 'Ulla, a rabbi of the Talmud, who at the prospect of the carnage that would herald the advent of the messiah, cried out: "Let him come, but let me not see him!" [2]

2

Reknitting the
Severed Connection

THE LONG HISTORY of Christianity's wrangling with Judaism has been marked by sharp and momentous discontinuities. When Christians were a sect in Judaea, the relations were those of a genetrix and her wayward progeny. But when Christians turned to the pagan gentiles to win converts, they deliberately separated themselves from the ongoing history of Judaism. The repudiation of the Jewish law and its commentaries was the center of the Christian controversy during the period of the Apostles and the Church Fathers. Modern scholars have remarked upon how few of the Fathers who formed the Church knew Hebrew—the trilingual Jerome was an exception. Though Philo Judaeus and Flavius Josephus, both of whom wrote in Greek, were readily assimilated by the Church, rabbinic interpretations of Jewish law were pushed aside, as the Church relied increasingly on Greek philosophy for its intellectual frame.

In the early history of the Church, the Bible was the sacred connection between Western Christendom and Judaism. Even when there was a falling off in the study of Hebrew and Aramaic, this remained true throughout the thousand years after Jerome's heroic translation of the text into Latin from the Hebrew original (with the aid of a Jew as guide during his sojourn in the Holy Land). After some tergiversation, Augustine accepted the new translation, and though he knew no Hebrew himself he led the way in establishing Jerome's Vulgate as the "Hebrew truth." As knowledge of Greek declined in the west, the Septuagint and Latin renderings of the Bible earlier than Jerome's virtually ceased to be cited as authorities in determining God's word. Jerome's text had generally striven to respect the literal meaning of the Hebrew Bible, but Augustine's interpretations were predominantly allegorical in the tradition of Philo the Alexandrian Jew, and the method of this most revered of the Church Fathers was fixed for Christian scholars well into the twelfth century. Judaism lost its significance as a separate entity that could cast light on the Scriptures when Augustine denounced its literal corporeality in the reading of the Bible and the performance of ceremonials devoid of spiritual content. The Jews continued to be targets for conversion, an extension of the apostolic mission—they were to be persuaded with love and not subjected to force—while the Old Testament was transformed into a repository of testimonies foretelling the coming of Christ and was stripped of much of its literal and historical meaning. The voluminous commentaries that generation after generation of rabbis had been compiling were no longer of interest to the Christian world, except insofar as they secreted blasphemies against Christ and had to be denounced.

In the constant flow of treatises against Jews, there was a repetitive rejection of Jewish renderings of the sense of Old Testament prophecies, psalms, proverbs, and canticles, without much reference to specific rabbinic sources. The Christian attack on Jewish literal interpretation became a stereotype that hardly varied from one patristic diatribe to another. The term Talmud, in the rare instances when it appeared in the early Middle Ages, was used as a coverall for whatever Jewish interpretations of Scripture entered the Christian world, and these readings were dismissed in the name of the new dispensation, which denigrated the crass, material exposition of Mosaic law.

Christian arguments against Jewish exegesis were embodied in formulas that barely changed through the ages. In the earliest Christian polemics, as in *Justin against Trypho,* a Jew was sometimes introduced and allowed to represent the Mosaic view; but as the centuries wore on, the Jewish protagonist was often eliminated and the Christian held forth without the impediment of contradiction. It is tempting to see the arguments as diffused from one manuscript to another, but it is unnecessary to establish actual contact between Christian authors or their knowledge of one another's works, since they dealt with a limited number of subjects and depended on the same Old Testament texts for sustenance. The dialogues or works of apology were addressed sometimes to Jews as potential converts and sometimes to

Christians who might be called upon to defend the faith. The subjects ordinarily covered were repeated without much thematic variation: Christian abandonment of Judaic circumcision and the Jewish sabbath, refusal of the dietary laws; proofs that trinitarian conceptions were common whenever the Old Testament referred to the name of God; assertions that the messiah mentioned or implied in Jewish texts was Jesus, with a thousand prefigurations of the actual events in his birth, life, passion, and resurrection; the futility of the Jews' awaiting their messiah when the destruction of the Temple was evidence that God had forsaken them and Christians were now the true Israel; the duration of the Jewish diaspora—so much longer than the Babylonian captivity—as incontrovertible proof that the crime of deicide was unforgivable; the contention that total observance of the law, which was founded on the Jewish covenant with God, was now impossible since temple sacrifice had perforce been ended; baptism as the replacement for circumcision; numerous references in the Old Testament to the imminent coming of a new order; the vanity of the Jews' expectation that their messiah would raise the dead and establish hegemony over the whole world after the restoration of the kingdom in Palestine; the assumption that the rabbis knew the Christian truth implicit in their own works but continued to deny it because of a curse they had taken on themselves in calling for the crucifixion.

Traces of Medieval Christian Hebraists

Knowledge of either Hebrew or Aramaic among Christians was so infrequent before the twelfth century that their textual interpretations of Jerome's Vulgate were often gross distortions; and though the clerisy was occasionally infiltrated by Jewish converts who brought with them familiarity with the Hebrew original on which the Vulgate was based and echoes of midrashic and even protocabbalist traditions, there are few indications that these fragments substantially altered the Christian perception of Judaism before a new school of Christian glossators and interpreters began to be established in the early twelfth century. From time to time even in the period before 1100, a novel rendering of a biblical phrase in glosses that have been preserved in cathedral school texts suggests that Christian scholarship was not hermetically sealed off from rabbinic commentaries. But consistency both in the choice of Old Testament passages and in the patterns of allegorical translation attests to the fossilization of the Christian views.

Intermittent outbursts of popular violence against the Jews, who enjoyed relative prosperity in their isolated communities, were often bloody. And relationships between the higher cultures of Jews and Christians were sparse before the rise of the Christian monastic orders of Franciscans and Dominicans that, by infusing vigor into the efforts of the Church to revivify and reform itself, took cognizance of the studies of rabbis living in their proximity. In the twelfth and thirteenth centuries, the number of Christians who sought ties with rabbis multiplied, and the tenor of the Christian perception of Judaism began to change. There was a renewed attempt to proselytize the Jews, and the study of Hebrew was undertaken by a small number of Christian scholars, a few of whom wrote treatises that became landmarks in the history of Christian understanding of Judaism. Copies of their manuscripts have been preserved in monastic libraries. When the printing presses became the major agencies for the diffusion of Christian thought, works on Judaism by medieval friars achieved a new life and continued to fashion Christian conceptions well into the seventeenth century.

The Abbey of St. Victor in Paris became a center of biblical scholarship, and the Victorine method of interpretation has been regarded as a break with the allegorical tradition of Augustine and a return to the literal and historical approach that underlay Jerome's translation from the Hebrew. Hugh (d. 1141), Richard (d. 1173), and Andrew (d. 1175) were masters in the cathedral school of St. Victor. Their glosses on the biblical text, superlinear and marginal annotations, as well as their more extensive commentaries on entire books of the Old Testament, were imbued with a new spirit and imaginative originality, which allowed for idiosyncratic renderings that departed from long-accepted tradition. Andrew, who left for a time to become abbot in a Welsh monastery, later returned to Paris, where he continued to produce manuscripts that a few centuries later might well have been condemned as heretical. Modern scholars have recognized in his novel literal interpretations the marked influence of the writings of Rashi of Troyes (1040–1105), the most popular medieval Jewish interpreter, who dominated Jewish exegesis of both Scripture and Talmud.

Though his name is rarely mentioned by Andrew, who does not always agree with his Jewish source, his many glosses, gathered together
by Beryl Smalley in *The Study of the Bible in the Middle Ages* (1941),
lead to the conclusion that at least in the Abbey of St. Victor the
rabbinic commentary tradition was taken seriously and was discussed
with students. Often the Jewish interpretations were introduced without ascription to specific rabbis: there are generic formulas such as
"the Jews assert" or "the Jews maintain" or "the Jews believe."

Andrew probably went further than his master Hugh and his colleagues in juxtaposing traditional Christian renderings with contradictory Jewish opinions. The passages in which he introduces con-
flicting Jewish readings involve crucial verses in Isaiah presumed to
foretell the virgin birth and passion of Christ. These passages, which
most Jewish commentators interpret as references to the sufferings
and humiliations of the people of Israel, are set forth by Andrew in a
manner that hints at accord and represents a sharp deviation from
patristic tradition. A question remains as to whether Andrew read
rabbinic commentators himself, whether he knew enough Hebrew to
examine the original text of the disputed passages with the aid of a
rabbi, or whether he relied solely on the verbal elucidations of rabbinic friends or acquaintances. The intimacy of relationships between
Christian masters and rabbis in the high Middle Ages is problematic.
They doubtless varied widely from center to center and period to
period.

Three works are significant enough to warrant special consideration because the ripple effect of their revelations lasted for centuries
and they involve important intellectual figures: the Latin translation
of Moses Maimonides' *More nevukhim* (Guide for the Perplexed),
probably made in southern Italy or Provence in the middle of the
thirteenth century, Raimundo Martini's *Dagger of the Faith against
Moors and Jews,* and the postillae of Nicolas de Lyre (c. 1270–1349),
a Franciscan who taught in Paris. Martini's learned diatribe infiltrated
Judeophobic and antisemitic literature through the Nazi period. De
Lyre's commentaries became one of the most cited Christian exegetical works in the late Middle Ages and a crucial agent in the transmission of Rashi's commentaries to European scholars. The translation of
parts of Maimonides' *Guide for the Perplexed* has been found in
nearly a score of manuscript versions in repositories spread through-

out Europe. These three works bear witness that their authors either knew Hebrew or had access to rabbis well grounded in a long tradition of philosophical, talmudic, and later midrashic learning. If to these major writings are added those of converts to Christianity, the generality that Western Christendom was completely cut off from Jewish learning appears to require emendation. And yet the extent of diffusion of the ideas embodied in the works of Martini, de Lyre, and the anonymous translator of Maimonides is not measurable. Often the works by Christians were used for polemical purposes, in a spirit of negation, and did not enrich the collective Christian view of Judaism. These isolated instances of penetration of rabbinic thought into medieval Christianity, though significant, pale before the outpouring of Christian Hebraist writings that began in the latter part of the fifteenth century, seeped into the institutional structure of universities, publishing houses, and even clerical assemblies, and with varying fortunes in different countries became an integral part of Western European culture.

The postillae of Nicolas de Lyre, commentaries on the Bible published posthumously in many editions, became a subject of raillery among such adulators of Greek studies as Thomas More, who told of playfully making up quotations from the commentaries that bewildered an ignorant cleric who had come to revere de Lyre's glosses as if they were Holy Writ. Mere reference to late medieval Hebraicians was no signal of approval, particularly in the Erasmus-More circle, where Hellenic studies of Plato and the Greek text of the Bible were preferred to the nascent preoccupation with Hebrew. The Hellenists notwithstanding, the infiltration of Rashi at second hand brought Judaic and Christian commentators closer together in the reading of many disputed biblical passages. This proximity did not exclude de Lyre's rejection of many rabbinic interpretations. Jewish investigators have often been overly eager to cite instances of confluence when the main lines of Jewish and Christian commentary continued to diverge.

Martini's work was not translated into a vernacular language until the twentieth century, but its modification of the Christian perception of Judaism was in many ways the most subtle and enduring of the medieval texts, especially when it opened up the aggadic literature of the rabbis to christological inquiry. Later Christian writers cannibalized his work, which in its printed form ran to more than seven hundred folios.

Martini had been recruited by Ramon de Peñaforte in his effort, with papal blessing, to renew the apostolic mission of conversion. Martini had been schooled in Arabic before his departure for duty among the Moors of Tunis, where he narrowly escaped martyrdom. Upon his return, he was encouraged to prepare a work of Christian apology conceived on a grand scale: *Dagger of the Faith* was to become a companion piece to Thomas Aquinas' *Summa against the Gentiles*. Though Martini never achieved the fame of Aquinas, he exercised an influence on Christian polemists for almost seven hundred years and was often plagiarized or denounced as a fraudulent purveyor of rabbinic texts.

Martini contended that the rabbis themselves admitted Christ's divinity and confessed to the doctrine of the Trinity. He documented his arguments lavishly with quotations and paraphrases from ancient Midrashim, some of them so rare that they have been discovered in no other manuscripts. The suspicion that a fertile imagination supplemented his scholarship was laid to rest only when a renowned modern scholar of rabbinics found Martini's references to the Talmud and later Midrashim to be painstakingly accurate, and suggested that those appearing to be inauthentic may well have harked back to earlier manuscripts that have since been lost. Martini's idiosyncratic interpretations of Old Testament prophecies, passages in the Talmud, and glosses in the *Midrash Rabbah* collection became a rich treasury for generations of Christian polemists dedicated to refuting Jewish denial that the messiah had already come—the crux of debates between rabbis and priests for more than twelve hundred years.

Whether Martini was himself enough of a Hebraist to control and manipulate the texts on which he relied, or whether he employed Jewish converts and assistants, remains open to question. His work was used in medieval contests and was clumsily pilfered by his contemporary Victor Porchetto de Salvatici and by the Italian Renaissance mystic Pietro Galatino (Pietro Columna) in his *Opus toti christianae reipublicae maxime utile, de arcanis catholicae veritatis, contra obstinatissimam judeorum nostrae tempestatis perfidiam* (A Work of the Greatest Usefulness to the Whole Christian Republic, Concerning the Secrets of Catholic Truth against the Most Obdurate Perfidy of the Jews of Our Time; Ortona, 1518). That, at least, is a traditional accusation. Comparison of Galatino's published work, which assumes the form of a colloquy among Galatino himself, Reuchlin (who appears as Capnio), and the Dominican Jacob Hoochstraten (his enemy), with the 1687 printed text of *Dagger of the Faith* should soften the outright allegations of plagiarism, though there are similar passages and ideas. Both works are polemics against the Jews' rejection of Jesus as messiah and make frequent reference to Jewish sources; but while Martini concentrated on Midrashim, Galatino drew primarily from the Talmud, and Reuchlin the interlocutor is given ample opportunity to defend the rabbis of the Talmud by insinuating hidden allegorical meanings into their dicta. Further editions of Galatino's *Opus* were published in Basel (1550, 1561, 1591), in Paris (1602), and in Frankfurt (1602, 1612, 1672), testimony to Galatino's role in transmitting the trinitarian arguments of Martini. (It required the authority of the humanist Joseph Justus Scaliger [1540–1609] to mark Galatino's *Opus* as a corrupt rendering of *Dagger of the Faith*.) By the seventeenth century, Martini had become a recognized Christian authority on rabbinic thought. Basic editions of his work were published in Paris by Joseph de Voisin in 1651 and by the famous Leipzig Hebraist Johann Benedict Carpzov in 1687. Since Luther, too, had lifted arguments from the *Dagger,* Martini became the fountainhead of Christian rediscovery of rabbinic Judaism in both the Catholic and the Protestant worlds, especially because of the paucity of Latin translations of aggadic texts. Martini, a thirteenth-century Catalan of the Order of Preachers, is an example of the complex fate of medieval men of learning who dealt with Judaism. While a book may be rooted in a particular theological ambiance at the time of its composition, its fortunes in later ages are varied, and the transplantation of a treatise like Martini's to Leipzig in the year that Newton published his *Principia* bestows new meaning on the text.

Though Christian knowledge of philosophical Judaism was paltry during the interval between Jerome and the Renaissance, ignorance was not complete. References to Moses Aegyptius—Maimonides—in the works of Albertus Magnus and Thomas Aquinas were first signaled by nineteenth-century German Jewish scholars associated with the learned enterprise called the Science of Judaism, and led them to make the intellectual leap to an assumption of Maimonides' influence on scholastic thought. The very mention of his name was sometimes adduced as evidence, even when the citation was nothing more than a curt dismissal of a Maimonidean idea as stupid. Nevertheless, the eighteen Latin manuscripts of the whole or parts of the *Guide for the Perplexed,* a Spanish translation by the convert Pedro de Toledo, *Mostrador e Enseñador de los Turbados* (assigned to the first decades of the fifteenth century and only recently reproduced from a manuscript in the National Library in Madrid), and a dozen citations in Martini's *Dagger* testify to the penetration of Maimonides in various forms in Christian Europe.

A learned publication by the German Jewish authority Joseph Perles in 1875 raised the possibility that a Latin translation of the *Guide for the Perplexed* had been available in Europe as early as the mid-thirteenth century. A Munich manuscript without a title page, identified by Perles, bears enough similarity to the Latin text published with the title *Dux Neutrorum* by Agostino Giustiniani, bishop of Nebbio, in Paris, 1520, to allow for the hypothesis that the two were in some way connected. Giustiniani's publication—his role as translator or compiler was not firmly established—quickly became a rarity, since most Christian scholars in the seventeenth century, when the Maimonides cult among Christians was at its height, used a new translation by Buxtorf the Younger. Allusion to a Latin, or "Christian," translation of the *Guide,* found in a commentary on the work by Moses ben Solomon of Salerno, indicates that the translation was composed in the middle of the thirteenth century and was probably put together in southern Italy; it has been suggested that the translator may have maintained amicable relations with Jewish scholars. A further theory relates the Latin translation to other works of transmission prepared under the patronage of the Holy Roman Emperor Frederick II and his son Manfred. But the whole matter of this Latin text remains shrouded in obscurity. Was it the work of a Jew, a Jewish convert to Christianity, or a Christian? Was it a loose rendering into Latin of Samuel Ibn Tibbon's Hebrew version of Maimonides' original Judeo-Arabic? Was it based on Yehudah Al Harizi's contemporaneous translation from Arabic into Hebrew, or were the two versions mixed? Was the original text of Maimonides resorted to on occasion? Was the final text, now housed in Munich, the work of one man or members of a study circle in which both Christians and Jews participated? And, lastly, was this thirteenth-century Latin translation really the basis of Giustiniani's 1520 publication?

In recent years, citations to Maimonides have been laboriously

gathered from the writings of Alexander of Hales, William of Auvergne, Roland of Cremona, Thomas of York, and Giles of Rome,
supplementing those from Albertus Magnus and Aquinas found in
the nineteenth century. Most of the references have to do with Maimonides as an expositor of Aristotelian physics, though of late it has
been claimed that Master Eckhart favored his exegetical ideas on
scriptural interpretation.

The references to Maimonides, without explicit mention of his
name, in texts of William of Auvergne and Alexander of Hales (d.
1245), an Englishman who taught at Paris and was the author of a
Summa universae theologiae, date to the third decade of the thirteenth
century. In the *Summa* of the Dominican Roland of Cremona, written
in 1232–1234, the mention of "Rabi Moses philosophus Hebraeorum"
who wrote a work against the antiquity of the world is specific
enough, though quotations from him are imprecise. The most extensive treatment appears to be in Giles of Rome's *Errores philosophorum*
(Errors of the Philosophers), which includes two full chapters on
Maimonides in a general attack on Aristotle's physics, with which the
Hebrew philosopher is identified—although Giles recognizes that
Maimonides leaves room for divine revelation. But despite these indications that Maimonides the philosopher, as distinguished from the
exegete, was known and even appreciated in the thirteenth century, it
seems farfetched to introduce him as a major element in the construc-
tion of medieval scholasticism.

Martini, de Lyre, the translators and excerpters of Maimonides,
and a few other figures are outstanding exceptions to the sparseness
of medieval Christian knowledge of Judaism, all the more threadbare
when juxtaposed with the erudition of Christian Hebraic virtuosi
from the fifteenth century on. Uses of Jewish sources by Christian
exegetes going back to the twelfth century are constantly being discovered. Herbert of Bosham (fl. 1162–1186) relied on two Spanish
Jews, Menahem Ibn Saruk and Dunash Ibn Labrat, and frequently
quoted from Rashi of Troyes in his commentary on Psalms. Sporadic
encounters aside, however, Christian Bible interpreters and Jewish
rabbis, while referring to the same Old Testament, proceeded along
different paths during the centuries of estrangement, from Jerome in
the fifth to Pico della Mirandola in the fifteenth century. Perhaps in
the future the empty space will be filled in with additional instances

of Christian knowledge of rabbinic sources, but for the present the record remains scanty. As the fifteenth century approached, Christian Hebraists—later the term often applied to anyone who knew some Hebrew—became more numerous. For all that, the trickle did not swell to a steady flow until the latter part of the century, when Hebraism became an integral part of the European recovery of antiquity.

Iberia: The Facade of Coexistence

On the Iberian peninsula, the history of Christendom's medieval relation to Judaism is unique, a gruesome magnification of cruelties that had been practiced before and a prefiguration of horrors to come. Both the intellectual and the economic encounters of church and synagogue assumed a character so radically different that events south of the Pyrenees appeared to take place in a spiritual landscape alien to other countries of Western Europe, where different complex relationships had evolved. Though there are resemblances, what transpired in the Iberian peninsula constitutes a separate episode in the confrontation of Christianity with Judaism. The Spanish Inquisition, authorized in 1478 by Ferdinand and Isabella (with Rome's approval), had roots in the papal Inquisition of the thirteenth century, but it quickly developed an institutional and intellectual format so monstrous that analogies tax our credulity. And yet Spanish Christendom, later regarded as abhorrent in its relations to Judaism by large segments of Western Christianity, was a prototype for the aberrations of human behavior that cropped out in twentieth-century European society.

The parallel between fourteenth- and fifteenth-century Spain and twentieth-century Germany obtrudes upon the historical imagination, despite the commonsense realization that comparisons between circumstances half a millennium apart must be strained and arbitrary. In both cases the dominant cultures were confronted by Judaisms seeking to assimilate themselves, in the secular sphere, into the society of the overlords. They succeeded only in spawning social hybrids, bastards that were relentlessly hounded. The *conversos* of fourteenth-century Spain and their descendants in the fifteenth, sixteenth, and seventeenth centuries were never accepted into the Christian body politic; and the emancipated nineteenth-century Jews of Western Europe, whether or not formally converted to Christianity, were never

cleansed of the stigma of their origins. Christendom failed to devise a
way of adopting these anomalous Jews—or anomalous Christians—
either theologically or politically. Both in old Castile and in modern
Germany, the final solution to the existence of Judaism had tragic
consequences for the hosts as well as for the victims.

As the Christian kingdoms of the Iberian peninsula reconquered
territories formerly occupied by Islam, they inherited Jews who had
served in administrative posts under the Moors and were prepared,
when allowed, to perform the same functions for Christian monarchs.
By the fourteenth century, the hostility of ordinary Christians in urban
and nonurban areas assumed significant proportions, and the Jews
became a problem from which there was no disentanglement. Sporadic outbursts that ended in massacres or in forced conversions were
the outward signs of deep-rooted animosities in which social, political, and religious elements were intermingled. Jewish converts, the
unwilling and the willing, created a class of New Christians who,
though their individual destinies were varied, raised the antagonism
between Christians and Jews to another level. In a world where religious and personal identities could not be disguised, the New Christians were lost in a spiritual no-man's-land. The rich among them were
able to marry into old Christian families, often with titles of nobility,
but the mixture of Jewish blood with that of pure Christians was not
readily forgotten. The brutal Seville uprising of 1391, which initiated
widespread pillaging of Jewish communities and the imposition of
mass conversions, was preceded in other areas by isolated incidents
of violence and baptisms forced and voluntary.

On the Iberian peninsula, fourteenth- and fifteenth-century Jews
who had willingly converted often became the most vocal antagonists
of their former correligionists, creating a polemical literature that has
a long history in the west. The zeal of the turncoat is an obvious tool
of self-justification both within religious establishments and among
secular revolutionary ideologists. The anti-Judaic writings that appeared in the Iberian peninsula during this period are largely the
work of New Christians; they have only begun to be studied and may
complicate the traditional cosmeticized portrait of life among Christians and Jews in the fourteenth and fifteenth centuries. Long before
the edict of expulsion in 1492, Christians were learning about the perils of Judaism from the converts. Fray Alfonso de Spina, later bishop

of Orense, in his *Fortalitium fidei contra iudeos, sarracenos aliosque christiane fidei inimicos* (Fortress of the Faith against Jews, Saracens, and Other Enemies of the Christian Faith), written in Valladolid (1459–1461) and printed in Strasbourg (1471), threatened lapsed New Christians with eternal hellfire. Alfonso de Valladolid, born Abner de Burgos (1278–1346), was the author of *Mostrador de la justicia y Libro de las tres gracias* (Teacher of Justice and Book of the Three Graces). Pedro de la Caballería, whose family was long a target of the Inquisition, wrote *Zelus Christi contra judaeos, sarracenos et infideles* (Zeal of Christ against Jews, Saracens, and Infidels). The most influential figure was probably Pablo de Santa María, once the doctor Solomon ben Levi and later the archbishop of Burgos, whose accusations against the Jews were comprised in a work entitled *Scrutinium Scripturarum libris duabus contra perfidium judaeorum* (Scrutiny of the Scriptures in Two Books against the Perfidy of the Jews; Mantua, 1475). Recent scholarly publications of the writings of Alonso de Cartagena (1384–1456), *Defensorium unitatis christianae* (Defense of Christian Unity; 1943), and Cardinal Juan de Torquemada (1388–1468), *Tractatus contra madianitas et ismaëlitas* (Treatise against Midianites and Ishmaelites; 1957), have only scratched the surface of the spiritual turmoil created by the Spanish Inquisition to which the writings of the conversos bear witness.

When New Christians found a place in communal, royal, or ecclesiastical offices, they did not become immune to envy and the enduring suspicion that their conversions were not genuine. Transitions from one religious definition to another could not be effected overnight without leaving residues in legal and economic ties, in custom and habit. When laws were passed at the end of the fourteenth century excluding New Christians from communal and ecclesiastical offices, their enforcement wrought havoc among the upper classes. The tracing of ancestries led to such publications as the notorious "green book" of Aragon that charged the most illustrious families with concealing the taint of Jewish blood. When the Inquisition assumed control of investigations into the behavior of Jewish converts rumored to have lapsed or accused of heresy, conceptions of what Judaism meant to official Christendom assumed a frightening cast. The mere regular performance of Christian ceremonies was not considered sufficient evidence of sincere conversion, and inquiries turned to the uncovering of secret Jewish practices. Most interrogations appeared to avoid abstract theological questions, since many New Christians were educated enough to provide stock answers; instead, inquisitors concentrated on concrete examples of judaizing behavior. Avoidance of work on the Jewish sabbath could be substantiated by witnesses.

When New Christians suspected of being secret Jews were rejected by Christian authorities, they did not always find refuge among the unconverted Jews who, until the formal expulsion of Jews from Spain in 1492, still found a place for themselves in Spanish society and sometimes even in the royal service itself. The attitude of the rabbis toward converts was often as ambivalent as that of Christians. During the mass forced conversions that accompanied the Crusades in the Rhineland in the eleventh century, respected rabbinic opinion, recorded in responsa, had been understanding of the awesome alternatives that confronted Jews. Martyrdom was not expected of all of them. In the Iberian peninsula of the fourteenth and fifteenth centuries, the rabbinic posture was not fixed. Some rabbis refused to recognize the reality of conversions: once a Jew, always a Jew. Others considered the convert an irredeemable apostate. In any event, close relations of Jews with converted Jews were dangerous because an implication that a Jew was fostering the return to the fold of a former correligionist placed them both in jeopardy, within the jurisdiction of the Inquisition.

There is a whole vocabulary of denigration that was concocted to describe the New Christians, the most common term being *marranos* (an enigmatic word probably meaning pigs). When after the expulsion Jews and marranos were dispersed over the Mediterranean basin, the Christian and the Jewish communities outside Spain inherited many of the religious and economic dilemmas that had plagued the Iberian peninsula. Individual Jewish converts faced difficulties in the cities of Western Europe to which they gravitated. The image of the forced Iberian converts surviving the hazards of migration, reunited with their brethren and joyously embracing again the religion of Moses, has long since been modified. Marranos who had been practicing Christians for a number of generations often did not know with whom to identify. Sometimes the exiles passed as members of the "Portuguese nation" and ultimately were established as a separate entity. In the Bordeaux area they finally received a privileged status in the 1550s, despite prohibitions against the residence of Jews in France. In Italian city-states there were marranos who were accepted into the synagogue, but the arm of the Inquisition made them a threat to the indigenous Jews who received them; at the same time, others who appeared to live as Christians were scrutinized with mistrust by the Church. Those who managed to find refuge in the Turkish territories of the east solved their immediate problem because they were tolerated; when they returned to Christian lands as traders under Turkish protection, they enjoyed privileges as Levantine Jews.

Marranos who shifted from one religious body to another and then back again as expediency dictated ended up uneasy members of all communities. If Paris was later worth a mass to Henry IV, acceptance of a shower of chrism, the sanctified oil of baptism, did not trouble many worldly Jews. There were gradations between martyrdom and indifference. Summaries of trials conducted by the Spanish Inquisition suggest that artisans and simple folk had a more tragic fate than many rich Jews, who could enjoy, at least for a time, the protection of grandees and members of the royal household. A blanket generality cannot cover those struck by the edict of expulsion: the chief rabbi of Castile, Abrahám Senior, converted; the financier Don Isaac Abravanel went into exile, where his biblical commentaries and apocalyptic writings were published and, paradoxically, exerted considerable influence on Christian theologians.

After the expulsion of the Jews from Spain and the dispersal of conversos during the ensuing centuries, the coexistence of Sephardic and Ashkenazic Jews in the same communities, with their own rites and synagogues and lifestyles, bewildered Christian authorities, and in great commercial centers like Venice they even set up nominal boundaries to confine Jews of different origins in separately demarcated quarters. In the seventeenth and eighteenth centuries, most Christians and most Jews still confronted each other as an undifferentiated mass. But it was precisely in this epoch that Christian scholars, in far greater numbers than in the Renaissance and the Reformation, parted the curtains and peered into the Jewish sanctuaries. A similar curiosity was exhibited by isolated Jews who read Christian polemists; their inquisitiveness was more dangerous, however, because they were the weak spying on the habits of the strong who exercised dominion over them. In both cases the audacious ones were stepping into forbidden territory, and severe punishments would be meted out by their respective communities to those who crossed the line and converted.

Converts from Judaism to Christianity disseminated some knowledge of the Talmud and later rabbinics, which friars of the thirteenth, fourteenth, and fifteenth centuries adapted in their diatribes against Judaism. In spectacular forensic exercises, as in the Tortosa debates of 1413–14 sponsored by the antipope Benedict XIII, rabbis summoned by command were forced to argue about blasphemies in the Talmud and the validity of evidence on Jewish doctrine in Midrashim with friars led by Jewish converts. Hieronymus a Sancta Fide, formerly the pope's physician, who had been persuaded to become a Christian by Fray Vincent Ferrer, was the chief protagonist in the Tortosa debates and focused the disputation on the key question: had the messiah already appeared, as implied in rabbinic Midrashim he interpreted with abandon, or was he yet to come, as the rabbis insisted? The contention of the rabbis that Hieronymus drew his proofs from Martini's "fabricated" Midrashim was to no avail, nor were their arguments that Midrashim were imaginative sermons, not authoritative legal decisions (the same objection that Nachmanides had voiced in a similar Barcelona confrontation in 1263). Summaries of the Tortosa disputations have survived in two versions, one Christian and one Jewish, that are partisan and divergent; the conclusion was foregone, a condemnation of the Talmud. The circumstances of a solemn assembly inevitably required at least a modicum of theological, albeit hostile, converse; but with the rarest exceptions, the utterances of the friars were only primitive, sketchy, and shadowy reflections of the Judaic corpus.

The significance of Jewish translators who knew Greek, Arabic, and Latin as well as Hebrew was recognized in the nineteenth century by the virtuoso of Hebraic bibliography Moritz Steinschneider and by Ernest Renan; and Ludwig Geiger briefly summarized what was then known of Christian Hebraists in medieval and Renaissance Italy in an extensive footnote to the third edition of Jacob Burckhardt's *Civilization of the Renaissance in Italy* (1877–78). When all the materials are assembled, they illuminate the acquisition of Arabic scientific and philosophical ideas through Jewish intermediaries, but reveal little about Christendom's acquaintance with rabbinic Judaism. In the realm of science, the role of Jewish scholars in making available to Christendom Greek and Arabic texts has long been recognized, and the presence at the court of Alfonso X, king of León and Castile, of men of learning from Arabic, Christian, and Jewish communities is well documented. Yet the infusion of a knowledge of traditional Judaism into the Christian world through the agency of rabbinic conversos, which served a specific polemical purpose, hardly affected the intercourse between the main bodies of Jewish and Christian men of learning. The converts brought to Christianity a wealth of debating techniques, but few novel perceptions. It is difficult to conceive of tightly closed enclaves of thought during the period of coexistence (*convivencia*) among Muslims, Christians, and Jews in medieval Spain, but the interpenetration of intellectual currents, beyond scientific treatises, remains conjectural and is still based on inference.

The writings of Spanish conversos fueled the fires of the later autos-da-fé, and their prejudicial Latin treatises exposing the dark, blasphemous nature of Judaism ultimately seeped into Western Christendom north of the Pyrenees. With the invention of printing, many of these works by Spanish authors became sourcebooks on the teachings of Judaism that competed with the learning of Christian Hebraists published in the sixteenth and seventeenth centuries in Italy, Germany, and Holland. The works by Spanish friars and conversos, often prized for their purported intimate knowledge of Judaism, properly belong to the history of Judeo-Christian polemics of the baroque age, when the printing presses of the more northerly lands, which produced them in many editions, gave them a significance they may not have had at the time they were first written in Aragon and Castile.

The End of a Thousand-Year Estrangement

Of the scriptural religions Judaism and Christianity, the golden words of Ecclesiastes, modified with academic license, still hold: commentary of commentaries, saith the Preacher, all is commentary. While the complete text of the Old Testament might be taught in medieval cathedral schools, with commentaries described by Christian glossators as literal, allegorical, analogical, and anagogical, relations with the great centers of rabbinic learning that flourished in Spain, France, and Germany were restricted, if they existed at all.

When in the ancient world postbiblical Judaic commentaries had come within the ken of Christians, they were usually dismissed as tainted with the dead letter of a superseded law and were denigrated as corporeal, fleshly, in sharp contrast with Christian readings, which were animated by the Holy Spirit. This Christian perception of the underlying opposition between Christianity and Judaism—spirituality against corporeality—persisted through the ages. Augustine's *Tractatus adversus judeos* had set the tone and content of the argument. Though almost all the Church Fathers wrote treatises against the Jews, their polemics were usually reduced to the accusation that the Jews stubbornly refused to believe their own prophets and misinterpreted Old Testament texts clearly foretelling the advent of Christ the Messiah, born of a virgin, and his passion. When the works of the Fathers were printed in the sixteenth and seventeenth centuries, the old diatribes against Judaism were diffused in a new medium. Simultaneously, a spread of Hebrew learning, which had begun in the Renaissance, opened to Christians broad areas of Jewish thought that had not been examined before.

In the late fifteenth century, Hebrew studies burst upon the consciousness of a literate Christian elite as a novelty. Earlier, the conversions to Christianity by educated Jews, an apostasy whose dimensions are not measurable, ensured some awareness of Jewish thought; but its cultivation was at most sporadic until the burgeoning of Jewish learning serving Christian purposes toward the end of the fifteenth century. The reception of Judaica among Christians was by no means peaceful. In some quarters the study of the Hebrew language and Hebrew and Aramaic writings aroused violent antagonism; among humanists like Thomas More and Erasmus, infatuated with Greek studies, what they deemed the excesses of absorption in Old Testament commentary appeared as a distraction from the spirit of Christ embodied in the Greek New Testament. The Renaissance introduction of those books of the platonic philosophy that had not undergone a period of gradual acceptance in the Middle Ages, as had Aristotle, provoked similar opposition.

Before the sixteenth century, acquaintance with the Hebrew language in university centers was scant. The decision of the Church Council of Vienne (1311–12) that professorships in oriental languages should be established in Paris, Oxford, Salamanca, and Bologna, the better to propagate the Christian faith among Jews and Muslims, largely remained a dead letter. (Not until 1540, at the instance of Henry VIII, were Regius professorships of Hebrew inaugurated at Cambridge and Oxford.)

The early resurgence of the Hebrew language occurred on a one-to-one basis. A Christian scholar possessed with a zeal to learn the language of the accursed Jews, at the risk of his soul resorted to a rabbi or rabbinic convert who would teach him the rudiments. This was the experience of sixteenth-century Italian scholars, a number of whom, when conditions became too precarious in Italy, migrated to France; there they were well received by the French court and nourished the Hebraist fashion. The German scholars Reuchlin and Münster left testimonials of gratitude to their rabbinic mentors. Perhaps the most famous teacher was Elias Levita (c. 1468–1549), who exchanged lessons with Cardinal Egidio de Viterbo—Hebrew for Greek.

As Christianity, after a hiatus of a thousand years, began to reknit connections with the ongoing history of Judaism, new inquiries into rabbinic sources were stimulated by a series of changes in the intellectual atmosphere of Western Europe. The free-floating curiosity of the Renaissance encouraged cardinals to learn Hebrew and made its study fashionable even among courtiers. The Reformation diffused the text of the Old Testament to previously untouched strata of the population, and the establishment of printing presses made accessible a host of Hebrew and Aramaic commentaries. The appearance first in Venice and other northern Italian cities, later in Amsterdam, of Jewish exiles from Spain and Portugal who were learned in Latin and vernacular languages provided Christians with skilled communicators and intermediaries. The multiplication of biblical manuscripts from the east in many languages, soon incorporated in a series of polyglot bibles, revealed countless discrepancies among the texts, and a search for religious truth, fortified by a sheer thirst for knowledge, led Christians to consult rabbinic interpretations of the Hebrew original. The Reformation ferment of new denominations and sects provoked scholarly wrestling with biblical texts and raised questions of grammar and syntax with which Jewish rabbis had been preoccupied for centuries. The practices of Judaism, which became more visible with the infiltration of Jews into European cities, were included in huge compendia of all the world's religions, along with descriptions of exotic savage ceremonies, an interest kindled by geographic exploration and conquest.

The interweaving of these many strands makes the recovery of Judaism overdetermined, much like the earlier rebirth of a passion for Greek and Roman literature and art. The Hebraic renaissance in Christendom, coming later, profited from many of the structures that had already been built around the study of the classics: the publishing houses, princely libraries, patronage systems for scholars, university chairs. The trilingual man became a humanist ideal.

The Italian Printing House, Chrysalis of Hebraica

Before a critical mass of Christian Hebraists could be shaped in western societies, the accumulated manuscripts of the two Talmuds and fifteen hundred years of rabbinic literature had to be made available in a significant number of copies. The printing houses of Italy became the scriptoria of Judaica, and in the course of less than a century beginning in the latter part of the 1400s they reproduced a substantial portion of the philosophical and exegetical writings that were the mainstay of Jewish religion and learning. Prayer books and Old Testaments were chief sources of sustenance for printers who specialized in Judaica, as were Christian missals and breviaries in the houses reputed for their editions of classical and vernacular literature; but a number of families risked their fortunes in the far less assured markets for the Talmud and the commentaries of later rabbis. Since at the outset the primary purchasers of Judaic books turned out by the great presses were Jewish readers, their parochial demands determined which works would be readily available to Christian Hebraists when a sufficient number of them acquired the linguistic skills needed for the study of rabbinic literature. The folio editions of the Old Testament, the Talmud, the major medieval commentators, and the *Zohar,* in their original languages, are creations of the fifteenth- and sixteenth-century printing houses of Italy, and their acquisition by Christian scholars was a slow process.

Very early attempts at Hebrew printing have left a few traces, in the form of stray leaves, in Spain and Portugal, but the first printed Hebrew book that has survived is a copy of Rashi's commentary on the

Pentateuch, which appeared in Reggio di Calabria. It is a rare work that Giovanni Bernardo de Rossi, the late eighteenth-century Christian bibliographer of Hebrew typography in Italy, left to the grand Ducal Library of Parma. Other isolated examples of early Hebrew books have been discovered, but it was not until the family of Samuel and Simon ben Moses established a printing house in Soncino, a town in northern Italy belonging to the Sforzas, that publishing Hebraica became a major enterprise. Two publishers in succession dominated the field, the Soncinos and Daniel Bomberg. The first were Jews, the second was a Christian, though in the golden age of Hebrew printing in Italy, the great publishing house was a forum in which Jews and Christians intermingled.

When in 1454 Samuel and Simon ben Moses left the German city of Fuerth and settled in Soncino, they adopted the name of the town as their surname. Their descendant Joshua Solomon (d. 1493) set up a press that in 1484 issued the first Soncino book, the tractate *Berakhot* of the Talmud along with marginal commentaries, in a format that became the prototype for later editions. There followed a completely voweled Hebrew Bible in 1488, a *Mahzor Minhag Roma* (Prayerbook according to the Roman Rite), and a series of famous medieval rabbinic works. A nephew, Gershom ben Moses (d. 1534), branched out to become one of the most prolific publishers of the late fifteenth and early sixteenth centuries, with a list of books in Hebrew, Judeo-German, Latin, Greek, and Italian. He traveled in search of rare manuscripts and was the first to print the *Tosafot* (Addenda) of the thirteenth-century Eliezer of Touques, to introduce woodcut illustrations into Hebrew books, and to publish a secular Hebrew work, the *Mahberot* (Miscellany) of the poet Immanuel of Rome (born c. 1272). The content of Gershom Soncino's Latin publications seemed not to trouble him even when they were devoted to Christian polemics against Judaism—he issued Galatino's *Opus de arcanis catholicae veritatis,* for example. The Soncino printing presses were subject to the vagaries of civil and ecclesiastical politics and had to be constantly on the move as the political and theological winds shifted; but the independent city-state system of Italy allowed for the survival of marginal groups, and those evicted from one place could find succor in another. The Soncino publications bear a variety of place names: Soncino, Castelmaggiore, Brescia, Fano, Pesaro, Ortona, Rimini, Ancona, Cesna. When finally forced out of Italy, the family took refuge in Salonica and Constantinople, where they continued their "holy work" (printing had been endowed with an aura of sanctity in Judaism). The Italian field was left to Daniel Bomberg, a native of Antwerp who established himself in Venice.

Bomberg, who died sometime between 1549 and 1553, set up close to two hundred works of Hebraica. In 1517–18 the apostate Jew Felix Pratensis prepared for him the first edition of what came to be known as the rabbinic Bible, *Mikra 'ot Gedolot,* four volumes of text along with the Aramaic Targum and the standard commentaries of Rashi, Kimchi, and Abraham Ibn Ezra. A later edition (1525) by Jacob ben Hayyim Ibn Adoniyah became the model for subsequent versions. With the approval of Pope Leo X, Bomberg issued the first complete editions of the two Talmuds (1520–1523). Among his printers, editors, and proofreaders there were apostates from Judaism as well as such learned Jews as Kalonymus ben David and Rabbi Elias Levita, who had once been the master of Christian Hebraists but had fallen on evil days.

Both the Soncinos and Bomberg managed to weather the early sixteenth-century onslaught on the Talmud directed by the Dominicans. When the Council of Trent renewed the attack during the Counter Reformation, those houses that had replaced Bomberg and the Soncinos were confronted in 1553 by confiscations and ceremonial burnings of the Talmud and later rabbinic writings in Rome and Venice. The efforts of Italian rabbis to agree on a method of self-censorship that would excise any passages the Church might consider blasphemous were fruitless, and the Holy Office was left in full control of what could or could not be printed. But the previous seventy or eighty years, though marked by intermittent harassment of the great printers, had allowed for the production of a corpus of rabbinic literature that became the foundation of Christian Hebraist learning in the seventeenth century.

Latin translations of parts of the Talmud and a few of the rabbis began to be published in the sixteenth century, but most educated Christians became acquainted with the names of rabbinic writings from the side- and footnotes of Christian Hebraist works that appeared in Latin. Within about a hundred years after the invention of printing, a substantial portion of the talmudic and later rabbinic corpus was set into Hebrew type in European cities and in Constantinople. Despite the widespread reproduction of rabbinic writings from all ages in Italy, Germany, Polish centers of Jewish settlement, and cities under the domination of the Turks, the profusion of Hebraica should not lead to an exaggerated estimate of the penetration of the third culture into Western Europe. The dispersal of presses that were capable of turning out Hebrew type was a guarantee of survival for many rabbinic manuscripts that might otherwise have perished, but the number of works that came to be known among literate Christians was still limited. A selection had been made early, in Bomberg's rabbinic Bible of 1517–18, and the commentators he printed fixed the parameters of most Christian Hebraists' acquaintance with the rabbis well into the seventeenth century, when Buxtorf's edition of the Bomberg Bible became the foundation of Protestant knowledge.

For two centuries the presses kept turning out Hebrew rabbinic commentaries, supercommentaries on the most famous medieval Jewish writers, and translations, annotations, and refutations of the rabbis by Christian university professors, not to speak of publications accompanying the internecine learned quarrels among the Christian Hebraists themselves. The active commerce in Hebraic books during the seventeenth century among Western European centers, Salonica, Constantinople, and Polish cities as a factor in long-term intellectual development has only recently attracted the notice of historians. Personal relations among the pioneer Christian Hebraists can sometimes be followed in their correspondence, but the pivotal role of the printing houses in the diffusion of Hebraism is yet to be fully appreciated. As the history of the book comes to occupy its rightful place in the historical order of western culture, the vicissitudes of Hebrew printing may yield fresh insights into the network of intellectual relations among Christians and Jews. The productions of the great houses have begun to be investigated; the chronicle of the individual rabbi intent upon the preservation of his name through the private printing of his responsa, glosses, and commentaries—an undertaking he often financed himself—remains to be explored. The relative success of Manasseh ben Israel's printing press in Amsterdam was an exception rather than the norm, and even he had to secure the approval of a number of his fellow rabbis, among whom clerical backbiting was as prevalent as among their Christian neighbors.

In printing establishments that became houses of Judaic learning, eminent scholars—Jews, converts from Judaism, and Christians—gathered in informal discussions. As the vagaries of war and Renaissance court politics drove scholars from the protected refuges of secular and ecclesiastical princes, the printing house was sometimes also a haven, as Daniel Bomberg's was for Elias Levita. Publication of Hebrew bibles and rabbinic commentaries could be a profitable venture; or it could be a hazardous undertaking whose outcome was business failure for both Christians and Jews. But whatever their efforts to achieve commercial success, the men who participated in the production of Hebrew books were driven by the same enthusiasm for learning that motivated the famous printers of the Greek and Latin classics.

When Christian authorities encountered Judaism anew after the invention of printing and the publication of the major works of rabbinic commentary, philosophy, and law that had existed only in a limited number of manuscripts, they had to deal with vexing questions and determine an appropriate course of action. Should Judaic books be destroyed if they contained blasphemous utterances? Should printing be allowed or prohibited, or permitted after the scrutiny of censors? The printing presses were multiplying sacrilegious opinions and enormously increasing the dangers of contamination. But the enterprise of famous printers who were not Jews could not easily be curtailed; and even if some control might be exercised over the publishing houses of Western Europe, imports from Poland and Constantinople could not be effectively stopped. When in the course of a century a good portion of the rabbinic corpus had been set in type, the most venerable of the Jewish commentators were made safe from the depredations of would-be exterminators. The problem of how to treat Jewish writings had arisen in earlier periods, and there are medieval reports of burnings of Hebrew manuscripts by the cartload. But such destruction, however frenzied, was spasmodic, circumscribed in time and place. By the third decade of the sixteenth century, incinerating the total production of scores of printing presses that dotted the continent and turned out Hebrew books was beyond the power of the Inquisition.

3

Rival Interpreters in the Renaissance and Reformation

THOUGH in the Middle Ages there had been individual Christians who studied and quoted Hebrew rabbis and converted Jews who had varied degrees of proficiency in Jewish learning, the emergence of Hebraic studies as a third humanist culture was an event of the Renaissance and Reformation. Four scholars stand out in a growing body of Christian Hebraists in Italy and Germany: Giovanni Pico della Mirandola, Sebastian Münster, Johannes Reuchlin, and Paul Fagio. But the minor figures who translated rabbinic commentaries and parts of the Talmud, the *Zohar,* and other cabbalist literature also helped to lay the foundation for a Hebraic humanism that came into full flower only in the seventeenth century. The sixteenth-century scholars still had to fight for the recognition of their studies as a legitimate part of Christian education. Both Guillaume Postel and Jean Bodin were castigated as judaizers, and anyone who knew Hebrew was at first suspected of being a recent convert. Christian Hebraists had to distinguish themselves from the Jews whose works they were popularizing and refute charges of heresy when their interpretations of Jewish writings appeared to be too favorable.

Pico della Mirandola and His Jewish Mentors

During the Renaissance revival of interest in all aspects of Hebraic thought, the Christians who plunged into the turbulent sea of talmudic, rabbinic, philosophic, and cabbalist writings were confronted, broadly speaking, by two modes of scriptural interpretation, two faces of Judaism. One, Halacha, tended to be literal, juridical in its practical purposes, homiletic in its teachings; the other took off on the wings of allegory, constructing grand systems of cosmology and theosophy that have been called mystical and in the thirteenth century acquired the name "Cabbala" in the restricted sense now commonly used.

Both Cabbala and Halacha were ancient traditions that traced their origins to Moses and among Jews were not ordinarily conceived as contradictory. A Jewish adept of the Cabbala would normally fulfill every one of the Halachic decisions of generations of rabbis who preceded him. But Christianity sharpened the distinction to serve its own esoteric purposes, going so far as to create in the late Renaissance what has been called a Christian Cabbala, which a small number of Christian scholars assimilated with the Renaissance hermetic or neoplatonic currents of thought nourished by the revival of ancient culture. The Cabbala was seized on as fitting in with the myth of a primeval theology that could shelter under its canopy the writings of Pythagoras, Plato, neoplatonists and Hermes Trismegistus; the Sibylline Oracles; and the works of Dionysius the Areopagite.

Christian Cabbala, a veritable potpourri, attracted among its early adepts the young Count Giovanni Pico della Mirandola (1463–1494), who created a scandal in the Roman Catholic world by openly declaring his adherence to the new religious philosophy. Christian humanists in other lands took inspiration from his work: in 1494 Johannes Reuchlin published his first cabbalist treatise, *De verbo mirifico* (On the Wonder-Working Word); Heinrich Cornelius Agrippa's *De occulta philosophia libri tres* (Three Books of Occult Philosophy; 1533) was dependent on Reuchlin's version of the Cabbala that in turn derived from Pico.

Christian Cabbala exerted a certain fascination on poets and artists and philosophers of nature even when the name cabbalist became associated with the arts of black magic and sundry heresies. Historians of the occult have discerned its influence in many Elizabethan forms. By the seventeenth century, the images in cabbalist systems and the Cabbala's terminology—*ein soph* (that which is without end) and the attributes of God identified with the ten *sephirot* (spheres), and the tripartite division of things into natural, celestial, and supercelestial realms—had been picked up by theosophical writers such as John Dee and Robert Fludd. Elizabethan poets adopted some cabbalist conceits either directly or indirectly from Pico and Agrippa and intermingled them with an agglomeration of occult ideas liberally spiced with neoplatonic and hermetic phrases. Still a lingering force in the seventeenth century, here and there even in the eighteenth, Christian Cabbala raised its head among mystics such as Louis Claude de Saint-Martin of Lyons, and in the nineteenth century theosophy and other esoteric cults touched its periphery.

There is a broad chasm between this Christian Cabbala and the Jewish Cabbala, the complex body of literature illuminated in our time by Gershom Scholem and his disciples. The book that became the sacred work of the Jewish cabbalist tradition was the *Zohar* (Book of Splendor), written in pseudo-Aramaic, which made its appearance in late-thirteenth-century Castile and remained unpublished until editions in Mantua and Cremona in the mid-sixteenth century. A significant collection of authentic cabbalist writings translated into Latin, including part of the *Zohar,* was not printed until Knorr von Rosenroth's two-volume compilation (1677 and 1684), the *Kabbala Denudata.*

To Christians who sought the core of truth that lay hidden in Judaism, the Cabbala emerged as an alternative superior to the juridical tradition of Jewish expositors and antithetical to much that was customarily associated with polluted talmudic commentary. They favored the Cabbala because it was not legalistic and did not deal with myriad petty ceremonials or inconsequential rituals; in short, it was not a circumcision of the flesh. The Cabbala, as read by Renaissance Christian scholars and the Jewish converts in their circle, was turned into the Judaic form of a pristine theological truth that strove to define the nature of God and contained wisdom long antedating the redaction of the Pentateuch. Cabbala was a secret oral tradition that went as far back, perhaps, as Adam. It unlocked the mystery of Genesis and of God's attributes, and could be interpreted as harboring a Jewish belief in the Trinity, thus becoming a persuasive instrument for the conversion of the Jews.

But it would be difficult to argue that the Cabbala was the face of Judaism most Christians turned to when they began to study Hebraica in earnest in the sixteenth century. The Hebraism that flowered in Christendom in the seventeenth century centered on the halachic tradition, on the legal system of Judaism, its rationalist philosophical writings, its interpretation of the text of the Scriptures, its attitude toward Christ and Christians, its political theory, its ritual and ceremonies. With the acquisition of new philosophical instruments, Christendom renewed its polemics with Judaism over major principles of faith embodied in the Bible.

Serious preoccupation with the Cabbala was restricted to a relatively small number of Christians. It could figure in a poetic image and a few terms might penetrate the theosophical vocabulary, but it did not reach to the heart of Christendom. Talmudic Judaism and its expanding legal system entered the university and the seminary, and through the oral preachings of priests and ministers and translations into the vernacular, Hebraic thought transmitted at second and third hand won a considerable audience. The massive compendia of the seventeenth and eighteenth centuries did not include abbreviations or condensations of cabbalist works, which were rarely translated (many remain in manuscript to this day).

It was the young Pico della Mirandola who explosively inaugurated the heroic age of the Christian rediscovery of Judaism, when in 1480 he published nine hundred *Conclusiones* and offered to defend them before an assembly to be convened in Rome. The propositions set forth by this prodigy of learning, which covered all known theologies and philosophies ancient and medieval, pagan, Christian, Muslim, and Jewish, grouped by authors and schools, showed virtually the whole of ancient wisdom to be in harmony with the underlying truths of Christianity. Contradictions were reconciled in Pico's synthesis, a universal system to which all men of reason could subscribe, as hidden meanings in alien theosophies were revealed. When the pope had these affirmations examined by theologians, some were found to be heretical, and Pico fled to the protection of the French court until death brought the ascension of a new pope who exonerated him.

Among the propositions considered dangerous to the faith, those grouped under the rubric "Cabbala and natural magic" figured prominently and were defended by Pico at length in an extended *Apologia,* which cited both Christian and Jewish authorities. His Christian version of the Cabbala embraced talmudic rabbis like Shimon bar Yohai and, oddly, pillars of medieval Judaic rationalism like Maimonides. The writings Pico left behind when he died at the age of thirty-one have had a checkered history in western thought. His propositions on the Cabbala continued to be debated in the Church throughout the next centuries as disciples expounded and often distorted his ideas to the point of heresy. The precise meaning of his cabbalism still baffles commentators seeking to recapture the theological moment in which he wrote and tracing his sources to cabbalist manuscripts whose meanings are themselves subject to diverse scholarly interpretations.

Pico's preparation in Hebraic studies included areas of the Jewish tradition totally neglected by most Christian thinkers. With almost unlimited resources at his disposal, he acquired rare manuscripts and even had Jewish texts written in Arabic translated into Latin. His guides in these studies have been tracked down and their relationship to him investigated, even though the precise nature of their influence and the works they prepared for him require further exploration. Perhaps Pico's first and most important teacher of Hebrew was Eliyahu del Medigo, a native of Candia in Crete, with whom he spent some years at the University of Padua; surviving correspondence attests to the intimate friendship between the two men. Del Medigo, a doctor, was not an adherent of what had come to be considered the cabbalist tradition (though his heterodoxy in other respects led him into trouble with the Jewish community), but he introduced Pico to Hebraica and familiarized him with a wide range of rabbinic texts that included cabbalist compositions. Another Jew whose ties with Pico have been established was Johanan Alemanno, of German origin, a man of great learning who gave a solid base to Pico's thought. By far the most flamboyant figure in the circle was Flavius Mithridates, born Raimundus Moncada, a Sicilian convert from Judaism to Christianity whose many names have bedeviled modern scholars. He is usually regarded as the major source for Pico's acquaintance with Jewish Cabbala in the version of Menahem di Recanati. Flavius Mithridates has been identified as the eccentric preacher who delivered a cabbalist sermon before the pope in 1486, and the Vatican library contains a voluminous collection of Mithridates' Latin translations from late medieval cabbalists.

With the recent publication of Chaim Wirszubski's study of Pico's encounter with Jewish mysticism, the complex phenomenon of the relationship of Renaissance Christianity and the Cabbala has been illuminated with details hitherto obscure. Though Pico was ready to defend some seventy-two propositions on Cabbala and magic, along with the rest of his nine hundred theses on all aspects of philosophy and religion, before a learned convocation in Rome, it is now clear that his knowledge of Hebrew at the time he issued his quixotic challenge was at most elementary, and his pronouncements on the Cabbala were based on three thousand folios of translations into Latin from Hebrew and Aramaic that Flavius Mithridates poured out in 1486, during the period when he was patronized by Pico. The principal authors of the works Flavius translated have been identified as the cabbalist rabbis Abraham Abulafia, Menahem di Recanati, and Joseph Gicatilla. It is doubtful that Pico, who at this time was absorbed in an amorous adventure with a Sienese widow related to the Medicis, could have fathomed the intricacies of the Jewish cabbalists without the constant guidance of Flavius Mithridates. Pico was learning some Hebrew and Aramaic in order to enter the world of Jewish Cabbala, but he had already propounded his audacious theses. That Mithridates bargained with Pico before he revealed his secrets is attested by the strange conditions he stipulated: they included Pico's oath not to teach Aramaic to anyone else and the delivery of a *na'ar yafe* (handsome boy). Mithridates' christianizing commentary intruded into his translations of the cabbalist texts, which he further obfuscated by esoteric references to the bottom (*tahat*) of a boy—all of which Wirszubski carefully traced back to Gicatilla's fourteenth-century manuscripts.

Wirszubski has explicated Pico's dicta that fell under the general rubric Cabbala and has revealed cabbalist influences in other theses groping toward a universal Christian philosophy. Scholars have noted that, simultaneously, similar attempts were being made in the 1480s to fashion a Christian philosophy in which Ficino's platonic commentary would play a central role and that would relate esoteric Greek thought to Christianity as a primitive theology. Pico's discovery of Jewish cabbalist writings can be fitted into this theological synthesis as a cohesive element.

The fate of Pico's grand undertaking has been long studied: the papal condemnation of his *Conclusiones,* the flight to Paris, the lifting of the ban against him, the publication of an oration on the dignity of man that was intended to be his opening harangue before the aborted Roman convocation, and the posthumous appearance of his mammoth *Conclusiones.* Pico's later intimacy with Savonarola and his early death have compounded the perplexity of those who have tried to comprehend his all-encompassing amalgam of ancient and Christian thought. Though Pico did not use the term "Christian Cabbala," he inaugurated a perception of Judaism that would have a complex history for three centuries. But his friendship with Jewish scholars and his immersion in the Cabbala should not draw attention away from the Christian core of his thought and an attitude toward Jews that was in the spirit of the age. In his work against astrology, there is a passing reference to the fate of the Jews expelled from Spain in 1492 that praises Ferdinand and Isabella for their action, though he admits that even Christians were moved to pity by the calamities of the sufferers, devastated by shipwreck, pestilence, and hunger.

Pico's native genius, buttressed by the great fortune that allowed him to acquire translations from Greek, Hebrew, and Aramaic; his voluminous writings; his amorous adventures; and his untimely death combine to make him an enigmatic scholar whose intellectual sparks dart in all directions. His essay *De hominis dignitate* (On the Dignity of Man), which included favorable references to the Cabbala, was frequently reprinted, and Thomas More translated into English the biography composed by Pico's nephew. Pico was a monumental figure, but the weight of Christian Cabbala in Christendom's assessment of Judaism is arguable. Christian Cabbala was primarily a Renaissance phenomenon, and despite the residues it left in later centuries, it had no lasting significance in the Christian rediscovery of Judaism. In the age of the baroque, Christian learning was always far more absorbed in Jewish ritual, laws, literal exegesis of the Bible, rationalist philosophy, basic principles of the faith, even political theory, than in the Cabbala. But the constantly replenished body of Jewish esoterica, reduced to its proper dimensions, remained a part of Christendom's perception of Judaism, mocked by many, assimilated by adepts of the mystical vision.

Jewish Cabbala was only one aspect of Pico's vision of ancient theology, but the uproar it provoked indicates that from the very beginning Christendom's recovery of Judaism was surrounded with controversy. Pico died prior to the eruption of the Lutheran heresy in the north, but even before the Augustinian monk nailed his theses to the church door, a Judaic component in the tumultuous theological quarrels shaking the Christian world was dragged into prominence.

Charges of judaizing were flung about whenever unorthodox opinions were expressed or suspect rituals were observed. Contradictory Christian views of Judaism were persistent elements in the disputes that marked the formative years of the Reformation.

Johannes Reuchlin in Defense of the Talmud

During the Reformation, each of the major Christian denominations regarded the religion of the Jews in its own way. The relations of Christians and Jews had a variety of meanings, in keeping with the theological distinctions preserved within the churches. Depending on its own requirements, a Christian sect singled out one or another tradition in the long history of the religion of the Jews and made it their own. Enthusiasts, whether radical sixteenth-century reformers like Thomas Müntzer or the Ranters and Fifth Monarchy Men of seventeenth-century England, saw their religious trials as counterparts of those of ancient Judaism and regarded themselves as contemporary embodiments of prophecy or chosen interpreters of prophecy who were equivalents of the original prophets. Identification with Israel was almost complete among them (though they stopped short of circumcision). In denial of this identification, rationalist Anglicans stressed the uniqueness of ancient Israel, an epoch clearly delimited in a diachronic sacred history, a chapter that was closed with the coming of Christ. Between the two poles were dissenter sects that recognized varying degrees of similitude between their beliefs and Mosaic Judaism. Grand politiques of the Cromwellian persuasion could accept the generality of the equation, but bridled when followers became too zealous in institutionalizing the formula. They spoke in biblical rhetoric, resurrected Old Testament names, enlisted biblical events as metaphors, but found Deuteronomic punishments out of place among the customs of England. We cannot measure the intensity with which a likeness between England, Old or New, and ancient Israel was actually experienced. The dried-out stereotypes to which later generations give only lip service were once images vibrant with feeling.

While the existence of Jewish enclaves in Italian, German, and other Central European principalities cannot be singled out as a factor in the development of the great schism in the Church, Judaism as a repository of methods of scriptural interpretation, especially prophecy, came to play a vital role in Christian disputations. The printing houses of Italy, Germany, and Switzerland, which in a brief period of time turned out thousands of copies of Hebraic texts, were arsenals of war for the Christian world, though this stockpile of weapons held dangers for the religion that tolerated their manufacture and wielded them in verbal combat. As the Reformation approached, some Christians became alert to the spiritual hazards of a Judaism that had survived in Europe and was now preserved in print.

In the early sixteenth century, the toleration of Hebrew books became enmeshed with the general issue of allowing the publication of pagan literature. If absolute prohibition of Hebrew books were decreed because of their blasphemies, how could the Greek and Roman literature that the great humanists were editing escape censorship? If the Dominicans were permitted to expurgate the Talmud, what would happen to the classics? Johannes Reuchlin, a Stuttgart civil administrator and jurist as well as a scholar possessing Latin, Greek, and Hebrew, led the movement against the confiscation of the Talmud and the censorship of Hebrew books, scheduled to be carried out under an imperial mandate by the converted Jew and popular pamphleteer Johann Pfefferkorn, with the support of the Dominicans of Cologne.

Reuchlin's well-reasoned brief in response to the emperor's request for his opinion on the issue, and subsequent polemics in answer to clerical attacks, attracted to his side Christian humanists who ardently defended their profession. These scholars, however, were far from unanimous in their attitude toward the Talmud: Erasmus refused to give his protection; Ulrich von Hutten compiled *Letters of Obscure Men,* which helped to exonerate Reuchlin from the Dominicans' charge of heresy. What had begun as a vindication of the Talmud turned into a denunciation of obscurantism. Reuchlin, who studied Hebrew for a time with Elias Levita, maintained in his original brief to the emperor that he was aware of only two Hebrew books that were blasphemous. If a few books violated the law, they could be condemned under existing statutes, Reuchlin pointed out, without wholesale confiscation of the property of Jews who, after all, enjoyed special status under municipal or imperial jurisdiction. But Reuchlin's ultimate victory in his Roman trial, instigated by Inquisitor Hoochstraten, was not a definitive triumph for the Talmud, and the contest continued until the papal decree of 1553 ordering its confiscation and burning, by that time more effective in Italy than in Germany.

Reuchlin's defense of the Talmud, with which he confessed only casual acquaintance, was more juridical than scholarly. His contribution to Christian Hebraism was in the tradition of those who, like Pico, espoused a Christian Cabbala, and his two works, *On the Wonder-Working Word* and *Three Books on the Cabbalist Art* (*De arte cabalistica libri tres;* 1517), drew mockery and shrugs of disbelief from Erasmus and Luther. These writings concentrated on the cabbalist techniques of gematria: reading words and whole texts by identifying letters with numbers—beginning with aleph as one and proceeding through the alphabet—and then substituting one word for another by virtue of their equivalent numerical values. Reuchlin appears to have been acquainted with the more intricate techniques of cabbalist word and letter combinations and claimed to have discovered the miraculous secret word for God. His cabbalist writings were totally out of keeping with the cool logic and mordant wit of his polemics against Pfefferkorn, and they appealed to very different audiences. Reuchlin remained in the Catholic Church and did not participate further in the wars over the interpretation of Scripture that soon absorbed the sects and denominations dividing the Protestant world, as new images of Judaism were created by Christian scholars' unprecedented use of rabbinic commentators. In Judaic historiography, Johannes Reuchlin usually finds a place of honor as a defender of Judaism, in sharp contrast to Martin Luther, who looms as the prince of darkness and one of the founders of German antisemitism.

Martin Luther, Sebastian Münster, and John Calvin

Fundamentally different attitudes toward the rabbinic traditions of Judaism ultimately came to characterize the Lutheran Evangelical and the Calvinist Reformed Churches. This bifurcation of Protestantism during the Reformation was many decades in the making. It does not always take into account the individual positions of Protestant leaders, the views of dissident groups within the Lutheran and Calvinist camps, and the idiosyncrasies of theologians like Servetus, burned at the stake by Calvin, so flagrantly radical that they cannot be fitted into any category.

Luther himself is in many ways the most baffling figure of the Reformation, and no displays of exegetical skill can reconcile his theological posture of the 1520s, when he proclaimed that Christ was born a Jew, with the violent phobic utterances of the mid-1540s, which could be interpreted as calls for a massacre. One should not wholly impute the transformation to the change from an early expectation that Jews would convert en masse to a later conviction that their stiffneckedness and blindness in rejecting Christ were irremediable. Luther had a profound sense of the chasm separating the law of the Old Testament from the gospel of Christ, and the christological centrality of his belief should not be ignored. His translation of the Bible became the lifeblood of the Evangelical Church, for whom the relationship between the Old and the New Testament is the sole key to understanding both texts. There were scholars of Hebrew and Greek in his inner circle, and while he availed himself of their knowledge of rabbinic literature, especially the grammatical works of David Kimchi in interpreting the Hebrew Bible, in his final rendering of the text into German he was insistent that the spirit of Christ be kept alive in every verse of the Old Testament, irrespective of scholarly glosses, which he dismissed as pedantry. In the beginning was the gospel of Christ in the New Testament, and the books of the law of Moses and the prophets were empty vessels, worthless unless they were filled with the spirit of Christ.

Once the new dispensation had been proclaimed, the old one lost its independent existence, and rabbinic interpretations of the Talmud, let alone the Cabbala, were seen as a mere multiplication of follies. Lutheran scholarship could discover the distortions of Old Testament texts deliberately introduced by the Jews to deny the clear references to Christ, and dicta that blasphemed against Christ in rabbinic writings had to be laid bare. Thus in the Lutheran world Hebraic scholarship ended up as a search for error, a ferreting out of falsifications in the Talmud and rabbinic literature, a revelation of the lies of the Jews. No truths meaningful to Christians were to be discovered in the postbiblical creations of Judaism.

Doubtless the economic well-being of Jews in many German states aroused envy, and the vehemence that pervades Luther's *Von den Jüden und jren Lügen* (Of the Jews and Their Lies; Wittenberg, 1543) reflected the popular hostility. Early rumors, spread by Catholic propaganda, that Luther's heresy was a Jewish conspiracy to destroy Christianity may have strengthened the anti-Jewish phobia of the evangelical churches. But however complex the origins of this brutal summons to the persecution of contemporary Jews, the theological consequences of the Lutheran stance lasted for centuries in the Germanic world. Elements of nineteenth-century German nationalism merged with Lutheran doctrines to foster an antisemitism that had antecedents in the sixteenth-century amalgam of Lutheran theology and appeals to local bigotry. Luther's tirades of the 1540s and the hackneyed arguments that Jews were unproductive and lived on the sweat and blood of the German peasantry were joined to demands that the Jews' houses and synagogues be burned and the enemies of Christ be driven into the wastelands to scratch the soil for sustenance. Lutheran eschatology in its mature form held out little prospect that Jews would be converted to Christ at the end of the days. In the interim their suffering was justified by the crime of deicide and the curse they had wished upon themselves.

But this simple statement of the Lutheran position does not account for the emergence of the most significant Christian Hebraist of the first half of the sixteenth century, who left the Franciscan order and went over to the Reformation camp. The German Reformation, though dominated by the person and theology of Martin Luther, spawned many deviations, from the radical biblical prophetism of Thomas Müntzer, whose subversive uprising Luther suppressed with a bloody appeal to the German princes, to the scholarly virtuosity of Sebastian Münster, whose prodigious linguistic skills kept alive a tradition of encyclopedic learning to which Luther himself was relatively indifferent.

Münster, who was born in Ingelheim in 1489 and died in Basel in 1552, was known as the German Ezra. His enormous output of works included Hebrew and Aramaic grammars that derived from the writings of Elias Levita; translations of the "Hebrew Josephus," *Yosippon,* ascribed to Joseph ben Gorion; an annotated Latin translation of the Hebrew Bible (1534, 1535); a trilingual dictionary in Hebrew, Greek, and Latin (1530); a *Catalogus omnium praeceptorum legis mosaicae, quae ab Hebraeis sexcenta et tredecim numerantur* (Catalogue of All the Precepts of the Mosaic Law, Which the Hebrews Count at 613; 1533); *Fides christianorum et judaeorum* (The Faith of Christians and Jews; Hebrew and Latin, 1537); *Messias christianorum et judaeorum* and *Christiani hominis cum judaeo, pertinaciter prodigiosis suis de messia opinionibus addicto colloquium* (Messiah of the Christians and Jews, and Dialogue of a Christian and a Jew Stubbornly Addicted to His Own Strange Opinions about the Messiah; 1539), a two-part volume in Hebrew and Latin that betrays a measure of contempt for Judaic messianic expectations, though the dialogue is rather civil in tone and unmarred by Luther's Judeophobia. Among Münster's scientific writings were *Cosmographia universalis,* which appeared in German (1543), elementary works in arithmetic, a study of Rabbi Abraham Zacuto on the sphere (1546), and *Horologiographia* (1533).

Münster made Basel the center of his teaching and writing. Though he began his academic career without a formal professorial title, teaching theology, philology, and mathematics, he gave up the first subject to concentrate more on the others. His linguistic prowess was phenomenal. As one moves into the seventeenth century, the combination of Hebraic studies and science in the same person becomes less frequent (Schickard, Kepler's teacher, proficient in astronomy and Hebrew, was an exception). The elder Buxtorf appears to have continued the Münster tradition of Hebraic learning in Basel, though he did not quite equal Münster's production of more than forty volumes.

John Calvin, born in Noyon, 1509, who at one point in his wanderings studied Hebrew in Basel with Sebastian Münster, is a puzzle to those who seek to define the relationship of the sixteenth-century reformers to historical Judaism. There appears to be a flagrant contradiction between the utterances of Calvin himself and the positions later adopted by learned members of the Reformed Church in Holland, by Huguenots, and by Puritans in England and New England. Though the philosemitism of the Calvinists may have been exaggerated at times by modern scholars, in fact the conduct of the Calvinists in power and their absorption in rabbinic literature has little connection to the Calvin who derided Jews as "profane dogs" and ignoramuses. Calvin had begun his Hebrew studies in Paris along with Greek and Latin, and in many respects he was the model of a humanist who remained loyal to the trilingual ideal of the Erasmians; in the academy founded in Geneva in his last years, Hebrew was included in the required curriculum along with Greek and Latin, so that the

Bible and the classics could be studied in their original languages. He was determined to bring forth an erudite clergy, and in large measure he succeeded. But there is no indication that his knowledge of the Talmud and rabbinic literature was any deeper than Luther's, and his mockery of what he had heard of the cabbalists was in the Erasmian vein. He seems to have known few Jews, though there is record of a private disputation with a learned Jew on the nature of Christ that resembles the medieval tourneys of rabbis and priests far more than the later friendly colloquies of rabbis and Calvinists in seventeenth-century Holland. In debating the meaning of the vision of the four kingdoms in the seventh chapter of Daniel, Calvin ridiculed the absurdity of the Jew's interpretation, which foretold Israel's world dominion, and he concluded with a Luther-like verdict that condemned the whole people of Israel to damnation.

But aside from these obiter dicta, there is a significant respect in which Calvin may have affected the Christian view of ancient Israel: his unique reading of the Old Testament in a free and easy spirit makes the text approximate the speech of ordinary people. This approach, which has its origin in the talmudic dictum that the Torah speaks in the language of Everyman—though there is no reason to believe that this was Calvin's source—allowed him to make light of minor inconsistencies in the Bible without much ado about exegesis, to teat metaphoric language as a normal way for the authors of the final text to express themselves without use of elaborate allegorical interpretations. The gates were opened for the acceptance of the new science when Calvin argued that Moses knew the facts of creation and other secrets of nature but made his language conform to the understanding of the common people. The same undogmatic way of reading the Bible led Calvin to render biblical heroes like Moses and David psychologically plausible. Calvin's training in classical rhetoric permitted him to appreciate the art of persuasion, to dramatize biblical events, and to instill passion into sermons without resort to the allegorical fantasies he abhorred. Though the outcome was unintended, his humanizing of the Bible may have made Jewish commentators and philosophers, who had long been introducing similar reflections into their writings, more accessible to Christian readers in the next century.

French Hebraists in a Time of Troubles

While France was in the throes of its own religious wars and persecutions, Michel de Montaigne, a moderate in the conflict, wrote with compassion in his famous *Essais* (1580) of the plight of Jews who sought refuge from the Spanish edict of expulsion in 1492 and were so cruelly treated by the Portuguese monarchs. Narrating the forced conversion of Jewish children, Montaigne, who probably had some Jewish blood, abandoned his customary equanimity: "They say that the sequel was horrible . . . It was quite common to see fathers and mothers making away with themselves, and—a still ruder test— driven by love and pity, throwing their young children into the wells, to evade the law." [1]

During the religious wars in France, scholars and politiques on both sides of the divide extended their perceptions of Judaism by continuing to publish biblical commentaries and to translate into Latin excerpts from the rabbinic corpus. France's relations with the Ottoman Sublime Porte facilitated the transfer of manuscripts from the east to Paris, which fed the ongoing efforts of the great Parisian printing houses to reproduce biblical and patristic texts. Apart from the Bible, Hebraica was not a favored province of French publishing—but the dissemination of Church Fathers in critical editions brought to the fore many of the ancient Christian diatribes against Judaism.

In sixteenth-century France, the acquisition of Hebrew and Aramaic as tools was still a goal of the Christian Hebraist as a necessity for sectarian polemics. And here and there linguistic geniuses sprouted on French soil in the midst of the civil war. The Huguenot Joseph Scaliger (1540–1609), who had a passion to learn languages for their own sake, became proficient in Hebrew and other "oriental" tongues, in addition to Greek, without the aid of tutors. This "bottomless pit of erudition," as he was called, was persuaded to leave his native France and accept a professorship in Leiden, which became a center for the study of languages considered cognate to Hebrew. Though his major textual works were on Greek literature and he edited writings on ancient medicine, chronology, and mathematics, he was consulted by scholars from around the world for his knowledge

of Aramaic, Syriac, Arabic, Coptic, and Persian. In the eulogy delivered at Scaliger's funeral, Daniel Heinsius left an account of his phenomenal power of concentration, the hallmark of the true humanist
scholar. Heinsius recalled hearing from Scaliger's own lips that while
the Massacre of Saint Bartholomew (1572) was raging, he sat so intent
upon his Hebrew that for some time he did not hear the clash of arms,
or the cries of women and children, or the clamor of the men. A
similar tale of scholarly dedication is told of an older French Hebraist
on the Catholic side, Gilbert Génébrard (1537–1597), Regius Professor at Paris, who translated commentaries of Rashi and Abraham Ibn
Ezra on the Song of Songs and the chronicle *Seder Olam Zutta* by Jose
ben Chalafta: he trained a dog to rouse him if he should nod during
his studies. But though there were many Hebraists in France, there
were no towering figures devoted principally to the recovery of rabbinic literature. French prowess lay elsewhere.

An understanding of Judaism that went far beyond the perfection
of philological skills was exemplified by two Frenchmen whose visions continue to baffle modern scholars, as they did their contemporaries—Guillaume Postel and Jean Bodin.

Of the forty-two works of Postel (1510–1581) printed during his
lifetime, the overwhelming number, written in either Latin or French,
appeared in Paris from 1538 through 1579. This is perhaps the only
identifiable focus in the turbulent life of the Norman orphan. The
role Postel allotted to Judaism in the establishment of a universal harmony among all religions and sciences is in part derived from Pico
della Mirandola, but half a century separated them and the religious
schism in Christendom lent an urgency to Postel's projects that
marked, and perhaps scarred, everything he wrote. Pico's princely
scuffles with the Catholic Church, always buffered by his wealth, were
of a different order from the harassment to which Postel was subjected. When as a young man he managed to make his way to the
College of Sainte-Barbe in Paris, he quickly demonstrated his linguistic virtuosity, learning Hebrew by himself after having been taught
only the alphabet by a rabbi in the neighborhood. At Sainte-Barbe
Postel became linked with a group that formed the nucleus of the
Society of Jesus.

Attached to a diplomatic mission to Constantinople, Postel learned
Arabic and rekindled the perennial hope of the Church for Christian

conversion of the Orient. On his return journey he stopped in Venice, visited Daniel Bomberg's printing house, and began to write of Hebrew as the original language of mankind before the confusion of Babel, a theological cliché to which he brought empirical evidence by publishing illustrations from twelve Balkan and Near Eastern languages. Back in Paris he was appointed a royal reader, a comfortable post he held until he became embroiled in a court intrigue. Pushed out into the cold in the terrible winter of 1542–43, he took solace in scholarship and set about writing his major work, *De orbis terrae concordia* (On the Harmony of the World; 1544). When the Sorbonne returned the manuscript without formal comment, he sent it for publication to the Protestant Johann Oporinus in Basel, a strange destination for a work intended to convert the world to the Catholic faith.

In 1544 Postel was received into the Society of Jesus, was soon expelled, embarked upon studies of the Cabbala, translated parts of the *Zohar,* and discovered a Venetian virgin, Jehanne, who became his "mater mundi." After another voyage to the Near East he returned to Europe, where he was possessed by the holy spirit through the mediation of his Mère Jehanne, who had died in the interim. In pursuit of his grand design to bring universal harmony to the world, he made overtures to the king of France, the Holy Roman Emperor, and Lutheran scholars. For decades before his death in 1581, he was shunted from the prison of one religious or secular authority to another, with intervals of freedom during which he continued to propagate his millenarian doctrines among kings and printers and sundry Protestant sects. The Inquisition declared him mad, not heretical. In 1563 an order of the Parlement of Paris sequestered him in a monastery, where he lived for eighteen years under conditions that allowed him some liberty of movement and permitted him to receive learned and royal visitors.

Since Postel left no disciples and his books were rarities, it is difficult to assess his significance in the creation of a novel Christian interpretation of Judaism. In his idiosyncratic history of Jewish thought, he distinguished between two types of biblical commentary prevalent among Jews before the time of Jesus: one was allegorical and was preserved in the two Talmuds; the other was esoteric and anagogical and was a revelation of the highest mysteries, restricted to those Jews who led the holiest lives. According to Postel, these esoteric doctrines survived as the Cabbala. Though on occasion he cites the Babylonian Talmud, his commitment to the truth of this source is not nearly as constant as his veneration for the Cabbala as the fount of scriptural interpretation. (In a letter to the German scholar Konrad Pellikan in 1553 he even called the Babylonian Talmud the utmost perversion of truth.) There is nothing in the literature on Postel to indicate any serious acquaintance with the Halachic tradition of the Talmud, and there is little evidence that his knowledge of rabbinics went much beyond what was included in Bomberg's rabbinic Bible, the standard fare of Christian Hebraists. His familiarity with a number of writings in the cabbalist tradition is far better authenticated: he published a Latin translation of the *Sepher Yezirah* (Book of Creation) in Paris (1552) and an interpretation of the symbolism of the candelabrum in Venice (1548), but his translation of parts of the *Zohar,* which remains in manuscript, to my knowledge has not been studied.

In sum, Postel's use of cabbalist literature in the elaboration of his world religious synthesis does not seem to have equaled that of Pico, who had available the translations of Flavius Mithridates. Whether Postel could have immersed himself in the intricacies of cabbalist tradition without a Jewish mentor is open to question. This eccentric genius, who fostered Syriac and Arabic scholarship that found its way into Christoph Plantin's polyglot Bible, belongs in that galaxy of Christians who were fascinated by what they believed to be the Jewish Cabbala, discovering in it trinitarian mysteries. But as a Hebraist he is not on the same level as his younger contemporary Jean Bodin, who controlled much of the Halacha of the Talmud as well as the tradition of Christian Cabbala.

It is thought that Jean Bodin was born in Angers in 1529 or 1530. He joined and subsequently left the Carmelite order, traveled to Geneva in 1552, where it is conjectured that he observed Calvin's burning of Servetus and quickly abandoned any sympathy he may have had for the Protestant cause. Ten years later he was practicing law in Paris, where he had to take an oath of loyalty to the Catholic faith. After a brief imprisonment for heterodoxy, he was released and became a counselor to Francis, duke of Alençon, of the Politique party. In 1576 Bodin was a leader of the third estate at the meeting of the Estates General. After the death of Alençon, Bodin frequently fell under the suspicious eye of the Catholic League; as a moderate he ultimately joined the royalists supporting the converted Henry IV. Bodin has been known best for his *Methodus* on history (1566) and *Les Six livres de la république* (1576). His other works, especially a treatise on demonology (1580), have bewildered many. Bodin's serious preoccupation with Judaism is prominent in the *Colloquium hepta-plomeres de rerum sublimium arcanis abditis* (Colloquium of the Seven about Secrets of the Sublime), completed in 1588 but not published until 1857 after circulating in the European republic of letters in manuscript for almost three centuries.

The seven participants in this imaginary discussion, which takes place in Venice in the luxurious home of one Paulus Coronaeus, range widely over the field of religious and philosophical thought, ancient and modern. A variety of opinions and different degrees of zeal are displayed, though the argument veers toward the prospect of a society that would tolerate a multiplicity of religious views short of atheism. The guests include a convert from Catholicism to Islam, a Calvinist who stresses the inner piety of the Reformed religion, a Lutheran mathematician, a skeptic who wittily insists that all religions are good, and a speaker who maintains what would later be called a deist position, that rites and ceremonies are superfluous and that adoring God and following the plain laws of nature are sufficient. The oldest interlocutor is a Jew named Salomon Barcassius, whose bearing and erudition command general respect and who argues that the religion of Moses, the most ancient, remains superior to all others. In the free-roaming conversation, Salomon feels at liberty to attack frontally, with Hebrew quotations from the Bible, the traditional Christian interpretation of Isaiah 7.14, the prophecy of the virgin birth: "Isaiah did not ever suppose anything about Jesus, much less about his mother, Mary. He uses these words: *Hinneh ha'almah,* that is, 'Behold, a young girl!' for *ha'almah* does not mean a virgin, but one whose love a man [husband] enjoys. Even Christian theologians who know Hebrew now are forced to admit this." [2]

Modern readers of the *Colloquium* have debated about which protagonist is the mouthpiece for Bodin's own beliefs. He had clearly moved beyond the position implicit in the *République*, where religion serves the purposes of the state, and was seeking solutions to religious questions that agitated this nominal politique throughout his tumultuous life. The learning revealed in Salomon's presentation is witness to Bodin's absorption in both Testaments; and his scores of citations from Philo, Josephus, the Talmud, the *Zohar,* Rashi, Maimonides, Gersonides, the Aramaic paraphrasts (targums), David Kimchi, and Abraham Ibn Ezra bear the marks of a Hebraist culture far superior to the platitudes of mediocre Hebraists who drew their knowledge from thumbing Bomberg's rabbinic Bible. References to Pico della Mirandola and the Cabbala have led commentators to surmise that Bodin was ultimately aiming for a higher synthesis that would transcend the literal interpretation of the Old and New Testaments in a religious vision bordering on the Cabbala.

The *Colloquium* ends with a paean of praise for religious brotherhood, rare in the bloody epoch of civil strife in France: "All . . . withdrew, having embraced each other in mutual love. Henceforth, they nourished their piety in remarkable harmony and their integrity of life in common pursuits and intimacy. However, afterwards they held no other conversation about religions, although each one defended his own religion with the supreme sanctity of his life." [3]

Rabbinic Transmitters and Christian Receptors

The privileges granted Jews in French enclaves, in some German and Italian cities, and in Holland made possible interchanges of erudite Jews and Christians in sixteenth- and seventeenth-century Europe in a measure never before deemed possible outside a compulsory religious tourney or an inquisitorial chamber. Benchmarks of change cannot be fitted neatly into the chronology of Christian centuries: the eye necessarily moves backward and forward across a shifting landscape. In Venice, rabbinic Jews assimilated the classical literature, and sometimes the vices, of their Christian neighbors: Rabbi Leone Modena (1591–1648) learned to rhyme drinking songs in the Italian manner and to gamble. In the Roman inquisition of the Christian heretic Tommaso Campanella (1568–1639), the records refer to the sinister influence of a Jew, a ubiquitous Abraham. No meeting place equaled Amsterdam, the New Jerusalem, for the free and easy intercourse of Jewish and Christian scholars.

The rediscovery of Judaism in a sense restored the converse that had existed among the Jewish and Christian schools of Syria during the early centuries of our era. The threads had unraveled during the ensuing thousand years, but now the growing mass of rabbinic writings from Jewish settlements throughout Western Europe and the Ottoman Empire, on subjects ranging from commentary and supercommentary on the Bible and the Talmud to philosophical dialogues and treatises of astronomy, was opening up to Christian scrutiny.

With the Reformation, the quarrels of the major Christian denominations and intramural disputes among members of the same sect about the precise meaning of God's word ended up, paradoxically, with recourse to the despised rabbis as arbiters. This did not necessarily lead to general acceptance of what a particular rabbi said, and often as not Christian contenders could find support for contradictory opinions in the treasury of Judaic learning. But in the course of the search, personal ties were established with rabbis that led to further investigation of the rabbinic corpus. Even as the conquerors and colonizers of new lands—new only to the invaders—coopted and used friendly natives, Christians venturing into the thickets of Judaica found rabbis to serve as mentors. Sometimes the conquerors turned on their guides once they had acquired their knowledge. The discovery of new territories, either physical or intellectual space, inevitably transforms both the discoverer and the discovered. Judaism was being profoundly amended even as it was being examined, though its fluidity has frequently been ignored.

By the seventeenth century, a number of Jewish works were recognized by Christians as compendia of rules of religious conduct; all of life among the Jews appeared to ordinary Christians to be a succession of ritual acts. The Spanish inquisitors tracking down judaizers among the New Christians invariably collected evidence of residual Judaic practices, such as changing undergarments for the sabbath and shunning pork. Learned Christians knew that there were books and utterances by noted rabbis that set forth the fundamental tenets of belief (*Ikkarim*). These compilations, which were used by Christian Hebraists in the seventeenth century, did nothing to dim the impression among many literate Christians that rabbinic thought was a *magna turba*.

The attitude of Christian scholars toward Judaism was riddled with contradictions. On the one hand, inimical Christians wanted to see Judaism as a stagnant pool of dogma and empty ceremony so that Jewish thought historically and in the present could be refuted and dismissed once and for all, making it easy to characterize the religion in simple pejorative terms. On the other hand, as they became fairly well versed in rabbinic disputations, rival sects, and theological conflicts among Jews, scholarly Christians could not remain indifferent to the Jewish quarrels. What occurred in Judaea at the time of Christ was pertinent to Christians, because an understanding of their own religion was related to the beliefs of the Judaic sects. And when a messiah, Shabbetai Zevi, arose among the Jews in the year 1666, sowing bewilderment in their communities that lasted for more than a century, the question of the true and the false messiah, which had divided Judaism from Christianity since Jesus, was pointedly brought to the forefront of European consciousness by deists, who used the event to make fun of all messiahs.

The rediscovery of Judaism should be considered against the backdrop of prevailing curiosity about all the religions of the world. Accounts by friars and noble warriors and educated natives such as the Peruvian Garcilaso de la Vega featured sections on the religious practices of conquered peoples and tribes. By the seventeenth century there was a great vogue for books devoted to non-Christian religions or superstitions that juxtaposed beliefs and rituals from different lands. Scholars such as John Selden, whose learning bridged the classical and the Judaic fields, groped in their fashion for a science of comparative religion. The practices of Judaism were included in compendia of universal religions along with descriptions of more exotic savage ceremonies. Such compilations concentrated on rituals, actions, performances, and avoided complicated theologies. The books were often illustrated, and their engravings are among the rare pictorial representations of Judaic ritual practices, not countenanced by some Jews because of prohibitions against the making of images (though portraits of the Sephardic rabbis of Amsterdam were beginning to be common and there are group paintings of prosperous Dutch Jews celebrating a circumcision).

When in the early sixteenth century Christians examined the contents of the Talmud—and printing subjected the text to formal censorship—some friars, with the Dominicans in the lead, singled out blasphemies against Christians in unexpurgated copies. Though attacks against the Talmud were renewed with vigor, the sixty-odd tractates survived and remained an impregnable stronghold of rabbinic learning, a foundation on which generations of commentators built structures that were at first incomprehensible to Christians. In addition to Rashi and Maimonides, three major Jewish agents for the transmission of post-Talmudic rabbinic knowledge merit special consideration: one is the sixteenth-century scholar Elias Levita; the other two, medieval rabbis who became living presences among Christian Hebraists, are David Kimchi and Abraham Ibn Ezra.

During the sixteenth century, German Jews like Elias Levita had crossed the Alps into Italy, where they became the teachers of a generation of Christian scholars, playing a significant role in the transmission of Judaic learning alongside the Sephardic exiles, whose migration from the Iberian peninsula continued even after the expulsion in 1492. Born in Neustadt an der Aisch, near Nuremberg, Levita sojourned in Padua and Rome before moving on to Venice. There he died in 1549 at the age of eighty, having been despoiled of his goods in the wars that erupted in central and southern Europe. In addition to teaching Hebrew to eminent Christian scholars such as Egidio de Viterbo and Paul Fagio, Levita was a prolific author. In writing scholia to David Kimchi's Hebrew grammar, he became part of a tradition that linked a medieval rabbi (d. 1235), born in Narbonne of Spanish ancestry, to Hebrew learning in southern Germany, to the Christian Hebraist Münster, and to Bomberg's printing presses in Venice. Levita's lexicographical works covered the Aramaic of the Talmud and the targums, and his book on the Massorete tradition, *Massoret ha-Massoret,* which supported the Catholic position that the diacritical marks and vocalizations in the Hebrew text of the Bible were not integral to the divine revelation, was authoritative among both Catholics and Jews. Levita was probably the outstanding intermediary between Christians and Jews in the first wave of the Hebraic renascence. His numerous Hebrew grammars, dictionaries, and commentaries were translated into Latin and adapted by Sebastian Münster, who became the schoolmaster of Christian Europe. Many generations were brought up on these textbooks, which monopolized the field until the publication of a new set of major guides by the Buxtorfs in the seventeenth century. Not that there was a dearth of scholars trying their hands in the composition of a Hebrew grammar—writing one was the brevet of a Christian Hebraist.

The writings of David Kimchi (1160?–1235?) occupied a unique role among Christian Hebraists. Luther, ordinarily no friend to rabbinic commentators, once told his followers that if he wished to become a Hebrew scholar—which he confessed he was not—he would start with Kimchi the commentator and grammarian. Over the next two centuries, Kimchi's Hebrew grammar—the *Sefer Michlol* (1522)— and his biblical commentaries, excerpted, abbreviated, and combined with other medieval commentaries, were translated into Latin by an array of Christian Hebraists, Santes Pagninus, Reuchlin, Konrad Pellikan, Rudolf Bayne. No denomination rejected David Kimchi.

Among Christian Hebraists who steered clear of the mystic way of Pico della Mirandola and Guillaume Postel, the surviving biblical commentaries of Abraham Ibn Ezra, preserved in the Bomberg Bible, were highly prized. For over two centuries there was a steady flow of translations into Latin in all parts of Europe, though many of the authors failed to grasp his subtleties. In the introduction to his commentary on the Pentateuch, Abraham Ibn Ezra castigated those of his predecessors who presumed to insinuate into their expositions discussions irrelevant to the text, those who gave themselves over completely to allegorical and mystical readings (he meant the Christians), and those who followed Midrashim, ignoring the straightforward meaning of the Scriptures. Abraham Ibn Ezra (1092–1167) opted for literal readings in combination with an acceptance of the talmudic interpretation of the legal portions of the books of Moses. His practice did not always conform to his resolve and, though he generally stressed plain, grammatical explanations, he digressed often enough with reflections on human nature, gleaned during extensive wanderings in Italy and France after he left his native Tudela in Spain.

When Christian Europeans acquired Ibn Ezra's commentaries, they assimilated the learning of medieval Spanish grammarians who had originally written in Arabic, as well as Ibn Ezra's cryptic remarks casting doubt on the dogmatic position that every word in the Pentateuch was written by Moses himself. In his commentary on the Song of Songs, Ibn Ezra allowed himself to see the whole text as an allegory of the history of Israel, from Abraham to the coming of the messiah. In recognizing the second half of the book of Isaiah as the work of a prophet who lived during the Babylonian captivity, he opened the door to biblical criticism that would eventually become even freer.

The commentaries of Ibn Ezra were second only to Rashi's in their popularity among Jews, and Christian Hebraists made frequent reference to them. Despite Ibn Ezra's occasional moral homilies and astrological beliefs, he strengthened the hands of Christian literalists and counteracted the lucubrations of allegorists and cabbalists. His wit and satire sometimes bordered on skepticism where details of tradition were concerned, but this in no way detracted from his profound religious quest for God, which he pursued in a neoplatonic mode. His astrological-medical and arithmetic works were among the first of his writings to be translated into Latin, beginning with *De luminaribus et diebus criticis* (On Heavenly Bodies and Critical Days; 1496). When Ibn Ezra was not directly accessible, his grammatical and exegetical works penetrated the Christian world through the writings of Elias Levita, the master of Münster and Fagio.

Though Hebrew and Arabic studies had been formally approved at the Council of Vienne in order to facilitate conversions, Judaic studies required further justification. A number of stereotyped apologies were developed, with different nuances, in the several Christian denominations. The need to know the Judaic texts thoroughly in order to achieve success in the mission of conversion still assumed a nominal position of primacy; but this concern was soon overwhelmed by other considerations. That there was something to be learned from the rabbinic commentators was a concession that gained ever greater prominence as Christian scholars became acquainted with the texts.

By the seventeenth century, Christian scholars were able to pursue their studies in the Protestant universities of England, Germany, Holland, and Switzerland and within the precincts of Catholic orders with growing independence from Jewish mentors. The basic linguistic skills had been learned. And even when taught by famous rabbis like Manasseh ben Israel (1604–1667), Protestant scholars in Amsterdam usually read rabbinic interpretations of Old Testament texts in a critical, independent spirit, accepting some, refusing others. In the Netherlands this would hold for both orthodox Calvinists and Arminians. Of the rabbinic authorities, Maimonides and Abraham Ibn Ezra were most readily assimilated, but there was no blanket approbation of any single rabbi. The rejection of rabbinic commentary on those verses in the prophetic books where Christians traditionally discovered foretellings of the coming of Christ was taken for granted. But Christian skepticism extended also to Jewish glosses on Old Testament books that on their face were neutral.

As postbiblical Judaism, virtually ignored for centuries, became a subject of controversy among Christians, the theological issues were not ipso facto related to legal questions about the residence of contemporary Jews in the kingdoms of Western Europe. Though tolerance of a Jewish presence sometimes evoked a more favorable judgment of rabbinic Judaism, curiosity about or deep involvement with Judaism of any epoch could be joined with a dogged hostility to the admission of Jews into Christian lands on the part of burghers, secular authorities, priests, ministers, and scholars. A utopian, idealized vision of ancient Israel, such as the Abbé Claude Fleury's *Moeurs des israélites* (1681), might have a certain resonance in the toleration of visible, contemporary Jews. But fundamentally, Christian scholars delved into Judaism to further theological ends that could be dissociated from political and economic issues involved in the granting of limited residence to Jews, who in principle had been outlawed from the realm.

Whether an attitude toward Judaism was favorable or inimical did not depend on the orthodoxy of the Christian sect or its radical departure from the main current of one of the major denominations. The Socinians, followers of Fausto Socinus, despite their profound commitment to the text of the Old Testament, were just as vehement in their rejection of rabbinic Judaism as they were in their repudiation of the trinitarian conceptions of Christianity. By contrast, the Remonstrants, who were ejected from the orthodox brotherhood of Calvinists, conducted scholarly inquiries into the nature of Judaism and held colloquies with Jews in a spirit of amity. Lutheran pietists eschewed the virulent Judeophobia of Luther himself and most of his later disciples. And among the Huguenot exiles in Holland there were leaders such as Pierre Jurieu, whose messianic doctrine closely approached an orthodox Judaic interpretation of the coming of the messiah.

On the other side of the great schism, Catholicism covered a broad spectrum of views on Judaism. Under the Spanish Inquisition there was a cruel and relentless attempt to eradicate the slightest taint of judaizing, and a Hebrew work would be destroyed unless it was authorized as a weapon in polemics against Judaic ideas. Long after the Jews had been expelled from Spain, orthodox theologians continued to prepare treatises against Judaism that were ludicrous in their extravagant manipulation of purported citations from the Talmud and the Midrash. On the other hand, Père Richard Simon, who had a deep knowledge of rabbinic writings in the anticabbalist tradition, respected Judaism and defended its adherents against blood libels and other accusations.

It would be anachronistic to discover evidence of philosemitic sentiments of the order of Lessing's feelings for Moses Mendelssohn in the relationships of sixteenth- and seventeenth-century rabbis and their Christian students. Even favored pupils of Manasseh ben Israel were not eager to have his works dedicated to them, and the homage he tried to present to the city fathers of Amsterdam in one of his books was rebuffed. Manasseh was too sanguine in his expectations of the marvels that knowledge of the Hebrew language and his millenarian exegesis of texts could achieve in winning more than forbearance from famous Christian Hebraists in the universities of Holland. The chair in Leiden occupied by the learned Constantijn l'Empereur van Oppijck, who was Controversiarum Judaicarum Professor, was devoted exclusively to the refutation of Jewish religious contentions. And if this was true in Holland, it goes without saying that in Germany and Italy the diffusion of Hebraica failed to act as a charm in preserving Jewish residents from intermittent molestation and expulsion. Christian Hebraism perhaps contributed a mite to the dediabolization of Jews, but its part in the history of their toleration is more dubious. And there was always a possibility of the opposite consequence. Those rabbis reluctant to allow the teaching of Hebrew to gentiles may have had a point. Three German Christian Hebraists of the seventeenth century, Schickard, Wagenseil, and Eisenmenger, used their learning to cast a glaring light on those texts in the Talmud and later Jewish writings that were either blasphemous or full of hatred for Christians.

In one crucial respect the discovery of Judaism differed from the recovery of the Greek and Latin corpus. Despite expulsions from England, France, Spain, and Portugal, and periodic evictions and readmissions of Jews in German and Italian principalities and city-states, Western Europe had never been free of living representatives of Judaism. Islands of protected residence had always survived. And in the middle of the seventeenth century there was a reversal of the general movement of Jews to Poland and the east that had been going on for centuries; after the Chmielnicki massacres in the Ukraine and Poland, Jews began to trickle back to the west, living under conditions of doubtful legality. Christendom was aware of the existence of these settlements; they were known to vigilant church and princely authorities and were tolerated. In the seventeenth century, general inquiries into the whole body of knowledge that constituted the beliefs of the Jews began on a grand scale and reached a zenith at about the same time that Jews were beginning to migrate westward from Poland. Amsterdam was becoming a new Jerusalem, a place of boundless opportunity for Sephardic marranos from the Iberian peninsula, who were joined by immigrants from Poland and Germany, the three "nations" establishing separate and often warring communities.

The underlying ambivalence of Christendom toward Judaism assumed new forms. Rival Christian denominations were attracted to different Judaisms and fitted them into their particular theological systems and biblical hermeneutics. Christians mined the Judaic corpus as they had exploited the mines of Peru. And they found appropriate biblical examples to justify their recourse to forbidden books. Yet despite the vast learning of the Christian Hebraists, their translations or paraphrases of rabbinic writings were often many times removed from the originals. The spirit of the pristine text, its unique kernel, was covered over with linguistic layer upon layer alien to it; though there were doubtless more and less felicitous renderings, the ordinary Christian reader of a vernacular translation had before him a much adulterated document. Scholars and priests adapted these discourses, usually out of context, to purposes completely different from any intent of their authors. The Judaism that was transmitted was indeed a confused morass—but however the original Judaic text was misconstrued, the transmogrified version was all that was available and, who knows, it was probably not much worse than some of our twentieth-century renderings of the same rabbinic and cabbalistic writings, for all the critical apparatus with which they are now laden. The color of the lenses has changed, the distortions are different in nature and spirit, but discoverers of unknown continents are ruthless in their exploitation of whatever they find.

An initial impetus for planting the seed of Christian Hebraism can be discovered in the particular historical circumstances of the fifteenth and sixteenth centuries. But having started to delve into what the rabbis said, Christian scholars could not refrain from further inquiry. They were drawn by curiosity, antagonism to what they read, and the amenability of the rabbinic materials to their use in internecine Christian controversies. The movement gathered speed as it went along, and the fascination with Hebraica continued until it was broken in the eighteenth century by another force of great magnitude, the anticlerical crusade.

4

The Flowering of Christian Hebraism

THE FLOWERING of Hebraic studies in Western Christendom was hardly comparable in extent to the revival of Greek and Roman writings; nor was its impact on European culture so pervasive. Yet it was an intellectual movement of no mean proportions in the Christian world. Though I am not a great partisan of cliometrics, perhaps one number may suggest the magnitude of the phenomenon: in 1694 the Cistercian monk Carlo Giuseppe Imbonati, in his *Bibliotheca latino-hebraica* of all works in Latin relating to Judaism, listed some thirteen hundred Christian authors, many of whom had composed numerous treatises and translations—witness to the fecundity of Christian Hebraists in Western Europe. By the middle of the eighteenth century, when Christian Hebraism had passed its prime, Blasio Ugolino, probably a convert from Judaism, published in Venice a Latin *Thesaurus* of thirty-four folios of disquisitions and translations by Christian writers on all aspects of Judaism; in volumes of a thousand columns each, he assembled a representative sampler of the vast storehouse of Christian Hebraic learning accumulated over the previous centuries. The making of anthologies signaled the end of this initial age of discovery.

The Third Culture

In the early seventeenth century, the perfect Christian Hebraist who pretended to the control of the whole corpus of knowledge on the "religion of Moses" and related Judaica of all ages would have to be fluent in many languages, in addition to the scholarly Latin in which he normally wrote. The Old Testament was in Hebrew, the speech in which God and Adam had conversed in the Garden of Eden and the angels had communed with the patriarchs, and it was revered as the sacred tongue (though a considerable body of dissident linguists contended that the paradisaical language was Dutch or English or Hungarian). Christ had spoken in Aramaic, the lingua franca of Judaea in his time, and a few phrases in that language were preserved in the New Testament. Parts of the books of Ezra and Daniel were also written in Aramaic, and it was the tongue in which the later generations of rabbis known as Amoraim disputed over interpretations of the law, in contradistinction to the earlier Tannaim of the Mishna, whose opinions were codified in Hebrew about 200 A.D. The Aramaic translation of the Pentateuch by Onkelos, about whom nothing is known beyond the Greek form of his name, was especially valued by Christians because it illuminated the Old Testament text in a version purportedly free of the alterations of rabbis intent on obliterating any prophetic reference to the coming of Christ. Finally, the *Zohar* was believed to have been composed by Shimon bar Yohai in Aramaic (though it now seems reasonably well established that the author was a thirteenth-century rabbi of Leon who wrote in pseudo-Aramaic to heighten the air of antiquity of his work).

Midrashim and post-Talmud grammars, commentaries, and works on philosophy, principles of faith, astrology-astronomy, chronology, medicine, and botany were in rabbinic Hebrew, as were poetry, liturgical prayers, books of moral preaching, and responsa that gave authoritative rabbinic decisions on difficult legal cases. The writings of Philo Judaeus, the Alexandrian philosopher and commentator of the first century, were in Greek, as were the histories of the renegade general Josephus who defected to the Romans, works that were greatly valued by Christians. Today they are reminders of the Hellenic envelopment of culture among the Jewish elite in Judaea and the Mediterranean basin at the time of Christ. The original language of the medieval philosophical treatises of Maimonides and Yehudah Halevi (called Judah Levita in Christian texts) was Judeo-Arabic, though they are familiar to European Jews in the Hebrew translations of the Ibn Tibbons and Al Harizi. Spanish, Portuguese, and Italian, sometimes written in Hebrew letters, were used as languages of religious instruction in the Iberian peninsula, Italy, and especially Holland, where rabbis compiled popular works for conversos returning to the fold.

The rendering of the Old Testament into Greek (the Septuagint, about 200 B.C.) was esteemed for its antiquity and thus its presumed accuracy, as were translations into Syriac, Coptic, and Slavonic when they later came to light, contributing to the overwhelming number of discrepancies in the flood of manuscripts pouring into Western European libraries from the east and bedeviling the compilers of polyglot Bibles. The complete Christian Hebraist would also have to know some Old French because the most famous medieval commentator, Rashi, was from Troyes and he sometimes interpolated a French translation of a Hebrew term in order to make his meaning clear. Other medieval commentators used words in Provençal and Judeo-Arabic, the demotic speech in lands where Jews had settled. Yiddish, the Judeo-German of Ashkenazic Jews, had no serious literature that concerned a Christian, though the phenomenal seventeenth-century linguist Johann Christoph Wagenseil published a book on the language.

This portrait of the complete Christian Hebraist is an ideal that never existed. Most run-of-the-mill Christian Hebraists did not acquire a high degree of proficiency in all or any of these tongues. In the sixteenth and seventeenth centuries, ambitious scholars usually contented themselves with a working knowledge of biblical Hebrew and some Aramaic, which they called Chaldean.

Christian Hebraism today occupies a corner in the cemetery of seventeenth-century baroque learning. In that magnificent age of scholarship, the production of a hundred volumes in a lifetime was considered a feat, but not an unsurpassable one. The grand folios poured forth by the presses of Amsterdam, Venice, Leiden, Rome, and Frankfurt, preserved in university treasure rooms, are now rarely disturbed by intruders. Modern scavengers have not often bothered to pick the bones of these worthies or plagiarize them, or even savor the content of their works. An occasional essay or book on one has appeared, but who would venture to encompass the writings of John Selden, John Lightfoot, John Spencer, and Edward Pococke in England; Johann Buxtorf, father and son, in Basel; Père Simon in France; Wilhelm Schickard, Wagenseil, and Eisenmenger in Germany; the Dutchmen Jan van den Driesche (Drusius), Adriaan Reeland, Antonius van Dale, Pieter van der Cun, Willem Surenhuis, Philipp van Limborch, or the scholar who published in Leiden and bore the sonorous name Constantijn l'Empereur van Oppijck?

Frequently the Christian Hebraists were helped by rabbis or converts: Buxtorf the Elder housed two rabbis, for which he needed special dispensation from the Basel authorities since Jews were prohibited within the city. But sometimes the Christian scholars heroically confronted the rabbinic corpus alone, doubtless making egregious errors, but in solitude producing monumental works of interpretation which, in the prearchaeological world and in a primitive period of oriental philology, transmitted rabbinic thought to Christian divines, litterateurs, and ordinary lay readers impelled by a desire to learn about the religion of the Jews.

Despite the bloody religious wars of the seventeenth century, there remained the semblance of a republic of letters among Christian Hebraists. Awareness of sectarian differences was sharp, and when Imbonati in his *Bibliotheca* included Protestant writers, he was careful to identify them with appropriate warning signposts, such as "heretic of the first order"; but all the same, he recorded them insofar as he knew of their existence. While no single papal, royal, private, or university library contained all of the rabbinic and Christian Hebraist works, there were impressive collections in many parts of Europe (Imbonati lists them); and leading scholars traveled to consult them, even stepping over the boundary between Catholic and Protestant territories. The Vatican store of Hebrew manuscripts, which had its origin in the sixteenth century, was significantly augmented when Maximilian of Bavaria conquered the Protestant Palatinate, seized the great palatinate library, and gave it to the pope in 1623.

In the Catholic world, the College of Neophytes in Rome housed learned Jewish converts as well as old Christians. Seventeenth-century England produced linguistic prodigies, such as Selden, Pococke, and Lightfoot, who encompassed the whole range of Hebrew studies from the Talmud through contemporary rabbis. Protestant universities, notably those of Basel, Leiden, and Leipzig, witnessed the establishment of veritable dynasties of Hebraists, as professors succeeded one another for three and four generations in a family—the Buxtorfs of Basel, the Vossiuses of Amsterdam, the Carpzovs of Leipzig. Where succession from father to son was excluded, as it was in Rome, there were chains of disciples as students completed the work of masters:

Giulio Bartolocci, who died before finishing his *Bibliotheca magna rabbinica* (Great Rabbinic Library), organized according to the Hebrew alphabet in four gigantic folio volumes prepared for the Sacred Congregation for the Propagation of the Faith—he got lost in the letter yud—was followed by Imbonati.

The papal Inquisition had collected Judaic manuscripts of all sorts in order to stamp out sources of heresy, for writings had to be read or at least perused before they could be forbidden. Among secular collectors, the passion for accumulating Greek and Latin manuscripts often spilled over to all ancient writings. Christian scholars in universities and librarians attached to royal courts assembled works from all ages of Jewish thought. An Italian rabbi's library acquired by Oxford University became a nucleus of Hebraic scholarship. In 1647 Parliament appropriated £500 to purchase a library in eastern languages from George Thomason, the assiduous gatherer of Civil War pamphlets. The library, for which there is a printed catalogue, was eventually deposited at Cambridge University, where it nourished the writings of John Lightfoot.

Whereas previously the Hebrew parchments had merely been amassed, in the sixteenth and seventeenth centuries they began to be catalogued and studied. Once the Protestant reformers and Catholic scholars started to analyze the Bible manuscripts streaming in from the east, and ambitious translation projects and polyglot Bible enterprises were initiated under the patronage of cardinal, pope, or secular lord, it was inevitable that Christian scholars would turn to the works of rabbinic commentators and grammarians about passages difficult to interpret. The Buxtorfs, Selden, and Lightfoot assembled substantial private libraries of published Judaica. Buxtorf printed his catalogue, Selden's exists in manuscript; unfortunately Lightfoot's library, which had been sent to Harvard, was burned in an eighteenth-century fire. Richard Simon the Oratorian left a detailed evaluation of a selection of rabbinic commentators with Western European, Polish, and Constantinople imprints that he reviewed for his heterodox *Histoire critique du Vieux Testament* (Critical History of the Old Testament; 1678). Bartolocci's *Great Rabbinic Library* was by far the most extensive printed catalogue of Hebraica.

As the practice of accumulation became engrossing, scholars on both sides of the major denominational fracture competed, each denigrating the size of the other's Hebraic collections. The compilers of catalogues of rabbinic literature often included works to which they had only seen references, and rival erudits were quick to deflate one another's pretentions to completeness. The caustic Père Simon belittled the rabbinic descriptive catalogue published by Bartolocci in Rome, and accused him of passing off as his own the work of his teacher Giovanni Battista Iona, a Jewish convert. Simon was himself the cataloguer of the Hebrew and oriental manuscripts that the French ambassador to the Sublime Porte had sent back from Constantinople, following the practice that had brought rich harvests of Greek and Latin texts to Renaissance Italy.

By the seventeenth century, the patronage of Hebraic scholarship was increasingly concentrated in universities and royal libraries. In the sixteenth century, it had been assumed that Hebrew was included along with Greek and Latin under the rubric of professor of humanities. With time, Hebrew and Aramaic studies were split off and tended to be joined with other oriental languages in independent professorial chairs. Often Christian Hebraist studies were coupled with a cathedra in theology. Theological seminaries, especially those in French Huguenot communities and in Holland, became great centers of Hebraic learning. (The Christian Hebraists in Catholic religious orders had a natural means of support starting with the medieval movement to revive Hebraic studies for the defense of the faith and ease of conversion.) Under the title of professor of oriental languages or theology or Hebrew or Arabic, there was hidden a Christian Hebraist whose works were usually dedicated to the princely protector and supporter of the university. A Hebraist might even turn up as a professor of jurisprudence whose curiosity about ancient law had led him to delve into the Talmud and rabbinic literature. Sometimes young scholars attached themselves to nobles on tour and took advantage of the growing zest for travel to visit foreign libraries and converse with renowned scholars in other lands. In the Protestant universities where there were chairs of Hebrew and oriental languages, the kinds of dissertations required in the areas of Greek and Latin studies were soon adapted for Judaica. Any practice such as tithing, the rituals of temple sacrifice, or the levirate (the injunction to marry a brother's childless widow), could become a thesis subject. The seventeenth century was the golden age of the Latin university dissertation on

Hebraic topics, an enthusiasm that with some falling-off lasted into the eighteenth in Holland, Germany, and Sweden.

The same scratchiness that characterized competitiveness in the higher ranks of Greek and Latin scholarship was manifested in the rivalry among prominent Christian Hebraists. Scholarly correspondence kept the academic pot boiling with controversy, and the tone of the quarrels over matters great and small was usually as vituperative as that of contemporary scientific debates. Protestants and Catholics were generally aligned on opposite sides of the controversy over diacritical marks and vocalizations in the Hebrew biblical text, the Protestants opting for the integral relation of the marks to the letters, though as on all such battlefronts there were improbable alliances and strange defections. In a scriptural religion, the precise meaning of a text cannot be taken lightly, and new instruments of philology were soon brought into the fray as the study of languages considered cognate to Hebrew spread. The proliferation of royal academies occasionally provided new arenas of combat, but generally the learned societies avoided Hebraic studies, probably because of the hazards of involvement with theology.

Beginning in the early sixteenth century, translations of the Old Testament into the vernacular languages of Western Europe multiplied prodigiously. Some were renderings of Jerome's Latin Vulgate, others had recourse to the Hebrew Bible, the Greek Septuagint, and the rabbinic commentators. Luther's version dominated the Germanic world and came to exert a profound influence on his denomination, the Church of the Augsburg Confession; its force derived less from the accuracy of the translation than from the passion infusing the text. Though he consulted such competent Hebraists as Matthaeus Aurogallus, and the Greek scholar Philipp Melanchthon was by his side, Luther never pretended to be a slave to literalness. The King James version, a cooperative venture of English men of learning, possessed the conception of the Old Testament in Anglo-Saxon culture as Luther's did in Germandom. No French, Italian, or Spanish version ever succeeded in achieving a supremacy remotely approaching that of Luther's Bible or of the King James version. When the Council of Trent declared Jerome's Vulgate to be the "authentic version" and reaffirmed the exclusivity of church tradition in dictating interpretation, vernacular translations were under a virtual ban in the

Catholic world, and the Protestant and Catholic territories came to view pre-diaspora Israel through different lenses. Though prohibition of access to the Old Testament was never absolute in Catholic countries, the role of the Old Testament and its rabbinic commentators was always more problematic in Catholic than in Protestant lands. The voluminous *Cambridge History of the Bible,* published in the 1970s, failed to illuminate significantly the different sectarian colorations of the hundreds of Latin and vernacular translations of biblical texts, on which so many Christian doctrinal positions depended.

A random sample of Christian Hebraists from the sixteenth and seventeenth centuries would find them in all countries, employed in universities, churches, royal and aristocratic courts; piling up translations of rabbinic commentators, warring with them or composing biblical glosses of their own; engaging in printing-house controversies over the correct textual reading of biblical manuscripts, their vowels and points; compiling dictionaries in Aramaic, Hebrew, Syriac, Ethiopian, Persian, and Arabic. By the end of the seventeenth century, their labors had put at the disposition of Europeans who read Latin a sizable body of postbiblical rabbinic learning. In addition to the whole Mishna, presented with parallel Latin and Hebrew texts by the Dutch scholar Willem Surenhuis, translations had been published of some fifteen tractates of the Talmud, numerous Midrashim and Yalkutim, a large segment of the writings of Maimonides, the Bible commentaries of David Kimchi, Rashi, Abraham Ibn Ezra, Levi ben Gershon, Isaac Abravanel, the *Sefer ha-Ikkarim* (Book of Principles) of Joseph Albo, sections of the *Zohar,* parts of the Lurianic Cabbala, and the Targum of Onkelos, not to speak of new translations into Latin and the vernacular of books of the Old Testament. A bit of Maimonides was even done into English by Ralph Skinner. And there were many translations of Josephus into various European languages. Occasionally Hebrew treatises on chronology, astrology, botany, medicine, and mathematics also appeared in Latin. The two medieval works of Jewish philosophy most frequently quoted by Christian Hebraists, Yehudah Halevi's *Kuzari* and Maimonides' *Guide for the Perplexed,* were rendered into Latin by Buxtorf the Younger. (The older translation of the *Guide,* whose authorship is open to dispute, had been published in the early sixteenth century but was superseded in the scholarly world by the younger Buxtorf's version.) A long, if not complete, catalogue of translations available at the end of the seventeenth century can be drawn up from Imbonati's *Bibliotheca*.

The adjective "rabbinic" was applied by Christian scholars somewhat indiscriminately. Bartolocci idiosyncratically included in his *Great Rabbinic Library* even reputed biblical authors and anyone who wrote in Hebrew or Aramaic; Jewish converts to Christianity were especially welcome. But ordinarily the term rabbinic was reserved for postbiblical literature. Only in the more learned treatises were the rabbinic generations of Tannaim and Amoraim differentiated; the Massoretes were not consistently recognized as a separate group of authorities, though Elias Levita's history of these transmitters of biblical emendations was widely accepted as authoritative. Sometimes the "Talmudists" were distinguished from the later rabbis. The cabbalists were often singled out (by the seventeenth century, with a few noteworthy exceptions, the word *cabbalist,* noun or adjective, had acquired pejorative connotations among many Christians), but no distinction was ordinarily made between a philosopher, a grammarian, a commentator on the Bible and the Talmud, a writer on mathematics, and a poet; all were designated as rabbis if they were Jewish scholars. Some compilers reckoned Karaites and Samaritans among the rabbis, and their texts were often preferred to rabbinic versions as more ancient and unadulterated.

Before the Reformation, the sacred text was seen as an indivisible corpus, the whole inspired by God. When the critical spirit that possessed Christian humanist scholarship began slowly to nibble away at the sanctity of the Old Testament, demarcation lines were drawn more clearly between the five books of Moses or the Torah proper, the books of the prophets, and the hagiographa. Christian scholarship distinguished between the direct word of God transmitted by Moses and the "histories" of the Old Testament, which were not quite so sacred as the Pentateuch. The books of prophecy and psalms, crucial as witness to the truth of Christianity because they foretold the coming of Christ, acquired a paramount authority in Christendom. Often Jewish stubbornness in rejecting the messiah was imputed partly to the fact that there was no regular reading of *all* the prophets in the synagogue, whereas a portion of the Pentateuch was recited on every sabbath in the year until the cycle was complete. As prophecy became central to the rationalist Christian world view, subordinating the role of miracles, two Jewish thinkers appeared in Christendom as its lead-ing guides, Maimonides and Spinoza, albeit each appealed to differ-ent and often violently hostile Christian camps. Maimonides was widely and openly acclaimed as a defender of religion; Spinoza—in particular his *Tractatus theologico-politicus* (1670), which assumed that individual books of the Old Testament were composed in differ-ent centuries—was active in the underground, present but unmen-tionable, dreaded as a father of heresy and atheism.

The absorption in Jewish learning was sparked not only by desire to illuminate Christian doctrine and belief, but by inquisitiveness about the Jews themselves. Christians were curious about the rites and ceremonies of this strange people who were becoming ever more visible in the major European cities—Venice, Amsterdam, London, Hamburg. The synagogues of Amsterdam and London drew eminent visitors: Samuel Pepys, bewildered by the disorderly religious services he observed in the London synagogue; Marie de Medici, welcomed with great pomp by the elders of the Amsterdam synagogue; King William III of England, a visitor to the nearby synagogue when he stayed at the Amsterdam home of Jeronimo Nunes da Costa, the Se-phardic Jew who was an agent of the Portuguese court.

There was a certain looseness to some Christian Hebraist scholar-ship in the universities. Professors would allow their philological fan-cies to roam free, and there was little of the rigor that characterized Greek learning. The precision of quotations from the rabbis varied widely among Christian scholars, and faulty typesetting of Hebrew characters was common in publishing houses. Since there were thou-sands of biblical manuscripts in many eastern languages dispersed throughout the Continent, and the Massoretic text that contented most Jews was by Christian definition corrupted in key passages refer-ring to Christ, a critical Christian scholar could venture extravagant hypotheses without immediate reprisals. Wilhelm Schickard of Tüb-ingen—Hebrew scholar, mathematician, and astronomer—arbitrar-ily transposed Hebrew letters in obscure biblical verses; and having learned the art of gematria from the Jewish cabbalists, he used all manner of letter combinations to discover *Jesu* in Hebrew in the Old Testament. By the latter part of the eighteenth century, when Chris-tian Hebraist scholarship had fallen to a low point, Moses Mendels-sohn, who normally avoided debates with Christians on Judaic subjects, could not refrain from attacking pretenders to a knowledge of the Talmud for their flagrant misinterpretation of texts. When in seventeenth-century correspondence or public utterance a Christian professor is praised for his Hebraic and Aramaic learning, his reputation should often be examined with caution; though acrimonious academic fights were as common among Christian Hebraists as among scholars in other branches of learning, sloppiness and error were countenanced far more easily in Judaica than in Greek and Latin studies. Jews did not usually deign to look at what was published by *goyim,* though there were exceptions: Azariah de Rossi and Spanish marranos who escaped to other European lands kept abreast of some Christian scholarship and engaged in polemical refutations; and there were about a dozen Jews who corresponded with Buxtorf the Younger. A trinity of German Hebraists, Schickard, Wagenseil, and Eisenmenger, were tarred as outstanding antisemites in nineteenth-century Jewish apologetic literature; no one bothered to analyze them carefully or differentiate among them. Paradoxically, some of the most virulent Judeophobes were also among the most learned Hebraists.

Scholars and Popularizers

Though rarer than renderings into Latin, there were some translations of rabbinic literature into the vernacular languages of Western Europe. And from the sixteenth century on, works appeared that depicted contemporary Jewish rites and ceremonials with circumstantial detail. Well-received Latin books on Jewish history and political thought were normally translated into French, Dutch, and English. By the end of the seventeenth century, extensive histories of the Jews were composed in French, syntheses like those of Jacques Basnage, voluminous narratives that immediately became the targets of specialist scholars intent on demolishing them. The attacks of the learned seem to have had little effect on the circulation of these general works among a public interested in Hebraica and Jewish history in a language they could understand. For the incorrigibly indolent, there were journals and periodicals in French that abbreviated the contents of the vulgarizations and removed the learning another step further from the original seventeenth-century fonts of Christian Hebraism. The "universal libraries" of Jacques Basnage's elder brother, Henri

Basnage, Sieur de Beauval, of Jean Le Clerc, and of Pierre Bayle, published in French in Amsterdam, enjoyed a European reputation. The Leipzig *Acta eruditorum,* which covered all branches of learning including Hebraica, stubbornly clung to its Latin idiom.

Along with the more weighty and recondite researches of Christians in Protestant universities and Catholic monastic orders, there was a progressive popularization of information about the practices and beliefs of Judaism in European society. A number of Jewish rabbis who wrote in both Latin and the vernacular expected to attract Christian audiences. Rabbi Leone Modena of Venice explained Jewish rites in a book originally composed for James I that became known throughout the Continent and was frequently republished, with illustrations, in the eighteenth century. Rabbi Manasseh ben Israel of Amsterdam, renowned in the Christian world as "philosophus" and "theologus," directed his works of apology to Christians with an evident political purpose, to facilitate the admission of Jews into England.

The task of popularization was often performed by Christians themselves. Books like the elder Buxtorf's *Synagoga judaica,* in German, and Thomas Godwyn's *Moses and Aaron,* in English, were widely circulated, running to ten or fifteen editions and many translations. There were attempts to attract readers with provocative titles. The implicit assumption in some of these works was that Judaism had managed to keep itself concealed from Christian eyes. Christian Knorr von Rosenroth's *Kabbala Denudata* has something of a voyeur's tone. And Johann Andreas Eisenmenger's *Entdecktes Judenthum* (Judaism Uncovered), written in a spirit of profound hostility to Jews and Judaism, used the same language of scandal. Wilhelm Schickard of Tübingen thought his *Jus regium hebraeorum* (Statute of Hebrew Kings) was "plucked from rabbinic darkness and exposed to the light." Buxtorf advertised his work as a disclosure of beliefs and ceremonies that were in secret usage, customs hidden from Christians. Judaism was being revealed, uncovered, unveiled. Jewish arcana were being opened up.

The Jewish rabbis who wrote in Latin or the vernacular and expressly addressed Christian audiences about the prevailing practices and beliefs of Judaism in European society were careful to present a sanitized version of their religion. When Leone Modena's *Historia de gli riti hebraici* first appeared in Paris in 1637, without the consent of the author, he took fright that some of its utterances would bring him to the notice of the Inquisition, and after months of anguish he voluntarily presented himself to the Venetian inquisitor in order to confess. As it turned out, the editor, Jacques Gaffarel, had discreetly attenuated the misdemeanors before publication and the inquisitor exonerated Modena, allowing an Italian edition to be printed in Venice in 1638. Père Richard Simon, who published a French translation under the pseudonym Don Récared Sciméon, quoted John Selden's report that he had seen a more extensive version of Modena's original manuscript in an English library. Rabbi Simone Luzzatto chose to write in Italian his apologetic treatise on contemporary Jews, *Discorso circa il stato de gl'hebrei* (published in Venice, 1638), designed to support a petition to avert a threatened expulsion of the Jews from Venice. Jews who published books about the tenets of their religion for Christian readers were often censured by their coreligionists on the ground that their revelations might lead to slander and false accusations, thereby further endangering the tenuous civil status of their community. Who knew what chance observation could be twisted by ill-intentioned Christians as a pretext for persecution? The fear of Christians was hardly a phobic fantasy, but it did not deter the seventeenth-century Venetian rabbis, who placed at least limited trust in the protective utility of the defenses of Judaism that they wrote in the vernacular.

At times the Jewish apologists made efforts to ingratiate themselves with the dominant religious denomination of the host country. Luzzatto's *Discorso* attempted to prove that many doctrines of the "Hebrew nation" were closer to the Roman Catholic than to the Protestant church. The Hebrews, like the Catholics, were convinced that numerous passages in Scripture were unintelligible without the light of tradition (in contrast to the Lutherans' fixation on the letter of the text). They too held that good works accompanied by faith were meritorious in the eyes of God. They considered the exercise of free will a fundamental article of faith, as against Calvinist predestination. They were confident that the accumulated good deeds of their brothers were transferable to sinners, and they prayed for the souls of the dead. Their penitents could receive real absolution, not merely the "putative" kind described by Calvin. And even though they did not use the term "purgatory" explicitly, their rabbinic authorities divided the souls of the departed into those deserving beatitude, finite punishments, or eternal torments in Gehenna, again bringing Judaism closer to the three-tiered Catholicism of the next world than to Protestantism.

By the same token, on the other side of the great divide, Manasseh ben Israel in dealing with the Cromwellian Puritans resorted to arguments that clung to the literally interpreted text of the Old Testament and joined in the Puritan condemnation of papist Catholicism as idolatrous. In accepting the doctrine of the millennium, which Augustine had rejected, the Jews could find themselves much closer to Calvinism than to the papist Whore of Babylon. The seventeenth-century apologetic position taken by Jews in Calvinist and Anglican lands appears more convincing than the theological arguments of Luzzatto on the similarities between Judaism and Catholicism. This did not remain true, however, in the eighteenth century and surely did not apply to the orthodox Lutheran world.

Thomas Godwyn's *Moses and Aaron* (1625), more than any other work diffused a knowledge of Judaism in the seventeenth- and eighteenth-century English-speaking world. (John Weemse's *Christian Synagogue* [1623?] was clumsy and ill informed by comparison.) In his dedication to the Earl of Pembroke, Godwyn, an English schoolmaster who had published a popular Roman history, wrote a classical apology for Christian Hebraism that departed from the conventional conversion argument: "That many have no better acquaintance with Christ and his Apostles, is because they are such strangers with Moses and Aaron: were customes antiquated thorowly knowne, many difficulties in Scripture would appear elegancies, and the places which now (through obscuritie) dishearten the Reader, would then become sweet invitements to an unwearied assiduitie in perusing those sacred Oracles."[1] To understand the New Testament better, it was necessary to know the laws and practices described in the Old. This was one of the chief motives for the careful examination of the religious rites and even idolatrous lapses of the Jews. Godwyn's compendium included descriptions of their government in the ages before Christ, their feasts and holy days, forms of worship, consistories, and punishments.

Though Godwyn had some faint recognition of the institutional changes that had taken place between the first and the second Jewish commonwealths, his tendency was to view all of Hebrew history as a block and to describe rituals as if they were unaltered from Moses to Jesus. Judaism of the diaspora was the same as it had been in Jesus' lifetime, a pretension to which many orthodox Jews themselves would subscribe (except for the abolition of temple sacrifice). As a result, in examining a law or ritual, Godwyn could cite Jewish authorities from any period—the two Talmuds, the *Zohar,* Philo, Rashi, Maimonides, Moses de Coucy (the thirteenth-century rabbi whose compendium of Jewish commandments and prohibitions was published by both Soncino and Bomberg)—without paying attention to their chronological sequence. Godwyn was aware of the diversity of opinions among Jewish authorities, which many Christians used to illustrate rabbinic confusion, but he stressed underlying uniformities. Along with his fellow Anglicans, he showed a preference for the rationalist and literalist Jewish interpreters. He also displayed his acquaintance with a host of Christian Hebraists—Bodin, Buxtorf, van der Cun, Reuchlin, Nicolaus Serarius (the early seventeenth-century Dutch historian of Jewish sects at the time of Christ), Joseph Scaliger, van den Driesche. In *Moses and Aaron* rabbis of all centuries rubbed shoulders with Christian Hebraists from different parts of Europe who had written since the Renaissance—a measure of integration. Only occasionally did they jostle one another rudely in side- and footnotes.

Unlike the popularizations about Jewish institutions and practices, learned books in Latin by the English scholars Selden and Lightfoot carefully distinguished between ancient Israel and modern Jewish communities. In Selden's three-volume *De synedriis & praefecturis iuridicis veterum ebraeorum* (On the Sanhedrin and the Judicial Magistrates of the Ancient Hebrews; 1650–1655), a parallel was drawn between the Sanhedrin and the English Parliament. Lightfoot appeared to be more interested in the precise interpretation of passages in the New Testament through reconstruction of the ecclesiastical and political life of Judaea at the time of Jesus and the Apostles. But both English scholars were keenly appreciative of the riches of the talmudic and rabbinic sources upon which they relied. In Dutch and in English scholarship, specialization had proceeded far enough to bring forth studies of individual topics such as Selden's *Uxor ebraica* (Hebrew Wife; 1646) or Dionysius Vossius' translation of Maimonides' *On*

Idolatry (1641). While the treatment of Jewish laws on marriage and divorce was an objective, scholarly rendition of talmudic opinion, the deeper motive behind Selden's exhaustive analysis was to revamp contemporary British divorce laws. John Spencer's *De legibus hebraeorum ritualibus et earum rationibus libri tres* (Three Books on the Ritual Laws of the Hebrews and Their Reasons; 1683–1685), by all odds the most comprehensive work on Jewish ritual laws, was really an organized presentation of Maimonides' summation of a perennial theme of rabbinics and philosophy—the reasons for the various commandments. Spencer's masterpiece became fundamental to the Anglicans' understanding of Judaism and their rationalist conceptualization of prophecy.

As the seventeenth century wore on, ancient Judaism could be perceived either through the eyes of Maimonides, who made plausible the tenacious clinging of the Jews to every one of the 613 commandments—essentially an attempt to differentiate the people of God from the heathens who surrounded them—or through the eyes of Christian comparatists who, with the aid of travel literature and the study of the classical corpus, were constantly discovering similarities between the practices of the Jews and those of the heathens. This was no minor scholarly dispute, because the question of Hebrew uniqueness was at stake. In Herbert of Cherbury's work, which argued that philosophical minds among all the gentile nations from remote antiquity on entertained the same underlying principles of religion, Judaism was stripped of its special character. If the basic principles of all religions were identical, the ceremonials of the ancient Hebrews were on the same plane with the rites of pagans and savages and had no intrinsic worth. Except as a way of demonstrating the universality of essential deist beliefs, Jewish studies were not worth pursuing. Deism was in a measure responsible for the decline of Christian Hebraism in the eighteenth century. But in the seventeenth, the majority of divines and scholars rejected Herbert of Cherbury's encapsulation of religion into a few principles, and the Old and New Testaments continued to be revered as a true recording of the word of God.

The overwhelming number of the famous Christian Hebraist works were weighty tomes written in Latin, with citations in Hebrew, and were incomprehensible even to most educated Christians; but their impact on the minds of seventeenth-century Europeans cannot be adequately measured merely by counting their readers and identifying them in terms of social class. Initially the ponderous Christian writings on the Jews were read by the priests and pastors of the various denominations, by university professors, and by an indefinable yet existent body of gentlemen-scholars. The ideas then seeped into sermons, conversations, journals, and popularizations. Since the sermon was still a major form for communicating ideas on sacred history and Judaism, the learning of the Christian Hebraists ultimately reached a far wider audience than might at first be surmised.

Christian commentary was rarely constant in tone. The same Hebraist who had been studiously following his Jewish sources could abruptly break into a denunciation of the "oriental imagination" and Jewish superstitions. But there is a discernible general trend away from Jewish mystical and allegorical readings, and a persistent mocking attitude toward the multiplication of minor observances related to dress and dietary laws. Appreciation of Judaism was reserved for its rationalist laws as explicated by Maimonides. Crudities and anthropomorphisms in the Old Testament were often attributed to the fact that the Scriptures were originally addressed to "rather boorish and unruly people" (Galileo's version of the accommodation argument that justified Moses' failure to use scientific language in describing planetary movement).

The next century witnessed a violent reversal in the appraisal of biblical literary images. When the poetic nature of the Bible was recognized by men like Bishop Lowth, what a seventeenth-century Anglican had derided as enthusiasm came to be admired as vigorous expression, sublime and noble. As the estimation of the primitive underwent a transformation in European culture from the pejorative to the adulatory, the biblical prophets were reinterpreted, at least in some quarters. There are no seventeenth-century assessments of ancient Judaism that eulogize the Old Testament for its "primitive" qualities, attributes associated with barbarians.

The Buxtorfs of Basel

When the number of Christian Hebraists increased in the sixteenth and seventeenth centuries and rabbinic writings became accessible to them, penetration of the uncharted seas of Jewish commentaries on the Old Testament and the tractates of the Talmud was uneven. Learned Christians who read the Talmud were more comfortable with those parts written in Hebrew, the Mishna of the generations of rabbis known as the Tannaim (ending about 200 A.D.), and less at ease with the Gemara of the Amoraim, whose debates were preserved in Aramaic (codified about 500 A.D.). Few Christians could comprehend the pseudo-Aramaic of the *Zohar.* A knowledge of mishnaic Hebrew did not go hand in hand with an understanding of either the language or the complex arguments or spirit of the Aramaic Gemara. The paraphrases of the Bible in the Aramaic targums—the Chaldee Paraphrast, for example—were studied more frequently; but the whole of the Hebrew Mishna was available in Latin translation long before all the tractates of the Talmud—Aramaic Gemara as well as rabbinic Mishna—were known to gentlemen-scholars or even professors. To surmount the Aramaic barrier, the *Lexicon hebraicum et chaldaicum* (1607) of Buxtorf the Elder, professor at Basel and spiritual heir to Sebastian Münster, became the crucial instrument—it was his boast that he had made the entire Talmud available to Christendom.

The monumental works of the Buxtorfs, father and son, loomed over Christian Hebraic scholarship in the seventeenth century and were still being reprinted in the eighteenth and nineteenth. They served a heterogeneous audience, those who knew only German, Dutch, or English as well as those who could read Latin. The Buxtorf grammars were adopted as textbooks throughout Protestant lands, and their specialized treatises nourished scholars and divines of all denominations. The elder Buxtorf prepared the basic dictionaries of Hebrew and Aramaic that made intelligible the Talmud and the Cabbala to those who worked independently or with tutors who were rabbis or Jewish converts to Christianity. In the previous century Sebastian Münster had provided elementary tools for the study of Hebrew and Aramaic, but his pioneering works were now superseded, making it easier to understand the Gemara of the Talmud and to justify learning Aramaic as another sacred tongue in which the sages had spoken. This was Buxtorf's gift to Christian Hebraists.

Johann Buxtorf the Elder (1564–1629) was born, the son of a minister, in the town of Camen in Westphalia. He was educated in Marburg, Herborn, Heidelberg, Basel, and Zurich, and at the age of twenty-seven was named to his professorship of Hebrew at Basel, where he settled permanently and became the founder of a dynasty of scholars. His marriage to the daughter of a Basel patrician, Leo Curio, provided him with independent means to travel, assemble a large library of Hebraica, and employ rabbis as assistants and guides through the intricacies of rites and commentary. In his lifetime he enjoyed the prestige of being the outstanding Christian Hebraist in the Protestant world. Viewed in retrospect, the solidity and accuracy of his famous works are perhaps approached only by those of John Selden, though the purposes of the two scholars differed fundamentally: Buxtorf was in search of the precise literal meaning of words; Selden had a far broader concept of Judaism as a legal and religious system.

Buxtorf took his mission seriously. Perhaps his single most important work in the diffusion of Hebraic knowledge was his edition in 1618 of Bomberg's traditional rabbinic Bible, published in Venice a century before with the commentaries of Rashi, Kimchi, Abraham Ibn Ezra, and the Targum. Pastors of Protestant sects throughout Europe and in America who had some familiarity with Hebrew availed themselves of Buxtorf's new text, and in this way rabbinism infiltrated the sermons of Protestant Christendom. The Buxtorf Bible became the sourcebook for displays of Hebrew learning by scholarly gentlemen, such as John Milton and Isaac Newton. Many a reputation was founded on the capacity to make use of the text and commentaries of the Buxtorf Bible, frequently with the aid of a dictionary.

Christian Hebraists often confused the two Buxtorfs, and in the hundreds of letters addressed to father or son it is not always clear who was the intended recipient. The roster of letter writers, now arranged by nation in the Basel University Library, includes the most eminent scholars of western society—Germans, Dutchmen, Englishmen, Frenchmen, Italians, Poles, Swedes, Danes, Hungarians, and Jews—and affords an insight into the complex network of seventeenth-century Christian Hebraists. With rare exceptions, the letters are written in Latin, but these trilingual scholars habitually embellished their writing with Greek and Hebrew phrases. In addition to the normal shoptalk of their profession as Hebraists, they lift a curtain on the curious world in which works on recondite Judaic subjects were printed. The correspondents are avid for information about books and manuscripts in all parts of Europe, and they intermingle their elaborate baroque compliments with sad tales of their trials in finding skilled editors, typesetters, and proofreaders for Hebrew and Aramaic texts.

The Hebrew grammar of the Buxtorfs, originally written in Latin but translated into vernacular languages and republished in many Protestant countries, was frequently abbreviated and adapted for schools. The Buxtorfs' *Lexicon,* more a concordance than a mere dictionary, was excerpted and revised in many editions well into the eighteenth century. Parts of the great Buxtorf Bible were lifted from the whole, translated into Latin, and published separately. Sometimes the adapters and abridgers acknowledged their Buxtorfian source; often they kept silent. While many works were mercilessly compressed, as well as pirated, with the passing of time others swelled by accretion. Buxtorf the Elder's original *Lexicon,* a weighty tome of 983 pages, was expanded with a *Lexicon breve rabbinico-philosophicum* in a 1615 edition, and in Buxtorf the Younger's 1639 folio edition the work was further enlarged to 2680 columns.

While descriptions of Jewish ceremonials in Western Christendom answered to a growing inquisitiveness about religious practices all over the world, often there was a covert secondary intent in writing about Judaism from which the elder Buxtorf was not free: to cast odium on the superstitions and ceremonies of the Jews living in Christian Europe. With the rarest of exceptions—John Selden perhaps—the Christian Hebraists were continually on the defensive for engaging with rabbinism. But their attitude was not always merely cautionary, and ambivalence toward the creators of their subject surfaced in the writings of the most eminent professors.

Buxtorf the Elder's comprehensive description of Jewish beliefs and rituals, a volume of 730 pages, first appeared in 1603 under the title *Synagoga judaica: das ist, Jüden Schul: darinnen der gantz jüdische Glaub und Glaubensubung, mit allen Ceremonien, Satzungen, Sitten und Gebräuchen, wie sie bey ihnen öffentlich und heimlich im Brauche: auss ihren eigenen Bücheren und Schrifften, so den Christen mehrtheils unbekandt unnd verborgen sind, mit vermeldung jedes Buchs ort und blat, grundlich erkläret: item ein aussführlicher Bericht von ihrem zukünfftigen Messia: sampt einer Disputation eines Juden wider einen Christen* (Synagoga judaica: that is, the Jewish synagogue, in which the Jewish religion and religious practice, with all the ceremonies, precepts, customs, and usages, as they perform them openly and in secret, are thoroughly illuminated from their own books and writings, which are mostly unknown and hidden from Christians, with the citation of place and page in every book; also a full report on their future messiah; including a disputation of a Jew with a Christian). It was later published in Latin by Hermann Germberg, along with a letter from Ludovicus Carreto describing his conversion to Christianity. An authorized Latin version by David Le Clerc was edited by Buxtorf the Younger in 1661, and further emendations were made in 1680. The work was reprinted in Latin in Blasio Ugolino's *Thesaurus antiquitatum sacrarum* (1745) and was abridged and translated into English in 1748 by the Reverend John Stehelin, who performed the same function for Eisenmenger's *Entdecktes Judenthum.*

The *Synagoga judaica* was the most popular compendium of its kind in the Germanic world. It boasted all the trappings of scholarship and abounded in quotations from tractates of the Talmud and the Midrashim as well as from later rabbinic attempts, such as the *Book of Principles* of Joseph Albo, to fix norms for belief. Buxtorf's authority was conceded even by his rivals and enemies; he had, after all, compiled a Hebrew and Aramaic-Latin dictionary with meanings of words elucidated by quotations drawn from the whole corpus of Judaic writings, deciphered the bewildering acronyms that made the reading of a rabbinic treatise a trial even for those who knew Hebrew, and was the possessor of a famous library of rabbinic literature, for which he printed a descriptive catalogue along with a key to the acronyms. After his death his son, who corrected and expanded his father's works in new editions in Latin and in the vernacular tongues of Europe, made the name of Buxtorf synonymous with Christian Hebraism on both sides of the Atlantic. In the *Synagoga judaica* the elder Buxtorf oscillated in his summaries of rabbinic works between formulaic denigration and occasional grudging praise. Casual midrashic opinions were reported as if they were on the same level with fundamental principles and requirements of Jewish law. The distinction between halachic conclusions of the rabbis and the imaginative excursions, moral sayings, and poetic fancies of the Aggadah, which were not considered "obligatory" by Jews, was not respected.

The ostensible aim of Buxtorf's *Synagoga judaica* was to provide a guide to Christian outsiders. In fact this popularization was a caricature of the synagogue that sustained with a show of learned evidence one of the common reactions of Christians who chanced to visit Jewish places of worship—that Judaism was a confused and disorderly religion. Buxtorf the Elder also punctuated his narrative with snide remarks on Jewish deceptions. Judaism was represented as essentially a haphazard conglomeration of ceremonies, an impression that was sharply engraved on the minds of literate Europeans and reappeared in the writings of the deists, who declared Mosaic Judaism devoid of noble sentiments about God or immortality. Neither Buxtorf had any sense of the historical transformations of Jewish rituals through the ages, and the elder had a marked inclination to highlight what was shocking and ridiculous in Jewish rituals, or his version of them, often garnered at second hand.

In the thirty-sixth chapter of the *Synagoga judaica,* "On the Future Messiah of the Jews," Buxtorf put together what purported to be the orthodox Jewish conception of the messiah from selected passages of the Old Testament, excerpts from the Talmud (the tractates Sanhedrin, Babba Batra, Hulin, Berakhot), and Rashi. In Buxtorf's portrait, the Jewish messiah was a mere man, though far superior to others in virtue. Polygamous, he would invite daughters of kings to be his brides, but his choice would fall on Jewesses. He married, ruled a temporal kingdom, and sired children who inherited his dominion. Buxtorf conflated stories about a mortal Messiah ben Joseph, a warrior, with a Messiah ben David about whose being the Jews were in dispute. This dual messiah did not represent any consensus among Jews, and neither Buxtorf's sources nor common belief bear out his extravagant notions. The conception of a tyrannical messiah, a potentate governing with an iron rod who would ultimately vanquish the powerful Christian enemy, explained for Buxtorf why Jews refused to recognize gentle Jesus as the true messiah. Jews were convinced that their messiah had been born on the day Jerusalem was destroyed and that he lay hidden somewhere, perhaps in paradise, bound with a woman's hair. Among the ten formal signs of his imminent advent would be the sudden appearance on earth of creatures with two heads and seven eyes.

In Buxtorf's version of the Jewish messianic age, all sickness and suffering would depart from the Israelites, who would live many hundreds of years as they did in the generations from Adam to Noah and would be able to see God face to face. Inclinations and provocations

to evil would be dissipated. The messiah would gather the Jews together from the many lands of the world, and in Canaan he would
prepare a great banquet: it was there that Leviathan, after cavorting
before them, would be slaughtered and eaten, and quantities of fowl
and fish would be consumed, washed down with wine grown in paradise and preserved in Adam's cellar. Tourneys would be staged to
entertain them. The gentiles would build houses for the Jews and
plant their gardens; the air would be purified; war would be abolished. Buxtorf's treatment of Judaic messianism emphasized the ma-
terialistic aspect of the hoped-for fulfillment, and with obvious relish
he thrust into his account outlandish folktales, in order to render the
Jewish prophecy of the messiah and his reign gross by contrast with
the spirituality of the Christian messiah and the Christian heaven.

Johann Buxtorf the Younger (1599–1664), a child prodigy who succeeded his father as professor of Hebrew at Basel, lived in his shadow.
The younger Buxtorf edited and amended his father's works before
striking off in a different direction. Part of his scholarly activity was
devoted to a defense of his father's thesis that the vocalizations of the
Hebrew text of the Old Testament were as ancient as the words themselves. The younger Buxtorf's polemic with Louis Cappel, who insisted on the relative modernity of these signs, kept the scholarly
world buzzing for decades, as the learned were astonished by the te-
merity of a critic who ventured to challenge the opinion of the omni-
scient Buxtorfs. But though Buxtorf the Younger fully discharged the
obligations of filial piety, editing and republishing his father's dictionaries, textbooks, and the *Synagoga judaica,* he eventually forsook his
father's spirit. In later editions of the *Synagoga* he dropped parts of
the original work and incorporated long sections of Leone Modena's
Jewish Rites, with the result that he supplied his readers with a better-
arranged and markedly more accurate description of Jewish belief
and worship.

The mood of the younger Buxtorf's scholarship was in the end radically different from that of his father, as he initiated a new trend in
the Protestant estimate of Judaism, discovering a rational philosophical Judaism totally alien from the literalist, niggling Judaism presented in the *Synagoga.* In addition to a new Latin translation (or
more correctly, paraphrase) of Maimonides' *Guide for the Perplexed*
in 1629 and the first Latin translation of the *Kuzari* of Yehudah Ha-

levi, with the title *Liber Cosri, sive colloquium de religione* (1660), he published selections from Isaac Abravanel's commentaries, particularly his interpretation of the dream of Nebuchadnezzar in Daniel, which gave rise to a Jewish version of the Four Monarchies doctrine that was widely quoted by Protestant millenarians. He compiled a *Florilegium hebraicum* (A Hebrew Flower-Culling; 1648) of proverbs, apothegms, and elegant excerpts; collected an *Exercitationes ad historiam* (Historical Exercises) that included studies of the ark of the covenant, the urim and thummim, manna, the holy fire, sacrifices, and other mysteries of the ancient Hebrews, about which scholars and learned gentlemen had an inordinate curiosity. His treatises, almost neutral in tone, described Jewish rites in the way that abbés in the French Academy of Inscriptions and Belles-Lettres would later discuss the beliefs of Egyptians, Greeks, and Romans.

Understandably, there was a far greater readership for the shallow ridicule and sarcasm of the *Synagoga* than for the philosophical subtleties of Maimonides and Halevi. The translation by Buxtorf the Younger of the two most noteworthy works of philosophy inherited from the Judeo-Arabic world, the *Kuzari* and the *Guide for the Perplexed,* revealed another face of Judaism. While these philosophical works may not have exerted a powerful direct influence on western thought, through the Buxtorf translation knowledge of them was diffused more widely among the learned than has often been recognized—Leibniz, Newton, and many Anglican theologians made reference to Maimonides, for example. Buxtorf the Younger maintained in his introduction to the *Guide* that the Jewish thinker provided solid arguments against atheism and was a bulwark of faith against false philosophy.

Buxtorf the Younger's rendition of the *Kuzari* fitted in neatly with an older Christian tradition that featured three-cornered discussions among a Christian, a Muslim, and a Jew. Abelard, Ramon Lull, Sebastian Münster, and Jean Bodin had each tried his hand at a similar rhetorical device (though the number and identity of the interlocutors varied), but none of their works had an effect on seventeenth-century Christian scholarship that was comparable to the younger Buxtorf's tour de force. After the publication of the new translation, the earlier Latin translation of the *Guide* (Paris, 1520), ascribed to Agostino Giustiniani, was rarely quoted by Christian Hebraists.

In the dedicatory epistle to his *Kuzari,* Buxtorf the Younger offered an apology for spreading Jewish philosophical ideas among Christians: nothing in this world was so good but that it contained an element of evil and nothing was so evil but that there was not in it an admixture of the good. No one would banish the writings of the Greeks and Romans from the schools, even though they contained matter contrary to the principles of Christian morals. In justification of his *Guide for the Perplexed* translation, Buxtorf quoted Rabbi Meir in the Talmud tractate Hagiga: one could even hold converse with heretics if one followed the admonition to eat the meat of the pomegranate and throw away the rind. For both philosophical books Buxtorf provided biographies of the authors, extolling them as exemplary religious thinkers who vindicated religion from the attacks of unbelievers, and he included a list of citations from authorities Christian as well as rabbinic singing their praises. Maimonides and Halevi would teach Christians to be wary of the sophistries and seductions of the pagan philosophers.

Buxtorf the Younger was by no means a judaizer, but in choosing to translate the two greatest works of medieval Jewish philosophy he moved far from the contempt of his father's most popular book. From the same Christian Hebraist family, Christians could thus receive two contrary impressions of Judaism: the father portrayed an obsessive devotion to empty rituals, underscoring the image of Jewish carnality and an absorption in acts bereft of spiritual meaning; the son showed a complex philosophical view of the world that supported rationality in religion. While later the disdain of the deists and philosophes for Judaism found sustenance in the elder Buxtorf's compilation, the Anglicans drew arguments from his son. The effect of the *Synagoga judaica* was immediate, especially among those in the Germanic world who could read only the vernacular; the influence of Buxtorf the Younger's translations was generally limited to an elite that could comprehend philosophical Latin, and they ultimately fed the German Enlightenment.

The story of the *Kuzari,* an amicable presentation of the relative merits of the Christian, Muslim, and Jewish religions, which finally led to the conversion of the king of the Khazars to Judaism—a theme extending back to the eleventh century—ended up in Lessing's *Nathan the Wise* (1779) as the parable of the three sons looking for the true ring in their father's legacy. But the great chasm between Buxtorf the Younger and Lessing should not be glossed over. Buxtorf had to prefix his translation with an admonition against judaizing, while Lessing's play became the classical literary pronouncement on religious toleration.

There exists a substantial seventeenth-century literature of selections from rabbinic writings, thesauruses, and florilegia by professors of Hebrew who translated excerpts from the Talmud and the rabbis that might be of interest to Christians. These relatively popular books were sometimes written in the vernacular, such as Christophorus Helvicus' *Jüdische Historien* (Jewish Stories; 1612), but often they appeared in Hebrew and Aramaic with Latin translations, like Buxtorf the Younger's *Hebrew Flower-Culling*. In the preface to this work Buxtorf deplores the fact that appreciation of the Greek and Latin classics led many of his contemporaries to dismiss the writings emanating from lands of the orient, especially Palestine, Babylonia, and Arabia. His collection of proverbs and sayings would be especially pleasing to those scholars who studied and loved oriental languages. This type of literature was to be read for its substance, not only as a stylistic model. It illuminated aspects of antiquity not understood even by cultivated minds and transmitted wisdom accumulated through long experience. The ethical, political, and economic precepts in the *Flower-Culling* could serve also as a set of teachings for the ordering of life. Buxtorf the Younger was particularly interested in demonstrating the excellence of the later Hebrews, those who came after the times of the prophets—no one in his right mind would dispute the worth of the Sacred Books themselves. The postbiblical Hebrew writings that may have seemed obvious and trite to the uninitiated could bring pleasure and utility to those able to penetrate their riddles.

In both their erudite and popular publications the Buxtorfs broadened concepts of Judaism in western Christendom, especially in the Protestant world, beyond the traditional bounds. And with Buxtorf the Younger, Christian Hebraism was on the way to scholarship for scholarship's sake, based on careful textual analysis. The holiest rites of the ancient Hebrews were depicted as any other non-Christian religious practices might be; the treatment was bookish and literary. Explicit conformities with pagan customs in antiquity or in newly discovered lands were discreetly avoided. The perception of resemblances among Judaic, Greek, and American Indian religions did not become really significant until the publication of La Créquinière's writings in the early eighteenth century, though there were some precedents in the seventeenth-century treatises of comparatists (John Selden), deist philosophers (Herbert of Cherbury), and scholars of world renown (Hugo Grotius). Once Hebrew ceremonials were depicted in a matter-of-fact manner, analogies and similarities between pagan and Hebrew rites struck the eye of the perspicacious. And when ancient Judaism was desacralized in this way, Christian practice did not long remain immune from similar examination.

Amsterdam, the New Jerusalem

The theoretical position of eminent Dutch theologians and publicists with respect to the legal status of their Jewish communities was not uniform, and a hard line of policy was never established. Imprecision appears to have suited the Jews well enough; neither in Holland nor in England, which followed the same style of leaving a gray legal penumbra around the Jewish presence, did Christians or Jews show an inclination to force the issues. Erasmus had advocated tolerance among Christians by severely restricting the concept of heresy; but he would not extend the idea to Jews, who were satanic violators of Christian peace. Dirck Volckertsz Coornhert (1522–1590) in the next generation favored toleration on the principle of allowing religious conscience free rein, and he would encompass in Christian mercifulness Turks, Jews, and even atheists. In 1619 Hugo Grotius, who had been asked by the States of Holland to draft a Jewish statute at a time when he was embroiled in the bitter controversy between Arminians and orthodox Calvinists, produced a document that satisfied no party. His *Remonstrantie* has enjoyed greater repute in the history of toleration than its rather involuted argument deserves. Amsterdam practice was superior to the theory of its most famous jurisconsult.

Except in a few instances, the ecclesiastical authority of the Calvinist Church in Amsterdam did not intrude upon the administration of the civil magistrates, who, without a comprehensive Jewish policy, adopted a set of procedures under which the Jews usually exercised a measure of autonomy over what were regarded as religious affairs and were treated as burghers—again, with exceptions—in most civil matters. There was no specific ordinance permitting public worship in a synagogue; instead, for their house of worship the members of the "Portuguese nation" built a structure to which a city councillor was given title. Private religious observance was never explicitly prohibited. By dealing with individual cases on an ad hoc basis, the magistrates allowed the Jews to live comfortably in Amsterdam and to engage in a good number of occupations in which they were not considered competitive with existing guilds. In this way a certain de facto tolerance came into existence without a broad-gauged theory or the passage of detailed legislation. There was no formal edict of toleration that applied to Jews, nor were all disabilities removed until the age of the French Revolution; but they could live unmolested so long as they did not disturb the public tranquillity. In the course of the seventeenth century, the Christian city fathers, when they did interfere with the Jewish community, tended to strengthen the power of their *parnasim* (notables). From time to time Jews violated rules against sexual converse with Christians, but the sanctions against such infractions were trivial—usually fines. The Reformed Church exercised a far harsher authority over transgressors among its own members, as in the case of Rembrandt's mistress accused of living in sin, than over Jews.

Emancipation of the Netherlands from Spanish dominion and their ensuing prosperity, in which Jews played a prominent role, had a counterpart in the spiritual realm. A new Christian perception of Judaism was largely mediated by Sephardic scholars and wealthy merchants who lived in great style in their splendid mansions. The internecine, often savage, quarrels within the Amsterdam community of Jews were generally veiled from Christian eyes. An exception was Rembrandt, who in his drawings and etchings immortalized the poor among the Ashkenazic immigrants disdained by their Portuguese coreligionists. The Jews of Amsterdam ended up divided into three separate congregations, Portuguese, Germans from the Rhineland, and Poles, differing from one another in some details of ritual and prayer, and so jealous of their autonomy that they negotiated virtual treaties with one another governing work relationships. The Sephardic Portuguese considered themselves the aristocratic founders of the community and usually had the ear of the Calvinist magistrates.

Rembrandt moved into a Sephardic neighborhood in 1639, and many of his paintings, drawings, and prints that used Jewish models are endowed with a deep spirituality, as in the drawings of *Nathan Admonishing David* (c. 1653) and *Tobias and His Wife Sara Praying* (c. 1648–1650). Rembrandt was a friend of Manasseh ben Israel, and he did four illustrations for the rabbi's book on the coming of the messianic age: *Even Yekara. Piedra gloriosa, O, De la estatua de Nebuchadnesar* (1655). Three of the etchings revolve around the symbol of the "glorious stone," which appears in different contexts in the Bible: the stone on which Jacob rested his head when he saw the angels on a ladder ascending to heaven, the stone with which David slew Goliath, and the stone that destroyed the colossal statue of Nebuchadnezzar. The fourth etching drew forth the messianic implications of the glorious stone in a composite portrayal of the four beasts of Daniel's vision, interpreted as representing the four kings who ruled the world before the triumph of the people of the saints of the most high. In Rembrandt's original etching, an Ancient of Days—his garment white as snow, his hair like pure wool—proclaims his triumph over the beasts. Millenarians, Jewish and Christian, differed in their understanding of the meaning of the enigmatic Ancient of Days, which in the Rembrandt etching could be God. Rembrandt's rendering of the image in Daniel was preserved in the copy that Manasseh presented to a friend, the Hebraist Isaac Vossius, and the book is now in the Leiden University library. In other copies of Manasseh's work, the Rembrandt etchings were replaced by crude prints from the hand of one Salom Italia, and an aureole was substituted for the figure of the divine in Daniel's vision. The alteration exemplifies the compelling force of Jewish commandments, even when there were bonds of friendship between Christians and Jews: latitudinarian though he was, Manasseh could not violate with impunity the prohibition against reproducing the image of God in a printed book.

Amsterdam was unrivaled as a place for the uninhibited intercourse of Jewish and Christian scholars. Isaac Orobio de Castro, from a Jewish family that had converted to Catholicism in Spain, studied metaphysics and medicine at the great Spanish universities, was seized by the Inquisition as a lapsed Christian, and was tortured in a Seville prison. He made his way north, first to France, where he lectured in Toulouse and served as physician to French noble families. When he finally reached Amsterdam he returned to Judaism, was circumcised, changed his forename from Balthazar to Isaac, and joined a group of intellectuals interested in Spanish poetry and the sciences. With the Remonstrant Philipp van Limborch he conducted a friendly colloquy on the beliefs of Judaism, and he left in manuscript many refutations of Christian doctrine. Such open discussion was possible nowhere else on the Continent. The reclusive Spinoza published his *Theological-political Tractate* (1670) anonymously in Latin, but this revolutionary treatise on biblical Judaism by a scholar steeped in the talmudic and Jewish philosophical tradition soon appeared in French and English, and its authorship was well known to Christian scholars. The *Tractate* was denounced in a stream of writings by orthodox Calvinist theologians, but when he was excommunicated by the rabbis of the Jewish community of Amsterdam, Spinoza managed to survive by living obscurely outside the jurisdiction of the Amsterdam magistrates.

In many ways the Latin translation (1698–1703) of the whole of the Mishna by Surenhuis was the Dutch Hebraist work that exerted the most profound influence in the diffusion of knowledge of rabbinics among Christians, both believers and unbelievers, in the next century. Surenhuis' introductions to the various parts of the Mishna argue the reasonableness of most of its legal provisions and demonstrate how they fostered peace and tranquillity in the civil society of the Hebrews. Through the commentaries of Maimonides and Rabbi Obadiah de Bartenora, Christians were offered a commonsense interpretation of the Mishna. Each of the beautifully printed codices is ornamented with medallions illustrating the tractates in the relevant *Seder* (Order) and is enlivened with pages of illustrations lending concreteness to the abstruse legal discussions. The figures in the illustrations are dressed in the Turkish manner, signifying their "oriental" character, but their posturings are those of European nobles. The landscape is dotted with palms, and the buildings of Jerusalem are lofty. Agricultural scenes of hardworking Hebrews alternate with cities of magnificent grandeur and opulence. The cumulative impression created by the engravings is that of a prosperous Judaic society under the reign of law.

Surenhuis' dedication in his first volume is a celebration of the Mishna and of Amsterdam, the New Jerusalem, whose consuls had patronized the work. The dedication is an eloquent justification for tolerance toward the Jews and for the study and preservation, in the modern Dutch Republic, of the tradition of the ancient Tannaim:

> It is on this account, most merciful fathers, that you are tireless in pre- serving this people, fallen not principally because of greed, or some depravity, but because of religious opinion that is indeed bad, but cer- tainly not impious, and because of a kind of ignorance. They are wit- nesses who occupy an important place not only with me but also with the Apostles of our Lord. Among them Saul stands out, the disciple of the once very renowned Gamaliel (rather often mentioned in this our Mishna, and to whom the rites of the Hebrews owe much), called Paul after his conversion. I readily proclaim the divine Paul the chief of all the Apostles of Christ. After he was educated at the feet of the great Gamaliel and became learned in the Mishnas (as he himself is happy to testify) and was touched by a celestial fire, the flow of his genius was so full, the vigor of his speaking and writing was so great, and his elo- quence was so abundant in his speeches delivered before the people, that he would pierce with darts the minds of his hearers, and snatch the palm of victory from all rivals in proclaiming the glory of God. For this reason he even dared to proselytize—with the utmost confi- dence—the Christian faith among the Roman people, learned in all arts and especially sciences, and proud of so many great conquests, there- fore most difficult of all to convince.[2]

Like most Christian Hebraists, Surenhuis believed that his absorption in rabbinic studies required an explanation, and he was careful to assure prospective readers that there was nothing in his compendious work that would endanger their faith.

Surenhuis' translation of the Mishna drew on the living and the dead. He dwelt close to Jewish rabbis in Amsterdam and frequently conferred with them about difficult passages. The Mishna itself was Rabbi Judah ha-Nasi's compilation and redaction, in the beginning of the third century, of legal arguments that had long been discussed orally and were later embodied in the two Talmuds. In 1158 Maimon- ides began his Judeo-Arabic commentary on the Mishna that expli- cated not only readings of the Tannaim whose opinions Rabbi Judah had codified, but the gist of discussions of the Amoraim. The com- mentary of Maimonides was translated from Judeo-Arabic into He- brew by the Sephardic scholars Yehudah Al Harizi and Samuel Ibn

Tibbon of Provence; the work was completed about 1297. Toward the end of the fifteenth century, Bartenora composed a matter-of-fact commentary on the Mishna in Hebrew that was published in 1548–49 in Venice. Surenhuis' translation of the Mishna into Latin was based in part on a manuscript by Jacob Abendana that had been sponsored by Cambridge University scholars and was deposited in the university archives. In addition to the commentaries of Maimonides and Bartenora, the Surenhuis edition included a preface by Isaac Abravanel to his remarks on the *Sayings of the Fathers,* as well as introductions and addenda by Christian scholars: Selden, Pococke, Gusius, Sheringham, Leusden, Fagio, L'Empereur, and Wagenseil. Surenhuis' work, in which the original Hebrew text was also reproduced, thus became in and of itself a repository of rabbinic culture extending in time over a thousand years and in space from the Near East across Africa to Spain, Provence, Italy, England, and Germany. It made it easy for Protestant preachers and scholars, even those who knew little or no Hebrew, to adorn themselves with the trappings of talmudic and later rabbinic learning. In the eighteenth century, Surenhuis' work was ransacked by Voltaire—his copy is preserved in Leningrad—and turned on its head to ridicule rabbinic Judaism.

The Surenhuis text incorporated so many different elements of Jewish learning, though all were in the rationalist tradition, that the Judaism it conveyed was afloat in a sea of scholarship without specific historical anchors. A similar compilation of diverse elements can be found in Knorr von Rosenroth's *Kabbala Denudata,* in analytic historical studies of ancient Israel such as Pieter van der Cun's *Republic of the Hebrews,* and in Dionysius Vossius' translation into Latin of a portion of the *Mishneh Torah* of Maimonides, "De idololatria," a text that was a showpiece of baroque Christian Hebraism, resplendent with commentary and erudition. In such major seventeenth-century texts, rabbinic authorities and Christian Hebraists from different ages were juxtaposed in a spirit of equality.

The influence of the theologian Jacobus Arminius (1560–1609) was strongest in Holland, England, and America. In 1610 his followers presented a remonstration to the Dutch state that set forth their five fundamental articles, including a demand for freedom of conscience. They were called Remonstrants and condemned at the Synod of Dordrecht. When Hugo Grotius failed to win over James I of England to the Arminian cause, their leader Jan Oldenbarnevelt was rejected by the Synod, a decision in part determined by the political alignments of the opposing theological factions. Two hundred Arminian pastors were also banned and only allowed to return ten years later, when they founded the Remonstrant Brotherhood. Simon Episcopius (1583–1643) and Philipp van Limborch (1633–1712) were respectively rector and professor at the Remonstrant seminary in Amsterdam; Stephen Curcellaeus (1586–1659), Johannes Clericus (1657–1736), and the biblical scholar Johann Jakob Wettstein (1693–1754) were of the same general orientation. The seminary, started in 1634, became a major center of biblical and theological research that was more latitudinarian than the orthodox Dutch university faculties, which enjoyed overt state approval. As was to be expected, the Remonstrant Brotherhood merged with liberal Protestantism in the nineteenth century, and English Arminians moved into the unitarian current.

Christian Hebraists such as Gerhard Johann Vossius were Arminian and tolerant of Judaism; others, among them Constantijn L'Empereur, were strongly orthodox Calvinists and antirabbinic. The tendency of popular Jewish historiography to equate a knowledge of Hebrew with Judeophilia is based on an old misconception that goes back to those prominent Amsterdam rabbis who argued, like Manasseh ben Israel, that the fascination of the Hebrew language by itself would lead to tolerance, respect, and even affection. When rabbis were allowed to teach Christian scholars, the consequences were in fact unpredictable: the study of rabbinic thought could nourish an Eisenmenger as well as a Vossius.

Bartolocci among the Neophytes

Giulio Bartolocci was born in Celleno (Viterbo) in 1613 and entered the Order of the Cistercians in 1632, assuming the name Julius a Sancta Anastasia. He later wrote an encomium of the convert Jehuda (called Giovanni Battista) Iona of Safed, the professor at the Archiginnasio Romano who had initiated him into Hebraic studies. Bartolocci's career was spent in Rome, where he occupied a series of posts that allowed him to pursue his bibliographical studies of rabbinic literature and to compose voluminous catalogues and apologies for Christianity against Jewish criticism. His published works ranged over a wide area, and his tendency to digress resulted in the accumulation of many unfinished fragments. In 1651, on the way up the Vatican ladder of preferment, Bartolocci was appointed reader in Hebrew and rabbinics at the College of Neophytes in Rome and *scriptor hebraicus* in the Vatican library. He became abbot of San Sebastiano ad Catacumbas and, shortly before his death in 1687, was named by Pope Innocent XI as one of the *consultori* of the Sacred Congregation of the Index.

Bartolocci's fame rests primarily on the four folio volumes of his monumental *Bibliotheca magna rabbinica. De scriptoribus et scriptis rabbinicis* [the title page of the first volume reads *hebraicis*] *ordine alphabetico hebraice et latine digestis* (Great Rabbinic Library of Authors and Writings, Alphabetically Arranged in Hebrew and Latin), which appeared in 1675, 1678, 1683, and 1693, published by the Sacred Congregation for the Propagation of the Faith. The posthumous last volume, which was left to his disciple and biographer Imbonati to complete, covered the letters from kaf through tof, making a rather lopsided collection since Bartolocci had not progressed beyond the tenth letter, yud. In 1694 Imbonati added an extra volume of his own under the title *Bibliotheca latino-hebraica* comprised of works on Hebrew subjects composed by Christians and converts to Christianity, which constitutes a mammoth appendix to his master's rabbinic library and, for all its inaccuracies, remained the foundation for studies of Christian Hebraism until the appearance of Johann Christoph Wolf's bibliography in the eighteenth century.

In these grand folios, the use of Hebrew characters for titles and their transliteration, as well as the incorporation of Hebrew excerpts with their Latin translation, provided for professors with pretensions to Hebraic learning erudite adornments at a minimal cost in cerebral labor. The folios did not succeed in standardizing the names of rabbis and commentators, and references to Hebraic texts remained as chaotic and arbitrary as ever in Christian scholarship.

In his numerous addenda, Bartolocci conducted a running polemic with rabbinic commentators. In the Christian scholarly war over the date of the Jewish massoretic vocalizations of the Bible, he opted for their late introduction. Among his many supplements there is a catalogue of all the bibles ever printed in Hebrew and in translation. Five of the biographies that accompanied his listing of authors were republished separately in Utrecht by Adriaan Reeland in his *Analecta rab-binica* (1702): Rashi, Abraham Ibn Ezra, David Kimchi, Gersonides, and Abravanel, a selection of the outstanding commentators remark-able only for its omission of Maimonides. In addition to his published bibliography of Hebraica, Bartolocci drew up catalogues of Hebraic books and manuscripts in the Vatican that remain unpublished. One was titled "Index librorum omnium hebraicorum, tam impressorum quam manuscriptorum qui anno MDCL in Bibliotheca Vaticana ex-tabant"; the other, prepared with the aid of Giovanni Battista Iona, was called "More Makom, Index materiarum, authorum et titulorum librorum manuscriptorum ebraicorum Bibliothecae Vaticanae, Pala-tinae et Urbinatis, in tres partes distributus." Bartolocci also left many works of Christian apologetics directed primarily to Jews.

In the second part of the *Bibliotheca magna rabbinica* (1678), dedi-cated to Pope Innocent XI, Bartolocci justified his preparation of a multivolumed descriptive catalogue of rabbinic works with an argu-ment often repeated after the imprisoned Campanella had proposed to convert the Jews with evidence from their own writings in ex-change for his freedom. Attitudes toward the preservation of rabbinic texts had undergone fundamental changes since the medieval cere-monial disputations that took place before popes and kings between rabbis and priests, the latter often converts to Christianity. Usually the great public debates centered on the demand of Christian zealots that the Talmud and other Hebrew books be burned, on the ground that they concealed blasphemies against Christ and might seduce Christians into apostasy. By the seventeenth century, however, the hope of converting Jews outweighed the fear of contagion from their works. As the chosen people of the Old Testament, Israel had to be bound to the Church with chains of charity. The sponsorship of Bar-tolocci's colossal descriptive catalogue by the Sacred Congregation of the Faith was inspired by a renewal of the proselytizing mission, but as in many such enterprises the scholar possessed could lose sight of his ultimate goal and fall prey to the lust for accumulation. Though the conversion of the Jews remained the prime mission of Catholic Hebraists, the original impetus could produce extraordinary results once the collector's passion was set aflame.

The evil doctrines of the Hebrews had to be known to be combat-ted, Bartolocci argued. In its own way his *Bibliotheca* was peculiarly impartial: Hebrew writers of all times and places were ranged alphabetically. Thus the Vatican collector of Hebrew books and manuscripts demonstrated that a measure of "scientific" neutrality had guided the compilation, even though the alien word was not used. A work by Daniel Cohen the Rabbi on astronomy, astrology, and judicial astronomy was followed by an article on Daniel the Prophet. Each item was numbered and adhered to a fixed pattern: the author's name, a brief Hebrew summary of the book followed by a Latin description, with the publisher's name, place, and date of printing according to both the Hebrew and Christian calendars. If Bartolocci had not seen the item himself, the source of his information, Buxtorf's *Bibliotheca rabbinica* for example, was meticulously cited. Authors to whom books of the Old Testament were traditionally ascribed (David, composer of the Psalms) were smothered with talmudic references or citations from Maimonides and Abraham Ibn Ezra. Bartolocci was not one to evade difficult questions, such as "Was Daniel a eunuch?" And he boldly entered into polemics on sacred chronology, pitting one Jewish authority against another.

Bartolocci's obiter dicta tell something about the relation between monks and Jewish converts to Christianity in the College of Neophytes: he paid homage to Joseph Ciantes Romano, one of his own preceptors in rabbinics, who was as well versed in the Talmud as in the secrets of the Cabbala and who translated into Hebrew three of the four books of Aquinas' *Summa against Gentiles*. Full details of the role played by Jewish converts have not been gathered together, though references such as those in Bartolocci's writings are substantial evidence that converts and rabbis were active agents in the transmission of Hebrew learning. When Christian monks in Italy consorted secretly with Jews, both risked trouble from the Inquisition; but converted rabbis housed in establishments of the Catholic Church were in a protected category.

The Broad Expanse of Judaica

Sir Thomas Bodley gained a knowledge of Hebrew at an early age when he was a student in Geneva. After he dedicated himself to the restoration of the Oxford University library, the acquisition of Hebrew and Arabic books and their proper cataloguing became one of his principal occupations. As early as 1607 he complained in correspondence about the difficulties of finding a Jew in England who could assist him and of acquiring a Hebrew font; indeed, his hope of publishing a Hebrew catalogue was not realized in his lifetime. Through most of the seventeenth century, scholars had to content themselves with a handwritten listing of manuscripts and printed books known as the "Bibliotheca rabbinica," a late copy of which is extant. When the printed catalogue of Thomas Hyde, a Hebrew and Arabic scholar, appeared in 1674, England was endowed with a list of Hebraica which, though hardly as full as the Vatican work Bartolocci was preparing, or equal to Buxtorf's printed catalogue, was a sound base on which to build. The two outstanding Christian Hebraists in England, Selden and Lightfoot, acquired libraries of orientalia on their own.

Bartolocci's *Bibliotheca magna rabbinica* remained the most impressive catalogue of writings in Hebrew and Aramaic compiled in the seventeenth century. It far outstripped Buxtorf the Elder's few-hundred-page bibliography of rabbinic literature, which was more generally available in Europe. If added to these two works are the Hebrew books in the contemporary catalogue of the Bodleian Library, Selden's manuscript catalogue of his own collection, and Imbonati's great folio of 1694 listing works in Latin on Hebraic subjects, a conception may be formed of the totality of printed books and manuscripts, both primary and secondary sources, to which a Christian scholar might theoretically turn. Of course only part of the corpus would ordinarily be accessible to a learned Christian Hebraist or a rabbi. The Buxtorf correspondence affords an insight into the obstacles encountered even by wealthy scholars in the acquisition of Judaica. The complexity of their relations with agents in Poland and in Constantinople testifies to a zeal in pursuing the instruments of learning that is reminiscent of the great patrons of the Renaissance.

In the latter half of the seventeenth century, extensive Latin compilations of commentaries on the Old and New Testaments, consisting of passages from the eminent Christian theologians of the previous age, began to be published. Such a work was the *Critici sacri, sive annotata doctissimorum virorum in Vetus ac Novum Testamentum* (Critical Writers on Sacred Subjects, or Commentaries by the Most Learned Men on the Old and New Testament), the first edition of which, in nine folio volumes, was issued in 1660 by Cornelius Bee, a

London bookseller, as an appendage to Walton's polyglot Bible. (The work was reprinted in Frankfurt in folio and in quarto; an Amsterdam edition, 1698–1732, is an expanded version, with four volumes of a "Thesaurus" not included in the original.) The process of excerpting and condensing continued when the *Critici sacri* was itself abridged by Matthew Poole's *Synopsis criticorum* in five volumes, 1678–79, which offered Protestant divines of modest means a selection of Christian Hebraists.

An overview of the Christian Hebraist studies to which "Hebraicians" had access in the seventeenth century can also be gathered indirectly from an analysis of eighteenth-century catalogues and compilations, such as Dom Calmet's hundred folio pages of bibliography that included seventeenth-century writings on all aspects of ancient, Judaism; Johann Christoph Wolf's magnificent *Bibliotheca hebraea* in four volumes (Hamburg, 1715–1733); and Blasio Ugolino's *Thesaurus antiquitatum sacrarum complectens, in quibus veterum hebraeorum mores, leges, instituta, ritus sacri et civiles illustrantur* (Complete Thesaurus of Sacred Antiquities, in which the Customs, Laws, Institutions, Sacred and Civil Ceremonials of the Ancient Hebrews Are Illustrated), which was published in Venice in thirty-four volumes over a period of twenty-five years, 1744 to 1769, and followed much the same pattern as the *Critici sacri.* By the eighteenth century, lists of Christian Hebraists are plentiful, as in the preface to Johann Gerhard Meuschen's *Novum Testamentum ex Talmude et antiquitatibus hebraeorum illustratum* (Leipzig, 1736); Meuschen had planned an extensive "Bibliotheca antiquitatum." The Venetian *Thesaurus,* however, ranged widely in the authorities it reproduced, though in theory its subject matter was exclusively focused on ancient Hebrew rites and institutions. Each volume of Ugolino's selections and excerpts consisted of more than a thousand folio pages, many of them devoted to internecine scholarly debates.

Ugolino avoided the Judeophobic works of Eisenmenger, but in his very first folio he reproduced the introduction of Martini's *Pugio* with the detailed observations of Joseph de Voisin, who took a passing swipe at Galatino:after praise of Martini's book as a "work for all the ages," the accusation was repeated that Galatino had filched passages from it for his *Secrets of Catholic Truth.* Ugolino's collection concentrated on the special topic dissertation rather than the more general treatises of an author. A large section of the compendium is given over, understandably, to Ugolino's own translations into Latin from the Jerusalem Talmud, the Tosephta, Midrashim, and Maimonides. Works as recent as Robert Lowth's *De sacra poesi hebraeorum* find a place, while selections from the sixteenth century are bypassed. The texts of famous Christian Hebraists in the Renaissance and Reformation—Pico, Génébrard, Münster, Reuchlin, and Fagio—virtually forgotten by that time, are absent, though the justifications of their calling as Hebrew scholars were repeated in almost identical rhetoric.

The dinosaurian yet elegantly printed *Thesaurus* is characteristic of Christian Hebraism of the later Enlightenment, with its penchant for compilations and for excerpting previously published works. Though a few of the early volumes were miscellanies, Ugolino tended to dedicate an entire volume to a single topic, throwing together seventeenth- and eighteenth-century writers to illustrate an individual subject. In the end the *Thesaurus* covered the whole domain of Christian Hebraist studies in sacred history, seen through the scholarly eyes of an impressive roster of men of learning in France, Germany, Holland, and England—Lowth, the Carpzovs, Thomas Godwyn, Schickard, Michaelis, Spencer, Selden, Wagenseil, the Buxtorfs, Hyde, Prideaux, Huet, Isaac Vossius, Hulsius, Reeland, Bochart, Morin, Vorstius, Lightfoot, Bertram, de Cun, Sigonio, J. C. Hottinger, L'Empereur, Dassov, Conring, Compiègne de Veil, Voisin, Jean Le Clerc, and scores of minor Hebraists. Except for the considerable number of his own translations, Ugolino rarely included Italian scholars—the omission of Bartolocci and Imbonati is remarkable. Cabbalists, popularizers, and philosophers were excluded from the *Thesaurus,* which Ugolino considered a serious work of erudition and embellished with citations to post-Talmud rabbis. Assisted by a volume of indices as a guide, a curious reader could browse through authoritative treatments on the republic of the Hebrews, sacred chronology, the geography of Palestine, the terrestrial paradise, the tabernacle in the wilderness, the two temples, the candelabrum, the Jewish calendar, the priesthood, sacrifices, tithes and the jubilee, synagogues and seminaries, circumcision and lustrations, Israelite and Canaanite idolatry, the Sanhedrin, oaths and punishments, weights and measures, numismatics, clothing, marriage and adultery, Hebrew poetry, music and musical instruments, concluding with funeral rites.

By mid-eighteenth century, Hebraic studies were coming to resemble more and more the dissertations on Greek and Latin subjects current in royal academies and to strike the same passionless note; but Greek and Latin scholarship found a Gibbon who rescued the pedantic treatises from oblivion and used them to create a work of genius. The ancient Hebrews fell into the hands of Jacques Basnage, the plodding Huguenot preacher of Rotterdam, whose general history of the Jews differs from the academic dissertations it cannibalized less in spirit than in the multiplication of errors.

The extent to which rabbinic and early Hebraic knowledge was available to seventeenth-century Christians depended on how well they could read Aramaic, Hebrew, or Latin. Measuring the spread of Hebrew by social class, religious denomination, or state unit is an impossible task; the difficulties entailed in the estimate of literacy in mother tongues are compounded many times over. Learned men like Isaac Newton could follow the text of the Bible or even a rabbinic commentator with frequent resort to Buxtorf's dictionary, but his study of Jewish history depended on writings in Latin. Greek was becoming less important for Hebraic studies because Josephus, as well as parts of Philo, had been translated into Latin and the vernacular. By the eighteenth century a good deal of information about Judaism could be garnered from works in modern languages alone.

The great divide between a popular and a scholarly view was the possession of Latin. When easy familiarity with Latin began to diminish even among the literate sometime in the eighteenth century, Hebraic studies suffered a parallel fate. The decline was not total, since there was an increase of publications on Judaica in the vernacular. As learned journals and academic memoirs appeared more frequently in native languages, Hebrew was the first of the three ancient tongues to be abandoned. By the early eighteenth century, there were general histories of the Jews in English and French, descriptions of Jewish rituals in German, English, Italian, and French. In dissenter England and in America, learned clergymen still sprinkled their sermons with occasional references to Hebrew writers, though one sometimes wonders whether this was mere fashionable display, as today Latin and Greek phrases are tossed into lectures. As the clergy became less educated and lost their Greek and Hebrew, laymen had to depend more on popularizations, and the way was open for the litterateurs of the radical Enlightenment to turn their antipathy to ancient Israel into a battering ram against revealed religion. But in the seventeenth century, Hebraism was still an intrinsic part of the higher culture of Western Europe, along with Greek and Latin studies.

In the course of the sixteenth and seventeenth centuries, the printing press made available to Christian Hebraists who had mastered Hebrew and Aramaic the major medieval commentators. This substantial body of literature, however, constituted only a portion of the rabbinic writings being steadily produced by presses throughout Europe and the Near East wherever Jewish settlements were tolerated. The writings of even the most erudite Christian Hebraists show only a sparse acquaintance with the supercommentaries of rabbis less celebrated in Christian centers, either medieval disquisitions first printed hundreds of years after their composition or the contemporary novellae (*hidushim*) that eminent rabbis were publishing as they pored over the tractates of the Talmud in search of solutions to legal conundrums. Rabbis renowned for their learning, issuing opinions in reply to thorny questions of interpretation and practice sent to them from various parts of the world, had collections of these responsa turned out by local presses; but like the novellae, the responsa, which fed on each other, rarely found their way into Christian hands. They dealt with refinements of legal judgments and decisions that were of little interest to scholars outside the confines of the Jewish communities. The conclusions reached in the responsa, whose comprehension required detailed knowledge of the whole corpus of precedents covering centuries of rabbinic thought, were beyond the ken of even the towering figures of seventeenth-century Christian Hebraism, and references to them are normally absent from their side- and footnotes. Often the feats of rabbinic virtuosity were dismissed as trivia, and indeed they were, from the vantage point of Christian scholars. The minutiae of the dietary laws, which in everyday Jewish life were continually breeding new perplexities that demanded resolution, could hardly occupy Christians indifferent to which foods were or were not forbidden and in what circumstances. Joseph Karo's *Shulhan Arukh* (The Prepared Table; 1565), a code setting forth what was allowed and what was prohibited in daily life, was not a favorite with Christian Hebraists. Whether it was permissible to ride in a gondola on the sabbath raised problems that had little import outside the Jewish quarters of Venice. Christians could not fully grasp the intellectual and religious meaning of ritual Judaism any more than Jews could act freely in the world beyond the boundaries of their ghettoes.

Thus the ongoing life of everyday Judaism was not a primary concern of Christian scholars, and their conception of the religion tended not to heed the cantankerous disputations that regularly took place behind Jewish walls. Intramural conflicts sometimes grew so fierce that partisans resorted to Christian authorities for help in trouncing a rival, defying terrifying anathemas pronounced against them in rabbinic decisions for their perfidy. Though the evidence is by no means firm, it is reported that in medieval Provence the Jewish opponents of Maimonides, turned informers, betrayed him to the friars and denounced his works as atheistic, a charge that resulted in their condemnation and burning. As with all religious sects, zealotry among the Jews has led to bitter internal quarrels and fratricide; the annals of such wars usually remain sealed, hidden from Christian eyes, and the episodes are erased from communal memory. To the extent that Christians were aware of rabbinic contentiousness, it served only to nurture their perception of Judaism as a vortex of acrimonious controversies.

5

Seventeenth-Century Uses
of Historical Judaism

IN THE AGE of the baroque, the uses that Christendom made of its
scholarly acquisition of Judaism ramified in many directions.
Some made possible western forbearance of Judaism; others inflamed
what in the nineteenth century became antisemitism. Though haphazard curiosity is not excluded, a good deal of Christian Hebraism
served specific Christian purposes, not all of them articulated, that
were quite indifferent to the fate of Judaism in itself. The missionary,
political, exegetical, Judeophobic, and eschatological arguments of
Christian Hebraists disclose the multiplicity of the ends to which
Christian thinkers put Judaism and Jewish thinking.

Conversion, the Apostolic Mission

The mission to convert the Jews to Christianity remained alive among
the major denominations, and direct knowledge of Jewish writers was
conceived as a powerful instrument of persuasion through its access
to the Jewish conscience. This was one of the principal justifications
advanced for maintaining converse with Jews and Judaism. For those
who accepted the decrees of councils and popes against the outright
killing of the Jews, refutation of Jewish beliefs was the only allowable
measure against them, and a thorough familiarity with rabbinic writings, it was imagined, would permit Christian propagators of the faith
to search out their opponents' weaknesses in their native territory.
Grand virtuosi of learning such as Tommaso Campanella were convinced that theological arguments drawn from the rabbis themselves
would prove unanswerable by the Jews and were bound to convert

them. There was a presupposition that once a rabbi was converted the rest of his congregation would follow, a notion still harbored in eighteenth-century England, with the role of the rabbis supplanted by that of wealthy Jews. Campanella, blessed with a touch of megalomania, was prepared to perform the same services for the Muslims and for the pagans of Asia, if only the pope would free him from the dungeon in which he had been incarcerated by the Inquisition. Though his memoranda on how he would go about converting the Jews were not published until the twentieth century, they were influential in establishing the Sacred Congregation for the Propagation of the Faith. In a lower key, Anglican societies for spreading the Gospel operated on the same presumption and won the patronage of eminent scientists such as Robert Boyle.

Catholic theologians disputed among themselves about the line where persuasion ended and the impermissible constraint of Jewish conscience began. Enforced attendance at sermons in which preachers exercised their converting skills was favored in the Catholic Church; but despite pious resolutions to foster the practice, it was followed only sporadically. Whether the conversion of minors was legitimate was a theological question not definitively resolved even in the nineteenth century, when a Christian maid's baptism of a sick Jewish child in her care was accepted by the Church despite widespread protests (the Mortara case). Christian behavior often bore little relationship to canon law and papal decrees, as the compulsory mass conversions in Spain and Portugal attest.

The resistance of Jews to conversion baffled churchmen from the early days of Christianity onward. When Protestant proselytizers in the seventeenth century asked themselves why they had failed, they would point to moral deficiencies among the Christians themselves: Christians, especially papists, had used force against Jews, had massacred them, and these cruelties, so flagrantly contradictory to the teachings of Christ, prevented Jews from seeing in the gospel of love anything but hypocrisy. Christian behavior in general was so barbaric that Jews could not believe the messiah had in fact already appeared among men on earth. Simon Bisschop (Episcopius), the Dutch Remonstrant, in his *Conciones duae, de causis incredulitatis judaeorum* (Two Discourses on the Causes of Jewish Unbelief; 1650), offered an explanation in this vein for the Jews' stubborn rejection of Christ:

from earliest childhood they were taught to hate all things Christian, and Christian molestation of Jews fortified this animosity. The conduct of Christians repelled many Jews, and persecutions by the papists robbed Christ's gospel of credibility. The doctrine of transubstantiation, the senseless internecine wars and sectarian conflicts among Christians, contributed to Jewish loathing and contempt. If Christians would practice charity, forswear persecuting Jews, and establish unity among themselves, the Jews would be more amenable to conversion. The German scholar Eisenmenger also laid part of the blame for the failure to convert Jews on Christian shortcomings: Christian apologetic writers were so ignorant of Talmudic and rabbinic learning, and their citations were so careless, that Jews despised them and remained steadfast in their own faith. If an impeccable scholar like himself were in control, a new chapter in the history of Jewish conversion would be opened.

Catholics and Lutherans taught that God had not only permitted the continued existence of the Jews, but preserved their nation as living witness to Christ's crucifixion, and ordained their suffering as punishment for that heinous crime. (The legend of Ahasuerus the Wandering Jew embodies this idea.) Theologians quoted a text from Augustine as authority; since he was accepted as the greatest of the Church Fathers by both Catholics and Protestants, his verdict could not be impugned, which later led Moses Mendelssohn to reflect sarcastically that the Jews owed their very lives to a church father and should be grateful to him. The ambiguous status of the Jews in Christian theology was not resolved: the effort of the Church to convert them was a continuation of the proselytizing by the Apostles, and yet it was predetermined that the Jews would not be successfully converted until the second coming of Christ.

In the interim before the consummation of the times, it was the duty of true Christians to use every form of nonviolent persuasion, especially arguments from the sacred books of the Old Testament, to win individual Jews over to Christ. In no circumstances was coercion to be used, for conversion had to be an act of free will and conscience. This view was strongly entertained by Dissenters in England, other Protestant sects on the Continent, and American Puritans. It was accompanied by admonitions to Christians that their own faith forbade them to interfere with Jews in the practice of their religion or to insult the descendants of the people of Israel. Puritan preachers delivered homilies on what the Christians owed to Judaism. Jews were incomplete Christians whose existence was inextricably bound up with the ultimate fulfillment of the Christian promise.

When Jews were expelled from the Iberian peninsula, it was under the pretext that through wiles and satanic magic they were threatening the faith of Catholics. Jews were actively judaizing, or they were desecrating the host, or they were spilling the blood of Christians in abominable nocturnal ceremonials. Jews could not be burned at the stake simply for being Jews, but their malevolent activities against Christians and their seduction of conversos had to be halted; in the end, expulsion was the only effective measure in defense of the faith. As an inquisitor interpreted events, the rigorous interrogation and torture of Spanish Jews who had been converted did not violate Christian doctrine. After a conversion that had been "voluntary," many New Christians relapsed. Since they had become part of the Catholic Ecclesia, the Holy Office of the Inquisition had jurisdiction over them and decreed their punishment in accordance with canon law, turning them over to secular authorities for execution of sentence.

The converted Jew was a perennial problem to Christianity in its many subdivisions. Had the conversion been authentic and sincere, spiritual, unmotivated by venal interest? Neither in the countries where a state inquisition was in power, as in Spain, nor in modified theocracies like New England could a Christian be sure of his convert; nor could the New Christian feel secure in his adopted religion since he was the object of lingering doubt, suspicion, and apprehension. How could distrust be wholly dissolved? What was a true convert? One about whom uncertainty had been dispelled in the minds of the pure Christians and whose own soul was free of misgivings. The Spaniards passed laws excluding New Christians for a number of generations from holding public office or joining monastic orders; these laws of *limpieza* (purity) were manifestly intended to guarantee the authenticity of the conversion. When books of genealogy appeared in Spain showing that even the noblest families in the realm were tainted with Jewish blood, blackmailers seized the opportunity and the persecution of Jews brought in its wake the persecution of Christians.

In more recent centuries, Christian societies were generally reluctant to accept the validity of conversions as miraculous as Paul's on the road to Damascus. Gilbert Burnet (1643–1715), bishop of Salisbury, has left a cogent explanation of the uneasiness often provoked by converts to Christianity:

> The World has been so often deceived in many pretended Converts, who make a Trade of changing their Religion, that it is no wonder if Men are not easily perswaded of the sincerity of those who come over from one Religion to another; since it is certain the prepossession of Education and Custom is so strong, that such as turn to a New Religion, must either be led to it by a clear Conviction, which will shew itself in other signal Effects, or are guilty of great levity and fickleness of Mind, that disposes them too easily to change for changes sake; or do it upon a baser account, of working upon the Compassions of those, who being very Religious themselves, are apt to deal their Charity liberally to such as seem to follow the steps of Abraham, who being called to it, forsook his Kindred and Country to serve the true and living God.[1]

When in 1722 one Judah Monis was formally converted to Christianity at a ceremony in Boston, the Puritan divine who officiated made a great point of the fact that the elders of the church and Harvard College, where Monis was to be employed as a teacher of Hebrew, were convinced of the sincerity of his Christian faith. Monis, in a sermon published as *The Truth, being a discourse which the author delivered at his baptism. Containing nine principal arguments the modern Jewish rabbins do make to prove the Messiah is yet to come; with the answer to each . . . and likewise with the confession of his faith*, demonstrated with citations from the Old Testament and Jewish commentators that Jesus was the true messiah. But as one reads the sermons of the officiating minister and the new convert, both appear to be protesting too much. Clearly, Monis felt some ambivalence: he married a Christian, but could not quite bring himself to violate the Jewish sabbath.

Spanish Inquisitors did not hesitate to consign to the flames those relapsed Jewish heretics who, through a passion for martyrdom, proclaimed at their final trials their belief in the God of Israel. The Inquisition had more difficulty with New Christians who vigorously maintained that they had *not* lapsed. The charge of judaizing in the interrogation of an accused convert affords an insight into what an inquisitor supposedly construed as the essence of Judaism. Usually the trials focused on residues of Jewish ritual performance as concrete proof, not on questions of doctrine. This was also in harmony with the general presumption that Judaism was a carnal, not a spiritual, religion. Witnesses at the trials of conversos were pressed to testify as to how long the remnants of Judaic observance had been honored; the importance of the rite was totally irrelevant. Judaizing was a deeply ingrained disease, and the records of the Inquisition go to extravagant lengths to trace the persistence of a habit over decades as the victim wandered from place to place and was tracked by the Inquisition's agents.

Outside the Iberian peninsula, Christian literature designed for converting Jews rehearsed time and again the same Old Testament passages, and the same interpretations were applied for almost sixteen hundred years, from the early Church Fathers through the eighteenth century: the Genesis texts that quoted the word *Elohim* in the plural, in order to prove the Trinity; chapter 53 of Isaiah foretelling the virgin birth; the promise of Jacob to Judah; the allegorical reading of the Psalms; the identification of Isaac and Joshua as types for Jesus.

In their zeal for converting the Jews, Christian clerics often relied on one small book that achieved world-wide fame, the translation of Rabbi Samuel of Morocco's confession of how he came to Christianity through the very words of the Old Testament. From an original edition in Sant'Orso, his witness was repeated for centuries in the principal languages of Western Europe, and, if the frequency of reprinting is a test of success, it must have been regarded by Christian missionaries as a marvelously effective instrument of conversion, though on its face it seems to be a pious fabrication. The tiresome chronicle of its triumph throughout the Continent, in slightly variant versions, illustrates the assiduousness with which the apostolic mission of conversion was pursued. Under the title *Epistola contra judaeorum errores* (A Letter against the Errors of the Jews), the apology of Rabbi Samuel appeared at least seven times in the fifteenth century, separate editions being published in Sant'Orso (1475), Paris (c. 1495), Florence (1479), Naples (1480), Bologna (c. 1475), Rome (1480), and Nuremberg (1498). Latin editions continued through the first half of the sixteenth century with various titles: *Tractatus cōtra iudeos* (Treatise against the Jews; Paris, 1510?); *Tractatus rabbi Samuelis, errorem iudeorum indicans* (Rabbi Samuel's Treatise Revealing the Error of the Jews; Ancona, 1516); *Quod judei messiam, qui venit, ceu venturum temere expectent* (Why the Jews Foolishly Await the Messiah, Who Has Come, As If He Is Yet To Come; Strasbourg, 1523); *Contra judaeos* (Against the Jews; Venice, 1535 and 1545). Italian translations appeared in Venice (1518) as *Requisitioni profundissime, et argumenti subtilissimi, del sapiente hebreo magistro Samuel* (The Deepest Probings and Most Subtle Arguments of the Learned Hebrew Master Samuel), and in Florence (1568) as *Epistola di maestro Samuelle ebreo* (Letter from Master Samuel the Hebrew). German translations were entitled *Ain beweisung* (A Proof; Augsburg, 1524) and *Sendbrieff Rabbi Samuelis des Juden* (A Communication from Rabbi Samuel the Jew; Frankfurt, 1544). In the seventeenth century there were two editions in Portuguese, *Carta que hum rabbino chamado Samuel escreveo a outro rabbino chamado Isaac* (A Letter Written by a Rabbi Called Samuel to Another Rabbi Called Isaac; Lisbon, 1651 and 1673), and an English translation, *The Blessed Jew of Morocco* (York, 1644). Eighteenth-century Latin editions continued to be published in various European centers—Venice (1702), Prague (1718), Mainz (1775), Vienna (1780), along with three Italian translations, *L'Ebraismo convinto dalli proprj errori* (Hebraism Convicted by Its Own Errors; Genoa, 1725), *Confutazione degli errori de' giudei* (Confutation of the Errors of the Jews; Venice, 1770) and *Degli errori dei giudei* (On the Errors of the Jews; Ancona, 1775). Doubtless other editions could be found in smaller centers.

Christian divines had to reckon with the writings of generations of rabbis who interpreted very differently the chief passages in the Old Testament cited as predicting the coming of Christ, and who derided the notion that the man on the cross was the glorious messiah foretold in Scripture. In the seventeenth century there was a running debate between Christian divines and Jewish scholars, sometimes friendly as in the case of the Dutch Remonstrant Limborch's published discussion with Orobio de Castro over the meaning of the key verses in question. This sort of contest, in circumstances far less favorable for Jews, had been going on for centuries. As in the Middle Ages, the Catholics who engaged in the polemic were often monks who had converted from Judaism and knew the Jewish commentaries well or who had access to converts. Since there are no global statistics of conversion, it is difficult to ascertain which side profited more from these exegetical tourneys. In the seventeenth century, Christian observers began to worry that as many monks were judaized as rabbis were christianized.

Anatomy of the Republic of the Hebrews

The nature of the ancient Jewish commonwealth as a political entity engaged eminent theorists from Jean Bodin through Thomas Hobbes. In a Christian world, the one government directly decreed by God and described in action in the Old Testament could be accepted as the most perfect, rejected as completely superseded by the law of Christ and thus of no contemporary validity, or respected as a historical experience from which there was still wisdom to be drawn. Christian Hebraists sought to reconstitute a political and institutional history of ancient Israel from its beginnings to the time of Jesus, and those with a knowledge of Hebrew appealed to rabbinic commentators as authorities to bolster views of the ideal polity that Christians had derived from Aristotle and to a lesser degree from Plato. The framework and the nomenclature remained Hellenic, but the infusion of examples from ancient Jewish history altered the spiritual content and force of the theory. One body of thinkers perceived the commonwealth of the Hebrews as a classical mixed government of monarchic, aristocratic, and democratic elements. Though it was conceded that the balance of those elements was not always preserved, especially during periods of corruption and persecution when the Hebrews were in exile, the mixed government was considered the essence of the Mosaic dispensation.

Parallel to the reliance on Hebrew precedents in treatises of abstract political theory was the recourse of Christian Hebraists to Jewish rabbis and philosophers for the sustenance of their own positions in sectarian conflicts over the relations of church and state. Israelite examples of the division between civil and ecclesiastical authority were cited as justifications, and the organization of priests and Levites was invoked as a model for settling controversial issues of church government that bedeviled the major denominations. Jewish writers were summoned to participate, in absentia to be sure, in debates over the relationship of church and state. At the Westminster Assembly of Divines in 1644, charged with reorganizing the religious establishment of England, Philo and Maimonides and Kimchi were quoted as witnesses in a gathering resplendent with the outstanding English Hebraists.

Machiavelli's idealization of Rome was replaced among the Christian Hebraists by the Jewish commonwealth. As confidently as Machiavelli had turned to Livy, Englishmen of the Civil War period seeking to establish a stable political order offered the citizens of their commonwealth the paradigm of ancient Israel. If the new English commonwealth could not be an exact replica of the ancient Hebrew republic since the conditions of life had changed, at least the underlying principles of government could be consistent with those of a polity that God himself had ordained. The numerous studies of the constitution of the ancient Jews that appeared in England and Holland served as a justification for the polities in which their authors were living, even though their societies were only similar or analogous to that of the ancient Hebrew kingdom. From the Bible, Josephus, the Talmud, and the rabbis, they reconstructed a Hebrew society that was a projection of their own. The scholarly evocation of ancient Israel lent divine sanction to their fragile governments, especially when they were new establishments like the Dutch republic and the Cromwellian commonwealth. Earlier, John Selden's treatise on the magistracy of the ancient Hebrews, *De synedriis et praefecturis juridicis veterum ebraeorum* (1650–1655), a scholarly tour de force well nourished with references to Jewish learning of all ages, had assimilated the Sanhedrin with Parliament, giving that body sacred authority and annulling any supposed divine right of kings.

Historical precedents and Israelite prototypes were enlisted to bolster the royalist as well as the popular party in the contentions over sovereignty that shook the states of Western Europe. Proponents of royal absolutism like Jean Bodin could find in the Old Testament numerous examples of sovereignty residing in a single person, to the detriment of both democratic and aristocratic elements. Bodin the renowned Hebraist, suspected at times of favoring Judaism over Christianity, in the *Six livres de la république* (1576) quoted Maimonides' "Law of Kings" to strengthen his cause. Thomas Hobbes filled the *Leviathan* (1651) with testimony for the predominance of secular power over the church by invoking the practices of the revered kings of Israel. To denigrate the pretensions of clerics, Hobbes peppered his text with more passages from the Scriptures than from traditional Greek and Roman sources. In chapter 40 examples of the exercise of absolute royal sovereignty by ancient Hebrew kings before the Babylonian captivity are strung along for page after page:

> Besides, we read (1 *Kings* 2.27) that Solomon *thrust out Abiathar from being Priest before the Lord:* He had therefore authority over the High Priest, as over any other Subject; which is a great mark of Supremacy in Religion. And we read also (1 *Kings* 8) that hee dedicated the Temple; that he blessed the People; and that he himselfe in person made that excellent prayer, used in the Consecrations of all Churches, and houses of Prayer; which is another great mark of Supremacy in Religion. Again, we read (2 *Kings* 22) that when there was question concerning the Book of the Law found in the Temple, the same was not decided by the High Priest, but Josiah sent both him, and others to enquire concerning it, of Hulda, the Prophetesse; which is another mark of the Supremacy in Religion . . . To conclude; from the first institution of Gods Kingdome, to the Captivity, the Supremacy of Religion, was in the same hand with that of the Civill Soveraignty; and the Priests office after the election of Saul, was not Magisteriall but Ministeriall.[2]

Puritan preachers and political leaders of the English commonwealth customarily interspersed their pronouncements on government with dicta from the Old Testament. Sometimes they identified themselves so closely with the Jewish commonwealth that they advocated the actual promulgation of the Mosaic code and prepared chapbooks based on the laws of Deuteronomy. Cotton Mather in his *Magnalia Christi Americana* (1702) regarded a virtuous contemporary divine in New England as a Bostonian incarnation of an Old Testament figure. It was no burden on a young member of the Massachusetts Bay Colony to go about with the weighty name of Shearjashub. In the wilderness of New England the colonists saw themselves as reliving the hardships of the Israelites in Sinai. Political adaptation was a natural consequence.

That Puritans in England Old and New clad themselves in the mantle of the Israelites has long been recognized. The consoling images of the city on the hill and the lamp as a saving light could have both spiritual and plain historical meanings. The imitation of Israel occurred on many levels; a noteworthy example is the covenant on the *Arabella* in which the Pilgrims accepted the harsh yoke of being God's chosen people and the terrible punishments that would ensue if they defected. To Roger Williams, however, the worldly identification of the national state of the Jews with the new dispensation was blasphemy.

In 1617 when the Dutch polymath Pieter van der Cun published the three books of his *Republic of the Hebrews,* he acknowledged the existence of only two predecessors who had treated the same subject, the Italian humanist Carlo Sigonio and the French Calvinist Corneille Bertram. The very idea of writing a treatise devoted wholly to the ancient commonwealth of the Jews, from its foundation to the destruction of the Second Temple and their dispersion, was thus thought to be a relatively novel departure in historiography. Renaissance scholars had written histories of Greece and Rome and commentaries on Roman historians; Italians had prepared narrative accounts of their own cities; Englishmen, of reigns of individual kings. And there was a long-flourishing European tradition of universal history, usually with the four monarchies symbolized in the book of Daniel as a framework, of which John Sleidan's little book of 1559, *De quatuor summis imperiis* (On the Four Great Empires), was the most widely quoted and adapted example. But Christian scholars had often shied away from writing a history of the Jewish state as an independent commonwealth.

Before the seventeenth century, there was great reluctance to turn the narrative parts of the Old Testament into a consecutive secular story or to analyze the institutions of the patriarchal age, the period of Moses' rule, or the kingships of the first and the second commonwealths, as if they were states with histories similar to those of other nations and with regulations for the maintenance of civil order that resembled contemporary royal decrees. Although the divine hand was recognized in the actions of all nations, there was something peculiar in God's relationship to the laws and vicissitudes of the Jews that made it prudent for the lay historian to keep his distance. The line between sacred and secular history was respected. Catholic theologians and Protestant divines discovered in the characters of the Old

Testament so many types of future Christian history that treating the leaders of the Hebrews like potentates who were no more awesome than contemporary European monarchs appeared to border on the sacrilegious.

But the subtle fluids of the secular spirit were penetrating into the most sacred places of Christendom, and the polity of the ancient Jews did not remain immune. Just as the critical techniques of humanist scholarship dealing with Greek and Latin authors would ultimately exert their force on the reading of the Scriptures, so the manner of conceptualizing the history of the Jews would become imitative of what Christian scholars were doing with the annals of Greece and Rome.

There was of course an exemplary history of the Jews, written in the manner of the Greek and Roman historians, that Christians valued highly and Jews condemned (though this was not uniformly true for Dutch Jews, and there was a medieval Hebrew adaptation of the work, called the *Yosippon,* attributed to Joseph ben Gorion): Josephus' *Jewish Antiquities* and *Wars of the Jews.* Flavius Josephus had approached the Old Testament as a narrative history and had described the civil and religious conflicts of the second commonwealth down to the destruction of the Temple. Many Jews could not mention without loathing the name of the former Jewish priest and military commander who had stood before the gates of Jerusalem in the army of Titus. But for Christians his treachery to his brethren only gave him authority and lent credibility to his narrative. In his text they also discovered one of the rare testimonies to the birth of Christianity. (This "testimonium Flavium" is now highly suspect as a later insertion.) In the sixteenth century, the few historical works dealing with the Jews were essentially amalgamations of the Bible with *Wars of the Jews.* Perhaps the very existence of Josephus' dramatic histories inhibited earlier Christian writers from composing original works, since they could not hope to surpass him.

The two late sixteenth-century polymaths whom van der Cun cited, Sigonio and Bertram, had boldly entered the field without extensive rabbinic learning. They abstracted from biblical texts, Josephus, Philo, and the Church Fathers those passages that could contribute to an orderly depiction of the government of the Jews. They had found a new reason for writing Jewish history. Since the laws and ordinances of the ancient Hebrews had been dictated by God himself, were they not worthy of emulation? Were they not superior to Solon, Lycurgus, Plato, and Aristotle as guides for modern polities? In these early histories the narrative was meant not to be entertaining, but to impart political lessons. True, the laws of the Jews had been superseded by the teachings of Christ and were decried as polluted with corporeality. But when the early writers stressed the civil order of the Hebrew commonwealth, the division of estates, and the underlying forms of dominion, they were celebrating a government that once had divine approbation; moreover, the society they portrayed was free from the evils of later rabbinism.

Van der Cun believed that he was introducing an entirely new viewpoint into the sort of treatises represented by Sigonio and Bertram when he discovered the works of Maimonides and other Jewish rabbis. His *Republic of the Hebrews* reproduced long excerpts from Maimonides in Hebrew, along with Latin translations, and made reference to Onkelos, Rashi, Zacuto, and Abraham Ibn Ezra. When the Dutch Hebraist Constantijn l'Empereur elaborately annotated and republished van der Cun's work, it became a treasury of rabbinic learning and Christian Hebraist scholarship, and was translated into Dutch, English, and French. In 1713 the popularizer Jacques Basnage's critical remarks on Josephus appeared as two volumes appended to the revised three-volume French translation of van der Cun, thus adding an analytical treatment to the narrative description of the Jewish polity.

Imbonati in his 1694 *Bibliotheca* lists some hundred volumes by scholars in France, Italy, England, Germany, and Holland published in the latter part of the sixteenth and the seventeenth centuries with titles that are essentially variants of *Republic of the Hebrews.* The more recent treatises drew directly from the biblical narrative, the Talmud, and later rabbinic commentaries, above all from Maimonides on the "Law of Kings" in his *Mishneh Torah.* Most of the works on the republic of the Hebrews divided their texts into sections on the ecclesiastical and the civil polities; once involved with the ecclesiastical order, or what Christians considered to be the organization of the Jewish church, they also tended to offer explanations of Jewish rites, ceremonies, and beliefs, especially doctrines about the coming of the messiah. By contagion, Christian divines became enmeshed in the why and wherefore of Jewish dietary and marital commandments that had the force of religious laws, particularly when at first glance these rules appeared outlandish or nonsensical. The long rabbinic history of "reasons for the commandments," a traditional field of inquiry from Saadia Gaon through Maimonides and beyond, came to the rescue, and the expositions of Jewish commentators were incorporated into Christian treatises.

As Christians began to write Jewish history, they drew political lessons from it, as they had from Greek and Roman history. Generally they followed Josephus' analysis of the breakdown of the second commonwealth, confirming the moral of his tale: internal sectarian strife had led to the destruction of ancient Judaea. Was it not possible that the wars among Christian sects would endanger the very existence of the Christian republic? In an indirect way, the new version of Jewish history came to serve the Christian pansophia preached by Comenius and the ecumenical ideal of Leibniz. Either the Christians would unite or they would suffer the fate of the bickering Judaeans. If there is one theme that runs through much of Christian historiography of the ancient Hebrew commonwealth, it is the proposition that discord brought about its downfall. While these Christian historians derived their original insight from Josephus' circumstantial depiction of the embattled Jewish sects under the Romans, the idea that internecine discord was the prelude to disaster was constant, whether the critical period was conceived to be the dissension after the breakup of Solomon's kingdom or the war of the sects at the time of Jesus. The same lesson for Christian contemporaries appears in historians as diverse as the Dutchman van der Cun, the French Huguenot Basnage, and the German philosopher Herder at the end of the eighteenth century.

In the preface to his book van der Cun, recalling the fate of the Zealots of Judaea, addressed urgent entreaties to the states of the Dutch republic to forswear factionalism and civil strife. For dramatic effect he began with a dithyramb to the ancient republic of the Hebrews:

I offer to your view a Commonwealth, the most holy, and the most exemplary in the whole World. The Rise and Advance whereof, it well becomes you perfectly to understand, be it had not any mortall man for its Author and Founder, but the immortall God; that God, whose pure veneration and worship, You have undertaken, and do maintain. Here you shall see, what it was that conteined the Hebrews so long in an innocent way of life; what rais'd up their courage, cherished their concord, bridled their desires. Indeed, that people had Rules of Government, excelling the precepts of all wise men that ever were; Which Rules, we have shewed, may in good part be collected out of the holy Bible. Only, of their Military Discipline very little is deliver'd to our memory: Yet must every one, that considers their victories and achievements, confess, that the Hebrews, for military vertue, were inferiour to none.

The moral for the cities of Holland was to maintain their unity, as the cities of Palestine had through the reign of Solomon:

> The Counsels of all provided for the safety of all; and the Cities, which were many, did not every one aim at their own dominion, but all used their best endeavours to defend the publick Liberty. That the Government might bee compleat and uniform, they had the same Laws, Magistrates, Senators, Judges, and the same weights, measures, mony. Wherefore, all *Palestin* might be accounted as one City, but only that all the Inhabitants were not shut up within the same Walls. Such a Community and Conformity there was between them all.

Then followed the darkness of disintegration. The discord and sedition stirred up by Jeroboam ended the unity, and divisiveness brought about the subjugation of the kingdoms of Israel and Judaea. The utopia of the Hebrew commonwealth vanished and the Jews never recovered from their enfeeblement. The states of the Dutch Republic were warned to learn from their fate and from the examples of Greece and Rome that internal discord, not conquest, destroyed nations. "Your own experience confirms you in it, since by divine favour, and your own vertue, and the conduct of your Invincible Leader, your Common-wealth, by many degrees, is at last arrived to that height, that your enemies can complain of nothing, but your greatness." At the very moment of triumph, however, they should be on guard against incipient civil conflict. "Many of your subjects are already gone into sides, and oppose each other with contrary opinions, since here sprung up amongst them some unprofitable controversies about mysteries of Religion, not understood by the most part of the people. The multitude are carried severall wayes by their affections, and every day the flame encreases." [3]

Though van der Cun harks back to the experience of the Jewish commonwealth, he is not uncritical of the rabbinic commentators; nor does he deviate from the time-worn Christian thesis of the ingrained blindness of Judaism. As a meticulous scholar, he is on the alert for rabbinic error. He can be censorious about Abraham Zacuto's "Judaicall trifles"[4] in his *Sefer Yuhasin* (Book of Generations; 1510), which contended that the accents and points in the Old Testament texts went back to the time of Ezra. The Jews' rejection of Christ made them foolish and obstinate. "They carry about in their own breast the cause of all their misery: and suppose, by some divine favour, they should recover *Canaan,* they would change their climat, not their mind. Whithersoever they turn themselves, their night goes along too, and overshadows them: nor shall it be dispelled, before they have thoroughly smarted for their ingratitude and their obstinacy, and the hardness of their hearts."[5]

But despite such strictures on contemporary Jews, van der Cun admonished Christians against persecuting them. Among Calvinists an appreciation of the ancient Jewish commonwealth was sometimes reflected in a certain tolerance of Jews in the modern state, though the two attitudes were not consistently linked even among Dutch scholars—witness the hostility of Constantijn l'Empereur to Jewish settlers.

British scholarship did not lag far behind the magisterial learned works produced in the Dutch and German universities. John Spencer's *De legibus hebraeorum ritualibus et earum rationibus, libri tres* (1683–1685) was rationalist and Maimonidean in spirit. In 1659 James Harrington published a small volume pretentiously called *The Art of Lawgiving.* It is far more succinct than his turgid utopia *Oceana,* which became better known and is said to have been admired by the framers of the American constitution. Harrington, like most of his contemporaries, relied on the Bible to prove the soundness of his arguments and invoked the republic of the Jews as evidence for the universality of the idea of balance in all human institutions ancient and modern, sacred and secular. The second book of *The Art of Lawgiving,* entitled *Containing the Commonwealth, of the Hebrews: As namely, Elohim, or the Commonwealth of Israel; and Cabala, or the Commonwealth of the Jewes,* illustrated his political principles by narrating the institutional history of Israel up to the establishment of the

Church by the Apostles ("Cabala" in this context meant simply "tradition").

In his descriptions Harrington often resorted to homely contemporary comparisons in order to make ancient Hebrew institutions comprehensible: patriarchs of tribes were like the clan leaders of Scotland. The political world of ancient Judaea became alive, albeit in a manner that neither Max Weber in his *Ancient Judaism* nor modern historical scholarship might countenance. The assimilation of Jewish elders with an aristocracy and the elements of a general election among the Hebrews with the democratic choice of representatives may appear farfetched to a modern reader, but Harrington saw them as analogous. Proofs from Jewish history would be expected to exert a particularly cogent appeal to the Puritan mind. That Harrington discovered the true principles of mixed government in seventeenth-century Venice and in ancient Israel is one of the stranger vagaries of western thought in search of historical precedents.

Among dissenting clergymen in England, the image of the republic of the Hebrews as a model of mixed government held sway well into the eighteenth century. In 1740 works still appeared that analyzed the constitution of the Hebrews as if it were the instrument of government in a modern state devised according to the political theories of Harrington and Locke. As a consequence, the republic of the ancient Hebrews, which meant the form of government prevailing before the Babylonian captivity, was painted as remarkably similar to the government of Britain viewed through Whig spectacles. The concept dear to Harrington and Locke and later elevated to the highest rule by Montesquieu, the principle of balance of powers, was discovered to have pervaded the Mosaic Hebrew polity.

Moses Lowman's *Dissertation on the Civil Government of the Hebrews in which the True Designs and Nature of Their Government Are Explained. The Justice, Wisdom and Goodness of the Mosaical Constitutions Are Vindicated* (1740) served as a double apology: British government in its innermost nature turned out to be modeled after the Hebrew and thus received an implicit religious sanction, and the Hebrew polity was imbued with the civilized spirit of enlightened England and removed from the cruel, barbaric rule of priests harped upon by the anticlerical deists. In this favorable exposition of the Hebrew government, the divine wisdom and goodness in a part of God's creation were vindicated, just as the exposition of Newton's laws demonstrated divine wisdom in the ordering of the physical universe. Though the Puritan identification of the Israelites with Englishmen did not continue with the same intensity in the eighteenth century, the underlying idea, that both the Hebrews and the English were chosen people, persisted.

Lowman's history in some respects resembled the history of any other nation, but it had a religious polemical undertone. Its author was really extolling the excellence of the Mosaic constitution and defending it from the denigration of deists and atheists who dwelled on the conformities between the Jews and the barbarous peoples of newly explored continents:

> The *Hebrew* Commonwealth is, without question, one of the most ancient of the World, and justly looked upon as a Model of Government of divine Original; it will deserve our Attention, as much sure, as any of the Forms of Government in the ancient times, either among the *Egyptians, Greeks,* or *Romans.* It should more especially deserve our Attention as Christians, who own the Laws delivered by *Moses* to the *Hebrew* Nation, to have been given by the Oracle of God, and established by Authority of the supreme Governour of the World; in which therefore, we may expect to find a wise and excellent Model, becoming the Wisdom of such a Lawgiver.[6]

Lowman's work is part of a running debate on the nature of the ancient Jewish state that continued for two centuries. Was it barbaric, even savage, or was it the manifestation of divine reason and wisdom? The answer had immediate relevance to a Christian's estimate of contemporary Jews. Were they an uncultivated and despised people who had inherited vicious habits, or did they continue to represent a noble tradition in abiding by the word of an ancient God? Lowman's conclusion was as positive as Voltaire's later answer was pejorative.

Lowman included frequent citations from Harrington's *Commonwealth of the Hebrews* and from Josephus, and made comparisons with the Spartan constitution in its Plutarchian version. Of the Jewish writers, Maimonides continued to be the favorite. Lowman's dissertation was not a work of original scholarly inquiry into the Torah and the Talmud, though he doubtless knew some Hebrew. He depended primarily on seventeenth-century works by Christian Hebraists in England, Holland, France, and sometimes Germany who had direct access to rabbinic learning and wrote their treatises in Latin—John Spencer, Adriaan Reeland, Elias Schadäus, Friedrich Spanheim, Wilhelm Schickard, Symon Patrick, Johann Heinrich Otho, John Selden, Joannis Stephanus Menochius, Thomas Godwyn, Hermann Conring, Thomas Sherlock, Adriaan Houtuyn. Thus Christian Hebraists of the seventeenth century were still being popularized long after they were first published; they enjoyed a longevity rare among scholars, for later generations did not approach their knowledge of Judaic commentators. The number of Englishmen who knew some Hebrew may not have decreased in the eighteenth century, but there were no giants of learning to tower above the multitude of mediocrities.

Referring to the commonwealth of Israel as a model continued to be common as late as the end of the eighteenth century. But there was also an important body of opinion that was refractory to this singling out of Israel as an exemplar for the whole world. When Spinoza wrote his *Tractatus theologico-politicus* he limited the Mosaic political law to God's design for a particular people. The laws were wise in God's wisdom, but they were not universally applicable. Orthodox Anglicans, in revulsion against Cromwellian bibliolatry and the Puritan identification of an ideal state with Israel, also upheld the idea that the Jewish commonwealth was sui generis: God was the direct ruler of ancient Israel in both civil and religious affairs, but with the coming of Christ to all the nations there was no longer one law. God could not undertake the practical rule in detail of every nation on earth as he once had of his chosen people. Civil government was a function henceforward performed by kings. One Anglican theorist, George Hickes, in his *Peculium Dei, a Discourse about the Jews as the Peculiar People of God* (1681), based his political conception of Israel on the idea of the "favored nation" in Halevi's *Kuzari,* which Buxtorf the Younger had translated into Latin: the laws of the favored nation could not be universalized. But however the ancient polity of the Jews was viewed, it was a subject of enduring intellectual concern.

Hebraic political theory, rooted in the biblical and rabbinic tradition, was throughout the long history of the Jews rather consistently monarchical. When the principle of kingship was called into question, some rabbis saw it as an implicit chastisement of Israel for demanding of the prophet Samuel the establishment of a kingship like that of their gentile neighbors, instead of resting content with the direct lordship of God himself, who had chosen them as his people on Sinai. An idiosyncratic departure from the general Jewish acceptance of monarchical theory can be found, paradoxically, in the biblical commentaries of the fifteenth-century scholar Isaac Abravanel, whose works were closely studied by Christian Hebraists. Abravanel spent a lifetime in the service of kings and potentates as he wandered from his native Portugal through Spain and Naples to Venice, where he died in 1506. In intervals between royal appointments, he composed long-winded, digressive commentaries on the early and later prophets, in which he included extensive reflections on the service of kings. This work, most of which was posthumously published in Christian and Turkish lands where Jews had sought refuge, was also interspersed with apocalyptic promises and astrological reckonings on the date of the coming of the messiah. A separate collection known as *Ma'yenei ha-Yeshu'ah* (The Fonts of Salvation; 1551) is a rich mine of often disenchanted observations on the rewards of fealty to kings in this world. Abravanel, who had experienced earthly success and access to the chambers of monarchs, drank the bitter cup of exile and entertained no illusions about kingship. His commentaries hark back nostalgically to an earlier conception of Judaism, when the bond between God and his people was direct and intimate, and an intermediary between them was superfluous, if not sinful. It may be stretching a point to discover a republican ideal in the writings of this courtier-financier, who chose exile rather than conversion in 1492—his early upbringing had exposed him to the corpus of Greek and Latin histories and political treatises—but whatever the secular influences that played upon him, he is a perverse and perplexing figure, difficult to locate in the century of the Iberian expulsions. That he ended up as an emissary of the doge and the Venetian senate in negotiations with Portugal is not easily explicable, any more than is the work on neoplatonic love written by his son, known as Doctor Leone Ebreo, about whose purported conversion to Christianity scholars have long been wrangling. Abravanel's antimonarchical posture may be a sport, but echoes of his Hebrew works on government, while not as common as those of Maimonides, are audible among Christian theorists of the sixteenth and seventeenth centuries.

Biblical Exegesis

When Christian Hebraists first examined rabbinic hermeneutics, one of their manifest purposes was to redeem the true meaning of the Holy Spirit from the erroneous biblical exegesis of the blindfolded Jews. Thorough knowledge of Hebrew and Aramaic was necessary to cleanse the words of the Old Testament of false rabbinism, represented by the Talmudists and their successors, and to restore the original significance of the Word, to separate the pure metal from the dross. This purification required a study of what the rabbis said in order to refute them effectively or, sometimes, reluctantly to accept them in small doses. In some of his moods Luther had refused on principle to engage with the rabbis on the ground that they were corrupt, dead, bereft of the living breath of the Holy Spirit. Nonetheless, during the review of his translation of the Old Testament, not only Greek scholars but Hebraists who knew rabbinic commentaries were present at the sessions over which he presided. Other Protestant denominations showed a greater willingness to inquire into the rabbinic meanings because the Hebrew words themselves contained elements of truth. Luther's antagonism to Jews does not seem to have prevented later members of his church from becoming outstanding Hebraist scholars.

Once inaccuracies in the Vulgate translation of the Old Testament were revealed, and travelers brought from the Near East variant manuscript versions in Aramaic, Coptic, Syriac, Slavonic, Greek, Latin, and Arabic, it was inevitable, at least in the Protestant world, that there should be a significant turning to the Hebrew original. For the full understanding of the word of God, major Protestant theologians applied to the rabbinic commentators, however vehemently the Jews had rejected Christian reading of the proof-texts in Prophecy and Psalms on the coming of Christ. The obligation to consult the original Hebrew text and learn about the laws and rites of the Jews doubtless touched clergymen more than their parishioners, but among those Protestant sects that insisted on the individual's pondering of the scriptural word, a knowledge of Hebrew and Hebrew customs was esteemed by both laymen and divines. In the English world before and after the Civil War of midcentury, the Anglicans, educated Puritans, and other Dissenters all regarded the study of Hebrew as a common responsibility. In that monumental enterprise of English erudition in the 1650s, Brian Walton's polyglot Bible, scholars and divines drawn from the whole spectrum of belief—from members of the Church of England through Independents and Presbyterians—managed to collaborate.

Though its spirituality was continually contrasted with Judaic corporeality, Christianity remained a scriptural religion, dependent on the exegesis of texts. Since the word of God had to be fathomed in its complete, true meaning, Jewish writings were studied in order to arrive at more accurate readings for the New Testament, as well as the Old. Despite intermittent outbursts against rabbinism, it was recognized that Jewish commentators and grammarians could shed light on the commonsense translation of words, on syntax, on the identification of offices and the duties attached to them, on conditions in Judaea at the time of Jesus that clarified the accounts of his life in the Gospels. Recourse to the talmudists and rabbis bred interest in other Jewish writings, such as the philosophical works of Maimonides and Yehudah Halevi, especially after Buxtorf the Younger's Latin versions appeared. The trickle of printed Latin translations from the rabbis in the fifteenth century—incunabula like the medical *Aforismi* of Maimonides and Rashi's commentaries on the Bible and the Talmud—by the sixteenth and seventeenth had swelled to a steady flow.

In their actual confrontation with the writings of the rabbis, the major denominations (Catholics, Evangelical Lutherans, Reformed Calvinists, Anglicans) did not present a solid phalanx; nor was there uniformity within the ranks of the deviationists (Socinians, Remonstrants, Puritans). As a rule, a fundamental difference obtained between Catholics, who insisted on interpretations of Scripture according to an accepted body of church traditions, and Protestants, who doggedly focused on the text itself. But even this division should be qualified: Anglicans gave great weight to the readings of the Church Fathers, and in the Catholic world the Council of Trent's decision to make the Latin Vulgate the *versio authentica* did not foreclose research and inquiry on the part of priests and monks into the proper sense of the Hebrew text. While Catholics were usually more reluctant than Protestants to appeal to the rabbis as aids in textual explication, for some the approval of the eminent Spanish Jesuit scholar and theologian Juan de Mariana (1526–1623) was a sufficient license to study rabbinic thought. In the quarrel over the antiquity of the vowel and accent markings in the Old Testament that troubled the world of Christian Hebraism, the Protestants generally followed the lead of Buxtorf the Elder and rejected the notion that the pristine Hebrew text had been tampered with over time. But the Catholic scholar Jean Morin envisaged all manner of emendations in the past; and his position was defended by Louis Cappel, a Huguenot professor from Saumur, to the consternation of the Buxtorfs. Such intellectual crisscrossing of confessional lines was becoming more frequent in the seventeenth century.

Believing that obscure parts of the Bible could be fathomed only with the assistance of Jewish sages, many Protestants prized talmudic and later rabbinic interpretations because admittedly the rabbis had a more thorough knowledge of Hebrew grammar and syntax than did Christians. The English doctor of divinity John Lightfoot used the rabbis dialectically. Those who hated the Gospel would be made through Lightfoot's talmudic scholarship its best interpreters, since they had lived in Judaea at the time of Jesus. The examination of New Testament phrases in the light of parallel passages gleaned from the Talmud and the practices of the Sanhedrin would allow Christians finally to settle on an accurate interpretation of the Greek text of the Gospels and would further peace and unity among the sects. In his *Hebrew and Talmudical Exercitations upon the Gospel of Saint Matthew,* Lightfoot expressed his feelings of love-hate toward the Talmud and the rabbis:

> When all the books of the New Testament were written by Jews, and among Jews, and unto them; and when all the discourses made there, were made in like manner by Jews, and to Jews, and among them, I was always fully perswaded, as of a thing past all doubting, that that Testament could not but everywhere tast of and retain the Jews style, idiom, form and rule of speaking . . .
>
> I cannot paint out in little a true and lively character of them better, than in these paradoxes and riddles. There are no Authors do more affright and vex the Reader, and yet there are none, who do more intice

and delight him. In no Writers is greater or equal trifling, and yet in none is greater, or so great benefit. The Doctrine of the Gospel hath no more bitter enemies than they, and yet the Text of the Gospel hath no more plain interpreters. To say all in a word, To the Jews their Countrymen they recommend nothing but toys, and destruction and poyson; but Christians, by their skill and industry, may render them most usefully serviceable to their Studies, and most eminently tending to the Interpretation of the New Testament.[7]

Lightfoot became one of the best-known English Hebraists on the Continent and in the American colonies. His many books on the harmony, chronology, and order of the New Testament and his minor works of learning were popular during the Cromwellian period. In his *Commentary upon the Acts of the Apostles chronicall and critical* (1645) he included a brief survey of the Jews and Romans at the time of Christ, and in one of his books, *The Harmony, Chronicle, and Order of the New Testament,* he added a "Discourse concerning the fall of Jerusalem and the condition of the Jews in that land afterward" (1655). But his outstanding contribution to the treasury of Christian Hebraism remained his illumination of the text of the New Testament through establishing a precise chronology of events in both Testaments, bringing to life the physical structure of the Temple and its service in the early Christian era, and combing the Talmud for passages that were parallel with dicta in the Gospels.

Lightfoot was born in Stoke-upon-Trent in 1602, the son of a curate; his spiritual father and patron, Sir Rowland Cotton, encouraged his Hebrew studies and brought him to London as his domestic chaplain. Though not indifferent to the political upheavals of his day, Lightfoot managed to survive the vicissitudes of changing regimes. He was a member of the Westminster Assembly, where he took an Erastian position on church government, and on numerous occasions in the years 1645–1647 he was called on to preach before the House of Commons. When the master of St. Catherine Hall at Cambridge was ejected, he assumed the post, and delivered a panegyric on Cromwell for his aid in completion of the polyglot Bible. Under the Restoration, Lightfoot was allowed to retain his mastership. Though he had sided with the Presbyterians, he signed the Act of Uniformity of 1662 and continued his scholarly researches until his death in 1675. His library of books in oriental languages was bequeathed to Harvard, a benefaction that may have persuaded the Mathers to treat him with special veneration in their writings. Though the publication of most of his works, he complained to his friend Buxtorf the Younger, had to be undertaken at his own expense, they appeared in a steady stream during the Cromwellian period and the early Restoration. A collection of the works was first published posthumously in English in two folios by G. Bright and J. Strype in London (1684), followed by a Latin edition in Rotterdam; its use was sufficiently widespread to justify an even more complete edition in eighteen volumes in London, 1825.

Lightfoot's works fortified the identification of midcentury English Christians with the precepts and practices of Judaism before the dispersion. Lessons of the talmudic rabbis found repeated in the New Testament dispelled the curse of rabbinism for those who sought help in the works of Jewish learning for understanding the Scriptures. While Lightfoot castigated the Jews for rejecting the true messiah and misreading the holy writings, his detailed recording of affinities between the Talmud and the Gospels inevitably altered Christian views of Judaism in the Protestant world. In the previous century Johannes Reuchlin had translated the book of Matthew into Hebrew, but the two religions were never brought closer than in Lightfoot's renderings of Greek New Testament teachings in Hebrew phrases drawn directly from the books of the Talmud. His *Horae Hebraicae et Talmudicae. Impensae I. In Chorographiam aliquam terrae Israeliticae. II. In Evangelium S. Matthaei* appeared in Cambridge in 1658, followed by volumes on Mark, John, and Luke. Carpzov considered their revelations significant enough to warrant a Leipzig edition of the *Horae Rabbinicae et Talmudicae in Acta Apostolorum* in 1679, and a collection of the *Horae* for all four Apostles in 1684. The German scholar Christian Schoettgen reprinted a large segment of the *Horae* in his own *Horae Hebraicae et Talmudicae in Universum Novum Testamentum* in 1733 and, in an awkward adaption of a couplet originally inspired by Nicolas de Lyre, celebrated Lightfoot in rhyme as the man who turned on the fountains of talmudic learning for the modern world: "Nisi Lightfootus lyrasset, / multi non saltassent."[8] Lightfoot's chronological writings found a place in Ugolino's *Thesaurus antiquitatum sacrarum*. The *Hebrew Talmudical Exercitations upon the Gospels, the Acts, some Chapters of St. Paul's Epistle to the Romans, and the first Epistle to the Corinthians* saw a new four-volume edition in Oxford as late as 1859.

In his *Mystery of Israel's Salvation* Increase Mather, for whom Lightfoot was a revered model, told his New England parishioners: "There is a multitude of places in the New Testament (and in the old too) which no one can clearly understand, except he be acquainted with the notions, customs, phrases, &c. which were formerly in use amongst the Jews."[9] Mather quoted Origen to the effect that *ubi bene nemo melius, ubi male nemo pejus* (when they do well there is nobody better, when they do ill there is nobody worse).

To write a commentary on the Bible continued to be the secret ambition of New England Puritans, whose destiny had thrust them into tumultuous lives of action. Those who realized this desire poured into their commentaries a fervid religious passion. In 1693 Cotton Mather recorded in his diary that toward the end of the "Summer now running, I began one of the greatest Works, that ever I undertook in my Life." What was to be his Biblia Americana was started "with many cries unto the god of Heaven." His hope was that "all the Learning in the World might bee made gloriously subservient unto the *Illustration* of the *Scripture.*"[10] Unfortunately for his design, though there are four hundred and forty separate titles in his published bibliography, no one has ventured to print the contents of the six massive volumes of his papers that now lie fallow at the Massachusetts Historical Society. Scholars who have dipped into the undigested material have sustained the judgment of reluctant publishers. Cotton Mather's commentary on Genesis is an example of the manner in which secondary and tertiary sources were cannibalized by divines with pretensions to great learning. In describing Creation, Mather randomly lifted sections from the writings of stale corpuscularians and such Newtonians as William Whiston.

Père Richard Simon, a member of the Congregation of the Oratory, was the most learned and heterodox critic of the Old and New Testaments and one who leaned heavily on Jewish sources, though he was denounced by Bishop Bossuet and out of caution felt constrained to burn many of his own manuscripts. When the French censors denied his books publication, they found a refuge in the Protestant printing establishments of Holland, where to his amusement they appeared under a variety of pseudonyms. Simon's *Histoire critique du Vieux Testament* had originally passed the French authorities and was already set in type in 1678 when Bossuet belatedly awakened to the heretical nature of this adventure in biblical criticism and suppressed the edition. But two years later the book was published in Amsterdam. The reaction of different Catholic orders to new readings of a biblical text often depended on the current status of quarrels among Jansenists, Jesuits, and Oratorians. Simon was not one to avoid ecclesiastical fracases by remaining an obscure closeted scholar.

When one Christian wished to refute the biblical interpretation of another, he commonly hurled the epithet "judaizer" at his adversary, an ancient practice revived in the Renaissance to defame men like Reuchlin and Postel. More than three hundred years after the Council of Vienne had decreed the establishment of chairs in Hebrew under the auspices of the papal curia and at the great universities of Europe, Catholic Hebraists were still introducing their major works with apologies for their absorption with rabbinic writings. Imbonati justified the study of Hebrew as a sacred language and defended consulting rabbinic works by analogy with the practice of the Israelites, who in fleeing from Egypt stole the utensils of their oppressors. If the Israelites were allowed to make off with material goods, a fortiori it was permissible for Christians to appropriate such spiritual goods of the rabbis as might be found illuminating. By the seventeenth century, rabbinic commentaries had become an important part of Christian exegetical equipment, though not all rabbis were equally respected. There were fashions in rabbinics.

In the Catholic world Père Simon left the most complete apology for consulting the rabbis in his *Histoire critique du Vieux Testament,* in which he included careful evaluations of each of the major rabbinic commentators he had studied. By all odds the most significant heterodox work on the history of Old Testament scholarship, the main body of the *Critical History* was supplemented with two analytic catalogues, one on the principal editions of the Bible in Hebrew and other languages, the other on Jewish authors referred to in the book. And though in many ways this unorthodox cleric is not typical of Christian scholarship in the seventeenth century, his likes and dislikes are indicative of the trend of opinion in both the Catholic and the Protestant communities.

It does not come as a surprise that in Père Simon's rabbinic catalogue the literal interpretations of Abraham Ibn Ezra are preferred, that Maimonides, though appreciated for his style, is found to be too philosophical and even too naturalistic when translating the biblical appearance of angels into dreams. Simon approved of David Kimchi the grammarian and rejected the famous thirteenth-century Spanish rabbi Nachmanides because of his cabbalist proclivities. In general, Simon looked askance on allegorists and even those whose commentaries shaded off into moral homilies. The cabbalists were disdained for their wild imaginings and the complicated systems they introduced into their commentaries on Genesis, which had little to do with a commonsense reading of the Mosaic text. Isaac Abendana passed muster. The most frequently quoted rabbinic commentator in the Christian world, Rashi—perversely known to Christians as Jarchi because they thought he came from Lunel ("yareach" being Hebrew for "moon")—was faulted by Simon for his excessive resort to talmudic interpretations of the Old Testament. Simon cited Abravanel's *Rosh Emunah* (Head of Belief) and claimed to have read his commentary on the early prophets (the Jewish way of referring to the historical books of the Bible) and on the later prophets and the Pentateuch. He made light of Abravanel's *Nahalat Avoth* (Heritage of the Fathers) and his *Miphaloth Elohim* (Wonder-Workings of God); his extensive messianic writings were passed over in silence.

Père Simon praised Elias Levita's *Massoret ha-Massoret,* his teaching of Hebrew to Christians in Venice and Rome, and his grammars (which were translated into Latin). He called him the least superstitious and the most worthy of being read among all the rabbis. With a few exceptions Simon treated talmudists, most later rabbis, and Christian Hebraists with either contempt or condescension; exceptions included Levita, Jacob ben Hayyim, who edited the Massoretes, and Joseph Albo, author of the *Book of Principles.* Simon particularly derided the attempt of Joseph ben Gorion (?) to compose a Hebrew equivalent of Josephus. Nor was he pleased with the *Book of Generations* of Abraham Zacuto, which he read in a Constantinople imprint; for him it was merely a compilation of chronologies and histories.

Simon's strictures on rabbinic commentators are restrained when compared with his attacks on the Christian scholars who were his contemporaries and rivals, Protestants and Catholics alike. He excoriated them in violent language for their ignorance of Hebrew, especially rabbinic Hebrew, and his criticisms were often well founded. No continental scholars escaped his scorn, not even members of the formidable Buxtorf dynasty and the learned Vossius family. In passing, he denounced one of the commonest failings of Christian Hebraists, their tendency to regard fanciful Midrashim and other collections of rabbinic moral tales and obiter dicta as serious textual interpretations of the law.

The underlying thesis of Simon's history, which purports to explain the major repetitions and contradictions of the Old Testament, lacks the quality of his critical estimates. His hypothesis that in the ancient commonwealth of the Hebrews there had been scribes who, like prophets, were divinely inspired and recorded what was most noteworthy in their times is a bold invention, suggested by the existence of scribes in Egypt. But its corollary, which imputes confusion in the Bible to the fortuitous mixing up of scribal scrolls by the early redactors, is not very convincing. His contention that Moses himself did not write every line in the Torah derives from Abraham Ibn Ezra's cautious comments on the passage in Deuteronomy describing the death of Moses. In its day Simon's scribal hypothesis was sympathetically examined by independent Protestant thinkers such as John Locke, whose analysis remains among his manuscripts. Despite Simon's attack on Spinoza's *Tractatus,* which he read at the time of its first appearance, the works of both men, steeped in rabbinic sources, each in its own way fed those currents of Christian thought that tended to move the history of the Hebrew republic out of the realm of the sacred and to push it, however gently, into the secular sphere. The divine inspiration of prophets and scribes was preserved, while the history as a whole was transformed into an experience understandable in worldly terms.

There is a question of how carefully Père Simon studied Abraham Ibn Ezra's commentaries, which enjoyed his general approval, and whether he was even acquainted with his religious treatises, poetry, or philosophical outlook, which clearly reveal a neoplatonic spirit alien to the matter-of-fact temper of the author of the *Critical History of the Old Testament.* Though in the introduction to his commentary on the Pentateuch Ibn Ezra had condemned allegorical and midrashic methods of interpretation, in the body of the work he too sometimes lapsed into imaginative digressions and symbolic readings that ignore his initial commitment. He mocked as baseless and irrelevant the foretellings of Christ that Christians read into the prophetic texts, but he was not altogether innocent of the intrusion of moral homilies that contradicted his own principles. When he turned the Song of Songs into a historical-philosophical narrative of the relations of God with his chosen people from the beginning of things through many trials to their final redemption, he made as adventurous a leap into the realm of symbols as the midrashic and christological excursions he dismissed with such biting sarcasm. But Simon and other Christian Hebraists seem to have blotted out these passages in their praise of him as an exemplary commentator. That they forgave him his trespasses is comprehensible, since the bulk of his commentary is in fact literalist, and he could be joined with David Kimchi in support of Jews and Christians who by the seventeenth century were inimical to types and figures and cabbalist fancies. These two rabbis were communicating to European scholars the accumulated fruits of a long tradition of Spanish Jewish grammarians, to whom Christians had had no access. A close reader of Ibn Ezra is aware that he did not wholly exclude hidden interpretations—such as a Philonic allegorical reading of the tree of knowledge and the tree of life—and that he often hinted at esoteric meanings at which traditionalists would have balked; but when Christian Hebraists resurrected rabbinic commentators who had been dead for more than half a millennium, they were looking for support of plain textual renderings that were in the prevailing spirit and provided them with linguistic information. For the most part they remained ignorant of the scores of supercommentaries on Ibn Ezra and Rashi and the occasional midrashic digressions in Rashi's commentary on the Talmud. Most of Ibn Ezra's commentary on the Pentateuch could be fitted with a little straining into the literalist company of Christian Hebraists.

Of course, a commentator's announcement that he was simply rendering the plain meaning of a biblical passage, while he resorted to all sorts of midrashic and allegorical sources, was not uncommon. Self-definition as an adherent of a particular mode of interpretation rarely involved an absolute delimitation of boundaries, among either Christians or Jews. An extravagant cabbalist reading or an immersion in number mysticism was one polar extreme, the unadorned translation of a passage into a foreign language the other; but in practice the categories were blurred. They were useful in polemics and in coining epithets, not in establishing methodological norms.

Rashi himself sought confirmation in earlier authorities, but as in all such enterprises he bent tradition a little for harmony with his own conclusions. Abraham Ibn Ezra, the wanderer, often quoted from memory and, marvelous as this instrument was, error was prone to creep in; his references to contemporaries or recent predecessors were also subject to alteration when he was engaged in battle with an adversary. In the end, Rashi was rich in citations to talmudic texts, and Ibn Ezra exuded a spirit of originality and an evident freshness. Grammar and philology were seen as neutral subjects by the Christian Hebraists, and adopting the literalist sense of Ibn Ezra offered protection from the stigma of judaizing.

Though he wrote no line by line commentary on the Bible, Maimonides ranked with Abraham Ibn Ezra in the eyes of English and Dutch Protestants. They esteemed him as an exponent of rational religion who gave plausible explanations for the customs and rituals of the Jews, downplayed the miraculous in biblical narratives, and made of the Old Testament prophet a sensible moral man, free from the stigma of enthusiasm. In John Spencer's Maimonidean *On the Ritual Laws of the Hebrews* they found a well-organized exposition of Jewish religious law that bolstered their own rationalist view of religion and could be used to debunk tinker prophets and men who spoke with tongues and saw visions, threats to the orthodox establishment. Maimonides was elevated to the status of an honorary Anglican. Buxtorf the Younger, Vossius, and Surenhuis joined the chorus of Maimonides' admirers.

Obviously not everything in Maimonides could win the approval of Christian Hebraists. In the twelfth chapter of "Laws Concerning Kings and Wars" in the *Mishneh Torah,* Maimonides characterizes the coming of the messiah as a natural, not a miraculous, event and conceives of his reign as a worldly restoration of Israel—an ideal epoch during which the Israelites would be able to observe all their laws without persecution by the gentiles: "Let no one think that in the days of the Messiah any of the laws of nature will be set aside, or any innovation be introduced into creation. The world will follow its normal course. The words of Isaiah: 'And the wolf shall dwell with the lamb, and the leopard shall lie down with the kid' (Isaiah II:6) are to be understood figuratively, meaning that Israel will live securely among the wicked of the heathens who are likened to wolves and leopards." [11]

The messiah is not a miracle worker and no signs are required of him. He is learned in Torah, a military hero, a rebuilder of the sanctuaries, and a preacher capable of converting the whole world to the worship of God, an act within the bounds of natural behavior. That he is the true messiah will be demonstrated by his achievements; his vindication will come in practice, leaving no room for doubt. Bar Kochba and Christ were demonstrably false messiahs because they failed and were executed. The true messiah will become a universal king as the mere report of his advent causes secular monarchies to fall. This Maimonidean evocation of the messiah could not be accepted by a Christian.

In one sector of seventeenth-century Christendom the Bible, once revered as the word of God down to the last letter and diacritical mark, was progressively appreciated as the historical document of a nation. New instruments for interpretation were now at the disposition of Christian scholars. There was a better understanding of Hebrew grammar as a consequence of the widespread acceptance of medieval Jewish grammarians (Kimchi) and Renaissance scholars (Levita). A more extensive knowledge of cognate languages such as Syriac and Arabic furthered the development of biblical Hebrew philology. Postel's crusade for the study of Arabic, which had once aroused the ire of Calvin, by the seventeenth century had borne fruit. Great arabists of Pococke's stature worked in English universities alongside the Hebraists, and undertakings like Walton's polyglot Bible encouraged the comparative philological studies. Christian Hebraists usually led the way in the new orientalist fields. The same techniques that had been used in dealing with textual variants among surviving classical manuscripts were adopted to make sense of the variations in Greek, Latin, Hebrew, Coptic, Slavonic, Armenian, and Arabic versions of the Bible—Isaac Newton's friend John Mill claimed to have discovered some 30,000 discrepancies among them—that were inundating Europe, as chaplains of embassies and trading companies in the Near East scooped up whatever biblical manuscripts came to their notice.

Surely as significant as the new tools of scholarship was the altered spirit of the inquiry. More and more the Bible, or at least parts of it, were treated as history, privileged and sacred perhaps, but in certain respects subject to the same critical analysis as the Greek and Roman historians. With the beginnings of a desacralization of the biblical text, even churchmen no longer believed that all of the five books of Moses had been written by the prophet himself under the direct inspiration of God. Isaac Newton, Richard Simon, and many other scholars distinguished between the prophetic and the historical books of the Old Testament as a matter of course. Treating the books of Samuel and Kings as straightforward history tended to make the kingdoms less sacred, and the motives of the monarchs of Judaea and Israel were scrutinized like those of any other potentates. This encouraged comparisons between Jews and gentile nations. The uniqueness of sacred history inevitably diminished as the Jewish kingdoms of this world were stripped of a mystical aura. The biblical protagonists were men whose intentions were comprehensible in terms of the prevalent theories of the passions. It was no longer incumbent upon a commentator to explain away as allegory the reprehensible conduct of King David. Among Christian scholars, biblical events had to be situated in time and place. There was a steady increase in the identification of place names occurring in the Bible and their location on a map, while heroic efforts were made to establish a world chronology that would define the relationship between Egyptian, Greek, Persian, and Roman history on the one hand and the history of ancient Israel on the other. The Jewish chronologist David Ganz of Prague, who had been close to Tycho Brahe, was highly regarded by so eminent a chronologist as Isaac Newton, who made an attempt to anchor comparative chronology in the solid matter of astronomic dating and measurement of the precession of the equinox.

If a magical practice or an idolatrous rite was mentioned in the Bible, how was it to be described? By featuring conformities in remnants of the classical corpus and in the travel literature recording pagan ceremonials, men like Selden, in his treatise *De diis syriis* (The Syrian Gods; 1617), gave substance to the practices of the biblical idolaters. The comparative mode of interpretation was in harmony with the general drift of a businesslike and scientific civilization, in which accuracy and matter-of-factness were becoming prime virtues. This is not to say that allegorical, moral, theosophical, and other imaginative readings of Scripture were cast out of the exegetical arsenal at one fell swoop. They coexisted, and sometimes in the works of the same scholar.

The desacralization of ancient Jewish history as presented in the Bible was a long-drawn-out development whose intellectual landmarks are hard to establish. Among some Christian denominations it never took place, and even among men who appear to have headed the new movement of ideas, the divestment of the sacred was not complete on all levels of consciousness. But historical biblical criticism was solidly founded in the seventeenth century and rose to new heights in the daring eighteenth-century hypotheses of Dr. Jean Astruc in France and Michaelis and Eichhorn in Germany. By that time, Jewish contributions to the process had long since been assimilated by Christian scholars. Spinoza's *Tractatus* in the end was probably the most revolutionary document of seventeenth-century exegesis, but for most Christian as well as Jewish scholars—even for the enlightened Leibniz—Spinoza remained outside the pale.

Latterday Christian Cabbala

By the end of the seventeenth century, Christianity had been infiltrated by traditional Judaic concepts both halachic, those treating of the law, and cabbalist, esoterica that lent themselves to all manner of adaptation in Christendom's quest for an occult philosophy. Poets and theosophists were receptive to cabbalist imagery and the manipulation of word-number equivalents, secret anagrams, hidden meanings, while most university scholars and members of religious orders tended to draw on halachic learning. Within the Judaic world there were mighty disputes among adepts of the two ways; but often as not these were two souls in the same rabbinic breast. A devotee of cabbalistic inquiries and contemplation of the works of creation or the nature of God still adhered to the talmudic rules that controlled all aspects of his everyday conduct and were the foundation of the legal system governing public life in the Jewish communities. In the mid-seventeenth century, when Manasseh ben Israel wrote his *Conciliator sive De convenientia locorum Sanctae Scripturae, quae pugnare inter se videntur* (1633), reconciling apparently contradictory opinions in the Old Testament—a work well received among Protestants in the Old World and the New—he evenhandedly cited scores of writings by both cabbalists and legalists, referring to them by name under these rubrics.

The distinction between Cabbala and juridical Halacha became a breach at the height of the quarrels over acceptance or rejection of the messianic pretender Shabbetai Zevi in 1666. In the aftermath of the Shabbatian movement, which had assimilated cabbalist ideas, many Jewish settlements in Europe and the Near East were torn asunder as rival partisans flung thunderbolts at one another. But though Christians were cognizant of these quarrels (ambassadors to the Porte sent home circumstantial reports), they were not directly involved in them.

The role played by Jewish Cabbala in the Christian intellectual life of early modern Europe is complicated by the fact that the word itself came to cover a multitude of conceptions. Of the thousands of Hebrew and Aramaic cabbalist manuscripts and printed texts identified by Gershom Scholem, the great twentieth-century scholar of the Jewish mystical tradition, only a handful were ever known to Christians, and their interest in what they vaguely associated with the central family of cabbalist writings varied widely. The mere appearance and usage of the term Cabbala, like so many of the building blocks of western culture, tell little about its content. Christians used the word promiscuously when it was in fashion: a writer often praised or attacked it without having touched a cabbalist work of any epoch.

Since in many Jewish communities the "secrets" of the Cabbala were surrounded with taboos and their revelation was restricted to Jews worthy of initiation into its mysteries, allowing Cabbala to be taught to alien Christians, who might be merely curious, was under severe sanctions. Christian Knorr von Rosenroth, the erudite Lutheran poet from the Palatinate who in 1677 and 1684 printed two volumes of excerpts of Abraham Herrera's neoplatonized version of the Lurianic Cabbala (the traditions of Isaac Luria, called the Ari, or Lion) along with explications of cabbalist terminology, advertised the hazards of his undertaking: the rabbi who taught him the rudiments of Cabbala lost close members of his family, and Knorr refused to reveal the name of this daring mentor even after his death, lest there be further reprisals against his relatives. In the face of the belief that knowledge of the Cabbala bestowed supernatural powers, the misgivings of the Jewish authorities were comprehensible. Knorr was by no means free from the apprehension that a curse might attach to his divulging cabbalist esoterica.

If the murky streams of Christian Cabbala—the composite term was introduced by Knorr in a communication from Franciscus van Helmont printed in the *Kabbala Denudata*—are followed from the time of its invention by Pico della Mirandola in the late fifteenth century through the seventeenth, it becomes as clear as anything can be in this vaporous intellectual atmosphere that the main concern of Renaissance Christian cabbalism had faded by the seventeenth century. Pico, Reuchlin, and their disciples believed they had discovered, in the Jewish cabbalist manuscripts at their disposal and the lessons of their rabbi-teachers, an arsenal of arguments for the conversion of the Jews to the dogma of the Trinity. The christological weapons Reuchlin adapted from the Jewish Cabbala were primarily mechanical, number-letter techniques of scriptural interpretation known as gematria, notarikon, and temura, which led to the revelation of the name IHSUH and fundamental trinitarian dogmas in Old Testament texts. The allegorical interpretation of the book of Genesis, one of the mainstays of cabbalist thought, was a lush garden in which Christian conceptions of creation and the nature of the godhead could be plucked from every verse. It was the contention of Christian cabbalists that Moses' hidden meaning in Old Testament prophecy was a foretelling of Christ, and that this was solidly demonstrated through letter mysticism. The method was still occasionally recommended in the second half of the seventeenth century by Henry More, the Cambridge scholar usually listed as a platonist in the chapbooks of western thought, who in trying to persuade Knorr to translate the *Zohar* in its entirety into Latin advised that he stress what he believed were trinitarian and christological allusions in the text. But generally in the seventeenth century the technical devices of Cabbala were not widely resorted to, except by Christian theologians and theosophists calculating the date for the inception of the millennium. While some Christian humanists of the Renaissance had seen in Cabbala an alternative to the rabbinic Talmudism that had prevented the Jews from recognizing the Trinity in their own secret traditions, by the late seventeenth century Cabbala among Christians had become a subject of philosophical interest related to the new natural philosophy as much as a vindication of the truths of Christianity.

The temper of European Christian esoterica had changed from the 1480s, when Pico published his first summaries of pre-*Zohar* excerpts, to the 1670s and 1680s, when Knorr prepared his compendium of post-*Zohar* fragments. During the interval there had been a wide diffusion of hermetic, neoplatonic, and philosophical alchemical systems, each of which, like the Cabbala, purported to communicate truths about the nature of God and his relationship to the created universe. The Jewish Cabbala presented in Knorr's Latin translations entered a culture saturated with speculative philosophies that both reinforced one another and competed for adherence among believers. Cabbala helped to free some of the builders of these grand speculative systems of nature from the quandary in which the new philosophy—science—had cast them by intensifying absorption in the material world at the expense of the spiritual. Henry More could refer to "cabbalist rubbish" and at the same time be convinced that precious philosophical gold could be mined there, elements for the creation of an integrated natural philosophy that would be consonant with both Descartes and Moses. Recent scholars have recognized in this preoccupation with natural philosophy a distinctive characteristic of English seventeenth-century Christian Cabbala, which was connected to modes of thought in philosophical alchemy and hermetic philosophy.

Natural philosophy was not at the core of traditional Jewish Cabbala: the "works of creation" figure less prominently there than the "works of the chariot," the contemplation of the nature of God. Christian Cabbala in the seventeenth century picked up from the various strata of Jewish Cabbala—the pre-*Zohar* systems, the *Zohar* itself, and the oral Lurianic Cabbala—a mystical nomenclature with which any number of theosophical natural philosophies were adorned. But the intricate mystical systems of the Lurianic Cabbala on the one hand and, on the other, hermetic philosophy, philosophical alchemy, and cognate theosophical systems have little in common outside of a few terms, an air of secrecy and occultism, and perhaps initiation procedures. Robert Fludd's *Philosophia Moysaica,* published posthumously in 1638, illustrates the banal manner in which stereotyped cabbalist phrases were adapted to lend mystery to a personal Christian theosophical system:

> The more secret Theologians and those most expert in true Cabbala say that just as Mind has domination in the human Soul, thus does Mettatron in the celestial world, where he rules from the Sun, and the

Soul of the Messiah in the Angelic world, and Adonai in the Archetypal [world]. And to the degree to which the active intellect of Mind is the light of the soul, even so the light of that same Mettatron or World's Soul is Sadai, and the light of the Messiah's soul is Elchai, which signifies the living God, and the light of Adonai is Ensoph, signifying the infinity of Divinity. The world's soul is therefore Mettatron, whose light is the Soul of the Messiah or of the Tetragrammaton's virtue, in which is the light of the living God, in which is the light of Ensoph, beyond which there is no progression.[12]

The self-conscious Christian cabbalist looking for concealed meanings in Scripture could believe that he would find truths known to Moses or even Adam; he might treasure the texts attributed to Shimon bar Yohai, the oral tradition of Isaac Luria, and the writings of Abraham Herrera and Moses Cordovero, and search for traces of Cabbala everywhere in Judaism. Without knowing it, the Christian cabbalist took sides in disputations that had wracked the Jewish communities for centuries, preferring the imaginative cabbalists to rationalists like Maimonides and Kimchi. Henry More, a reader of cabbalist texts—which did not make him a practicing, committed cabbalist— could even find passages in the sober *Guide for the Perplexed* that would transform Maimonides into a seeker after occult truths. Since before the appearance of Shabbetai Zevi Jewish rabbis did not draw a sharp line of demarcation between the Cabbala and other traditions, it cannot be expected that Christians, in surveying Judaism, would be absolutist or consistent.

Scholars have demonstrated of late that the Jewish cabbalist Luria's conception of *tsimtsum* was not the direct inspiration of John Milton in some of his verses on the creation in *Paradise Lost,* as once was supposed. In one particular instance (book 7, lines 168–169) the verse has been recognized as echoing Reuchlin's description of Pico's image of God during the act of creation as in a state of "retraction," withdrawing into himself. This reading is harmonious with neoplatonic ideas in Henry More, but not with either the text of the *Zohar* or the additions of the Lurianic Cabbala. It now appears that most of the details in Milton's narrative of the creation were influenced by the rabbinic commentators included in Buxtorf's edition of the Bomberg Bible, a commonplace of mid-seventeenth-century Protestant usage. Milton's verses thus derive from these literalist rabbinic commentators and not from Jewish or Christian Cabbala. If Milton had a "rabbi," it was his countryman John Selden, a talmudist, a scholar of rabbinics, but surely not a mystical cabbalist. The tendency to discern authentic cabbalist traces in seventeenth-century Christian writers, once a modish intellectual pursuit, perhaps should itself be "retracted."

While Jewish cabbalists could ascend to the higher stages of mystic communion with God, before the advent of the false messiahs of the seventeenth century they did not ordinarily deviate from obedience to the ceremonial laws of their faith. By contrast, many Christian cabbalists saw in these esoteric doctrines a way toward direct communion with God that bypassed the vain niceties of religious ritual and theology. A sect like the Quakers that stressed the inner life of a convert at the expense of scriptural religious truth might be amenable to the secret religious experiences promised by a Cabbala that in its original form was oral (Luria, the last great cabbalist of Safed, never wrote out his doctrine). Franciscus van Helmont, who inherited a predilection for cabbalism from his father, the well-known iatrochemist, was converted to the Quaker doctrine and made some headway in winning prominent Quakers like George Keith to what he considered the Cabbala. George Fox put an end to the liaison; and in any case, neither the younger van Helmont nor Keith should be reckoned in the roster of true Christian cabbalists merely because they mouthed cabbalist phrases and pretended to magical powers. There is nothing resembling the ascetic mysticism of a Jewish cabbalist of Safed in the behavior of the adventurer van Helmont, who frequented the courts of the Continent and for years was a house guest of More's friend Lady Conway.

In the seventeenth century, the Renaissance fascination with the Jewish Cabbala and the Christian Cabbala created by Pico and Reuchlin no longer prevailed among Christian Hebraists, who had become increasingly absorbed with the historical and philological refinement of the Scriptures. Whatever free-floating theosophical predilections they had appear to have been sopped up by philosophical alchemy and pansophic projects. Knorr von Rosenroth, who seems to have dabbled in both Cabbala and philosophical alchemy, is in many ways a throwback. His *Kabbala Denudata* came to represent Cabbala to Christian outsiders, but it was rarely read with assent and approval.

When More, whose letters to Knorr are included in the *Kabbala Denudata,* wrote his rather playful *Conjectura cabbalistica* in 1653, he was not associating his own neoplatonic thought with the *Zohar* or the Lurianic Cabbala, but seeking for inner meanings in the scriptural text. More was expressing dissatisfaction with plain literal reading and sought a more profound moral significance in sentences that, literally construed, he found dry, inconsequential, and irrelevant to religion. Essentially he was engaged in defining the rational theology of the Anglican Church by repudiating extravagant enthusiasts on one side and the atheist horde on the other. For More, Lurianic Cabbala as described by Knorr was an example of Jewish excess, and Spinoza was a Jewish representative of the atheists. On balance, More was perhaps less absolute in rejecting the spiritual vision of the Cabbala than he was the *Tractatus,* but he would have neither, any more than he would accept the Teutonic philosophy of Jacob Boehme. In most of More's writings, Jewish philosophy is a foil for the rationalist, Anglican middle way. Though he reproduced in his own later writings Knorr's diagrams and explanations of the Lurianic Cabbala, there is no reason to confound More with the Christian cabbalist followers of the Hebraic mystical tradition and their intricate theosophical systems.

In his younger days at Cambridge University, Isaac Newton knew More well and they spent many hours discussing the true meaning of the books of Daniel and Revelation. But in his mature years Newton stood with the rationalist Anglicans such as John Spencer, who read Maimonides as an exemplar of sound, sensible, nonenthusiastic religion; the cabbalists, gnostics, and platonizers in ancient and modern times were decried as the obfuscators of the plain truths of primitive Christianity. Newton was more inclined than More to accept some aspects of Spinoza's biblical criticism, and to reject forcefully all gnostic and cabbalistic system building. It reminded him too much of Descartes' vortices and Leibniz' universal harmonies. He would remain on the hard, solid ground of the literal interpretation of Scripture, turning Daniel and Revelation into histories of things to come, but avoiding mystical lucubrations. In his manuscripts Newton made mention of the *Kabbala Denudata* in order to attack it as an example of the survival of gnostic and platonizing proclivities. His was a scriptural religion, and he and his friend John Locke read the Bible first by their own lights and then with the aid of straightforward commentators. Among Newton's lesser-known works there is in manuscript a key to Revelation, but the spirit of this lexicon is anything but allegorical or cabbalistic. Newton was engaged in discovering political and worldly historical equivalents for the strange creatures in Revelation and the dreams reported in Daniel. He leaned toward demystification. In the tradition of Abravanel and Joseph Mede, he politicized and historicized the images in both the Old and the New Testaments.

Most Christian scholars saw the rabbinic cabbalist tradition as confused gropings. In the universities and the ordered religious establishments, Cabbala was a term of denigration. The poet Milton might use a phrase with overtones of a cabbalist concept; Newton, scientist and theologian, might read Knorr's *Kabbala Denudata;* the theosophical vocabulary of the age became cluttered with cabbalist terms—*en soph, sephirot, tsimtsum;* a rosicrucian in his flights of fancy might sound like a cabbalist. But the dominant trend of biblical interpretation was matter-of-fact, contextual, linguistic, and it moved away from the allegory and the fantasy associated with the commentary on Genesis in the *Zohar.* When the university professor Buxtorf the Elder or the Judeophobic scholar Eisenmenger summarized what they called cabbalist doctrine, their underlying purpose was to make fun of it and to mock the Jews who believed such superstitions. Europeans were kept abreast of the activities of Shabbetai Zevi and his prophet Nathan of Gaza in Smyrna, Jerusalem, and Salonica by Christian diplomatic agents, and a few were aware that the messianic movement was steeped in cabbalist thought. But after the great fiasco of Shabbetai's conversion to Islam, Christians paid little attention to the internal repercussions of the events in Jewish communities throughout the world. If anything, antics of the false messiah became a subject of ridicule that spilled over into the general Christian perception of Judaism.

Throughout the seventeenth century, reference to the *Zohar* and cabbalist cosmology are for the most part mere echoes of cabbalist fragments that had been in vogue in the fifteenth and sixteenth centuries, peripheral and freakish, remote from the doctrines of any Christian denomination. What are called cabbalist manuscripts of the eighteenth century turn up in archives, and a converted Jew of Iberian origin influenced the Lyons mystic Louis Claude de Saint-Martin on the eve of the French Revolution. But aside from such esoterica, the main currents of Christian mystical tradition had little affinity to Jewish Cabbala. There was a rich enough legacy of Christian mysticism in Germany, Spain, and England without recourse to Jewish or Christian cabbalist systems. There may have been a minor recrudescence of interest in Cabbala in the eighteenth-century curiosity about a romanticized Spinozaic pantheism. But for all the allurements of such intellectual miscegenation, it had no lasting effect on Christian judgments of Judaism—that is, not until the twentieth-century Christian rediscovery of Jewish mysticism, in a culture avid for exotic systems of irrational fantasy.

Judeophobia

Jewish texts proved adaptable to either Judeophilic or Judeophobic ends: to justify lifting the ban against Jews, as in England, and refute accusations such as blood libel; or to provide a storehouse of evidence that Jewish hatred of Christians was ineradicable. One of the consequences of a growing knowledge of rabbinic Hebrew among Christians was increased attention to those passages in the Talmud, in Midrashim and Yalkutim, and in rabbinic writings of the post-Talmud period, where incidentally or as part of a serious legal discussion the appropriate attitude of Jews toward Christians was authoritatively set forth. In the sea of rabbinic commentary, expressions of loathing for Christians, curses, and blasphemous depictions of Christ, Mary, and the Apostles could readily be picked up by Christian Hebraists. Questions were raised about the validity of oaths taken by Jews in procedures involving Christians, about obedience to Christian magistrates, about the legality of usury, about whether Jewish doctors were allowed by their laws to heal Christians, about whether Jews could consort with Christians. Some of the texts were obscure and open to interpretation. The hidden names that had been applied to Christians in rabbinic writings to disguise the animosity of the Jews toward the dominant religion were a standard subject of inquiry. If deciphered, the coded epithets would unravel the enigmas of many passages.

Once the publishing of books was made subject to the grant of royal, princely, or municipal privilege in both Protestant and Catholic lands, and the censorship of printed books was instituted and a Cath-

olic Index of Prohibited Books established, the whole corpus of talmudic and rabbinic writings came under review. In Catholic countries
the practice of censorship varied widely with the temper of the local
Inquisition; the primary censors were often converted Jews, whose
excessive zeal sometimes had to be bridled by their ecclesiastical su-
periors. The flow of Hebraic books from Turkish Constantinople
could not be stopped, nor could their importation into Catholic
countries from less rigid Protestant states be cut off completely. The
correspondence of Richard Simon reveals the assiduousness with
which a Catholic scholar in Paris would track down all kinds of Hebrew books and manuscripts. Expurgated editions of the Talmud,
however, indicate that official censorship had a substantial measure of
success. In the writing of new books, Jews exercised self-censorship,
but Christian Hebraists who spread their net over a broad area could
uncover Jewish blasphemies in these works as well.

Christian scholars used their immense, sometimes phenomenal,
learning to warn their brethren about the rising Jewish peril, and signaled particular rabbinic books as notorious repositories of sacrilegious utterances. In 1681 the erudite orientalist and jurist Johann
Christoph Wagenseil assembled a number of these blasphemous writings in two volumes entitled *Tela ignea satanae sive arcani & horribiles
judaeorum adversus Christum Deum & christianam religionem libri*
(Fiery Darts of Satan, or Secret and Horrible Books of the Jews
against Christ our God and the Christian Religion). There he reproduced the original Hebrew and Latin translation of a *Sefer Nitsahon*
(Book of Victory) by the fifteenth-century rabbi Yom Tov Lipmann,
replete with anti-Christian malevolence, along with a summary of the
medieval Tortosa debate on the Talmud, and, most scandalous of all,
the *Toldot Jeshu* (History of Jesus), whose authorship is still open to
question. This scurrilous account, which narrates the seduction of
Mary by a lustful Johanan despite her betrothal to Joseph, made a
mockery of the virgin birth. Jesus is portrayed as a bastard, brilliant
in his studies but arrogant, and his miracles are attributed to his theft
of the secret, unpronounceable name of God from the Temple. The
bizarre tale of Johanan's trickery in intoxicating his friend Joseph and
in duping Mary, who allows herself to be fornicated by Johanan during the prohibited menstrual period, is a gross parody that outraged
Christians. That Jews would continue to propagate this history of Je-

sus in the bosom of Christendom fortified the loathing for them already inflamed by their role in the crucifixion as set forth in the Gospels, countless sermons, paintings, and music. In the age of the baroque, the *Passion According to John* by Johann Sebastian Bach served to exacerbate the Judeophobia of Christians.

Repugnant though its individual pieces might be, as a whole Wagenseil's collection was not comparable to the revelations in the volumes of Johann Andreas Eisenmenger, one of the most persistent gatherers of anti-Christian texts in the latter part of the seventeenth century. His *Entdecktes Judenthum* (Judaism Uncovered) of 1700, a two-volume work in quarto of about two thousand pages, boasted a veritable taxonomy of special terms devised by Jews to avoid direct reference to Christians, language that was perfectly understandable to fellow Jews. *Minim, Nosrim,* Esau, Edom, Rome, Amalek, strangers, foreigners, goyim, corrupt ones, swine, were some of the more common ways of denoting Christians. Eisenmenger's narration of cases of ritual murder of Christians is among the more gory parts of the work—even Wagenseil refuted blood libel. When the accusation was repeated in learned works such as Eisenmenger's, Jewish apologists responded with denials, translated into European languages and phrased to appeal to Christian minds, that now appear tragicomic. (Earlier in the seventeenth century Manasseh ben Israel had already argued that, since Jews were forbidden to consume animal blood, a fortiori they could never eat matzoth made with human blood.)

Eisenmenger's book revived the question posed during the medieval debates and by Pfefferkorn in the sixteenth century as to whether the whole of the Talmud should be burned for its secret blasphemies. In the Barcelona encounter of 1263, Nachmanides had insisted that the offensive passages referred only to ancient heathen idolaters like the nations of Canaan, who fought against the Hebrews, that the curses did not apply to believers in an invisible God as the Christians were, that Jewish law provided for the salvation of the just among the gentiles, and that not all Christians were condemned to everlasting hell. Eisenmenger and other Christian compilers dismissed such rabbinic explanations as subterfuges. Eisenmenger's handsomely printed volumes had meticulous references to the 132 talmudic, midrashic, and rabbinic texts he had researched; the accuracy of his German translations could be checked since he cited the original Hebrew and

Aramaic passages at great length. When he referred to a manuscript treatise, he scrupulously noted the name of the rabbi who had lent it to him and the length of time it remained in his hands. Since his book was published in German, its influence was broader than that of Wagenseil's Latin work, and it was printed and excerpted throughout the eighteenth and nineteenth centuries.

An abridged and expurgated English-language edition, which first appeared in 1732–1734, was republished in London in 1742 with the title *The Traditions of the Jews, or, The Doctrines and Expositions Contain'd in the Talmud and Other Rabbinical Writings.* While praising Eisenmenger for his talmudic learning, the English translator and editor, the Reverend John Peter Stehelin, FRS, felt obliged to distance himself from the Heidelberg professor. The work demanded rectification, he wrote, but not because of any inaccuracies in its quotations. Eisenmenger's intent was to

> ridicule the Traditions of the *Jews,* mine is to explain them; his was to convince them of many Blasphemies against the Christian Religion, mine to prepare the Way for their Conversion, in bringing them back to the Religion of their Fore-Fathers . . . The best Method, in my Opinion, nay the only One, is to shew them, that they deviate from the Religion of their Ancestors, and that not understanding their Writings, but taking in a literal Sense, what was deliver'd to them in a mystical one, they are prepossess'd with many Prejudices, and can not see that the Substance of the Religion of their Fore-Fathers was the same with ours.[13]

Anticipating possible failure to convert the Jews, Stehelin at the close of his preamble took comfort that at least they would be convinced he had honestly studied their traditions and had not imputed to them outrageous practices and beliefs.

The original version of *Judaism Uncovered* has been treated contemptuously in Jewish historiography and figures prominently in histories of antisemitism. Its author's intent was clear: to warn Christians against the Jews in their midst, to highlight their age-old enmity against Christians at a time when Jews were beginning to occupy official posts in the administration of German principalities—the age of the Hofjuden, court Jews, had dawned. Though there are extant copies of Eisenmenger's book that bear a 1700 date on the title page, it was for many years sequestered and there was much haggling between Eisenmenger and Jewish notables about the purchase and suppression of the whole edition. It did not actually appear until 1711.

Eisenmenger's motives were complex. Doubtless there was a fear of conversion to Judaism, remote as this may seem; he is said to have witnessed the circumcision of two Christians in Amsterdam. If Jews wished to maintain that they never cursed Christians and pointed to prayerbooks that included supplications for the lives of reigning sovereigns, Eisenmenger ferreted out midrashic passages that bore witness to the contrary. The rabbinic citations that allowed for the violation of oaths to Christians—sometimes, though not always, removed from context—fed the image of the Jew as a disloyal subject. Quotations justifying the taking of usury from Christians were multiplied. Often accurate in detail and neatly presented under appropriate headings, Eisenmenger's texts swelled a body of Judeophobic literature that fed upon itself through the centuries. If the Jews were to bear witness to Christ through the mouths of their prophets, they also were to testify to the violence of their animosity against Christians and Christ. The great Selden in his *Table Talk* had taken a more worldly-wise attitude toward the Jews, observing that they never begged and praising their readiness to lend money to indigent princes. As for the antipathy they aroused in Christians, "my life for yours—Christians hate one another as much." [14]

These Christian attempts to keep hatred of the Jews boiling seems more virulent in the Germanic world than in other parts of Western Europe, though Spain of course, had achieved its own bloody final solution. Luther's diatribe *The Jews and Their Lies* had only been cosmeticized by Wagenseil and Eisenmenger. Both assumed a scholarly habit, and their books, which preserved the memory of ancient rabbinic hostility to Christians, were methodically organized by topic. Scientific Judeophobia was born. The republication of Martini's medieval *Dagger of the Faith against Moors and Jews* in Leipzig in 1687 was also grist for the Judeophobic mill. Carpzov's long introductory treatise to Martini's work, outlining the development of Judaic theology from the early talmudic period through the seventeenth century, was perverse and queer, though it revealed an astonishing acquaintance with Hebrew commentators, philosophers, grammarians, and cabbalists.

Eisenmenger proposed a radical reform of the methods of conversion. He cast doubt on the effectiveness of earlier Christian apologists such as Martini, Galatino, and Philippe Duplessis-Mornay, whose references were so erroneous that they could be scornfully dismissed by Jews. Unless the task of refutation were put into the hands of scholars like himself, the whole enterprise would defeat its own purpose. For centuries, violence had been employed to overcome Jewish obstinacy, but now more sophisticated techniques had to be devised. The vigilant protectors of the Christian faith should be professors of languages in universities, for they could publish incriminating Jewish works with precise textual annotations. The diffusion of books heavy with rabbinic excerpts would make the facts known and would alert Christendom to the ever present danger of Judaism.

As against Eisenmenger's vehemence, in another area the confrontation between Christianity and Judaism in the age of the baroque was relatively mild and matter-of-fact. From the sixteenth century on, there had been a growth of apologetic literature in defense of Christianity against the spread of what was called libertinism, originally a theological concept, and scores of works with titles that were variants on "The Truth of the Christian Religion" were written by gentlemen-scholars in both Catholic and Protestant countries. Though the primary target was epicurean doctrine and a variety of embryonic deisms, the authors, who were often such noted political personages as Hugo Grotius and Duplessis-Mornay, in their desire to present a full-scale account of their brand of Christianity battling all its enemies, included chapters on the Turks and on Judaism. The arguments were stereotypes and hark back to the Church Fathers and medieval diatribes like the ubiquitous Martini's *Dagger of the Faith*. This literary genre, often embellished with quotations from rabbinic writings, appealed to a broad segment of Europeans. References to Judaism were peripheral to the main objective, which was to strengthen Christians in their own belief. Polemical refutations of Judaism are to be distinguished from phobic attacks.

Eschatology

Christian millenarianism and the interpretation of prophecy, along with a rich eschatological tradition, were deeply marked by Judaic millenarianism and apocalyptic literature. A Jewish writer whose messianic foretellings were perennial subjects of disputation among Christian Hebraists was Isaac Abravanel. His posthumously published *Fonts of Salvation,* a sourcebook of messianism that was written in 1497 during his exile in Italy and comforted the Sephardim expelled from Spain, continued to influence Jewish thought through frequent Hebrew printings for three hundred years, while among Christians it became a common topic of millenarian controversy. Abravanel's readings of Isaiah 52 and 53, with their rejection of Christian interpretations, provoked a slashing attack by Constantijn l'Empereur. But Abravanel's elucidation of the visions in the book of Daniel were copied time and again by Protestant millenarians. More than a century after his death, prominent Christian Hebraists—Johann Buxtorf the Younger, Louis Compiègne de Veil, Anton Hulsius, Johann Carpzov, Johannes Friedrich Weidler, and Wilhelm Heinrich Vorst—still commented, with varying degrees of accord, on his version of the four-monarchies prophecy that foretold the end of the days.

Much of the attraction of Abravanel's writings lay in his citations from talmudic authorities, which lent a solid foundation to the extravagant prophetic utterances. The political manipulator and the fervid believer in the messianic advent, lodged in the same person, was a combination not uncommon among both Christians and Jews. Even Christian scholars who could hardly be classified as cabbalists resorted to number mysticism in order to prophesy the end of the days. In the sixteenth and seventeenth centuries, the spinning of eschatological fantasies was a major preoccupation in Christendom, and the role of the Jews in the final stages of the world drama assumed a new significance. Manasseh ben Israel and other members of the Amsterdam community who had emigrated from the Iberian peninsula were key figures in the transmission of Judaic apocalyptic thought to Christendom, inordinately thirsty for such visions.

In churches of Western Europe about the middle of the seventeenth century, a traditional part was assigned to the Jews and Judaism in the annals of the world before Christ, in the subsequent history of this world, in the age of the millennium, and in the final judgment. Since there was no uniform perception of Judaism, the several versions of the designated role of the Jews in the cosmic drama of sacred history differed in detail among the denominations and sects of Christianity; but there was a rudimentary consensus. The Old Testament provided an authentic record of the beginning of the world and of the early generations of mankind. The promises of God to Abraham and Moses were fulfilled when the tribes of Israel conquered Canaan and established a kingdom there, after destroying the idolatrous inhabitants. In the period that followed, the Jews broke the Mosaic laws, were punished, and were forgiven, only to resume their evil ways. During the course of their sinning, God sent them a series of divinely inspired prophets, whose words were preserved in the Old Testament.

In this Christian account, the central importance of the prophetic books of the Hebrews lay in their foretelling the advent of a messiah who was the son of God and who would end the sufferings of Israel and all mankind. When Jesus appeared, most Jews refused to recognize him as the true messiah, though his coming had been plainly set forth in their holy writings. They brought about his crucifixion, as reported in the Gospels. For this crime of deicide they were condemned to be dispersed and to suffer ignominy among the nations of the earth.

After the written laws of the Jews had been superseded by the teachings of Christ, the Jews continued to serve a Christian purpose: they were a living witness to the crucifixion and their books an irrefutable proof of the power of the Holy Spirit, since the prophecies of the Old Testament had been manifestly fulfilled. The Jews were not to be annihilated because they were of the same nation as Christ; their holy books could not be denied because they affirmed the reality of Christ's existence. Jews were not to be wiped out, but persuaded to convert by the explication of their own books of prophecy and of their own oral tradition, though it was foreordained that the Jewish people as a whole would remain obstinate and hard-necked—some believed until the end of the days.

Differences among Christians over the manner of the final fulfillment of the times, dating back to the Church Fathers, became pronounced in seventeenth-century Christendom. While there was general agreement among both Christians and Jews that the Jews had a role to play in the last days, eschatological controversies multiplied about the nature of that role. The futurist myth assumed different shapes among the denominations and sects of Christendom, and by the baroque age these variations were becoming central to the alternative perceptions of Judaism.

Jews expected a repossession of their land and the institution of political hegemony. Christians generally foresaw a conversion of the Jews, but disagreed over precisely when it would take place. Adherence to a specific periodization of history was involved. One projected series of events provided for an initial victory of Antichrist over all the nations, the Jews included; at this point Christ in his second coming would first convert the Jews alone, leading to the paradox that only Jews would be Christians, so to speak. Then would follow a universal conversion of the hosts of Antichrist. In the revolutionary Westminster Assembly of Divines in 1644, the "call of the Jews" became an explicit part of the Presbyterian catechism. In proclaiming a particular version of the end of the days, Protestants were not reluctant to adapt cabbalistic gematria that determined the final date of the millennium, or to rely for evidence on Abravanel's *Fonts of Salvation* and Manasseh ben Israel's *Hope of Israel*. Thus reticent Jewish predictions about the first coming of the messiah were applied, with emendations, to the second coming of Christ.

In Christian eschatological visions, the elements were combined in diverse patterns. Essentially they depended upon how the churchmen who spoke with authority interpreted the phrases in chapter 21 of the book of Revelation. Since the Church Fathers had left behind individual designs for the sequence of events, a seventeenth-century scholar of divinity in search of precedents to bolster his own description of things to come was faced with an embarrassment of riches. Not all the Church Fathers before Augustine were committed to a millennium, a thousand-year reign of Christ on earth before the final day of judgment; and Augustine peremptorily rejected the concept. Further complications were introduced by attempts to identify the Antichrist who would precede Christ's triumph. For many Protestants the domination of the papacy was in fact the rule of Antichrist. The fate of the Jews was intimately bound up with the reading of the crucial texts.

Perhaps the most surprising interpretation affecting the Jews came from no less awesome a figure than Pierre Jurieu, leader of the exiled Huguenots in the Netherlands, in *L'Accomplissement des prophéties ou la délivrance de l'église* (The Fulfillment of the Prophecies or The

Deliverance of the Church; 1686). In a radically heterodox explication of Isaiah 53, Revelation, and other prophetic verses scattered through the Bible, he maintained that the prophecies referred not to Jesus, the commonest Christian understanding of a virgin's son called Emmanuel, but to the triumph of the Jews in this world and their union of all the peoples on earth under a Jewish messiah reigning in Jerusalem, the commonest Jewish exposition of these texts. According to Jurieu, the promise of the prophetic books of the Bible that the appearance of the messiah would put an end to war and that all people would live in amity under Jewish hegemony had not been realized by the coming of Jesus, since the world was still torn by strife and, far from enjoying the headship of nations, the Jews were persecuted. Therefore Jesus could not be the messiah predicted in the Old Testament. For Jurieu this had no bearing on the nature of Jesus Christ, the son of God, and the truth of the New Testament witness. It only proved the obvious correctness of the Jewish interpretation of Isaiah and kindred prophecies.

Though Jurieu took it for granted that the Jews would ultimately recognize Jesus as the son of God, his overall interpretation of Old Testament prophecies was much closer to that of the rabbis than to traditional Christian readings, which related virtually all prophecies to Jesus. Among the papers of Richard Simon there is a copy of a purported joint statement (which may well be Simon's fabrication) addressed by the notables of the two Amsterdam synagogues to Jurieu, praising the accuracy of his textual interpretation and, while carefully excluding his references to Jesus of Nazareth, underlining the essential community of their views. Jurieu's original book had great influence among New England Puritans, whose sermons on Jewish survival mirrored some of his beliefs, though they were not generally credited in the Protestant world—surely not by the Lutherans, who grudgingly admitted a conversion of the Jews that would be severely restricted to a tiny minority of selected individuals. With the exception of visionaries like Guillaume Postel, Catholics had no sanguine expectations comparable to Jurieu's dream of massive Jewish conversion.

Other great religious minds of the seventeenth century invented formulas that highlighted traditional reasons for the survival of the Jews until the last judgment. The *Pensées* of Blaise Pascal includes an aphorism that demonstrates with compelling logic the need for the continued existence of the Jews as impartial witnesses to Christ: "If the Jews had all been converted by Jesus Christ we would no longer have had any but suspect witnesses left. And if they had been wiped out we would not have had any at all." [15] Total conversion before the end of the days or total extermination were both unacceptable solutions for most of Christendom. The fact that many Jews refused to believe in Christ the Messiah was not a sign of his weakness but was rather his crowning glory. Pascal was familiar with the rabbinic arguments against Christian expositors of Old Testament prophecies: according to the rabbis, the biblical passages foretold the coming of a magnificent messiah who would subdue all the nations; the Christians' messiah was a crucified wretch. But this was merely the carnal Jews' erroneous conception of Christ's triumph. They missed the spiritual meaning of the messiah's victory as they sinfully clothed him in warlike images. But the divine dialectic was at work, and by their very rejection of Christ Jews had become unimpeachable witnesses to him.

For Calvinists, it was only the continuing failure of the Jews to accept Christ that stood in the way of their total approval of the Jewish experience. Lutheran tradition was more tightly bound to the Judeophobia of its founder. For Lutheran theologians of the seventeenth century, the survival of the Jews was related less to their witness than to their punishment for the crime of deicide. Their suffering and wretchedness had to be eternal, commensurate with the wickedness of their deed. This reasoning served to justify their persecution as the fulfillment of God's will.

The New England Puritans had their own solution to the mystery of the survival. With the coming of the millennium, the redemption of the Jews would take place on this earth, a redemption that would be both spiritual and carnal. Spiritual salvation would entail the final success of steadfast Protestant efforts to propagate the gospel among Jews. The physical redemption would mean a movement of the Jews to the Holy Land, its restoration to them, and their assumption of a position of leadership among the nations. There were disputes about whether the physical or the spiritual redemption would come first. In their union of the spiritual and the worldly, the Puritans of New England were perhaps closer to orthodox Judaic thought than were most Christian sects.

Increase Mather gave temporal precedence to the physical redemption. He accepted Jurieu's explication of Ezekiel's vision of the coming together of the dry bones in the Valley of Death—the dry bones only later infused with spirit—to mean an ingathering of all Jews to Jerusalem and the establishment of a kingdom in the Holy Land that would precede the spiritual conversion of the Jews to Christ. While Mather did not go so far as to foresee a conversion of all the Jews, he was convinced that most of the nation would be illuminated by the light of Christ in this world.

Increase Mather had received word from various lands that the Israelites in great multitudes were already on their journey to Jerusalem, a movement accompanied by signs and wonders of the high and mighty hand of Providence. Jews on the march exhorted members of their nation in Europe and America to join them without delay. Though Mather did not name their leader, Shabbetai Zevi, he agreed with many other godly and judicious men that this was the beginning of the accomplishment of Ezekiel's prophecy. Mather preached that the calling of the Jews, their return to their own land, and their conversion were conditions precedent to the initiation of the final part of the sacred drama. Gentiles would benefit from the conversion of the Jews and their return to the Holy Land:

> The news of the *Jews* conversion will put life into all the Churches upon earth . . . It will be (unto the *Gentiles*) as life from the dead. For *Gentile* Churches shall be enlightened, and therefore enlivened from Jewish Churches. Then shall many dark and difficult questions be resolved, which at present cause sad thoughts of heart . . . "Upon the salvation of all *Israel* there will follow a reformation of all things, there will be a glorious renewall of the whole Universe." [16]

Increase Mather and his colleagues avoided falling into the trap of other millenarians who fixed the alpha and omega of the times, but the broad outline of events was clear and the signs were multiplying. "Not only Protestants, but Papists, Jews, Turks, Mohametans, and other Idolaters do expect some great Revolution of Affairs." [17] The survival and salvation of the Jews was a mystery greater than the original conversion of the gentiles. For 1600 years, from generation to generation, the Jews had continued to be the most obstinate despisers of Christ, and yet to this nation a glorious fate was foretold in Hosea.

The sounding of the seventh trumpet in Revelation was the calling of the Jews; it followed the enlarged powers of the Turk and the pope foretold by the sixth trumpet. "The *Jews* will be stirred up to joyn with the Christian Gentiles, to effect the final ruin of spiritual Babylon . . . This will be a time of great joy both to *Gentile* and *Jew,* when God shall be praised and glorified over and over in *Hebrew.*" [18] Mather quoted Church Fathers and schoolmen to sustain him in the belief that the ultimate general conversion of the tribes of Israel had been in some measure credited by the Church since the days of the Apostles. There has often been a kinship between Christian chiliasm and the restoration of the Jews to Israel, as if the perfection of the thousand-year reign of Christ required the conversion of the Jews.

Increase Mather's son Cotton believed that his prayers could serve to jog the high wheels of Providence in order to hasten the coming of the millennium and the second coming of Christ. He was leery of popular interpretations of the enigmatic books of the Old and New Testaments, and was convinced that apocalyptic studies should be undertaken only by those elevated souls whose heartstrings were somewhat finer-tuned than those of other men. A ninety-one page summary of his eschatological views, completed in 1703, generally follows the program for the end of the days laid out in the writings of his father and of Joseph Mede. In Protestant Bible expositors, harbingers of the millennium are differently conceived over the centuries. In Cotton Mather's day, the intimations would be the cessation of Turkish hostilities against Europe, the collapse of the papacy, and the conversion of the Jews. These major political-religious events were supplemented by the traditional signs—earthquakes, pestilences, eclipses—that every age had offered the zealous interpreters of the two principal prophetic books, Daniel and Revelation.

Christian doctrines of the last things were not cut off from Judaic visions of the end of the days. Images of the beginnings of mankind in an earthly paradise were perhaps more similar in the two religions, though the theological consequences of Adam's disobedience were radically different in Judaism and Christianity.

6

Transition to the Enlightenment

THE EIGHTEENTH CENTURY inaugurated a new epoch in Christian perspectives on Judaism. Jewish legal thinking and procedures became matters of special concern to kingdoms and republics consolidating their realms. Enlightened despotism on the Continent brought along with it a movement toward the codification of laws and a formulation of the rights and duties of citizenship that made the anomalous position of the Jews difficult to sustain. The Jews lived by a crazy quilt of privileges, grants promulgated and withdrawn at will. Enlightened despotism required uniformity, and Christian potentates questioned whether they could continue to countenance the de facto existence of another legal system with precedents of its own, in the very bosom of their polities. Since through royal or municipal privileges Jewish law was sanctioned within state boundaries, rulers could not long remain indifferent to what was going on behind ghetto walls. In order to determine the limits of Jewish autonomy that they were prepared to tolerate, sovereigns in modern states were obliged to heed Jewish legal injunctions, enforced by rabbinic courts, that were indistinguishable from religious duties.

Enlightened despots began to accumulate factual information about Jews. In 1784 Louis XVI decreed a complete census of Jews in Alsace—a roster, elegantly published, of the name, status, and residence of every Jew in the province. At the behest of the Prussian government, the head rabbi of Berlin directed Moses Mendelssohn to draft a summary of Jewish laws governing marriage and property. Dynasts were aware of outbursts of popular violence against Jews—the blood libel was endemic—and they had to evaluate the truth or falsity of general charges and inquire into such matters as the principles regulating their converse with Christians. In 1753 Aloys von Sonnenfels, a convert and Austrian civil servant, published in Vienna a defense of his former coreligionists, *Judaica sanguinis nausea, oder jüdischer Blutekel* (Jewish Aversion to Blood). By the end of the century, German princelets and French authorities were requiring Jews to prepare compendia of the laws that governed their private legal tribunals. But it was no easy task for the rabbis to communicate talmudic law to a French intendant looking for precepts expressed as clear and distinct Cartesian ideas. Compilations of rabbinic law, frenchified by legists, were incomprehensible potpourris.

Except for the Netherlands, the legal situation of Jews in Western Europe remained precarious throughout the century: there was expulsion from one German free city or principality, temporary admission into another; a remission of edicts, their reimposition. In Catholic France there were two religious minorities: the more important Protestant one, without legal status, and a lesser one, a few legally sanctioned enclaves of Jews in Bordeaux, Avignon, Alsace, and Lorraine. By the eve of the Revolution the lifting of disabilities of both stigmatized groups was being seriously debated within the councils of government. In England, the Jew bill of 1753 was passed and then withdrawn; there is more than a hint in contemporary pamphleteering that rich Jews were not wholly in favor of a general naturalization that would have attracted into the country many Jews from Germany and Poland. It is a truism of early modern Jewish history that prosperous Jews have often fought for discordant objectives: the acquisition of status for themselves and the careful circumscription of any minimal rights of residence that might be acquired by "foreign" Jews. The tale is sometimes an ugly one, as established Jews supervised the administration of exclusionary laws, making exceptions where money or extraordinary rabbinic learning and weighty personal recommendations were thrown into the balance. The meanderings of the Polish philosophical genius Solomon Maimon through the German principalities, narrated in his autobiography, are typical of the fate of Eastern European Jews trying to make their way into the enlightened west. But behind the legal discussions over citizenship and the vicissitudes of Jews seeking a measure of legitimacy in European societies lay the far knottier problem of the spiritual presence of Judaism in the growingly secularized world of enlightened monarchy.

A Brazen Reappraisal

It was not until the eighteenth century that the Old Testament generally came to be viewed by large numbers of literate Christians as an autonomous creation of the Jewish nation and not solely as a prolegomenon to Christianity. But when the sacred connection between the two Testaments was broken, Christendom's view of Judaism perforce underwent a profound transformation, in the course of which the Mosaic tradition often suffered denigration even as it won literary appreciation.

The weaving together of pre-Christian Judaism and Christianity had been relatively constant in the centuries before the Enlightenment. It was perhaps most complete in the Swiss, Dutch, and English (including the American) scholarly worlds of the seventeenth century. And if earnest believers did not themselves research the rabbinic commentaries for types, foretellings, and prefigurations, their pastors—usually chosen for their learning as well as their eloquence—poured something of this knowledge, garnered from the works of Christian Hebraists, into the willing and unwilling ears of members of their churches, who were subjected to a continuous round of sermons on the holy sabbath, on special fast days, and on days of thanksgiving.

In seventeenth-century Christian historiography, the binding of Jewish and Christian experience had been taken for granted. The greatest philosophical minds in the Catholic and Lutheran worlds, such as Malebranche and Leibniz, could not tolerate the idea of an independent Judaism, uncompleted by Christianity. Among the most enlightened thinkers the scandal of Spinoza's *Tractatus* was its attempt to establish Judaism as the religion of one people, not a universal religion; the point was highlighted in the title of its French translation, *Traitté des cérémonies des juifs tant anciens que modernes* (1678). The major state religions of Western Europe taught that though the Jews in their stubborn blindness balked at accepting Jesus as the messiah, there was a continuous sacred history from Adam through the present. With the insertion of apocrypha such as the books of the Maccabees and inclusion of the histories of Josephus, it was possible to join the Old and the New Testaments in an unbroken narrative. The universal history composed by Jacques Bénigne Bossuet, the official churchman of Louis XIV, was really a history of Judaic experience linked to the history of Christianity, with the Roman Empire subordinate to the future needs of the Church, and the Chinese and other pagan histories ignored as having no intrinsic worth. (This later drove Voltaire in a spiteful passion to overturn Bossuet's universe and start his world history with the Chinese.)

The philosophes-litterateurs of the Enlightenment first saw ancient Judaism through the spectacles of seventeenth-century Christian Hebraists. Whenever they found them too weighty in their original form, Pierre Bayle and Jean Le Clerc and Jacques Basnage, who spanned the two centuries, wrote in French, and published in Holland, acted as guides or transmitters. But the major French thinkers of the eighteenth century, educated before the expulsion of the Jesuits, read Latin fluently and did not always have to rely on *haute vulgarisation.* English deists of the early eighteenth century who had gone to Oxford and Cambridge had available the Latin commentaries and treatises of their seventeenth-century countymen, whose texts they translated with a certain license. Thus the later Enlightenment thinkers disseminated notions of Judaism that rested on information culled from respectable seventeenth-century Christian Hebraists at first or second hand. What the deists and philosophes did with the data effected a revolution in Christian Europe's perception of Judaism.

While the nature of Judaism—not only the physical existence of the Jews—remained a prickly subject for Christianity, in the age of the Enlightenment new ways of ending the ambiguous position of Judaism in the bosom of Christendom were proposed. An attempt among some literate elements of European society to cut the umbilical cord that had bound Christianity to Judaism from the moment of its origin was the most conspicuous break with tradition. More radical thinkers, reaffirming the historical tie with great fanfare, deliberately painted Judaism in gruesome colors in order to undermine the foundation of their own Christian religion. Others conceived of a new relationship between Judaism and Christianity that allowed for their coexistence through a redefinition of the nature of religion itself.

Christian perceptions of Judaism in the Enlightenment, as in the seventeenth century, should be individuated by country and status. A Catholic historian has called the Enlightenment the trial of Christianity; it was simultaneously a judgment of Judaism, and many different verdicts were handed down in various parts of Western Europe.

The assault on Judaism by English deists, Voltaire, the circle of Baron Holbach, and German philosophers in many respects departed from the traditional Christian attacks against the Jewish dispensation. Ancient religious ideas were wrapped in secular garments, even when the bearers of the ideas had not wholly divested themselves of the emotive baggage of Christendom. The English deists led the pack in the radical revaluation of Judaism. Voltaire learned from them during his apprenticeship of infidelity in London in the 1720s—many of his diatribes are paraphrases of deist tracts that he continued to devour avidly after his return home. And forty years later, the Holbachians still made it a practice to adapt English writers of the early eighteenth century for their anticlerical and anti-Judaic crusade. Across the Rhine a new view emerged in the Lutheran world of scholarship, philosophy, and literature, where strange overtones, born of pietism and romanticism, were introduced into the judgment of Judaism. The different natures of French and German antisemitism in the nineteenth century, when Judeophobia emerged as a "scientific" doctrine, can be traced to their eighteenth-century origins.

In the eighteenth century, trends that had been initiated earlier developed into idea systems which were to set new fashions in the study of Judaism. These modes of access were more "philosophical," daring, and often extravagant in their penchant for generalization, in the manner of the age. Commentary on specific details of Jewish doctrine and ritual continued, but a philosophical history of Judaism was beginning to supersede the textual glosses and disquisitions of the Christian Hebraist precisionists. There were Christians who now read the Old Testament as stories, court chronicles, natural histories. The Bible was discovered to be literature, not only sacred revelation; or, if the Christian critic was more cautious, without denying the divine inspiration of the text he nonetheless examined it for its poetic or prose excellence. This novel way of reading the Bible was consonant with other contemporary literary innovations: Persian and Indian epics were being introduced into Europe, and when northern literature was found wanting in dramatic epics, James Macpherson invented Ossian, whose wild barbaric character delighted the salons of sophisticated urban Europe.

When the Bible was read as literature, arid theological and philological argumentation could be discarded and the Old Testament could be appreciated for its sublime attributes, its beauty, the religious or primitive spirit it exuded, without the gentlefolk having to labor over exact meanings. Its poetry revealed the soul of the ancient Hebrews and that was what mattered. The Old Testament become literature could be compared to Homer and Ossian and was soon viewed as an expression of "oriental" society. Among philosophers, the theological refinements of meaning about which Christian sects had warred for centuries were bypassed; the Bible was turned into a book to be enjoyed for its literary qualities, or condemned for its barbarity and uncouthness. Subsidiary problems arose as the critics and professors of poetry were obliged to discover in Old Testament rhythms the rules governing the Hebrew poetic genius. This avenue of approach led Christians to a completely new Bible and a Judaism whose origins were not different in character from the religions of other primitive peoples.

Once inquiry was begun into the nature of the Israelite people as revealed in its literature, some commentators felt free to treat the Mosaic laws as a constitutional system that could be compared with similar systems both ancient and modern. There were sixteenth- and seventeenth-century precedents in the large number of treatises that fitted the Mosaic code into the constitutional typology of Aristotle's *Politics* and combed it for elements of aristocracy, monarchy, and democracy. But some eighteenth-century professorial works that dealt with ancient Israel as a *res publica* laid Aristotle aside and adopted aspects of the Montesquieu model as their guide. To understand the ancient kingdom of Israel, Christians looked for the spirit of its laws, not only forms of governance, and to capture this spirit they undertook investigations of the mores of contemporary Near Eastern peoples presumed to be still living like the tribes of ancient Israel. The comparative method had been used with some success to elucidate the meaning of Hebrew words; now the ways of the nomads of Arabia, one of the least explored stretches of desert, would be surveyed in order to clarify the spirit of the Mosaic law. The comparison could lead to praise of the Mosaic code as far superior to the laws of other tribes in the region. Ethnological inquiry bred a wholly new appreciation of ancient Judaism, as Moses the legislator was occasionally resurrected as a precursor of the Enlightenment whose governmental art was still worth studying. But it could also breed contempt.

Conformities of Judaism with Paganism Ancient and Modern

The discovery of new paganisms during the voyages of exploration aroused wonderment about strange, non-Christian religions. The friars who accompanied the fifteenth- and sixteenth-century conquerors left records of the religious behavior of the natives they encountered, and in the seventeenth century this information was brought together in grand illustrated compendia, where Judaism found a place along with other religions. The beginnings of comparative religion in a crude form are recognizable, as the writers dwell on the conformities of contemporary savage ceremonies with similar accounts in Greek and Roman literature and in the Old Testament. Ritual sacrifices and idol worship were common denominators. Rabbinic literature was combed for rationalist explanations of Jewish rites that bore resemblance to pagan ones, and a whole series of problems emerged about the origins of specific practices such as circumcision. A question arose as to whether the Jews had borrowed their ceremonials from the heathens or vice versa, a subject that had once been debated by the Church Fathers in establishing the chronological priority of Mosaic wisdom over Greek philosophy.

When in the seventeenth century the field of inquiry was extended to the whole globe, the comparison of rites of the ancient Hebrews described in the Bible with religious practices of pagan nations who were their neighbors or distant simulacres revealed the polytheist and idolatrous character of ceremonials into which the tribes of Israel occasionally lapsed, and diminished the reverence for Judaism as the first monotheistic religion. The antics of the savages in America, Asia, and Africa were understood in terms of the Bible and the classical literature that educated Europeans acquired early in life. Once the mechanism of association was set in motion, it ran rampant. The slightest similarity—a gesture, the sound of a word, a facial expression—became a conformity. Homebody scholars continued to establish identities or approximations of deities on the basis of the most remote auditory or visual relationships, as they had in the seventeenth century. Comparative mythology increased in quantity, though not in quality.

Outlandish hypotheses were constructed, demonstrating that remnants of the lost ten tribes of Israel still inhabited Tartary, China, or Peru. The notion of Peru, halfway across the globe, as a temporary place of refuge for Jewish exiles stemmed from Manasseh ben Israel's *Esperança de Israel* (Hope of Israel; 1650) with its account of descendants of ancient Israel stranded in the Andes, where they had been visited by a Jewish traveler who vouched for his report under a solemn oath to the heads of the Amsterdam community. Manasseh stressed the separateness of these Jewish exiles from the Indians who surrounded them, though the popularity of his book spread widely a supposition that all the American Indians were in fact descendants of Jews. Another thesis, which traced the lost tribes to Tartary where they had purportedly been driven by Shalmaneser, king of Assyria (d. 825 B.C.), discovered striking conformities between Jews and Tartars (Samarkand sounded like Samaria to receptive ears). It was conjectured that they had been pushed east from Tartary across the Bering Straits to America, for which confirmation was found in the writings of the "learned and judicious" Edward Brerewood, authoritative historian of all religions on earth.

The identification of American Indians as Jews, a perennial flower of European fantasy, spawned a large body of literature affirming or denying the connection. A work by Hamon l'Estrange, *Americans no Jewes, or, Improbabilities That the Americans Are of That Race* (1652), was written in response to Thomas Thorowgood's *Jews in America, or, Probabilities That the Americans Are of That Race* (1650). Maintaining that the Indians were Jews was a bold stance that solved two troublesome questions at the same time: it explained what had happened to the lost ten tribes and it found an origin for the American Indians. Isaac de La Peyrère, a Huguenot from Bordeaux, advanced the presence of the Indians in American as proof for his contention that men had been created before Adam on other continents and that Adam was the progenitor of the Jews alone; but he was forced to retract these views, published in his *Prae-Adamitae* (1655), when he converted to Catholicism. Orthodox Christians did not take kindly to a polygenetic thesis, since the beginning of mankind with Adam and Eve was so explicit in the Bible.

The literature establishing the identity of Jews and Indians was based on biblical texts presumed to hold the key to the controversy; it was bolstered by geographic argument revolving around the narrowness and easy crossing of the Bering Straits and, most persuasive of all, by the analysis of conformities between the customs and religious rituals of the Indians as reported by travelers and the practices of ancient and modern Jews. Many of the parallels drawn were hilarious. James Adair in his *History of the American Indian* (1775) presented twenty-three proofs, among them the Indian war whoop, which was recognized as "Hallelujah Jehova" if uttered in the appropriate manner with alternate pressure and release of the palm of the hand upon the lips. Hugo Grotius with some embarrassment quoted witnesses to the fact that American Indians were circumcised. William Penn thought Indians resembled Jews so closely in physiognomy that when he was in the New World he believed himself transported to the Jewish quarters of Duke's Place or Berry Street in London. That scalping was a Jewish custom was demonstrated by Psalm 68, verse 21: "God shall wound the head of his enemies, and the hairy scalp of such an one as goeth on still in his trespasses." Both Indians and Jews reckoned time by the moon. Jonathan Edwards thought the Mohegan language had affinities to Hebrew. President Ezra Stiles of Yale copied and left among papers now in the Boston Atheneum rock drawings by Connecticut Indians in which he discerned the names Adam and Abraham in Hebrew characters. In the literature relating Indians and Jews, the ancient Israelites were described as primitives not unlike the contemporary American savages presumed to be their descendants.

Travelers also found similarities between the American Indians and the ancient Greeks and between the Jews and the East Indians. The Jesuit Joseph François Lafitau's *Moeurs des sauvages amériquains comparées aux moeurs des premiers temps* (1724), and the gentleman-traveler La Créquinière's *The Agreement of the Customs of the East-Indians, with Those of the Jews, and Other Ancient People* (translated from the Brussels edition of 1704 by the deist John Toland), which advertised itself as the first essay of its kind, explaining difficult passages in Scripture and in classical authors through a comparison with present oriental customs, marshaled the evidence for the likeness of all non-Christian peoples. Once a Viconian type of cyclical thesis describing the growth and decline of nations became common in the eighteenth century, including the idea that all nations in their early stages had similar natures, diffusion was not required to explain the existence of primitive beast-men among the various peoples of the earth. Vico's account of the biblical flood, followed by the simultaneous genesis of different nations during a postdiluvian dispersion of mankind, could easily be credited. The American Indians might well be the sons of Shem who multiplied prodigiously after the deluge, a hypothesis that excluded their descent from the lost ten tribes.

Not all Christian scholars were equally possessed by the bulging catalogue of conformities between Jews and pagans. Leibniz never wrote a comprehensive treatise on Judaism; he was not a man to expose himself by taking a definitive stand on so hazardous a subject. A Christian with ecumenical longings though born a Lutheran, he served princes of various denominations; during one period of his life, settling in the Catholic France of Louis XIV was a recurrent ambition. His attitude toward Judaism can only be surmised from casual references in his correspondence, where he commented privately on the views of other men. Though his own opinions were often ambiguous, he rather consistently eschewed the theory that there were conformities between ancient Judaism and paganism. In writing to Lutheran princes he agreed with Bishop Pierre Daniel Huet that Jesus Christ was a fulfillment of Old Testament prophecies, but in a letter of August 1679 to Duke Johann Friedrich he criticized Huet's thesis that idol worship was a corruption of the Mosaic code:

> As for the various digressions showing that pagan idolatry was copied from the history of Moses, I consider them a jeu d'esprit . . . The history of the mythic gods is so confused that one can make of it anything one wishes . . . It seems advantageous to our religion to maintain that the erudition and theology of the pagans came from the Jews. Some of the ancients and Vossius in our time have said fine things on the subject. But one should not flatter oneself in these matters at the expense of truth . . . If I wanted to amuse myself with baseless jeux d'esprit, I could better sustain the thesis that Noah and Bacchus were really the same person, since both of them initiated the cultivation of the vine.[1]

In a Latin letter to Ludwig von Seckendorf in June 1683, Leibniz again ridiculed the notion that the philosophy and theology of the gentile nations came from "Judaica depravata"[2] and that Bacchus, Adonis, and who knows who else were derived from Moses.

Leibniz was immune to the etymological madness that filled hundreds of books tracing the genealogy of the gods; nor did he seriously participate in the debate over the priority of Hebrew or Hellenic wisdom. But his good sense was not communicated to his contemporaries. The presumed relations among the gods of Judaism, Hellenism, Egyptianism, and other beliefs and philosophies absorbed a substantial part of seventeenth- and eighteenth-century erudition among university, ecclesiastical, and independent gentlemen-scholars.

For obvious reasons the French Academy of Inscriptions and Belles-Lettres, which devoted hundreds of memoirs to the scholarly elucidation of pagan cults in antiquity, tended to keep away from commentaries on the sacred history of the Jews. That was the province of the theological faculty of the Sorbonne, and pensioners in the royal academies avoided tangling with the true religion. But this did not prevent them on occasion from proving that a particular Greek god was a corrupt translation of an Old Testament figure, and it was allowable for abbés to argue among themselves about whether Bacchus was really Esau or Moses in another form. In these academic dissertations deep-running cultural forces operated to favor the literal reading of the biblical text over allegorical interpretations and to support a euhemeristic reading of pagan myths as plain, matter-of-fact history of ancient kingdoms rather than as allegories of virtues and vices.

Judaism Supererogatory

As many of the exalted conceptions associated with the first dispensation were no longer restricted to the people of Israel, the need to sustain the monotheistic image of Israel as a bulwark for Christianity disappeared. When it was demonstrated that the Jews were imitators of surrounding peoples, borrowers instead of originators, their worth was lowered. In eighteenth-century royal academies, learned memoirs by more venturesome authors stressing the primacy of Egyptian and Persian origins for religious ideas became modish, and the position of ancient Israel as a civilizing force was depressed. Christian Europe owed the Jews nothing, or very little, and current Judaic rabbinism was denigrated as carnal, material, devoid of spirituality, a quibbling over words, a morass of superstitious practices. The devaluation of ancient Israel altered attitudes toward contemporary Judaism, even as contempt for individual modern Jews affected the portrait of ancient Judaea.

The philosophical Enlightenment has sometimes been considered an intellectual prelude to the legal acquisition of equal rights of citizenship by Jews during the revolution in France and in other parts of the Continent. The ideals of liberty, tolerance, and cosmopolitanism had to embrace Jews if the Enlightenment was not to be a sham. And in fact the political emancipation of the Jews, the lifting of restrictions on their freedom of movement, and their right to choose an occupation were benign consequences of the Enlightenment, which appeared to many Western European Jews as a form of salvation in this world. But the emancipation of slaves—and in the Middle Ages the Jews were juridically *servi* of the pope or the emperor and by extension of the princes who allowed them to exist in their territories—is a complex experience. In everyday life legal battles were fought as to who had jurisdiction over the former servi, a perennial struggle without resolution as long as there were Jews to mulct. Slaves have often been obliged to purchase their freedom. The ransom the Jews paid may have been heavier than anticipated by many of those who longed for emancipation.

The philosophical Enlightenment was prepared to accept the Jews if they were willing to be denatured, to deny the traditional practices of Judaism. From one viewpoint this was no more and no less than what historical Christianity in its various denominations had always demanded of the Jews. Even Immanuel Kant, the herald of a new secular morality, would permit Jews to enter his enlightened polity only if they abandoned their rabbinic law and ceremonials in favor of a civil constitution that would make them like all the gentiles. Napoleon, a latterday son of the Enlightenment, who once figured as a great emancipator in Jewish historiography, assembled a makeshift Jewish Sanhedrin in order to draw from the Jews commitments to renounce certain occupations such as moneylending, adopt productive professions, till the soil, and ignore traditional prohibitions against marriage with Christians. The Enlightenment put into a new cast Christianity's ambivalent relationship to Judaism.

The next chapters of this book touch only lightly on the mass of eighteenth-century Christian believers who dutifully performed their prescribed religious ceremonies, even when some of them secretly practiced pagan and primitive rites. My converse is with priests and bishops, doctors of divinity, professors of theology and ancient languages, writers in various conditions of independence—literary men who lived on their estates or survived by their wits, above all philosophes who published journals and were occupied in remolding what Thomas Jefferson called the opinion of mankind. What judgment did they pass on the ancient God of the Jews who lived among them, sometimes legally as in Holland, more often under murky arrangements as in France, but always on the margin of society? The responses constitute a revaluation of ancient and modern Judaism by Christians, many of whom were in the process of shedding the theological and dogmatic raiment of their own ancestors.

7

Assault of the
English Deists

TWO THEMES tended to dominate the deist perception of ancient Israel. One elaborated on the conformity of beliefs in all early religions; the other, a corollary, tackled the question of Israelite uniqueness directly. Once the great age of geographic discoveries had led to widespread recognition of the apparent resemblance between Jewish ceremonials described in the Bible and what explorers, missionaries, and travelers reported about the rituals of modern pagans dispersed over the face of the earth, a deep shadow was cast on the singularity of the Judaic dispensation, from which Christianity derived. The accounts of religious conformities throughout the world that had been accumulating since the early sixteenth century were grist for the English deists' mill. Their reading of travel literature and the narratives of missionaries sustained their many-pronged attack against Judaism. And the gathering together of texts about Jews from respected Roman historians and poets nourished their Judeophobia in the age of the Enlightenment.

The outpouring of studies in the seventeenth and eighteenth centuries on the nature of pagan myth and pagan religious worship might appear at first glance to constitute a wholly independent theme in baroque thought. But this perennial concern of the western mind connects by many avenues with the problems of Christendom's assimilation of Judaism. Much of the erudition devoted to paganism was produced under the auspices of a deist philosophy which taught that religions in all times and places held an element of truth, however material, immoral, and outrageous the beliefs and rituals might be when viewed in the pure light of Christianity. Paganism was a corruption and distortion of a primitive natural religion whose seeds were innate in human nature. The scholarly exercises were revealing the elements of true religion in paganism—for example, divine attributes of omnipotence in the most scandalous priapic cults. Such inquiries, which had their pornographic allurements, also seriously involved the nature of Judaism and Christianity. Both religions traditionally conceived of themselves as unique repositories of truth and regarded paganism as diabolical in origin and blatantly false. The discovery of conformities between pagan and Judaic practices deprived Israel of its birthright, its election among the nations, the exclusivity of its covenant with God. The surrender of a belief in the Israelites as the chosen people meant the abrogation of a fundamental article of Judaic faith that had been accepted by most Christians, even when they proclaimed that the once-chosen Jews had been superseded by Christians, who were now the chosen of God.

Uniqueness of Judaic Monotheism Denied

Lord Herbert of Cherbury (1583–1648), father of the deist gospel, thought he had demonstrated that the wise men of the gentile nations conceived of a single god and that polytheisms were merely popular superstitions corrupting the truth arrived at by heathen sages. This stripped Judaism of its pretensions to being the unique custodian of monotheism. In 1663 Isaac Vossius published in Amsterdam Lord Herbert's *De religione gentilium, errorumque apud eos causis* (On the Religion of the Gentiles and the Causes of Their Errors), where he traced the birth of his deism to his reluctance to accept the idea that so many just men of antiquity were condemned to eternal damnation because they had not recognized the true God: "This appearing to me too rigid and severe to be consistent with the Attributes of the *Most Great* and *Good God,* I began to consult the writings of the Heathens themselves."[1] He then came to reject the theory that among the ancients the word "god" had had a single meaning. Often they gave the name to mere imperfect, finite, and transitory powers of nature, and they even called "divine" in this limited sense emperors and other mortals of extraordinary status. But when they accompanied "god" with "optimus," "summus," or "maximus," the conception was the same as that of the Christian God. The ancients thus knew the true

God, but could be deflected from his worship by pagan priests who introduced superstitions and idolatry. The just men of every age, not only Christians, recognized five simple principles: "I. That there is one Supreme God. II. That he ought to be worshipped. III. That Vertue and Piety are the Chief Parts of Divine Worship. IV. That we ought to be sorry for our Sins, and repent of them. V. That Divine Goodness doth dispense Rewards and Punishments both in this Life, and after it." Those who resolved the causes of salvation or damnation into a mere exercise of God's will and a belief in Christ were entertaining base thoughts of God. "I could not understand how they could call that God *Most Good* and *Great,* who created Men only to damn them, without their knowledge, and against their will."[2] Lord Herbert's conclusion was that grace was always extended to those who believed in his five fundamental principles of deism.

Herbert of Cherbury tried to evade the idea that there were ages before Adam; nor would he fully accept an Egyptian origin for religious beliefs. Instead he demonstrated with a mountain of etymologies both the universality and similarity of all heathen and Hebrew rites. "What some do assert, That the *Hebrews* had the above-mentioned Names of God from the *Heathens,* seems to me very improbable, in regard almost all the Religious Worship of the *Greeks* and *Romans* came out of the *East;* though I do not deny but that some particular Rites were invented by their *Priests.* But, however the matter was, it is very apparent that the sacred Rites of the *Hebrews* and *Gentiles,* in most things differ'd very little."[3] Herbert's tract on the ancient religion of the gentiles was in effect a natural history that would be amended and reproduced many times in the eighteenth century.

Other deist writings about ancient Israel demeaned the Hebrews as latecomers among the nations, their customs and ceremonies mere adaptations and borrowings from neighboring pagans. The Jews were not the discoverers of monotheism. Other candidate nations were more ancient; in this sense the deists misread Thomas Hyde's *Historia religionis veterum Persarum eorumque magorum* (History of the Religion of the Ancient Persians and Their Magi: 1700). The Chinese, the Egyptians, even the Greeks were monotheists prior to the Jews, which deprived Judaism of its significance as the underpinning of Christianity. Were the Jews the peculiar people of God chosen for their particular nature, which made them prone to accept his law when all other peoples were idolaters? As a consequence of their election or because of their own genius, were they the actual founders of civilization and the originators of language, architecture, the polity, writing and literature, music? Deist tradition multiplied doubts.

Roman classical historians seemed to favor the notion that the Jews took their ideas from the Egyptians, and the deists followed in the Romans' wake. Since the Egyptians worshiped animals and the Jews lived long in Egypt, many of their rites were still tainted with the abomination of animal worship. The Bible itself offered numerous examples of the seduction of the people of Israel by Egyptian and Canaanite idolatry. Solomon's tolerance of the idolatry of his many wives cast a pall over his glorious reign. In effect, deism stripped ancient Israel of its purity and revealed it to be no better than the other eastern nations among whom Israelites dwelled.

Over the centuries a fierce battle was waged about the antiquity of nations. The implicit assumption was that the people who were first in time were nearer to God and thus superior, and that those who appeared later were lesser peoples living on the accumulated treasures of others. The debate acquired new vitality in the seventeenth century, when etymological virtuosity reached its height and when world chronologies (without archaeology) were being reconstructed at regular intervals. Isaac Newton produced hundreds of manuscript folios in defense of the priority of the Jewish nation in the inventions of civilization.

One of the oldest problems of Western Christendom was the relationship between Greek culture and the Judaic religion, both of which had become constituent elements in the spiritual synthesis of Christianity. Since there were similarities between these two embodiments of ancient wisdom, who had derived from whom? In the early centuries of the Church, the disputations were epitomized in the question: had Moses plagiarized Homer or vice-versa? Such issues involved technical problems of chronology and often degenerated into etymological puzzles, such as whether the Phoenician Moschus was really Moses in disguise.

Related to this axial question of priority was the baffling fact that Judaism was not mentioned by Greek authors prior to the Hellenistic period. Were the Jews too insignificant to be noticed? Indications that they were despised by the Egyptians—who had a very different version of Exodus—and the contempt with which Jews and Judaism were rather uniformly treated in Roman literature also sapped the prestige of ancient Israel among classically educated deists, who admired the noble Romans above all other nations. Aristocratic English deists who identified their very persons with the Romans inevitably condemned the fanatical Judaean zealots, who had given the great emperors so much needless trouble. Precious British Judeophobes have many eighteenth-century ancestors.

The Universality of Natural Religious Sentiment

English deism incorporated the apostolic stricture against Judaism that it had come to worship dead things, the letter of the law, and then underscored the equivalence of this Judaic word worship with the rites of primitive pagans all over the world who also adored dead objects and soul-less animals. Both Jews and pagans revealed themselves incapable of rising to the spirituality of a deist God. Awareness of conformities between Jewish sacrificial rites and the practices of East Indians, American Indians, and West African Negroes pointed in a number of directions. One path led the reflective scholar to conceive of a universal religious instinct or emotion that accounted for the "similarities," as they were called. The religious orientation of English deism was rooted in this presumption. Variety was explained as accidental or the consequence of error. The unity of religious experience and the resemblances between pagan and Judaic ceremonies had already been profusely illustrated by Herbert of Cherbury, and his followers merely amplified the doctrine. If the explanation for variability was insufficient to appease order-seeking men, the theory of the nation or people as an intermediate unit of religious expression was put forth. Though all men were endowed with the same religious propensities, individual nations, living in isolation, built separate identities that fostered differences in religion. Vico and Herder later stressed both the universality of religious experience and the multiplicity of religious manifestations. Herder found the roots of each Volk's religion in its geographic habitat and exalted the emergence of religious feeling in a specific body of men as the form-giving moment of its existence, but without in any way challenging the universal characteristics of religion.

If greater weight were given to the universality of religious sentiment, and the actions and beliefs of positive religions were minimized as fortuitous, deism was a perfect natural religion. Since the essence of all religions was the same as that of a purified, detheologized, and deritualized Christianity, one could be a comfortable Christian deist, believe in an underlying primitive monotheism, and dismiss the hordes of pagan gods as creations of weakness, ignorance, or power-lusting kings and priests who played on popular credulity. John Toland wrote in *Letters to Serena* (1704):

> Natural Religion was easy first and plain,
> Tales made it Mystery, Offrings made it Gain;
> Sacrifices and Shows were at length prepar'd,
> The Priests ate Roast-meat, and the People star'd.[4]

Such theories weakened the reverence for Judaism as stemming from a covenant between the one true God and his peculiar people. But it was still possible for orthodox Christians to cling to the belief that, before the advent of Jesus, the religion of Israel was the purest revelation of God and to stigmatize all other ancient religions as corruptions, adaptations, and borrowings from the Mosaic dispensation. The Church Father Clement of Alexandria had determined that Homer plagiarized Moses. Indeed, all the Church Fathers defended the chronological priority of Moses, a position maintained through the ages. But as the travelers and their reports accumulated, it became difficult to chart the routes along which the original doctrines of Moses had moved throughout the planet. In the seventeenth century, it was relatively easy to construct a conjectural system of the spread of ideas from Judaea to other parts of the closed world of the eastern Mediterranean. Plato traveled to Egypt, where Jeremiah had been exiled, and there the transmission of the Mosaic philosophy took place. But when travelers thought they recognized Jewish customs in the East Indies or among the American Indians, the learned were hard put to outline the paths and agencies of diffusion, and fell back on the universality of a natural religious sentiment.

Prophecy and Miracles Reconsidered

If the most relevant part of the Old Testament for theorists of the political state in Christian society was the history of kingship, particularly its cloudy inception under Samuel, for the theologians who were apologists for Christianity, as well as for those who would crush the infamous beast or at least cut its fangs, the heart of the matter was the nature of prophecy in ancient Judaea. It was here that the English deists and some radical French philosophes exerted their major effort in destroying the traditional historical connection between Judaism and Christianity.

Among orthodox believers, Christianity was proved both by the miracles that Christ performed, witnessed by apostles and the people, and by the evidence of what were considered the prophetic passages of the Old Testament in which the coming of Christ had been foretold. In orthodox Christian theology of the seventeenth and eighteenth centuries, there was a growing apologetic movement of ideas in one direction: miracles were substantially underrated, especially in the non-Catholic world, and the main witness, proof, or demonstration of the truth of the Christian religion inevitably shifted to prophecy. The written testimony of Old Testament prophets became the preferred battleground of believers and unbelievers.

The theological controversies over prophecy were a melee in which an outsider would often have had difficulty knowing on whose side the contenders were fighting. Did the proof-texts of Isaiah and Haggai and Malachi refer to the coming of Christ or to some more immediate political events in the history of Judaea? Or were they prophecies about a messiah who was yet to be? Ingenious commentators like Jean Le Clerc, the Genevan Remonstrant popularizer who ended up in Holland editing universal libraries for the learned, held that Old Testament prophecy might be at once a prediction of some immediate event, such as the Jewish release from the Babylonian captivity, and a heralding of a more distant messiah. Ultimately, deistic Christianity, which had assimilated much of this polemical literature, dispensed entirely with the philological refinements of rabbinic exegesis and flatly denied the relevance and utility of Old Testament proof-texts. Bereft of its primary function of prophesying the coming of Christ, the Old Testament lost much of its relevance for Enlightenment Christianity.

What was an Old Testament prophet? After Spinoza had answered the question in the *Tractatus theologico-politicus* in what appeared to many to be naturalistic terms, the character of the prophet became a key to the judgment of Judaism among skeptical Christians. In the seventeenth century, Christians like the Anglican dean of Ely, John Spencer, adopted Maimonides' portrait of the prophet as a man learned, rational, of impeccable morals, probably rich, who, after having shown himself worthy of divine inspiration, established a special relationship with God. While enlightened Anglicans embraced this portrayal of the prophet as a philosophical teacher, an eighteenth-century deistic reading of the prophetic books of the Old Testament dramatically transformed the character of the prophet even as he had become acceptable to a Maimonidean Anglican. In Anthony Collins' *A Discourse of Free-Thinking* (1713), the prophets of Israel, no longer recognized as foretelling the advent of either Christ or a Jewish messiah, were turned into agents of protest against priestcraft:

> The Prophets (who had the most learned Education among the *Jews* and were bred up in *Universities* call'd *Schools* of the *Prophets*, where they learnt to *prophesy*, and among means to *obtain* the *Prophetick Spirit*, play'd upon Musick and drank Wine) were great *Free-Thinkers*, and have written with as great *liberty* against the *establish'd Religion* of the Jews (which the People look'd on as the Institution of God himself) as if they believ'd it was all Imposture.[5]

The image of the prophets as social rebels had been propagated by Thomas Müntzer during the German Radical Reformation and had been adapted by Dissenters during the English Civil War. Collins' quotations from Isaiah, Jeremiah, Ezekiel, Hosea, and Micah stressed their anticlericalism. Among nineteenth-century radical dissenters, they were further metamorphosed into protosocialists and -communists.

Collins, the Oxford gentleman-scholar and friend of John Locke, accepted the challenge of orthodoxy that Old Testament prophecy was the easiest and most certain way of determining whether Christianity was true or false. In his *Discourse on the Grounds and Reasons of the Christian Religion* (1724) he posed the alternatives with compelling logic:

> *Prophecies fulfill'd* seem the most proper of all arguments, to evince the truth of a revelation, which is design'd to be universally promulgated to men. For a man, for example, who has the Old Testament put into his hands, which contains Prophesies, and the New Testament, which contains their completions, and is once satisfy'd, as he may be with the greatest ease, that the Old Testament existed before the New, may have a compleat, internal, divine demonstration of the truth of Christianity, without long and laborious Inquiries . . . On the other side, if proofs for Christianity from the Old Testament be not valid; if the arguments founded on those books be not conclusive; and the Prophesies cited from thence be not fulfill'd; then has Christianity no just foundation.[6]

Collins' riposte to the orthodox consisted of satirical thrusts, rather than quotations from modern scholars such as Orobio de Castro in the manner of the later Holbachians. In his *Scheme of Literal Prophecy Considered* (1726) Collins denied that there was any relation whatsoever between the books of Old Testament prophecy and the coming of a messiah, Christian or Hebrew. Among the Jews, he theorized, the expectation of a messiah was a rather late idea and was merely the natural fantasy of a persecuted nation, for which there was a contemporary parallel in the great expectations of the harassed Huguenots.

While orthodox Christian believers took comfort in the wisdom of the prophets who heralded the coming of Christ, the deists who wanted neither Christ coming once or twice nor a future Jewish messiah made the biblical prophets sound like the Protestant "prophets of London," those persecuted Huguenots from the Cévennes who were afflicted with glossolalia and held scandalous seances predicting doomsday. For the Enlightenment, Spinoza, whose works had been translated into the vernacular, had relativized prophecy and divine inspiration. Prophecy acquired a taxonomy: there were different types of prophets. Some heard voices, some had dreams. The Moses who saw God was the greatest, to be sure. But prophets were legislators of a particular people, and their admonitions lacked universal applicability.

The rationalist and relativist attitude toward prophecy diverted the argument from God's nature and intent to the nation of the Jews. A

Maimonidean theologian such as Newton had gone to great lengths to show the total concordance of all prophetic utterances, Judaic and Christian. For him the truths of the various Old Testament prophecies, which had been delivered at different times and places, derived their essential unity from God himself, who could harbor no contradictions. Later in the eighteenth century, acts of prophesying under the kings of Judaea and Israel were still widely regarded as historical events—the prophets were a distinct class—but for many English deists the prophecies became either the delusions of madmen and wild enthusiasts or the deliberate deceptions of priestcraft.

The English deists had a field day demolishing the miraculous nature of events narrated in the Old Testament, as they had the traditional Christian belief that the prophets of Israel foretold the coming of Christ. They regularly mocked ongoing Catholic miracles such as the periodic liquefaction of the blood of St. Januarius in Naples. Locke and Newton, for whom miracles were a subject of some consequence during their frequent religious colloquies, settled on a compromise: miracles had ceased after the first centuries of Christianity because thereafter further interventions of the divine will into the natural order would have been excessive, supererogatory, a violation of the scientific law of parsimony. Rationalism, skepticism about the accuracy of the senses, made reports of miracles that had occurred thousands of years earlier weak reeds to lean on, since men of sound mind doubted even contemporary accounts of prodigies.

William Whiston, Isaac Newton's successor in the Lucasian Chair at Cambridge before he was ousted for his heretical Arianism, was an important figure in the fashioning of a *physica sacra*, which wherever possible reduced miraculous divine interventions into the orderly running of the Newtonian universe to natural occurrences that were explicable scientifically. Interpreting the deluge as the consequence of a comet's very close approach to the earth—a near miss—was an example of such endeavors acceptable to Newton himself. In the eighteenth century the deist John Toland, a heterodox Irish adventurer with an acidulous pen, examined the details of Mosaic history in the Pentateuch and wrote his "Hodegus; or the Pillar of Cloud and Fire, that guided the Israelites in the Wilderness, not Miraculous" (1720) to show that the reported supernatural phenomena in the Bible were merely ambulatory beacons in the desert carried by Israelite sentries.

("Hodegus" was one piece in a collection called *Tetradymus*, containing also "Clidophorus," "Hypnatia," and "Mangoneutes.") The culmination of this pecking away at Old Testament miracles was the argument of the famous "Essay on Miracles" in David Hume's *Philosophical Essays concerning Human Understanding* (1748), which seemed to destroy once and for all the plausibility of miraculous breaches in the order of nature.

The Barbarous Hebrews

Seventeenth-century theologians had in all earnestness cited God's selection of the Jews, a rough primitive people, as a demonstration of his absolutely free will. The irreverent Collins mocked the choice of the Jews as unique bearers of the prophetic spirit. He called them an "Illiterate, Barbarous, and Ridiculous People," and quoted the Reverend Dr. South's tongue-in-cheek rationale for God's enigmatic choice: "They were all along a cross, odd, untoward sort of People, and such as God seems to have espous'd to himself upon the very same account that *Socrates* did *Xantippe;* only for her extremely ill Conditions above all that he could possibly find, or pick, out of that Sex; and so the fittest both to exercise and declare his admirable Patience to the World." [7]

The travel literature that described customs and habits of strange peoples in all parts of the world found many of them atrocious and cruel; but the question of whether the peoples were civilized turned on whether they had a system of laws. In this respect, once the Israelites had settled on both sides of the Jordan and occupied half of the eastern Mediterranean littoral, it was difficult for even rabid Judeophobes of the Enlightenment to deny them a measure of civility. But there were obdurate spirits who were intent upon likening the Jews to the wild Picts and Celts of Europe and the primitive Greeks. The parallel between the sacrifices of Iphigenia and of Jephthah's daughter was their stereotyped proof. They drew from the Bible the portrait of a barbaric, not a civilized, kingdom, and David was their exemplar monarch, a ruthless, faithless, sensual leader of a band of brigands. The psalm singer was denied or forgotten.

Though Bishop William Warburton was their natural enemy, the deists loved to quote from the inflated volumes of his *Divine Legation of Moses Demonstrated* (1742), which in a crude fashion propounded the thesis that the immortality of the soul was a lofty spiritual conception introduced into Judaism only after the Babylonian captivity, and rejected the very idea of a world to come among the Hebrews of the Pentateuch. That the ancient Jews did not believe in the soul's immortality became a deist historical-religious dogma and fed the time-worn Christian notion that Judaism in its origins was carnal, dependent on rewards in this world that were concrete, objective, and visible. The Jewish conception of God was material, fleshly, anthropomorphic. The temple was like a bourse: the Jews offered sacrifices to God and received equivalents in worldly goods. It was but a step from there to the accusation that the Jews' absorption with accumulating money was an offshoot of their religion and inextricably bound up with it—the worship of Mammon.

The God of the Jews was the national god of a tribe; like other tribal gods, he was cruel, vengeful, absolutist, bloody. The multiplication of ceremonials made Judaism one of the most superstitious of all religions. The kings and priests of the Jews were venal, lying, treacherous, hypocritical. The Apion-Manetho thesis—against which Josephus had argued—that the ancient Jews were originally a filthy band of lepers thrown out of Egypt was revived, casting aspersions on their progeny. While the carnal temper was often attributed to the absurd multiplication of rabbinic interpretations, an early proclivity in this direction was discerned in the laws of Leviticus and Deuteronomy themselves. On a more elevated plane, in *The Natural History of Religion* (1757) Hume jumped to the conclusion that unphilosophical monotheism, by which he meant both institutional Christianity and Judaism, was incapable of holding to its noble, abstract tenets and inevitably lapsed into the worship of concrete objects and idols, and into the fear of hell reified as a place full of pitchfork-wielding devils. Primitive Israelites were as barbarous as all other pagan idolaters—the Old Testament provided the evidence in profusion.

Bolingbroke's Lordly Contempt

While both Toland and Collins labored to dismiss the worth of Old Testament prophecy and miracles, they betrayed no particular animus against the Jews living in England in their day. In fact, Toland was intent upon granting them naturalization and wrote the most psychologically acute analysis of Judeophobia in the eighteenth century, *Reasons for Naturalizing the Jews in Great Britain and Ireland on the Same Foot with All Other Nations. Containing Also, a Defence of the Jews against All Vulgar Prejudices in All Countries* (1714). Whole passages from Rabbi Simone Luzzatto's seventeenth-century tract on the state of the Jews were adapted by Toland.

The same benevolent disposition cannot be attributed to the aristocratic Henry St. John, Viscount Bolingbroke (1678–1751), who mingled his denigration of ancient Israel with disdain for contemporary Jews. Lord Bolingbroke was an advocate of the "impostor theory" of the origins of all religion, and in his philosophical essays he brought up the case of "Sabatai Sevi" as a rather recent example of how a new messiah and a new religion could be imposed on a people. He concluded that whether a religion succeeded or not was no proof of its truth or falsity:

> Thus Mahomet, to go no higher, instituted a new religion in the seventh century of ours, and founded a great empire. Mahomet had intrepidity as well as address: and if a miserable Jew of Asia Minor, seventy or eighty years ago, had not wanted the former, we might have seen, very possibly, at this hour, a new spiritual and temporal empire established by the adorers of a new Messiah. But the courage of Sabatai Sevi, to whom the Jews resorted from all parts, in a firm persuasion that he was their true Messiah, failed him, and he passes for an impostor, merely because he durst not stand an impalement.[8]

Nor was the purported fulfillment of prophecy a warranty of the truth of Judaism and Christianity.

Bolingbroke impugned the veracity of the biblical priestly scribes on the ground that they had a considerable private interest in inventing falsehoods. Josephus, on whom Christians relied for collateral evidence in support of the Bible, trusted the accuracy of the scribes of Judaea simply because they recorded events in great detail, but he failed to meet Bolingbroke's standards of historical objectivity. After he had cast doubt on all the historical statements in the Pentateuch, Bolingbroke wickedly reminded his readers that "in all cases Christianity was founded on Judaism, and the New Testament supposes the truth of the Old."[9]

If the English deists were right and, as Matthew Tindal had announced, Christianity was as ancient as the world, it did not need the support of Judaism; on its own, Judaism could not survive an avalanche of testimony that laid bare its contradictions and thus destroyed any divine origin for the Pentateuch. Père Simon's contention in his *Critical History of the Old Testament* that Moses himself could not possibly have written every word of the Pentateuch, especially since it included an account of his own death, was quickly assimilated by the English deists. The laws of the Jews exacted from them fulfillment of the duties necessary to maintain peace and order among themselves—the Spinozaic formula vulgarized—but this was no mark of divine ordination, Bolingbroke argued, since robbers and bandits also abided by rules within their gangs. The laws of the Jews freed them from moral obligations to the rest of mankind. Legal injustice and cruelty characterized their conduct, and there was no part of their history without examples of both, authorized by their law and pressed upon them by their priests. Bolingbroke refurbished, with elegant mannerisms and the trappings of classical rhetoric, an old argument that Jews were explicitly enjoined by their rabbis to defraud Christians.

Thomas Morgan, the Moral Philosopher

In the writings of Thomas Morgan (d. 1743), who in a sense completed the chain of English deist teachers—Toland, Collins, Woolston, Chubb, and Tindal—Judaism occupied a central position as the foul source of everything in Christianity that was contrary to a pure, simple, reasonable, natural religion. This Welsh Dissenter, a minister who was expelled from his church and earned his living as a doctor, tackled the knotty problem of why Christianity, which in its primitive state was so close to what the weight of deist opinion considered natural religion, later fell into the quagmire of superstitious belief and persecuting behavior. He found his answer by turning around full face one of the oldest presuppositions of Christian theology. Far from discerning in Judaism a foretelling of Christianity, a foretaste of the truth, Morgan discovered in the Jewish remnants that survived in Christianity and penetrated ever deeper into Christian belief a poisoned source.

In a series of succinct paradoxes, Morgan formulated with biting sarcasm the orthodox version of the relation between Judaism and Christianity:

> Literal *Judaism* then, it seems, was figurative Christianity, and literal Christianity is mystical *Judaism*: the Letter of the Law was the Type of the Gospel, and the Letter of the Gospel is the Spirit of the Law; the Law was the Gospel under a Cloud, and the Gospel is the Law unveil'd and farther illuminated; *Moses* was the Shadow of Christ, and Christ is the Substance of *Moses*: But tho' this Sort of Connexion and Harmony between the Law and the Gospel, or between the *Old Testament* and the *New*, may give intire Satisfaction and appear perfectly just and beautiful to Men of Deep Discernment and Penetration; yet it must, as I imagine, be a little puzzling to vulgar Understandings.[10]

All that was fanatical, laden with ceremonials, against reason, everything that nourished priestcraft and powerlust, had been inherited from Judaism. A return to purity entailed identifying these polluted elements and expunging them from Christianity. The reams of exegesis that had striven to forge bonds of historical, allegorical, tropological, and anagogical interpretation between the Old and New Testaments were jettisoned. The purpose of Morgan's summaries of scholarly inquiries on Judaism was to trace idolatrous contamination. The Jews had transmitted abominable Egyptian superstitions to Christianity.

While the truths of natural religion could be arrived at by reason alone, so clear a revelation as Christianity was a way of convincing masses of mankind more readily and therefore enjoyed Morgan's approval. God was an immanent force in Morgan's deist world, not a mere one-time creator who abandoned his creation once the laws of nature had been incorporated into a system. The corruption of Christianity by Judaism was a historical reality that Christian deists were obliged to demonstrate—that is, true deists and true Christians like himself—if mankind was to be saved. He contrasted Philalethes, the authentic Christian of the *Moral Philosopher* of 1737, with the Christian Jew who was no real Christian at all but a judaized Christian. Voltaire and the Holbachians each in their own manner continued this train of thought, using rhetoric that no deist of the early decades of the eighteenth century would have dared resort to.

Judaizing was a heresy of which Christians had accused one another with regularity in the centuries of defense and propagation of the faith. The paradoxes of Thomas Morgan were the ultimate formulation of diatribes against Christian judaizers; the line from the Dominican friars of the Inquisition to Morgan is tortuous but unbroken. The deists and atheists of the eighteenth century twisted the dagger when they charged the orthodox believers of all denominations with the crime of preserving Judaism in Christianity. The magnificent edifice of Old Testament interpretations built up in hundreds of volumes of sermons and commentaries by Church Fathers, medieval saints, Christian Hebraists, and preachers was undermined by eighteenth-century heretics who were depriving Christianity of its most ancient witness. Morgan was not the inventor of this kind of argument, but he was surely one of its most powerful exponents.

In the seventeenth century, a learned Christian Hebraist would customarily attack Judaism on the ground that the rabbis had misread their own Scriptures. In the eighteenth, the radical deists latched on to the rabbinic interpretations and laws as the source of all evil in Christendom precisely because they had penetrated Christian ritual and dogma through their acceptance by Christian orthodoxy. Selden and Lightfoot had labored arduously to acquire Hebraic learning because they believed that the Jewish texts illuminated and clarified Christian doctrine. Within a century, the deists fell upon the similarities between Jewish and Christian dicta to prove that the original words of Christ had been distorted by Jewish influences.

Dissolving the Bond

The Enlightenment witnessed the falling apart of that uneasy Renaissance syncretism between the inherited traditions of Christianity and Graeco-Roman philosophical conceptions. In some quarters it also meant the disengagement of the Jewish and the Christian inheritances, which had once been linked by the bonds of Scripture and inveterate mutual loathing. As long as the Jews were condemned to continue their miserable lives as an eternal witness to the crime of deicide, they were a part of the world order with a role to play. Their existence had at least a satanic meaning. If the prophetic proof-texts of the Old Testament were miraculous demonstrations or prefigurations of the truth of Christianity, the Jews had deeper meaning, even if they refused to accept the overwhelming evidence of their own messianic writings. But what if the deists showed that the essential moral truths of Christianity were as old as creation? That the Jews were latecomers to the civilized world who had borrowed all their beliefs and customs from their venerable neighbors? What need was there then for Hebrews ancient or modern?

Judaism had not fulfilled any special theological purpose in the past, such as teaching the world monotheism, and was of no worth in the present. It was but an outlandish example of the heavy incrustation of man-made ceremonials and priestly impositions on a pure and simple set of deist principles. Judaism had accumulated more ritualistic prohibitions than other religions and was the more ridiculous for it. As a progenitor of Christian zealotry, it spawned one of the cruelest religions that had ever enslaved mankind. Since miracles were exposed as frauds and prophecies shown to be superstitions or errors, what was the point of studying the texts of the Jewish prophets to find evidence that Christ's coming had been predicted? The essential truths of deism were engraved in the heart and mind of every man, and the rout of ceremonials and dogmas about which men disputed were so much arrant nonsense.

When Judaism was no longer necessary for a rational religion in Europe, the Jews lost their place in the order of things and soon stood as naked aliens in a secular society. To the extent that deism triumphed, Judaism was devalued, and the Jews were left isolated, irrelevant, a sport in the history of Christianity. They became a mere remnant of ancient barbaric tribes, living on in the midst of civilized Europeans and preserving bizarre fanatical customs. Judaism had been deprived of its reason for further existence.

8

The French Philosophes: An Ambiguous Record

AUDACIOUS THINKERS of the Enlightenment embarked on a new examination of society with the assumption that the remote origins of a phenomenon or the early history of a collective body told what was quintessential about the thing itself. All nations and religions, like persons, had a primeval esprit that pervaded the organism and was relatively impervious to the ravages of time. The idea can be traced back to ancient theories of humors and characteristics and psychologies that implied the existence of a dominant passion in individuals and in groups. Montesquieu's *Spirit of the Laws* and Herder's doctrine of the *Volksgeist* were the form-imprinting bearers of this conviction on opposite sides of the Rhine.

While Montesquieu himself was not more involved with the study of Judaism than a casual reading of the Old Testament demanded, his writings exerted a powerful influence on eighteenth-century interpreters of ancient Israel in both France and Germany. The constant search for the unique spirit of the laws among different forms of governance and among individual peoples opened up the question of what constituted the esprit of the Hebrews. Montesquieu's utterance—laconic though it was—that the Hebrews were driven by a religious esprit, in contrast with the commercial spirit of the Phoenicians and the warrior spirit of the Romans, encouraged contemporaries and successors to invent a more elaborate thesis about the spirit of Judaism than he had ventured. A host of spirits were conjured up by eighteenth-century writers, who turned to new philological and ethnographic documentation in support of their contentions.

Voltaire, Gibbon, and Holbach among the Anglo-French anticlericals, Michaelis and Herder among the Lutherans, the Abbés Guénée and Bergier among the French Catholics, were judges of Judaism who derived their conclusions from a novel reading of the biblical evidence or what they believed to be fresh data that held the key to the enigma of Judaism. However the commentators differed from one another, they shared an implicit belief that concealed somewhere in the accumulating mass of information was the true esprit of Judaism, which could be simply defined and encapsulated in a few phrases. Eclectic conceptions were rarely espoused; natures were unitary. The esprit of a people was either benign or malignant, good or evil; there was no neutral or indifferent temper. The eighteenth-century psychology of peoples had inherited the categories of individual psychological types transmitted from the Greek world: a nation, like a man, had one humor. With monomaniacal insistence, the new philosophical commentators maintained that one idea alone would cast the most powerful light on the phenomenon and that all others were subordinate and subsidiary reflections, relegated to the shadows. The Newtonian quest for scientific simplicity, translated into Montesquieu's language, was adapted to the study of Judaism.

Two groups of French philosophes who were especially preoccupied with Judaism, often to the point of obsession, were the Voltairean theists and the Holbachian atheists. While both cliques were dedicated to the cause of freeing Europe from the toils of scriptural and theological Christianity, the line that separated them was marked, even when they temporarily joined forces in fighting superstition, religious cruelty, intolerance—in crushing the infamous one. But together they impressed upon a large segment of French society a monster image of Judaism that long outlasted their own internecine disputes. The hideous visage they imprinted on historical Judaism became a part of French culture. Sometimes the image was masked, sometimes paraded undisguised in the open. The full political consequences of the penetration of these conceptions are not measurable. Their survival, however, is evident in the Dreyfus case and in the antisemitic laws promulgated by the Vichy regime.

Voltaire's Obsession

To attack with violence the barbaric customs and punishments of the ancient Hebrews as profusely recorded in the Bible, to lay bare the treacheries and butcheries of the kings of Judaea and Samaria, to expose the falsehood of pretensions to miraculous performances in violation of the laws of nature, was a primary mission of the philosophes. In the writings of one of the *patres majores* of the Enlightenment, Voltaire, antipathy to Judaism took on the dimensions of a fixed idea, especially in the last fifteen years of his life. With the critical edition of the hundred volumes of his letters, it is possible to follow the exacerbation of his Judeophobia from a shadowy period in the 1720s, when he was flirting with Cardinal Dubois, with espionage, with court Jews in Germany deeply involved in the munitions business and thus having access to state secrets, through his final years, when this indefatigable defender of the rights of Protestants and freethinkers would ordinarily combine the word "Jew" with the adjective "execrable."

In May 1722 Voltaire was a witty Parisian fop in his late twenties who nurtured the illusion that he would become an important diplomat in the service of the Regency government. A letter to Cardinal Guillaume Dubois, the principal minister, shows the young literary lion trying to curry favor by purveying secret information about the spying of one Salomon Lévi, a native of Metz, who had been adroit enough to become the munitions supplier of the imperial army in Italy, a post from which he forwarded information to the French commanders. Voltaire purported to have intelligence that Lévi was an agent who operated simultaneously for the Holy Roman Emperor, the Lorrainers, and the French, and who counted on establishing relations with the court Jews Oppenheimer and Vertembourg, munitioners to the emperor. Voltaire charged that Lévi, in hiding somewhere in Paris, was also involved with a gang of criminals. Voltaire's summary judgment on Jews was fashioned early in his life. He wrote sententiously to Cardinal Dubois: "A Jew having no country but where he earns his money can betray the King for the Emperor as well as the Emperor for the King." [1]

Voltaire was an enthusiast who loved society and conversation about everything under the sun. When he traveled to Holland to try to arrange for the publication of his mock-heroic *Henriade,* he thought he was in paradise: he found a land of fertile fields where everyone worked, a port with a thousand ships, a city of half a million with no unemployed, no poor, no idlers, no arrogant officials and nobles. This middling way had its disadvantages, to be sure: the opera was abominable. But opinions were freely expressed. Voltaire ex-

changed theological ideas with Calvinists, Arminians, Socinians, Ana-
baptists, and Jewish rabbis, who all argued brilliantly and, so far as he
was concerned, were all equally right or wrong. To give the devil his
due, Voltaire adhered to this skeptical position for more than half a
century. Religious disputations were sport, like some plays, but were
essentially a matter of indifference to him; religious intolerance and
superstition were not. Mixing theology with the fumes of blood was a
bad habit that Christianity had acquired from ancient Judaism. And
if for brief periods in modern times this addiction has abated, both
Christians and Jews owe no small debt to Voltaire.

At the height of his Judeophobia, Voltaire insisted that the Jews,
like Rousseau, were crazy, but he never called for their burning, as the
Church had. On the other hand, writing to a friend about the outrageous behavior of a Jew, Voltaire dredged up the image of Negro
slaves with their names tattooed on their breasts and buttocks as precedent for marking all Jews on the forehead with the sign "fit to be
hanged."[2] At times Voltaire exulted in his hatred of Jews. In 1724,
when terrible sores erupted over his whole body, with black humor
he announced to his correspondents that he had been struck with
leprosy for maltreating the Jews. By some diabolical prefiguration of
events, in his select circle of friends one of his nicknames was "Goeb-
bels."[3]

Whatever his animus against individual Jews, when Voltaire published his universal history, he sounded the full blast of his Judeophobia in impersonal and generalized terms that obliquely cast aspersions
on Christianity and the religious establishment he worked to bring
down. Charles Bonnet, the Genevan scientist and Christian philosopher, immediately discerned the hidden purpose of Voltaire's narrative and wrote a friend: "The part of his history that deals with the
Jews is full of outrageous mistakes. It is clear that Voltaire intends to
render this nation odious and despicable, and to have the darts he has
let loose on *them* fall on the Sacred Scriptures."[4] Among other
charges, Voltaire accused the Jews of having offered up human sacrifices, which he said was proved by Jephthah's vow. Bonnet accused
Voltaire of deliberately aiming to perpetrate evil: to break the bonds
that joined men together, to shake the foundations of the Christian
religion that was the strongest support of society, and to deprive his
fellow men of the gentle consolations they had on earth. This philo-

sophe was no true philosopher, no friend of humanity, and no man of virtue.

In his voluminous writings on ancient Judaism, Voltaire constantly engaged in disputes over cultural priority, the standby of seventeenth-century scholarship. He claimed that the Chinese were six to seven hundred years older than the biblical flood and used this revised chronology to subvert the Mosaic account. The question of the antiquity of the Chinese was still being hotly debated among eighteenth-century erudits. Unless the Hebrews took chronological precedence over both the Greeks in the west and the Chinese in the east, their position as the chosen people of God would be shaken. The biblical account of Jewish origins was vindicated for the more orthodox when Joseph de Guignes published a treatise proving that Chinese characters derived from Egyptian hieroglyphs and that China was an Egyptian colony, not a venerable prior civilization. Voltaire always maliciously espoused the cause of the Chinese sages.

Voltaire was delighted with the Old Testament stories—there he discovered the original spirit of Judaism; they were more exciting than *Tom Jones* and a hundred times better than Homer if one wanted to have any understanding of wild barbarous ancient Asia. He desanctified the text of the Scriptures and treated them as literature. Of course he never expected the Marquise du Deffand, to whom he wrote jocularly of his enthusiasm, to take a fancy to the bloodthirsty Bible, but if she wished to learn something about the Jewish people, a subject of constant wonderment, she had to read the Scriptures. Imagine a people so stubborn, obtuse, and exclusive that for six hundred years it lived surrounded by the grand cultures of Tyre and Babylon and Egypt without having received from these lands any arts and sciences. Compared to their civilized neighbors, the Hebrews were a rude and primitive lot. In Voltaire's philosophy of history, nations were either barbarous or civilized, and he classified the Hebrews among the barbarians. They were comparable to the benighted Picts.

Voltaire is fair game for a freewheeling psychological exegesis that would tease remote and subconscious motives out of his tales and biblical commentaries. One cannot read in *Candide* the detailed descriptions of massacres and buttocks beatings, or the obvious relish with which the author describes Phineas the Levite entering the tent of the Israelite lying with a Midianite woman and piercing her belly and his private parts with one thrust of the spear, without being aware of the innate cruelty of the man, expressed through tirades against the cruelty of the Jews. Voltaire lived with daydreams of buttocks beating and spear heaving into the testicles of an enemy. When possessed by a thirst for vengeance, he was prepared to spread stories about a literary rival's purported homosexual behavior and in his mind's eye to watch him burning in ceremonial punishment. Much of Voltaire's ranting about the historical cruelties of the ancient Israelites was an opportunity for the release in fantasy of his own cruel desires. The Jews served a purpose in his psychic economy: they were a personal scapegoat.

Voltaire was a mesmerist with words, and the art of historical evocation and the hatred of Jews were pressed into the service of the "good cause," the destruction of theological Christianity. The historical world view that Voltaire built is perhaps the most elaborate outward evidence of his deeper passion. He had as slashing a way of dealing with Israel as had ever been devised by official apologists of the Church. The Jews were needed for sundry reasons that were consistently repeated by Church Fathers, popes, and councils: the Jews were there at the beginning of things and their prophets foretold the coming of Christ; they were necessary witnesses to the truth of Christianity; and their conversion was an important event in the drama of world salvation. The last great apologists of Christianity writing in French, Pascal and Bossuet, had highlighted the role of the Jews in universal history and theology. Voltaire's works were directed at destroying the structures Pascal and Bossuet had elaborated, and one of his war machines was trained on the elimination of the Jews from the early history of the Christian peoples and of civilization itself. If instead of occupying a central place in history, the ancient Jews were reduced to insignificance, the primary witness to the truth of Christianity would be denied.

The hatred that stoked the fires of Voltaire's revolutionary universal history may have originally been bred by experiences in the life of the young François Marie Arouet that can only be conjectured; his encounters with Jewish bankers and court Jews who fleeced him when they could, as Voltaire did others in his financial manipulations, kept alive his phobia. But much of his enmity assumed a rationalist form and was expressed as historical revelation and mock-serious biblical exegesis that with time assumed broad significance. Since no translation of the Bible ever possessed French culture with the pervasiveness of Luther's translation or the King James version, there were generations of Frenchmen who were brought up on Voltaire's Bible.

The factual errors in Voltaire's presentation of ancient Jewish history were legion. He was sloppy and did not copy straight from his sources; he adapted and plagiarized incorrectly, either through error or malevolence, covering his ignorance with witticisms that divert the eye and ear. Normally, in composing his anti-Judaic polemics, Voltaire perused, but did not read, the books from which he quoted. Sometimes he gave fictitious references as a joke. When he made up citations from Maimonides or Abraham Ibn Ezra to support an extravagant bit of biblical exegesis, he was poking fun at yokels who might waste their time trying fruitlessly to check his authorities.

Voltaire was a passionate monotheist who adored his God, but an eyewitness of his devotions heard him say that as for "Monsieur le fils et madame sa mère, c'est une autre affaire." Voltaire's weapons were crude. His underlying purpose—to attack Judaism and Christianity by conflating them—was plainly voiced in a letter of 1765 addressed to the Count and Countess d'Argental. He was commenting favorably on his own *Philosophie de l'histoire,* which had been published pseudonymously in that year in Amsterdam and Geneva as the work of the Abbé Bazin: "This book modestly shows that the Jews were one of the latest peoples to appear, that they took from other nations all their myths and all their customs. This dagger once dug in can kill the monster of superstition in the chambers of men of good will without the fools even knowing it." [5] On another occasion he had written: "It is good to know the Jews as they are and to see from what fathers the Christians are descended." [6] Out of unheroic caution, many, though not all, the philosophes considered off limits the early history of the Church, the lives of Christ and the Apostles. Most of the philosophes were determined to illuminate mankind without being martyred by it, to adapt Beccaria's formula. As a result, the particular God of the Jews and his chosen people were often surrogates that the philosophes fashioned to their own purposes and then lashed out against.

The twenty-odd volumes of the Benedictine Abbot Augustin Calmet's literalist commentary on the Bible provided the raw materials for Voltaire's biblical exegesis. Received as a distinguished royal historiographer in Calmet's monastery, Voltaire stayed for almost a month and has left an amusing description of the monks scurrying up and down ladders to search out texts that ultimately fed his bonfires of both traditional Christianity and Judaism. Beelzebub took the facts piously assembled by the monks and twisted them to fiendish ends. He also consulted original sources himself. Even a cursory examination of the collection of Church Fathers in his library, which has been kept intact in Leningrad from the time of Catherine the Great, bears witness to the assiduousness with which Voltaire pored over the sacred writings of early Christianity. In the dense forests of patristic literature he carefully set up his own markers, little dabs of thin paper pasted on passages that might some day be useful in the anticlerical crusade. He acquired the Dutch scholar Surenhuis' translations of the Mishna into Latin and a few other seventeenth-century respectworthy Christian Hebraist writings in Latin and the vernacular. But in this area his much-touted learning was fake; most of his gleanings were adapted to bolster hackneyed deist ideas to which his style lent glamor.

Voltaire used the dialectical skills he had learned from his Jesuit teachers to draw preposterous inferences about the behavior of the Israelites. If there was a biblical commandment forbidding sodomy with animals, he concluded that obviously the practice was prevalent—or else there would have been no reason to prohibit it in the Mosaic code. If a prophet threatened the sinners of Israel with a hunger so ravaging that mothers would devour their babes, he deduced that anthropophagy was common among them. ·

By adhering to the literal, factual meaning of the Bible, Voltaire rendered it inconsistent and contradictory, even repulsive. Reading in the book of Joshua that the victorious war leader circumcised all Jews who had been born during the decades in the wilderness and had been wandering about uncircumcised, Voltaire conjured up a veritable mountain of foreskins on Gilgal. What the Jews wrote about themselves was fiction and not to be believed. Then, in order to illustrate the cruelty of the Hebrew God, he reversed himself abruptly and uncritically accepted biblical statistics that pertained to the Hebrews on a slaughtering rampage of enemies and sinners. To Isaac de Pinto, an agent of the Sephardic community, who in a rather obsequious letter had protested some of Voltaire's remarks on the Jews, he wrote: "Remain a Jew since you are one, but don't masscre 42,000 men because they could not pronounce shibboleth right nor 24,000 because they slept with Midianites; be a philosophe." [7]

Though the bulk of Voltaire's references to Jews and Judaism are derisive, the philosophical Voltaire had moments when he stopped to contemplate more soberly the historical destiny of the Jewish people. His *Dictionnaire philosophique* includes an article on Jews that reiterates the constant themes of his Judeophobia, but a certain perplexity breaks through the wall of often monotonous and stereotyped witticisms. He joins the long line of Christian thinkers who have reflected on the profound ambivalence of Christianity toward Judaism: "The Jewish people is surely the most singular body that has ever existed in the world. Most despicable from a political point of view, in the eyes of philosophy [Voltaire means philosophical history in his manner] they are significant in many respects." [8]

In later writings Voltaire repeated the familial simile that first appeared in a notebook of his sojourn in England in the 1720s. In one passage of the notebook, written in rather quaint English, he remarked: "When I see Christians cursing Jews, methings I see children beating their fathers." [9] There is a temptation to discover a parallel between Voltaire's notorious hostility toward his father and his view of Christianity's enmity to Judaism, but in the very next sentence of his notebook the important familial bond is described in maternal terms: "Jewish religion is mother of Christyanity, and grand mother of the mahometism." [10] At another point he again combined the familial imagery with the language of physical abuse: "The Jewish religion mother of Christianity, grand mother of Mahometism, thrashed by her son and by her grandson." [11]

The family metaphor for the Judeo-Christian relationship is an old one. It was Montesquieu's way of expressing the singularity of the tie between Christians and Jews, though his tone was more neutral than Voltaire's. What is striking in Voltaire is his violence and, at the same time, his acute consciousness that, as with parent and child, the relationship could never be severed. The English deist Thomas Morgan, in trumpeting his enmity toward Judaism, conceived of his task as the eradication of the Jewish residue in Christianity. Voltaire would destroy Judaism, fully cognizant that since the two religions could not be rent asunder both would disintegrate.

If personal psychological and socioeconomic motives are left as a sort of grim obbligato, and the traditional Joshua-like bifurcation of Christians into Judeophobes and Judeophiles is avoided, there survive the images and arguments with which the Enlightenment responded to ancient Judaism. Granted that the perception of ancient Judaism cannot be divorced from the realities of eighteenth-century Jewish life in a hostile Christian world, the portraits of the God of the Jews drawn by Voltaire during this period outlasted the Enlightenment and became dynamic historical forces in their own right. In the confrontation of secular European intellectuals (emancipated or quasi-emancipated from Christian angels and devils) with ancient Judaism, men like Voltaire forged new cultural stereotypes that have endured for centuries. Voltaire concentrated on ridiculing the Israelites in the wilderness and holding up to scorn the barbarity of their early kingship. The moral of the tale was patent: nothing could be expected from present-day Jews when their origins were so polluted. Coming from the "king of the epoch," this attack colored one Enlightenment view of the religion of the Jews. Though Voltaire's was not the only Enlightenment portrayal of Judaism, it made the deepest imprint on European consciousness in the nineteenth century, when his works were regularly republished and he became the godfather of the French secular state. It was then that his Judeophobia merged with the main current of European antisemitism that drew on new pseudoscientific versions of ethnology, linguistics, and anthropology.

Baron d'Holbach's Synagogue

The clandestine publications of Baron Paul d'Holbach and his circle, which with playful self-mockery called themselves "the Synagogue," revived the formulas of the frank, militant, blatant atheism of the ancient world and added a virulent potion, the experience of Judaism. There was nothing in Christianity, deistic or positive, that Holbach wished to preserve. As a consequence, in describing the relationship of Judaism and Christianity, he argued that Christianity was simply reformed Judaism—and not much reformed at that. Voltaire and d'Alembert shuddered at the prospect of atheism when they read Holbach's writings and scribbled "dangerous work" on the flyleaves of their copies. Thomas Jefferson, who studied all the radical philosophes, vacillated about his own religious position, as the marginalia of his books show. What Voltaire and d'Alembert feared was *dix-sous* popularizations of Holbach's ideas, which might corrupt the populace and lead to anarchy. Holbach, secure in his conviction that society was protected by the hangman and not by God, pulled out all the stops. The Holbachians assimilated Judaism to other primitive religions, generated and maintained by fear and terror. And fear, they had learned from the ancients and were reminded by David Hume, obfuscated truth and bred cruelty. The analysis of fear in primitive religion was pivotal in the attack on Judaism by Holbach and by the engineer Nicolas Antoine Boulanger, who frequented his salon. The fear of God in Judaism, the *Gottesfurcht* that was the highest virtue among sixteenth-century Lutherans, became identified with cruelty in eighteenth-century associationist psychology. And if there was a single evil that the diverse branches of the Enlightenment joined in denouncing, it was cruelty.

When literate freethinkers of the Enlightenment weighed the witness of the Old Testament on the nature of Judaism against the evidence adduced by their favorite Roman historian, Tacitus, in his famous excursion on the character of the Jews in book 5 of the *Histories,* the scales tilted heavily on the side of Tacitus. For them he was a truly objective, pagan historian, not implicated in the quarrels of Christians and Jews. A first-century, civilized Roman official, he had sifted the tales about the Jews to ferret out the origin of their religion, their exclusiveness, the contempt in which they were held by other nations, and the hatred they reciprocated. Tacitus' account of how Moses instituted new religious rites in order to bind to himself the tribes of Jews driven out by the Egyptians was consonant with prevalent eighteenth-century theories about the origins of all oriental religions: they were inventions of a power-hungry leader or priest and had no divine sanction. The idiosyncrasy of an empty temple in Jerusalem without any representation of the invisible god was for Tacitus a patent demonstration of Jewish absurdity. There were those who, seeing vine-leaf ornaments in the temples of the Jews, thought they worshiped Bacchus, but they were wrong; Bacchus inspired joy, while the religion of the Jews was lugubrious. The Jews were contentious among themselves, though united in clinging stubbornly to their fatuous beliefs when the Romans attacked them. As a tribe in the Roman

Empire, they were peculiar, obdurate, and troublesome. Reading Tacitus, Enlightenment philosophes thought they recognized the Jews who were their contemporaries. One had to be wary of them.

A pseudonymous Holbachian work that appeared in 1769 with a fake London imprint and the pretended authorship of the late M. de Mirabaud, permanent secretary of the French Academy, was entitled *Opinions des anciens sur les Juifs* (Opinions of the Ancients on the Jews). It was a not-too-subtle attempt to show that Judaism was the religion of a people despised by all those nations of antiquity that the philosophes revered for their learning and understanding of human nature. With their sound classical education, the Holbachians assembled scores of citations to support a flat declaration: "Of all the ancients who discussed the origin of God's people, every one did it in a contemptuous and insulting manner."[12] Josephus was unsuccessful in his endeavors to refute the charges of the Egyptian historians Manetho and Apion that the Jews were lepers (*Against Apion,* book 1, chaps. 9, 11, 12). A passage in Lysimachus cited by Josephus in his *History* (book 5, chap. 34) and included in Photius' *Library* described the expulsion of the Jews from Egypt under King Bocchoris. Tacitus and Diodorus of Sicily, both quoted by Photius, had in common the tradition of the expulsion of the Jews from Egypt or some other country because of their infectious diseases.

Secondary evidence played up the ritual conformities between Jews and Egyptians: the frequency of priestly ablutions, the sapphire necklace of the priests, the cursing of the scapegoat to bear the sins of the people, the practice of circumcision, the abhorrence of pork, the fast days, the distinction between sacred and profane writings and between clean and unclean animals, the golden calf, the bronze serpent. Like many eighteenth-century writers, the Holbachians accepted the most superficial resemblances as indications of religious diffusion from one people to another. Their purpose was to diminish the reverence for Judaism as an ancient phenomenon and to present the religion as a mere derivation from Egyptian beliefs and rituals. Egyptians, once famous for their pyramids, had degenerated and become notorious for the crudeness of their animal worship, and among the ancients the Jews were often confounded with them.

Apart from the universal contempt in which the Jews were held by the ancients for their foolish rites, they were hated because it was believed that they despised all other peoples and constantly cursed the gods of other nations in the name of their invisible god. The pagans of antiquity called the Jews haughty and thought their hatred was ordained by the god they adored. This argument, revived by the Holbachians, was a translation of one of the most common Christian justifications for animosity against the Jews. Diodorus Siculus (book 34, in Photius) imputes Antiochus' desecration of the Jewish temple by sacrificing a pig on its premises to his resentment of Jewish hostility to other nations. Tacitus in the *Annals* (book 15, chap. 44) tended to confuse Christians and Jews, and thought it was easy to convict them of the crime of setting fire to Rome because of the general report that they loathed the rest of mankind, though their fidelity to one another was inviolable. Juvenal (satire 14, verse 103) repeated the same theme—Jews would show the way only to travelers who were coreligionists and point out springs only to the circumcised. Jewish misanthropy was sometimes explained as a desire for vengeance for their sufferings in Egypt (Diodorus Siculus, book 40, in Photius); loathing begat loathing. In *Saint Cyril against Julian* (book 6), the Holbachians found recorded Julian's opinion that Moses had ordered the Jews to exterminate entire peoples. The ill will of the Jews was universally recognized among the ancients, and during popular tumults they were always the first victims. The periodic massacre of Jewish communities in antiquity was retribution for the manner in which they had massacred the Canaanites (this appears to be based on the same passage in *Cyril against Julian,* book 6).

The Holbachians piled high the testimonies of the ancients. Jewish fasts, mournful prayers, sabbath-keeping were the butts of Roman scorn. Suetonius described Augustus praising his grandson Caius for not deigning to sacrifice in the temple of Jerusalem, a supreme Roman insult. The Roman poets joined the chorus. Juvenal and Perses ridiculed the credulity of the Jews, their superstitions, and their cheating. Horace made mock of their obsession with the sabbath. Marcellinus Ammianus always referred to the Jews as stinking (book 22). But above all they were derided for circumcision (though it was also practiced among Egyptians and Ethiopians). The derogatory names for Jews were *verpi, curti, recutiti,* all referring to circumcision. When Jews showed themselves in public baths, they were subject to such raillery that some resorted to strange and painful ways of disguising their circumcision. In the *Jewish Antiquities* (book 20, chap. 4) Josephus told of a Roman soldier on guard at the temple in Jerusalem who, to insult the Jews flocking to celebrate the feast of Passover, exhibited his penis. The offense roused the Jews to revolt, and more than ten thousand were killed.

The Holbachians reached the climax of their diatribes against the God of the Jews in *L'Esprit du judaïsme, ou examen raisonné de la loi de Moyse, et de son influence sur la religion chrétienne* (The Spirit of Judaism, or Rational Examination of the Law of Moses and Its Influence on the Christian Religion; 1770), a work often imputed to the English deist Anthony Collins. Actually it is a composite in which the rhetoric of Boulanger, Holbach, and perhaps Diderot can be detected. The twelfth chapter is an oratorical display in which the parallel between the God of Christianity and the God of Judaism is set forth with a passion rarely attained in anticlerical literature, even by Voltaire and Nietzsche. The full force of the battering ram is directed at the Judaic God, of whom the Christian God is a mere replica:

> Blinded by their legislator the Jews never had any sound ideas of divinity. Moses devised an image for them with the characteristics of a jealous tyrant, restless and insidious, who was never restrained by the laws of justice and who owes nothing to men, who chooses and rejects according to his caprice, who punishes children for the crimes, or rather the misfortunes, of their fathers . . . What more was needed to make of the Hebrew people a troop of slaves, proud of the favor of their celestial sultan, prepared to undertake anything without examination to satisfy his passions and unjust decrees? This ignorant, savage people, imbued with the idea that its God was amenable to gifts, believed that it was enough to please him to make him many offerings, to appease him with sacrifices, to enrich his ministers, to work in order to keep them in splendor, to fulfill scrupulously the rites that their cupidity dreamed up . . . These are the horrible features with which the legislator of the Hebrews painted the God that the Christians have since taken over.[13]

In this portrait the God of love and mercy is completely stricken out.

Explaining the burning of marranos in contemporary Spanish and Portuguese autos-da-fé, the Holbachians returned Christianity to its origin, Judaism. It was as if the Jews had willed their own eventual destruction: "In a word, all the ferocity of the Judaic priesthood seems to have passed into the heart of the Christian priesthood, which since it has established itself on earth has caused barbarities to be committed unknown to humans before." [14]

The Holbachians argued that in belief, in temper, in ecclesiastical organization, the Jews were the very model for Christianity. Where orthodox Christians had seen the sacrifice of Isaac as a type for the crucifixion, the Holbachians saw it as a despicable oriental child sacrifice that was imitated:

> Christians, like Jews, worship a cruel and gory God; they proclaimed one who demands blood to appease his fury. But is not cruelty a sign of weakness? Did God create his creatures in order to spill their blood? Nevertheless these abominable principles have been invoked to justify the atrocious persecutions that Christians have launched a thousand times against those whom they falsely imagined were the enemies of their God. Having made of this God a veritable cannibal, they have honored him by avenging his cause with the fumes of human blood. It is in accord with these atrocious ideas that they imagined this same God demanded of the patriarch Abraham the blood of his only son and then demanded that to redeem men, the blood of a God, the blood of his own Son, be shed on the cross. [15]

The shift from the seventeenth-century portrayal of the kingdom of the Jews as a model republic worthy of emulation by the nations to the Voltairean and Holbachian image of a savage and barbaric kingdom when it was independent, and an impotent client state when it was subjugated by a long line of imperial powers—Babylonian, Assyrian, Greek, Roman—was a dramatic reversal in the judgment of Judaism. Civil wars, divisive sects, and internecine quarrels marked this history of the ancient Hebrews composed by the eighteenth-century radical leaders of the anti-Christian crusade—a polity to be despised. Individual writers chose to dwell upon different epochs as quintessential expressions of the spirit of Judaism, but neither the much-touted reigns of David and Solomon nor the heroic epoch of the Maccabees escaped derision and censure.

In his *Histoire du Vieux et du Nouveau Testament* (History of the Old and New Testament; 1704) Jacques Basnage, the Huguenot exile who wrote what were probably the most popular eighteenth-century source books of secular knowledge about Jews and Judaism, had dropped the more licentious episodes from King David's life or psy-

chologized his misconduct to the point where the story of his iniquities became a morality play about the dangers of giving free rein to
the passions. Voltaire and Holbach presented the same biblical narrative in a different spirit, as a Tacitus or a Suetonius might in writing
about a wicked emperor of Rome. If measured by the standards of
Paris salon society or the club life of Hume's London, both the kings
of the Jews and their God turned out to be grisly characters.

The French anticlericals reveled in shattering the idealized image
of David. His orthodox apologists had celebrated the piety of the
Psalms; in *David, ou L'histoire de l'homme selon le coeur de Dieu* (David, or the History of the Man after the Heart of God; 1768), a translation of a work by Peter Annet, the Holbach circle turned to the
simple facts recorded in the books of Samuel and Kings as interpreted
by the radical English deist. In the previous century Rembrandt had
drawn David as a resplendent oriental monarch, repentant, deep in
thought, listening to the admonishments of an ascetic Nathan. For
the Holbachians, David the murderous lecher who had Bathsheba's
husband Uriah killed at the front and David the disloyal harpist who
betrayed Saul were more realistic portraits. They pictured David as a
leader of ruffians and his God as a capricious creature who poured
ointment about rather indiscriminately.

Pierre Bayle, who believed that their religion had impregnated the
Jewish people with a narrow, niggardly spirit, aroused such opposition among the orthodox with his article on David in the first edition
of the *Dictionnaire historique et critique* that he was forced in the second edition to suppress many of his acidulous comments; but they
were later restored, and the philosophes had regular recourse to these
passages. The brutal hacking of King Agag by Samuel graphically depicted in Voltaire's play *Saul* may reveal its author's delight in bloodthirsty episodes; but whatever their psychic motivation, his Old Testament scenes had a convincing goriness that the most persuasive
rabbinic apologies could not dispel. Not everything written in the
Enlightenment about the first dispensation was false or even distorted
in the light of a plain, straightforward reading of the Bible.

The English and French deists and the Holbachian atheists spear-
headed the movement toward the secularization of Europe, and in
seeking to extirpate a religious world outlook, they deliberately scandalized western society with a gruesome Judaism as the matrix of

Christianity. Voltaire's quips, in slightly different versions, fed the antisemitism of both the political right wing and a segment of the revolutionary left. The pamphlets that emanated from the Holbachian circle were translated in the nineteenth century and published in England and in the United States, where they nourished a popular atheism that continued to exist on a small scale throughout the Victorian age. The Holbachian writings, supplemented by halfpenny excerpts from Fourier, provided the documentation for village atheism, along with its dosage of Jew-hatred, in both England and America.

Diderot: A Patchwork Philosophy of the Jews

My account would be too strident if not rectified by the consideration of more temporate French secular thinkers of the eighteenth century such as Montesquieu and Rousseau, as well as by an overview of changing attitudes among clerics who became aware of the danger to Catholicism inherent in the philosophes' images of historical Judaism.

The extremist views represented by Voltaire and Holbach are balanced by fathers of the Enlightenment whose position was more neutral, at least in some of their reflections. Neither Montesquieu nor Rousseau nor Diderot devoted to Jewish writings anything like the amount of energy that Voltaire expended in his dogged hunt for Judaic iniquities. Considerations of Judaism were peripheral to the main body of their thought and usually assumed the form of casual observations. Montesquieu read the Pentateuch as the work of an ancient legislator worthy of respect, though not beyond criticism, and Rousseau saw in the Mosaic lawgiver the only predecessor deserving of the name. Though Diderot perused more learned secondary sources on the postbiblical history of the Jews and Jewish thought than had either Montesquieu or Rousseau, his function as an expositor of the history of Jewish philosophy was not brilliantly discharged in the *Encyclopédie.*

In later centuries, isolated phrases on Judaism from the pens of these great fathers of the Enlightenment were occasionally quoted as epigraphs, benign philosophical apothegms typical of the age, but their authors were not combed for insights into the nature of Judaism. The exception was Diderot's anonymous article on the Jews in the *Encyclopédie,* a piece that derived its importance not from any intrinsic excellence but from its inclusion in the summa of Enlightenment thought, and found its way into libraries ranging from those of provincial bourgeois professionals to that of the royal household. As usual, Diderot is the most difficult philosophe to pin down. On Judaism he whirled with the wind; of his literary hallmarks, only the customary wit is absent. Both Montesquieu and Diderot have left behind ambivalent depictions of ancient Israel before the final dispersion under the Romans. Montesquieu never abandoned his allegiance to the orthodox form of Catholic Christianity and thus was cautious in his treatment of Old Testament worthies; Diderot remained as inconstant and enigmatic in this matter as in virtually all others.

Diderot, editor of the *Encyclopédie,* who in his youth had briefly worn the tonsure and later was a member of Holbach's "synagogue," could not remain indifferent to the details of the relgous philosophy of Judaism. His major article on the ancient and modern history of the Jews and their philosophy, simply entitled "Juifs," appeared in volume 9. It is hardly an original performance, being essentially an abstract of Johann Jakob Brucker's and Thomas Stanley's standard histories of philosophy, mixed with smidgens from Basnage's popularizations. Plagiarism is perhaps too strong a word, but it comes close to being applicable to this twenty-five-page entry of double columns in folio. Diderot's piece became the text from which literate men of the Enlightenment derived their knowledge about the doctrines of Judaism in various historical periods. Further information on the subject was scattered in separate entries on Moses, the Prophets, the Karaites, the Rabbis, the Temple of Jerusalem, the Synagogue, and the Inquisition. Throughout the *Encyclopédie* are strewn incidental references to the doctrines and sects of the Jews, their government, customs, arts and sciences, and condition in Metz and Poland. Nowhere, however, is there a noteworthy appraisal of Judaism. Another piece, actually labeled "Judaïsme," is barely a column long and is of no significance. Diderot's youthful fragment, *La Promenade du sceptique* (1747), included a long-drawn-out parody of the history of Moses and his laws that portrays him as a wily leader playing on the credulity of an ignorant horde, but since it was published posthumously it was not comparable in influence with the entries in the *Encyclopédie.*

Voltaire by publishing in Holland, Switzerland, or German principalities was able to foil the censor. Diderot, issuing the *Encyclopédie* in France with an authorized publisher, had to be far more circumspect in his exposition of the origins of Christianity, the philosophy and religion of the early patriarchal Hebrews. Moses is hailed with adulatory ejaculations: "What a historian! What a legislator! What a philosopher! What a poet! What a man!" [16] After throwing the censor a few bones, avoiding any discussion of revelation and prophecy, giving lip service to the belief that the Jews were the most ancient people in the world—refuting by implication the claim to antiquity of the Egyptians and the Chinese—extolling the Jews for their direct discovery of the unity of God at a time when other nations harbored polytheistic superstitions, Diderot plunges into the main substance of his subject: the philosophy of the Jews after their return from the Babylonian captivity. Since he was borrowing heavily from Basnage, he included a history of the Samaritans, a topic that had been an obsession with the Huguenot historian. But most of the piece is devoted to a pedestrian exposition of the dogmas and doctrines of the Jewish sects during the second commonwealth, highlighting their quarrels and disputes, and a supercilious account of what was included in the Talmud. A few asides on the similarity between rabbinic and scholastic casuistry suggest that this history too served the anti-Christian crusade.

Diderot is meticulous when he describes artisans' manufacturing procedures—he had himself visited their shops—but in reporting on Jewish belief he relies on secondary sources that were at best sketchy. Always eager to display his learning, he quotes rabbinic dicta, but the names of the rabbis, their dates, and their doctrines are not accurately rendered, and he fails to distinguish among aggadic obiter dicta, parables, serious legal decisions, and fundamental articles of belief. When he polemizes against Christian Hebraists, lumping together men of the previous century who held widely divergent opinions, he produces a hodgepodge.

On the whole, the tone of the *Encyclopédie* articles relating to Judaism is passionless and factual (though the facts are often erroneous). In the general survey of Jewish philosophy, the method of presentation is plain historical. Critical examination of doctrines and rites is not entirely avoided, but it is infrequent. The narrative is not infused with Voltairean animosity; neither is there any tendency to blame the evils of Christianity on its Jewish origins, as the Holbachians did. Such sharply negative judgments as do intrude focus on the poverty of Jewish contributions to the progress of the arts and sciences and the addiction of the Jews to sectarian disputations over the minutiae of religious beliefs and to cabbalist fantasies. Diderot was unacquainted with Hebrew books on chronology, astronomy, medicine, or mathematics, though some of them had been translated into Latin, and he was as ignorant as Voltaire about Jewish participation in the scientific achievements of Arabic civilization in medieval Spain, the transmission of Greek and Arabic philosophy and science through Jewish intermediaries; for Diderot the Jews lacked even a semblance of objective science. In the middle of the eighteenth century, the philosophes, for all their pretense to universal culture, knew far less about Jewish works in astronomy, mathematics, and botany than had erudits like Selden or Bartolocci in the previous century. A reader of Diderot's articles was fed grossly distorted information about rabbinic Judaism, the numerous Jewish sects, and the zealotry of their convictions. A philosophe in search of clarity would have been repelled by the confusion of Jewish doctrines of different periods that Diderot treated as contemporaneous.

Diderot is coolly critical of the medieval kings of England and France who inflicted sufferings on the Jews, and he denounces the Inquisition, but without great vehemence. He displays a certain naive wonderment about the continued history of the Jews, who, he surmises, are as numerous as they ever were; but when he attempts to account for what Increase Mather called the mystery of the survival of the Jews, Diderot has nothing more profound to offer than "the nature and force of their laws." [17] The later intellectual history of the Jews as recounted by Diderot consists of nothing more than a succession of precepts and undemonstrated opinions of generations of rabbis.

Though in Diderot's religious history the Jews laudably skipped the stage of polytheistic idolatry and proceeded directly to monotheism, they made up for their early freedom from superstition by adopting a multiplicity of nonsensical theological dogmas. Passing gingerly over the period of the Old Testament in order to sidestep the censor, Diderot turned to an identification of the principal Jewish sects at the time of Christ—Sadducees, Pharisees, Karaites, Essenes, and the group Philo called Therapeutes. His history provided Christian readers with succinct, if rather fuzzy, definitions of the Mishna, the Babylonian and the Jerusalem Talmuds, and the Cabbala. His attitude toward the long rabbinic tradition of biblical interpretation is derogatory, though he concedes that on occasion the rabbis could be consulted with profit for a better understanding of the Scriptures. As a rationalist philosophe, he naturally preferred the exoteric Jewish thought of Abraham Ibn Ezra and Maimonides to the mystifications of the allegorists and cabbalists.

Among the meagre descriptions of Jewish rites borrowed from standard popularizations like those of Leone Modena, and of Jewish conceptions of the heavenly paradise and the immortality of the soul, Diderot includes a digression on the beauty of Jewish women, a subject about which he writes more feelingly. He accepts the explanation that Jews were forced into usury by being denied entry into other occupations, and he credits them with the invention of letters of exchange. A measure of respect is accorded the internal organization of their civil society as well as their seminaries of rabbinic learning.

While Diderot did not lead a crusade for Jewish emancipation, he refrained from publicly joining in Voltaire's tirades of vilification. He accepted the Jews as anomalies in European society and did not concern himself overmuch with their fate. In the opening of his *Encyclopédie* article on the philosophy of the Jews, Diderot plays the obedient son of the Church: the Jews were the oldest "nation"; the patriarchs spoke with God; as heads of large families leading a pastoral existence, they were occupied with practical things and had no leisure for scientific observations; David, Solomon, and Daniel were great legislators; the prophets were on a higher plane than the philosophers of Greece, the hierophants of Egypt, or the gymnosophists of India. But the initial paragraphs of Diderot's article are covertly satirical. The very hyperbole of the praise suggests that it was not intended to be taken literally. He becomes circumstantial only with his description of the warring sects during the second commonwealth, free territory for criticism.

One of the characters that makes an appearance in Diderot's *Neveu de Rameau,* unpublished during his lifetime, is a vulgar literary stereotype of the period, a rich sensual Jew of Avignon who is betrayed to the Inquisition by a Jewish convert to Christianity. The little Diderot knew about contemporary Jews seems to have derived from his acquaintance with the Portuguese Jew of Amsterdam Isaac de Pinto, a bizarre character who moved with a certain freedom between Bordeaux, Paris, and Amsterdam, acting as an agent of the privileged Sephardim, who were hostile to German and Polish Jews trying to acquire some legal status in France. De Pinto, an economist of sorts who wrote a treatise on money and credit, published a series of letters proving that England would never be able to surrender the American colonies lest it lose all consideration on the Continent. He also toyed with the paradox that cardplaying was an activity leading to the softening of manners and the spread of enlightenment, a conceit he printed and addressed to Diderot. Stopping at the Hague on his return from Russia, the aging Diderot visited this wealthy Jew and came away with the notion that his house was a gathering place for homosexuals. (Diderot reported a number of incidents revealing de Pinto's lasciviousness.) There are documents from the library of the Amsterdam Sephardic community (now in the Hebrew University of Jerusalem) that support Diderot's pejorative estimate of de Pinto as an unsavory character and give intimations that he was in the pay of Lord North—suspicions that de Pinto, proud of his illustrious Sephardic ancestry, vigorously challenged.

The court Jews with whom Voltaire had dealings in Prussia and the rich merchant princes of Amsterdam whom Diderot encountered led both of them to judge contemporary Judaism as begetting vice and corruption. Diderot's sketches have taken their place in the gallery of Jewish portraits drawn by French writers of genius, including Balzac, Proust, and Céline. Though Diderot's part in works of the Holbachian circle such as the *Spirit of Judaism* cannot be defined with precision, he clearly had something to do with them. Their bitter and flamboyant identification of Judaism with the vices of Christianity supplanted the indifferent presentation of the *Enclyclopédie.*

Rousseau on the Tenacity of Mosaic Law

Among the moving spirits of the Enlightenment, Rousseau, the religious changeling who worshiped in turn a Protestant and a Catholic God while harboring in secret a nature religion of his own, evoked an image of ancient and modern Israel that stood in striking contrast to that of most philosophes west of the Rhine. In the *Social Contract*

Moses was exalted as one of the three great legislators of the ancient world. Such a form-imprinting figure, who could shape a nation, would appear only once in its history. After decadence had set in among the Hebrews, all attempts at revival were doomed to failure— witness the futile effort of the Maccabees to reinstitute Mosaic law. There are other references to Moses in the *Social Contract,* as well as in *Considerations on the Government of Poland* and in a fragment entitled "Des juifs," where the Mosaic law is praised above all others for its duration: "The Laws of Solon, of Numa, of Lycurgus are dead. Those of Moses, which were more ancient, are still alive."[18] Of all the French Enlightenment thinkers, only the citizen of Protestant Geneva celebrated in a grand dithyramb the survival of the Jews, which he attributed to the excellence of the Mosaic code. "Des juifs" remained unpublished until recent years, but it is an integral part of Rousseau's conception of the supreme lawgiver who alone is capable of creating a nation, an idea that underlies the *Social Contract.*

Rousseau's eloquence rises in a crescendo as he marvels at the longevity of the Jewish people, a good fortune they owe to their first legislator:

> What a marvelous and truly unique spectacle it is to see an expatriated people having neither a place nor a land of its own for almost two thousand years, a people altered, burdened, mixed with strangers for even a longer period of time, having perhaps not a single offspring of the original race, a people spread, dispersed over the earth, enslaved, persecuted, despised by all the nations, that nevertheless preserves its customs, its laws, its manners, its love of country, and its first social bond when all ties to it appear to be broken . . . Zion destroyed has not lost its children. They are preserved, they multiply, they are scattered over the world and yet they still recognize one another. They mingle with all peoples but are never confounded with them. They no longer have leaders and yet are still a people. They no longer have a fatherland and yet remain its citizens.
>
> How great must be the power of a legal code capable of effecting such wonders, capable of braving the conquests, the dispersions, the revolutions, the centuries, capable of surviving the customs, laws, and dominion of all nations—a code of laws that, because of the trials it has already endured, gives promise of enduring everything, of overcoming the vicissitudes of human affairs, and of lasting as long as the world . . .
>
> The Jew and the Christian are in agreement in recognizing here the

finger of God, who according to the one preserves his nation and according to the other punishes it. But every man, whoever he may be, must recognize here a singular marvel, whose causes, divine or human, certainly merit the study and wonderment of the wise more than anything admirable that Greece and Rome have to offer us in political institutions and human establishments.[19]

Rousseau the eternal outsider had a deep understanding of this strange nation. Unlike Kant and so many of the French and German philosophes, he did not call for the euthanasia of Judaism as the price modern Jews would have to pay for their acceptance into European society. For Rousseau they would remain the perennial aliens. He never even raised the prospect of their eventual absorption by Christian society. When he was presented with Moses Mendelssohn's *Phaedon* (1767), an essay on the immortality of the soul, Rousseau expressed a desire to make the author's acquaintance. Nations capable of being imbued with a strong communal passion, whether Corsicans or Jews, readily won his admiration. He himself, alas, was a Moses without a chosen people.

Montesquieu's Spirit of Judaism

Though Montesquieu wrote no extended essay on Jews or Judaism, there are passing commentaries in his *Spirit of the Laws* (1748) that briefly characterized the temper of the ancient Hebrew republic and evaluated some of the articles of the Mosaic code. Montesquieu's most famous passage on the Jews is an eloquent attack on the Inquisition as a defilement of Christian principles, a speech that he puts into the mouth of a Jew addressing with sweet reasonableness the inquisitors who condemned an eighteen-year-old Jewess to be burned in an auto-da-fé at Lisbon. It is a moving piece of rhetoric, often cited in the eighteenth century as a classical plea for religious tolerance. (Outside Spain, the Inquisition found no staunch defenders in Christian Europe after 1700 until Joseph de Maistre's paradoxical apology in the next century.)

> You put us to death who believe only what you believe, because we do not believe all that you believe. We follow a religion, which you yourselves know to have been formerly dear to God. We think that God

loves it still, and you think that he loves it no more: and because you judge thus, you make those suffer by sword and fire who hold an error so pardonable as to believe that God still loves what he once loved . . .

We conjure you, not by the mighty God whom both you and we serve, but by that Christ, who, you tell us, took upon him a human form, to propose himself as an example for you to follow; we conjure you to behave toward us as he himself would behave were he upon earth. You would have us become Christians, and you will not be so yourselves.

But if you will not be Christians, be at least men; treat us as you would, if having only the weak light of justice which nature bestows, you had not a religion to conduct you, and a revelation to enlighten you.

If Heaven has had so great a love for you as to make you see the truth, you have received a singular favor; but is it for children who have received the inheritance of their father, to hate those who have not?

If you have this truth, hide it not from us by the manner in which you propose it. The characteristic of truth is its triumph over hearts and minds, and not that impotency which you confess when you would force us to receive it by tortures.[20]

There are also stray references to Jews in Montesquieu's travel notes and in his *Pensées,* comments that modern editors have grouped for publication. Ancient Judaea appeared to Montesquieu a society completely dominated by a religious esprit and, despite his superficial cultural relativism, he ranked it far below the level of a society dedicated to liberty. The laws of Deuteronomy, which required members of a family to denounce one another to the authorities for their sins, violated his concepts of freedom, privacy, and security *from* the state. Moses was a wise legislator who knew his people well, but not all of his specific ordinances won Montesquieu's approval. Montesquieu was acutely conscious of the peculiar historical relationship between Judaism and Christianity, the genetrix and its offspring who denied and hounded it. Since religious persecution was abhorrent on philosophical grounds and as a rejection of Christ, the existence of the Jews presented Montesquieu with a political and moral problem. According to his own precepts on the appropriate attitude of a religious majority to a minority that already resided within the confines of a polity, Judaism should be tolerated, but he was not favorable to the creation of a new religious pluralism.

There is no indication that Montesquieu had close relations with members of the "Portuguese nation," that small number of Bordeaux Jews, mostly exiles from Portugal, who lived not far from his chateau at Labrède and since the sixteenth century had enjoyed royal privileges of residence and commerce under the cover of a euphemism. The *Pensées,* however, includes a passing proposal that Jews be allowed to settle in an enclave somewhere between France and Spain, where they would be granted privileges of open trading similar to those of the Jews of Livorno in Italy. On his travels in northern Italy, Montesquieu visited a silk manufactory owned by a prosperous Jew, and described it in some detail as a praiseworthy example of productive industry; but he took no cognizance of poor Jews like the rag-peddlers of Metz. Most contemporary Jews were invisible to him. He pitied those still subject to the tortures of the Inquisition but evinced no particular affection for them, and he derided a German monarch who could appoint nobody better than a Jew as an administrator. Christian theology and the writings of the Christian Hebraists on Judaism held little interest for the Président de Montesquieu.

Montesquieu's significance for the history of Christian attitudes toward Judaism lies not in his direct engagement with the subject but in the application of his general theory of climate by a host of his contemporaries. No major thinker of Europe or colonial America escaped his influence. His aristocratic name reverberated through the century, stamping a Babel of ideas with at least the semblance of uniformity. In France on the eve of the Revolution, a number of works were published, reflecting Montesquieu's thought either directly or through intermediaries, that provided polemical answers to the diatribes of Voltaire and the Holbachians. Books like *L'Esprit des lois mosaïques* (Spirit of the Mosaic Laws; Bordeaux, 1785), by one Senger—his first name is unknown—is a curiosity of literature rather than a fountainhead of original ideas. With some straining it manages to enlist Montesquieu in the cause of Judaic apology. The epigraph of Senger's book, purported to have been written by a Christian, is "O people that I love, to you I address the Code of your Nation."[21] According to the author's foreword, the book is an adaptation of the *Mosaisches Recht* by Johann David Michaelis, the renowned professor of Göttingen and a pivotal figure in the contemporary German perception of Judaism. Outside Alsace and Lorraine, a French writer conversant with academic German is in itself unusual. Senger interspersed Michaelis' work with his personal fantasies and infused it with the spirit of Rousseau and Montesquieu, neither of them foreign to the German text. The result is a melange characteristic of periods of intellectual transition, when diverse currents flow into a common vat.

Traditional Christian universal history was reinterpreted by Senger in idiosyncratic terms. Instead of the catastrophic biblical account of the fall, Senger described a spirit of anomie (he used the Greek word) or disorderliness that at one time took possession of primitive mankind. Thereupon God chose a place, almost in the center of what was then the known world, that for a fixed period became the seat of a unique religion, and the Mosaic law, like a bark enveloping the trunk of a tree, protected the true religious nature of man. After an excursion on the land of Israel, the author ended with a millenarian prophecy: in the future, Israel would cease to be the mere repository of promises already fulfilled and would share with the rest of the world a salvation and a religion in which all worshipers would adore the Father in Heaven. Outlandish as it may appear, the mythopoeic frame of Senger's book enclosed serious, realistic reflections about the nature of Judaism that drew heavily from Michaelis' storehouse of Near Eastern ethnography and from Montesquieu's political philosophy.

A modern legislator needed to know the laws of all the nations, Senger cautioned, lest he imagine that his own were final and absolute, without realizing that every legislator had to accommodate laws to climate and "other considerations." It was natural enough that Montesquieu should be the inspiration in Bordeaux, where Senger's work was published, and his peculiar little book is a piquant example of the penetration of Montesquieu's esprit into a judgment of historical Judaism in the 1780s. The circumstances under which the laws of Moses had been proclaimed illustrated Senger's principle. The Mosaic was the oldest code, thus closest to the origin of things before corruptions, abuses, and the intrigues of political manipulators had set in. But the skies of the east were distant and different from those of France, and therefore the French legal system could not be a simple replica of that of the Israelites. Senger argued that the agrarian laws of the Old Testament were framed for the Hebrews exclusively—a chosen people in a chosen climate. Though the laws of the Jews could not bind present-day Frenchmen (despite the fact that European codes had preserved Mosaic elements), the political theorist had to study them, as did the theologian. Senger warned his readers against the antireligious trickery of the Voltaires and the Holbachs, who tried to identify Christianity completely with its Judaic mother, to damn Judaism as a snide way of condemning Christianity. If it were made clear that the religion of the Jews had a different esprit, the work of the great Montesquieu could be invoked to invalidate this line of argument.

Senger transformed Moses into the perfect examplar of Montesquieu's rationalist legislator, one who knew that it was wiser to leave intact much that was prevailing custom than to create an upheaval with wholly new ordinances. Rules governing divorce, polygamy, and concubinage could not suddenly be uprooted from the life of the ancient Hebrews. When an apologetic eighteenth-century thinker, still touched with religion, had to justify Mosaic laws that were not quite in harmony with Enlightenment conceptions, he tended to resort to Montesquieu: Moses was too prudent to institute at one fell swoop a complete code of laws that would violate the customs and esprit of his people.

In this apology for the spirit of Judaism, the original Mosaic law was freed from the encumbrances of the Talmudists and the medieval rabbinic commentators and valued as a magnificent creation in its own right. Though the existence of Moses was conceived as part of a providential plan and his inspiration was divine, many of the individual provisions he made were explicable in secular, human terms. Mosaic civil law, handed down at a specific historical moment, had as its primary purpose the abolition of certain noxious primitive customs, for example, the "eastern" practice of remarrying a repudiated wife after she had been wed to another and divorced. The Mosaic code was rationalist, molding the nation but not raising a revolution. The resulting constitution was not contradictory to the principles of eighteenth-century enlightened civilization, if allowance were made for the conditions of ancient life. It was not a cruel code. Until the Babylonian captivity, torture was unknown among the Jews, and in Beccaria's world eschewing the use of torture was one of the criteria for distinguishing a state of civility from barbarism. The destruction of the warlike tribes of Canaan was necessary to restore the land of the patriarchs to Israel—a divine promise as well as a once existing reality. The ancient Hebrew people had to be exclusive. With the exception of Canaanites, Moabites, and Ammonites, strangers could, after some generations, become part of Israel, but in general intermingling with other nations was discouraged. The purpose of this prohibition was to preserve the Jews from idolatry, since they were a lone monotheistic people in a sea of image worshipers. The echo of Maimonides' interpretation of many of the ritual commandments as defenses against idolatry had somehow penetrated late Enlightenment thought.

Simplicity, a modest way of life, marked the state of the ancient Israelites. Their cities were small, before the Babylonian captivity hardly distinguishable from villages. Each Israelite owned his plot of land, which was inalienable. All were poor but independent. There were no arts and sciences, nor was there any necessity for them. Savagery had been left behind and vices of urban civilization had not yet possessed the people. Senger situated the Israelites in that blessed interlude between the state of nature and the ravages of civilization in Rousseau's *Second Discourse*. He turned them into the inhabitants of popular French utopias, as though they lived in La Bétique of Fénelon's *Télémaque*. Voltaire had mocked the intellectual poverty of the ancient Hebrews; Senger made a virtue of their plain living.

Contemporary Arab mores, filtered through Michaelis' work, resembled those of Abrahamic times and afforded Senger an insight into the patriarchal epoch. The recent accounts of travel in Arabia and Syria illuminated the spirit of Mosaic law by providing analogies in practices that were presumed to have survived from pre-Muslim society. Arabs living isolated in their tents, remote from cities, had preserved a greater number of patriarchal customs than the urban civilizations of the Tigris-Euphrates, which had been mowed over by many conquerors. Senger, consciously imitating Michaelis, introduced comparative ethnology to make comprehensible the institutions of ancient Israel, without the malicious intent of Voltaire and his Parisian yardstick of civilized conduct. Senger depicted Israel as a predominantly pastoral society; to appreciate its esprit one had to look at other shepherd societies that had not changed radically through the centuries. The Israelites were destined from the beginning to be a pastoral and agricultural, not a commercial, people. As in many apologies of ancient Israel, Senger's description of the continent, laborious Hebrews refuted the common Judeophobic argument that the original seed of their national character predestined the Jews to be unscrupulous traders—all this without making explicit reference to their present status. Ancient Israel as utopia is one of the rarer late baroque images of Judaism, and it soon faded in Western Christendom, not to be revived until its brief resurrection in the mid-twentieth century.

9

❦

Catholic Vindications
of Israel

THERE WERE GREAT disparities among eighteenth-century
Catholic writings on Judaism in Western Europe, their tone and
temper depending on their country of publication and the proximity
of their dates of issue to the period of the French Revolution. The
novelty of French Catholic defenses of Israel at this time stands out
sharply against a background of more traditional attitudes in Italy and
Spain, and the bland, cautious neutrality of erudite performances in
royal academies and religious orders.

Residual Judeophobia in Italy and Spain

In Italy, the Christian bibliographical tradition of collecting rabbinics
continued, along with a capricious papal policy that alternated formal
exoneration of Jews from blood-guilt accusations with the imposition
of humiliating decrees on those residing in the Papal States. In 1800
Giovanni Bernardo de Rossi published in Parma a *Bibliotheca judaica
anti-christiana* that meticulously listed all books written by Jews
against the Christian religion. A substantial extension of Imbonati's
work of 1695, it had an apparent Judeophobic purpose. The same de
Rossi was a pioneer collector of Hebrew incunabula and the first historian of Hebrew printing in Italy. His books were bequeathed to the
ducal library in Parma, which thus became the repository of rare copies from the Soncino presses.

Within Italy there generally were no marked variations in the
underlying theological position toward Israel ancient or modern,
though practice was often arbitrary and capricious. The popes were

the official protectors of the Jews in the Papal States, a benefaction for which the protégés paid by providing the Roman populace with entertainments on set occasions. In theory, expulsions were prohibited, and the Jews of Rome remained a living reminder of the eternal punishment meted out to those whose ancestors had committed the crime of deicide. Ancient gladiatorial combats were replaced by more humane inflictions, according to Adolph Berliner, the nineteenth-century historian of the Roman ghetto. The sport-loving Romans were appeased with the spectacle of young Jews racing through the city, jeered at by onlookers—though commutation of this humiliating marathon into a money fine was sometimes arranged. In the Papal States the preaching orders enforced the attendance of Jews at formal sermons of conversion more assiduously than elsewhere. Though physical constraints were forbidden, the intricate theological question as to precisely what constituted an impermissible constraint of conscience in effecting a conversion was not resolved by the Catholic Church; the canonical rule shifted about.

In Spain, where the Inquisition was still actively functioning, seventeenth-century diatribes against Judaism were reprinted. The large number of polemics castigating Judaism that had accumulated since Martini's *Dagger of the Faith* in the thirteenth century were adapted and set in type north of the Pyrenees, bestowing upon the Spanish texts an unusual longevity. Spain without Jews remained the center of European theological Judeophobia. In the middle of the eighteenth century, 250 years after the expulsion of the Jews from the Iberian peninsula, substantial polemical volumes in the patristic tradition of treatises *Adversus Judaeos* continued to appear in Spanish with a Madrid imprint. An example was the *Centinela contra Judios puesta en la torre de la iglesia de Dios* (A Sentry against the Jews That Is Stationed in the Tower of the Church of God; 1736), a reprint and expansion of a 1673 work by Father Francisco de Torrejoncillo. For the most part it is standard fare. The Jews are and always have been liars; they are persecutors of the holy Catholic faith; those who favor the Jews will come to a bad end; the Jews crucified Christ and boasted about it, for which the clear evidence is a section entitled "Law of Kings and the Messiah" in Maimonides' commentary on the book of Judges. The Jews cannot be convinced that the messiah has already come and they still await him. That the religion of the Jews is carnal rather than spiritual—a central Judeophobic thesis—is tellingly illustrated by the portrait of their messiah:

> I ask you, what kind of person are they waiting for? Very rich. How greedy they are! He is to come with great pomp and worldly splendor. How vainglorious! With a vast entourage, greater than Solomon's. What sensualists! With lavish food and gifts. What gluttons! With an abundance of honey and butter. How avid for fancy tidbits! Very powerful in arms and war, to deliver them from the captivity they suffer. How cruel! There is no evil that the Jews do not desire, as they wait for their Messiah.[1]

The author of the *Centinela* gathered tales, purportedly derived from Jewish writings, of the messiah's activities while he delayed in coming. He was begging outside a temple in Rome; he was on Mount Caspio; he was living among the angels; he was preparing his advent in the shape of a fish by way of the Guadalquivir River. The *Centinela* chronicled the false Jewish messiahs that had appeared in Spain and Portugal over the ages. In chapter 14 the ultimate solution of the Jewish problem was predicted, a Spanish Catholic version of the end of the days. Antichrist (according to Jerome's commentary on the book of Daniel, chapter 11) would be born in Babylon of the Jewish people. He could not possibly be the offspring of old Christians, who were clear of the sins of infidelity; nor could he be of noble lineage, for the doctrine of *limpieza,* the invention of Spanish Catholicism, had it that those of good blood could entertain only exalted thoughts. By order of the Devil, Antichrist would be the son of fornication. The Jews would tout his excellence, "helping him, cooperating with him, leaving no stone unturned to get him possession of the Kingdom; proclaiming his deceptive virtues, magnifying his works, praising his prudence and wisdom, broadcasting his false miracles."[2] The lost ten tribes of Israel, crossing the Sambation River, would join their fellow Jews, who would flock to Jerusalem from Muscovy, Iberia, Russia, Galicia, Persia, Turkey. Jews living in barbarous lands would assemble great armies from their midst. Antichrist would restore the Temple in Jerusalem and reinstate the ancient rituals. A great massacre of Christians would follow. But finally Antichrist would be flung into hell body and soul. And only then would the Jews recognize their error and beg forgiveness and do penance for forty-five days. Thereafter the Church would dwell in eternal peace.

The English millenarian sectaries had a very different scenario of the coming of Antichrist and the role the Jews were destined to play in his triumph and defeat. Nor did the learned French abbés who populated the royal academies in the eighteenth century share the fanaticism of the Catholic monks of Spain.

Academic Dissertations on Jewish Antiquities

In France, the Royal Academy of Inscriptions and Belles-Lettres generally restricted its dissertations and learned articles to Greek, Roman, and Egyptian antiquities. The abbés who were members gingerly avoided serious entanglement with the touchy problems of Jewish history, which might have pulled them into dangerous biblical criticism and attracted the unwelcome attention of vigilant ecclesiastical authorities. But on a limited scale the clerical erudits allowed themselves to treat minor Jewish subjects as they did other aspects of ancient Mediterranean civilization. German universities like Göttingen, too, specialized in learned dissertations on concrete topics such as the classicist Christian Gottlob Heyne might write about Greece and Rome, but they did not shy away from similar factual subjects in Jewish history and chronology. Thus on both sides of the Rhine academies and universities produced scholarly treatises on Jewish musical instruments, aspects of government, modes of sacrifice, burial customs, or architecture, and made occasional attempts to relate Jewish names of God, customs, and marital laws to comparable practices among neighboring nations, though they remained leery of purely theological questions. Grand generalizations in the manner of Bossuet's universal history were not their province. They contented themselves with details, got lost in minutiae, and fought academic battles over wrong dates and the meaning and interpretation of words in fragments of texts. The nature of idolatry was sidestepped, as they busied themselves with identifying and classifying different types of idolatrous practices, of magic, of superstition, as if they were gathering specimens of flora and fauna.

If they could read Hebrew and Aramaic, which was infrequent, the academicians resorted to the Talmud and later rabbinic sources to give substance to their analyses of the strange customs mentioned in the Bible. It was no longer enough to say a word connoted a "magical practice"; the academicians now set their sights higher and looked for a circumstantial description of the specific actions involved. A new realism required them to check measurements, to iron out discrepancies in various biblical sources, and to have draftsmen sketch the ground plan of the Temple of Solomon or the ark of the covenant or a Solomonic palace. The same kind of activity had gone on in the seventeenth and early eighteenth centuries (Isaac Newton has left among his manuscripts a ground plan of the Temple), but while in the earlier period the numerical relationships of parts sometimes suggested a mystical or spiritual significance, in the eighteenth century the sole purpose of the drawing was to convey to the reader precisely how the structure or the object looked in an ordinary, secular sense.

Allegorical interpretation was not precluded or prohibited, but that function was left to preachers. The scholars, professors, and Benedictine monks who specialized in antiquities hungered after literal meanings; in fact, they became rather aggressive in their preference for unadorned reality and made derogatory remarks about allegorical readings. The texts they wrote were illustrated with pictures that showed Jews performing ceremonies, punctiliously observing sabbath rules, administering punishments, celebrating feasts. Mystery evaporated; Jewish ceremonials appeared merely as parallels of other, more familiar religious rites and could be regarded with objectivity. For readers of this literature, Judaism lost its terrors and the Jews became less diabolical. In some measure the demystification of Judaism prepared the way for the late-eighteenth-century acceptance of Jews as citizens.

The Jesuits of France who were engaged in putting out the *Mémoires de Trévoux,* a journal of learned articles launched to compete with the French periodicals of Hugenots like Le Clerc, Basnage, and Bayle that were appearing in Amsterdam, were not overly concerned with Judaism or with Jews. But along with other aspects of the arts and sciences, voyage literature, and history, the Jesuits included in their journal pieces on sacred philology and on the exegesis of difficult passages in the Old and New Testaments, all in the vernacular. This was in no sense the kind of Christian Hebraism that could hold a candle to the achievements of the previous century. In March 1703 Père Tournemine offered a hypothesis on the origin of differences between the Hebrew text of the Samaritan version of the Bible and the Septuagint with respect to the manner of counting the years of the patriarchs. Dom Pezron in June 1705 marked out, with pretensions to accuracy, the ancient boundaries of the promised land. Jean Bouhier and Bernard de Montfaucon wrote letters in 1712 for and against the assumption that the hermits known as the Therapeutes in Philo were Christians. Père Jean Hardouin was explicating the meaning of the Urim and Thummim in 1729. In April 1742 there appeared an anonymous dissertation on the first day of the world. The issue of May 1754 included a letter from Père Olivier on the usefulness of Hebrew for belles-lettres. Protestant histories of the ancient Jews by Prideaux, Leidekker, Metzger, Reeland, Basnage, and others were regularly reviewed critically, though without excessive sectarian vituperation. There were brief reports on Jews living in Paris and on Jewish resistance to conversion, but this material was communicated incidentally in the brief summaries of newly published books prepared for those too lazy to read the originals. On the whole, the *Mémoires de Trévoux* was a feeble voice. It survived the catastrophe of the expulsion of the Jesuits in 1762 and a series of name changes, until its extinction twenty years later.

In Dutch, German, Swiss, and Scandinavian universities, writers of treatises continued to approach their subjects in the neutral spirit of academic exercises, with no more passion than most late humanists brought to the description of social or religious practices in the Graeco-Roman world—barring a challenge of their assertions by some other scholar, in which event the barbs of academic malevolence were let fly. For example, in 1675 Theodor Dassov published in Wittenberg a *Diatribe, qua Judaeorum de resurrectione mortuorum sententia,* a learned discussion on the belief of the Jews in the resurrection of the dead. In 1713 Johann Conrad Hottinger of Zurich composed what he called a *Commentarius philologicus de decimis judaeorum,* whose full title, translated into English, would read: *The Law of Tithes; a Philological Commentary on the Tithes of the Jews. Complete in ten exercises. In which all things pertaining to the elucidation of this material are explained both from Holy Scriptures and from the very monuments of the ancient Jews, and various other subjects of sacred antiquity are incidentally treated.* Scholarly method had not fundamentally changed. The subject matter is first carefully defined and then neatly divided into parts. Hottinger wrote an introduction justifying his subject as casting light on the life and times of Christ—an idea that Lightfoot in the previous century had exploited with more profuse detail; but the apology is not an integral part of Hottinger's performance, which preserves a "scientific" form. Evidence is provided by Hebrew and Aramaic quotations from the talmudic or later rabbinic corpus, which are then translated into Latin. Where a Mishna or a portion of the Gemara or a section from Maimonides had already been rendered into Latin by one of the known Christian Hebraists (and Hottinger drew up an impressive chart of the *Ordines* of the Mishna and the Gemara sections that had been published in Latin), Hottinger adopted the existing translation. Dassov appears to have preferred his own versions.

Hottinger's apology for his interest in Hebraic studies is reminiscent of the justifications of the previous age:

> And whoever will rightly explain either the Mosaic law and the rest of the books of the Old Testament or very many places of the New without having consulted Jewish rituals, he will truly be for me the Great Apollo. Indeed, are not all the laws handed down about the worship of the Levites, or concerning the sacred places, or the sacred persons, or sacred things, or sacred times, typical and peculiar to Christians, cherished even by the more ancient Jews, to whom the whole mystery of salvation was revealed, though imperfectly? Whence it clearly proves Jesus, yesterday, today, and for eternity to have been, to be, and in the future to be, forever the same. Moreover, in what manner can the true relationship of antitype to type be shown, unless the literal meaning of the type is first brought to light? And in truth, how is that understood except from the rites of the Jews?[3]

Throughout the eighteenth century academic exercises such as Dassov's and Hottinger's continued to be produced, though at a diminished rate, as the great compilers took over and popular histories of the Jews won a wider and less-educated reading public.

The Biblical Encyclopedism of Dom Augustin Calmet

France was the seat of one of the last great Christian entrepreneurs of biblical exegesis and Jewish history, the Benedictine abbot of Saint-

Léopold de Nancy, Augustin Calmet (1672–1757), whose voluminous writings were distinguished by the new matter-of-factness character-istic of the philosophes, without their irreligion. Dom Calmet was by far the outstanding French Catholic scholar of Jewish antiquities who worked within the Church establishment. He left behind almost a hundred volumes, all pervaded by the same commonsense tone. Among them were: *Commentaire littéral sur tous les livres de l'Ancien et du Nouveau Testament* (Paris, 1724–1726, 8 vols. in 9); *Histoire ec-clésiastique et civile de la Lorraine* (Nancy, 1728, 4 vols.); essays en-titled *Dissertations qui peuvent servir de prolégomènes à l'Écriture Sainte* (1720, 3 vols.); *Trésor d'antiquités sacrées et profanes* (Amster-dam, 1722, 13 vols.); *Histoire sainte de l'Ancien et du Nouveau Testa-ment et des Juifs* (Paris, 1719, 2 vols.); *Histoire universelle sacrée et profane* (Strasbourg, 1735–1771, 17 vols.). French had driven out Latin, the traditional language of Christian Hebraism.

"We live in a century that one could call the century of diction-aries," began Dom Calmet in dedicating to the prince of Lorraine the magnificently printed and illustrated *Dictionnaire historique, critique, chronologique, géographique, et littéral de la Bible,* published in 1722 in two folio volumes. In the frontispiece, a figure lurks in the shadows, while another is gloriously illuminated by the Holy Spirit. A quotation from John 1:17 epitomizes the orthodox Catholic relationship be-tween the two dispensations: "The law was given by Moses, but grace and truth came by Jesus Christ." Since there were dictionaries of lan-guage, arts, sciences, history, geography, mathematics, poetry, juris-prudence, medicine, morality, preaching, why not a dictionary of the Bible? Calmet thus set knowledge of the Scriptures squarely by the side of other forms of information. It was time that data about Jewish antiquities, which had accumulated since the ancient endeavors of Philo, Origen, Eusebius, and Jerome, were assembled in a compen-dium that embraced sacred history, criticism, geography, chronology, the laws, ceremonies, and feasts of the Hebrews. The Bible would be made more comprehensible, with proper names identified by their French equivalents. Moreover, as in any learned work, a comprehen-sive bibliography of the authors who had written on the Scriptures was included. Biblical knowledge in all its detail would now be gath-ered up and put on display. It sounds as if the spirit that later infused Diderot's *Encyclopédie* had already penetrated the Benedictine mon-astery.

As it turns out, Calmet's dictionary articles are often far superior to many of the pieces on Jewish antiquities later written by the encyclopedists. But, at the same time, it is immediately apparent to anyone even casually acquainted with the seventeenth-century giants of Christian Hebraism—Selden, the Buxtorfs, Pococke, Lightfoot—that familiarity with Hebraic sources had suffered a sharp decline, though the standard commentators such as Rashi and Abraham Ibn Ezra are mentioned, and talmudic and later rabbinic writings are quoted when available in Latin. Spinoza's name appears, without the title of his work—a rare intrusion of the unmentionable disbeliever. The alphabetical arrangement of Calmet's dictionary allows readers to find quickly what they may be seeking, but the grandeur attained by the Hebraists of the previous century, for all their prolixity and digressiveness, is gone. Christian Hebraism had fallen on evil days. The covers of the books are rich with gold leaf and intricate decorations, but their content, though well written, is platitudinous. Hebrew had definitively ceased to hold even a modest place in the traditional triumvirate of Latin, Greek, and Hebraic studies. The vernacular was invading all fields of Christian learning, and Hebrew was the first citadel to fall.

Appended to Calmet's dictionary is a long bibliography that comprises writings and commentaries about all the books of the Old and New Testaments and the Apocrypha; it is the most complete assemblage of secondary works since Imbonati and Wolf. The bibliography was prepared primarily for Frenchmen, and includes both Catholic and Protestant writers in the principal Western European languages; Jewish writers are scant. A list of printed bibles in many languages is impressive; it is accompanied by a reflection that in general the Hebrew bibles printed by the Jews are more accurate but are surpassed in beauty by those of the Christians, a surprising criterion for the judgment of a sacred work. In addition to the commentaries on books of the Old and New Testaments, there are listed grammars, dictionaries, concordances, introductions to the study of Scriptures, books on the manner of interpreting Scriptures, and general works on Jewish antiquities. Calmet was not infallible, and even a novice can detect more than an occasional error. The great mass of material in the bibliography is rendered more tractable by its division into special topics such as the messiah, circumcision, the chronology of the Jews, precious stones, trees and plants named in the Bible, the music and musical instruments of the Hebrews. The number of books enumerated is sufficient to keep an army of doctoral candidates in Judaica busy for decades; but one comes away from the perusal of Calmet's monumental work with the feeling that Christian Hebraism had gained in the kind of ornamentation that might attract amateurs of curiosities, but not in scholarly depth.

The *Dictionnaire* boasts a series of detailed maps of the ancient world after the dispersion of Babel: a map of the earthly paradise, of the wandering of the Israelites in the desert, of the promised land at the time of Joshua, of the division of Canaan according to the vision of Ezekiel, of the places and lands where the Apostles preached. There are also illustrations of sacred events: a drawing of the nativity in the Bethlehem manger; reconstructions of the sacrificial altar in the Temple, with exact measurements; pictures of tumultuous consecrations of high places to idolatrous cults. Sites and monuments are featured: an eighteenth-century view of Jaffa; an engraving of a tomb of the Maccabees in Roman-Egyptian style, adorned by personages in oriental dress; a detailed plan of ancient Jerusalem; a two-page spread on the consecration of the republic of the Hebrews, with benedictions and maledictions; the cave of Engeddi where David hid from Saul, in a wild romantic setting. While in his Jewish histories the Huguenot Basnage presented the ancient Jews as highly urbanized, in Calmet's work stark landscapes are the background for sacred history.

Calmet warned potential readers that serious students of Jewish antiquities needed to know Hebrew, Greek, and Latin, as well as something of Aramaic, Syriac, and Arabic. But he did not scorn the less dedicated and less educated. Those who knew only French had at their disposal passable translators and commentators. They were quite all right for one who aspired to a modest level of edification— though Calmet could not suppress a measure of condescension toward them. He well understood that his own multivolume commentary on the books of the Old and New Testaments could have only a limited audience, and many readers were therefore directed to his lighter collected essays. Calmet had a keen interest in popularizing, in making available his learning to a large number of people; he was not writing only for closeted Benedictines. He called his dictionary a *bibliothèque des pauvres*. Its purpose was to provide "clear and distinct ideas of the terms and the things mentioned"—shades of Descartes.[4] Calmet aimed to be succinct; to avoid confusion; to introduce uniform standards for biblical geography, chronology, theology, and philosophy; to present convincing proofs of every statement. To sense how deeply the Enlightenment penetrated French religious culture, one has only to examine Calmet. His method was in the spirit of the age, detailed and down to earth. He concentrated on history, criticism, locating events exactly in time and space.

Calmet's treatment of David is a good example of the method he followed and of the new spirit of French Catholic biblical scholarship that informed his work. The leap from the Benedictine to the scoffing, debunking Voltaire is not quite so precipitous as might at first be imagined. Calmet sets the year of David's birth as 2919 after the world's creation. He then approaches David's murder of Uriah as if it were a contemporary scandal in Paris, an affair involving a royal mistress. Calmet's economy of language is not to be disdained:

> One day after rising from his bed after noon, while walking about on his terrace, he saw a woman who was bathing in the bath of her house. It was Bathsheba, the wife of Uriah the Hittite, who was then serving in Joab's army on the other side of the Jordan. David summoned this woman, slept with her, and sent her away. A few days later, she had David informed that she had conceived. Immediately David, to hide his crime and to protect Bathsheba's honor, had Uriah the Hittite come back to Jerusalem from his camp with the intention of getting him to pass the night in his house with his wife. But Uriah not having done so, David sent him back to camp with letters written to Joab, in which he ordered him to so arrange things that Uriah would be put to death by the Ammonites. Joab executed these orders, and in an assault against a city, Uriah, abandoned by the other soldiers, perished by the sword of the Ammonites. As soon as David was informed, he married Bathsheba and had her come to his house. This deed displeased God. The whole of Israel was scandalized by it, and foreigners took the occasion to curse the name of God.[5]

The same incident provoked in Bayle, Peter Annet, Voltaire, and Holbach unrestrained sneering at David, the well-beloved of God. But Calmet limited himself to recounting the facts as set forth in the Bible and exercising his critical intelligence on legends that had grown up around them. Reporting a story from the medieval Jewish traveler Benjamin of Tudela that, when David's tomb was opened about 1150 A.D., the workers found riches of gold and silver but were driven away by a voice, he commented drily: "This smells like a fable and it is pointless to refute it."[6] Calmet died before the complete triumph of the philosophes in France, and he had no inkling of the use to which his work would be put by Voltaire, who quoted him profusely but with his own rhetorical twist.

A decade after Calmet's death, amid the triumphs of the philosophes, a strong counterattack against their view of Judaism was launched by French Catholic clerics who had belatedly become aware of the grave implications for Christianity in the denigration of ancient Israel. In response to the onslaught of the philosophes, the Abbés Guénée and Bergier and Grégoire came forth as the defenders of Judaism against Voltaire and his cohorts. By the time the clerics entered the fray, the deists and the Holbachians were occupying the field. But the vindicators of Israel within the Catholic Church, though their influence may have been transitory, were effective in disengaging a part of French prerevolutionary opinion from the radical Judeophobes. The altered theological view of Judaism among some members of the French Catholic hierarchy helped to bring about a climate that made possible the civil legislation of the revolutionary assemblies. Those who believe that metamorphoses in religious outlook are of direct significance in social and political life will not spurn the evidence of intellectual efforts that admittedly were aimed only at a restricted audience. Once the grant of equal civil rights was on the floor of the revolutionary assemblies, official Catholicism, in contrast with Catholic friends of the Jews, assumed a hostile attitude toward the legislation. But in the 1780s orthodox Catholics could be counted among the apologists of Judaism, taking a stance that at first sight appears anomalous.

In the latter part of the eighteenth century, an idealization of Israel took shape in some official French religious circles—as distinguished from sports like Senger—that discovered in Judaism an esprit wholly contrary to that propagated by Voltaire and the Holbachians. The idealizing tone of the seventeenth-century Abbé Fleury's *Moeurs des Israélites* (Customs of the Israelites) was sounded again in a defense of ancient Israel among French clerics who came from disparate regions and had no connection with one another. Their apology of Judaism drew support from improbable sources: Louis XVI appointed a commission to review the status of the Jews; the confessor of Monsieur, the King's brother, drafted a treatise denouncing the philosophes' calumnies against ancient Israel; and one of the wayward nobles of France, the Count de Mirabeau, published a eulogy of the outstanding Jewish philosopher in the German world, the Berlin rabbi Moses Mendelssohn.

A paradoxical justification of ancient and modern Israel was thus fashioned in the very bosom of the French Catholic Church on all levels of the hierarchy, from the abbot of a great monastery down to the solitary parish priest. In the contest between the established church of France and the philosophes of various persuasions who assailed it on all sides, French clerics emerged as the most constant defenders of the Jews on the eve of the Revolution. Theirs was a dramatic reversal of traditional Catholic positions, though its seeds can be found in Fleury, in Pascal, and even in Bossuet.

Abbé Guénée, Secretary of the Jews

In 1769, when Voltaire was reigning as the uncrowned king of the epoch, a collection entitled *Lettres de quelques juifs portugais et allemands* (in later editions *polonais* were added), addressed to Voltaire, appeared in Paris. The German and Polish letters, which differed both in rhetoric and content from the Portuguese ones, were a flagrant affront to the acknowledged literary giant on the part of the most despised social group in France. The letters analyzed book by book and point by point whatever Voltaire had written on the Jews of antiquity. Though on rare occasions a rabbinic source was cited in the letters, they were based overwhelmingly on an explication of the Old Testament in the Vulgate and the French versions, supplemented by references to Josephus and Philo—Jewish writers long accepted by Christians—and data from the Greek and Latin corpus. They drew further support from memoirs of contemporary academies such as the Göttingen Royal Society and from the writings of the German scholar Michaelis.

In his attacks on the Jews, Voltaire had concentrated on the five books of Moses and the historical portions of the Old Testament, and his method was to reveal contradictions between one passage of the

Bible and another. The Jewish letters surpassed him at his own game; they were a stark confrontation of biblical excerpts presented by Voltaire, along with his observations, on the same page with the Old Testament originals. The juxtaposition revealed his flagrant errors in simple textual reading and his numerous contradictions, baseless interpretations, and false accusations.

The German and Polish collection was in fact the work of an obscure abbé named Antoine Guénée, who had previously specialized in rendering into French refutations of deism by English clergymen. When word got around that he was the author of the letters, he was rewarded with a tutorship in the royal household. During the French Revolution he retired to the country, where he quietly survived the turmoil. Only in later editions of Guénée's reply to Voltaire was a pamphlet by the Portuguese Jew Isaac de Pinto prefixed to the fictitious letters. The entire work went through five editions by 1781 and was reprinted at intervals throughout the Napoleonic period and the restoration; in the nineteenth century, it was published in translation by American fundamentalists continuing the holy war against Voltaire's perversion of Scripture.

Abbé Guénée stressed a commonsense reading of the Bible—cabbalists were disavowed. When driven to make an allegorical interpretation of a verse that Voltaire had ridiculed by maliciously taking every word literally, Guénée explained that allegory in his usage was simply a synonym for a poetic and imagistic manner of speaking. Voltaire had regularly indulged in drawing extravagant inferences, titillating his readers with sexual fantasies, and concluding, from the stern prohibitions against them, that homosexuality and sodomy had been rife among the Hebrews. Guénée attacked this kind of perverse reasoning: penitential guides in the Christian world included bestiality among the deadly sins, but did that constitute proof that it was widespread in Christendom? The sin was mentioned in the Bible because Moses was leading the Israelites into a land inhabited by pagans who practiced the abomination, and he was warning his people against its contagion. The admonitions against many other crimes for which dire punishments were set forth in Leviticus and Deuteronomy had the same justification. Voltaire relished the prohibitions as witness to the inherent depravity of the people of Israel. Following the Maimonidean tradition (which he knew from John Spencer's book),

Guénée held that almost all the ceremonial and ritualistic commandments of Judaism were instituted to keep the people of Israel uncon-
taminated by the pagan idolaters. Many of the dietary regulations
were rejections of modes of idolatrous sacrifice. Far from being nonsensical, the restrictions served a rational end: to insulate the Israelites from pernicious foreign influences.

The virtues of the Mosaic code were all the more striking when it
was set alongside the laws of any other nation of antiquity: "There are
in Mosaic legislation many laws in favor of the poor and insistent
exhortations to succor all those in need. Other systems offer nothing
comparable. When one recalls all these exhortations and these laws,
where the humanity of the Legislator is sensed very keenly, can one
without anguish see this great man Moses and all his legislation
charged with ferocity and barbarism by a celebrated writer who calls
himself impartial?" [7] With evident irony, Guénée, spokesman for the
Jews, took after Voltaire, calumniator of the innocent: "It is at least a
satisfaction for us to see that in the bosom of an *ignorant* and *crude*
people [Voltaire's phrase], there were anticipated so many centuries
ago the legal innovations of the most brilliant and far-seeing genius of
this our own philosophical century." [8] The Mosaic code was turned
into a perfect synthesis of a few Christian doctrines—without the theology of Christ—and the gentle virtues of the Enlightenment.

The pretense that the Abbé Guénée's letters were composed by
German and Polish Jews was sustained by a tone of deference whenever Christianity was mentioned. The letters did not at all harmonize
with a Portuguese Jewish apology that was attached to them. This had
initially been published in Amsterdam by Isaac de Pinto in 1762 as
Apologie pour la nation juive, and its inclusion with the letters violated
a biblical injunction against the harnessing of an ox with an ass. A
Portuguese Jew named Pereire, who acted as Paris agent of the Bordeaux Jews and was respected by the philosophes for his novel
method of teaching deaf mutes, was dismayed by Voltaire's diatribes
because of the authority his illustrious name bestowed on prejudices
and calumnies "capable of crushing this nation." [9] It was Pereire who
had encouraged the original publication of de Pinto's apology, an ir-
ritating document that reeks of intra-Jewish communal prejudice.

The Sephardic Jew de Pinto, who had access to the court of Ver-

sailles and used his influence to defend the exclusiveness of traditional privileges of Bordeaux Portuguese Jews from the aspirations of
Avignon and Metz Jews seeking similar rights, tried to answer the
Voltairean strictures. His primary thesis is that Voltaire failed to distinguish between the aristocratic, cultivated Portuguese Jews and the
crude German and Polish immigrants:

> A Jew of London resembles a Jew of Constantinople as little as the
> latter does a mandarin of China. A Portuguese Jew of Bordeaux and a
> German Jew of Metz appear to be absolutely different kinds of crea-
> tures. It is not possible to speak of Jewish manners in general without
> entering into greater detail and making specific differentiations. The
> Jew is a chameleon, who everywhere assumes the character of the dif-
> ferent climates he inhabits, of the different peoples he frequents, and
> of the different forms of government under which he lives.[10]

Voltaire ought to have known that Portuguese and Spanish Jews did
not mix by marriage or in any other way with the Jews of other nations. Their rites were different, they did not wear beards, they did
not dress like other Jews; indeed, Portuguese Jews were more elegant
in their habit than almost any other people. If a Portuguese should
marry a German Jewess, he would be excluded from the synagogue
and denied burial among his brethren. With studied amazement, de
Pinto, who considered himself one of Europe's most ardent admirers
of Voltaire, asked how this sworn enemy of prejudice and false denunciation could abandon reason to the point of writing that Jews were
"an ignorant and barbarous people, which has long united the most
unworthy avarice to the most detestable superstition and the most
horrible hatred for all the peoples who tolerate and enrich them."[11]
Voltaire owed amends to Jews, to truth, to his century, to posterity.
"Why does he not use his talents to destroy a prejudice that is a dis-
honor to humanity?"[12]

Isaac de Pinto's letter to Voltaire oscillates between groveling adoration of the god of philosophy and accusations of calumny. For a
moment he appeared to convince Voltaire that he had been unjust in
his portrayal of Sephardic Jews; in a letter to de Pinto Voltaire offered
to publish a retraction, a promise that was never fulfilled. Instead he
covered reams of paper defending his quirky biblical exegesis against

the meticulous criticism of Guénée, whom he contemptuously called the "secretary of the Jews." Guénée's work had ruffled him. Like many abrasive critics, Voltaire was sensitive to attack on his own writings.

Abbé Bergier: Restoring the Judaic Pillars of Christianity

In 1788–1790 there appeared the three-volume theology section of the *Encyclopédie méthodique,* under the direction of the Abbé Nicolas Sylvestre Bergier, canon of the Eglise de Paris and confessor of the King's brother. This wholesale revision of the articles on theological subjects in Diderot's *Encyclopédie* increased their number by a quarter, condensed some, eliminated an excessive emphasis on Arian doctrines, and replaced Greek and Hebrew words with French equivalents. Bergier's was a combative presentation at war with Socinians, deists, Protestants, and other heretics. The abbé saw himself as revitalizing the polemical tradition of the Church Fathers. A major theme running through the argument was that all Protestant sects, deliberately or not, had favored the enemies of Christianity. The work turned into a debate with the writings of the Lutherans Mosheim and Brucker, the Calvinists Beausobre, Basnage, Le Clerc, and Barbeyrac, and the Anglicans Chillingworth and Bingham. The ecclesiastical histories of the Catholics Fleury, Cave, Dupin, Tillemont, and Ceillier were pitted against those of the noted Protestant historians, and the palm of victory was in every case awarded to the Catholics.

One of Bergier's primary objects was to vindicate the venerable characters of the Old Testament vilified by unbelievers. The very close of the *ancien régime* thus witnessed the spectacle of an official scholar of the Catholic Church rehabilitating the Jewish biblical figures whom Voltaire and Holbach had maligned, and doing so in an encyclopedia that derived from Diderot and aimed to bestow on his work a more methodical format. Bergier felt that many articles in the original *Encyclopédie* were superfluous since their contents were covered in Calmet's dictionary of the Bible, and he did not intend to duplicate the biblical criticism of the English polyglot Bible or the prefaces of the seventeen-volume Avignon Bible. His treatment of Jewish ceremonies, sects, and the later rabbis is not very well informed; it does not even reach the level of the popularizers among the Christian Hebraists of the previous century, and it is not much of an improvement on the Diderot articles. But its tone is very different. Bergier steps forward as a Catholic champion of Judaism, doing battle against the philosophical infidels.

According to the *Encyclopédie méthodique,* Judaism was a religion given to the Jews by God through the ministry of Moses in the year 2513 of the Creation. Its divine sanction lasted about fifteen hundred years, until the destruction of Jerusalem. Ancient Judaism is lavishly praised: "All the Laws, all the practices of Judaism, tended to inculcate great truths."[13] The providence of God, the Jews believed, extended to all peoples, but they also rightly knew that God had chosen them, that he had a preference. Immortality of the soul and rewards and punishments in the next world were doctrines of Judaism from its inception. This was a refutation of Bishop Warburton's *Divine Legation of Moses,* frequently cited by the philosophes, and simultaneously ran counter to a host of Catholic interpretations that stressed Judaism's corporeal conception of rewards in this world. As for the Hebrew idea of God, Bergier took the same phrases in Tacitus and Dion Cassius that the philosophes had quoted as evidence of ancient contempt for the Jews, and used them to demonstrate the purity of Jewish belief in a supreme, eternal, invisible God. The philosophes lied when they maintained that the Jews had borrowed their conception of immortality from the Chaldeans and the Persians. Messianism, too, was an ancient belief in Israel, not a modern invention. On every major point of the philosophes' attack on ancient Israel, Bergier turned the argument around, denying the charges of the calumniators.

Mosaic law abridged in the Ten Commandments was natural law eternalized in writing. Though he gives little evidence of acquaintance with the works of Maimonides, Bergier accepted the Maimonidean idea that the ceremonial laws in the Mosaic code were aimed at protecting the Hebrews from idolatrous practices and at safeguarding the health of the people. Deists had claimed that the profusion of rituals and ceremonies among Jews was an impediment to the observance of the natural law and to the expression of sympathy for fellow humans. Bergier cited the golden rule in Leviticus 19:17 to demonstrate the contrary. The Remonstrant Jean Le Clerc, repelled by the harshness of many Judaic laws, in the Prolegomenon to his *Ecclesiastical History* had explained the multiplicity of restrictions as a necessary technique for keeping under restraint this hard, rough, intractable people, and had rejected the hyperbolic idealization of the Mosaic law; Bergier restored the image of its perfect role in preserving the Jews from the worst of crimes, idolatry. In his apology Bergier had recourse to Montesquieu's theory of climate:

> From whatever angle one examines the Jewish moral law, it turns out to be pure, wise, above reproach, appropriate in every respect to the time, place, genius of the people for whom it was destined, more perfect than that of the philosopher legislators . . . The unbelievers who censured and calumniated this morality and the laws of Moses understood neither its sense nor its spirit; they paid no attention either to the century, or the climate, or the national character, or the general customs prevailing among ancient peoples.[14]

It would seem that Michaelis, the theologian of Göttingen, had crossed the Rhine.

Bergier presented a series of explanations for the minutiae of Jewish ceremonial laws that derived from the Christian Hebraists of the previous century, who in turn had them from rabbinic literature—but Bergier was a long way from the sources. He argued that many of the ceremonial laws were introduced by Moses because the Jews had grown accustomed to pomp and ceremony in Egypt. By forcing them to heed rules of conduct, he made their manners gentler. The laws had to be detailed to prevent the adoption of Egyptian and Canaanite practices for which the Jews had a penchant. Some ceremonials were devised to commemorate the glorious acts of God. Finally, regulations were promulgated in order to promote cleanliness and health—an obvious new-fangled intrusion of the eighteenth-century doctrine of utility into religious debate. Tacitus had described the Jews of antiquity as robust; the same areas of Palestine and Egypt, no longer inhabited by the Jews, were now pestilential, proof positive of the medical soundness of the laws enforced by the ancient Israelites. Bergier, who had imbibed deep draughts of Fleury's pastoral utopia, saw even polygamy and divorce as tolerable institutions among a simple, uncorrupted people. Christian Hebraists of the seventeenth century had generally praised the original Mosaic code and reserved their criticism for the excessive multiplication of talmudic laws and interpretations. Bergier made a similar distinction: his apology for ancient

Judaism was accompanied by a critique of contemporary Judaism, which he contended had become so engrossed in ceremonial observances and petty regulations that it considered unswerving obedience to these rules superior to moral virtues.

The Socinians, who totally denied the meaningfulness of the Old Testament for contemporary religion, regarded Judaism as supererogatory after the coming of Christ. For Bergier, the books of prophecy and the Jewish witness were still indispensable to Christianity. Nor would he accept the fashionable notion that the Jews borrowed their ideas from their pagan neighbors. Like many of his brethren, he had come to realize that any attack on ancient Judaism held grave dangers for Christianity. Hence the irony that, at the end of the eighteenth century, orthodox Catholics in the highest places in the Church were the defenders of Judaism against Socinians, Remonstrants, deists, and unbelievers. On the eve of the French Revolution, the polemics led to a kind of transvestism between philosophes and clerical apologists. While Voltaire attacked the Jews for barbarities, Abbé Bergier extolled the purity of the original Jewish religion. Bergier's systematic refutation of the principal accusations against ancient Israel enjoyed only a brief influence, however; on the morrow of the Revolution, the Catholic Church returned to a more traditional position of hostility with the works of de Bonald and de Maistre, who led the romantic reaction in France.

The second volume of theology in the *Encyclopédie méthodique* was published in 1789, an inauspicious year for such literature. Its article "Juifs" was peppered with the intellectual paradoxes of the moment. The carefully ordered piece, which covered the spectrum of social-theological problems raised by Judaism among Christians, was divided into seven topics: the origin of the Jews, their manners, their propensities, the hatred other nations had borne them, the choice God made of them, their present state, their future conversion. In tone and substance it was a reasoned polemical answer to the position generally assumed by the philosophes in their treatment of Israel. In Bergier's vindication of the spirit of ancient Judaism against the animadversions piled up by the philosophes for half a century, direct mention of the names of anticlerical extremists was avoided, but the objects of the counterattack would have been patent to all literary men—though an avid readership for Bergier's writings on theology seems unlikely. If medieval formulas were still occasionally repeated by Bergier, the weight of his argument was in the spirit of the judeophile Mirabeau and against the phobic temper of the French deists. For the origins of the Jewish people, for example, Bergier drew upon a memoir in the fourteenth volume of the *Histoire de l'Académie des Inscriptions* that is a sharp refutation of Manetho and Apion.

The philosophes had perpetuated the classical image of the ancient Jews as a miserable tribe of brigands either neglected by the civilized nations of antiquity or loathed by them. Bergier granted that, before the translation of the Septuagint, the sacred books of the Jews were unknown in the Greek world; but this ignorance of the people and their ways, still reflected in the writings of Diodorus Siculus and Tacitus, created a false impression. By that time the Jews had already existed for thirteen hundred years, and the life of their republic was drawing to an end. It was as preposterous to rely on what the late Roman historians reported about Jewish origins as it would be to consult the first European travelers and merchants to China about Chinese antiquities. For both ancient Jews and ancient Chinese, their own historians were the only authentic sources.

Why God chose as his own this particular people, who were by nature refractory, rebellious, and ungrateful, had both theological and commonsense reasons. It was proof that when God elected to be good to men, his act was one of pure benevolence. If men were treated as they deserved, God would have to exterminate all of them. Moreover, there was no objective evidence that at the time of Moses there was any nation better than the Jews. In general there had been a tendency to exaggerate their crimes, atrocities, and moral depravity. The radical philosophes had dwelt on the violence and cruelty of the conquest of Canaan; but even if the Hebrews had not been given a divine promise of support, they had a natural justification for the conquest, since they were without means of subsistence and had no land of their own to cultivate. Population pressure and other utilitarian reasons were introduced to explain sacred history, a hazardous precedent. In any event, the Canaanites had no greater right to the land than did the Hebrews. Bergier conceded that this did not make the wars of Israel just in terms of seventeenth-century legal theory, but it modified the image of the Hebrews as exceptionally violent and barbaric.

The misfortunes of the Jews were always the consequence of a breach of their faith in God; he had never been wanting in fulfilling his promises to them. But the Jews were not the aggressors in their wars against the Assyrians, the successors of Alexander, or the Romans. Even the revolts of the Jews were a response to Roman tyranny. Bergier aimed his shafts directly at Voltaire: "Is it true that this people was ignorant, barbarous, stupid, without industry, without any knowledge of letters, of arts, and of commerce as one usually affects to depict them?" Drawing on the books of the Bible, he demolished this caricature and reverted to a common seventeenth-century view, exemplified by Isaac Newton, that the Jews were versed in all arts and sciences. "What is said in *Exodus* of the structure of the Tabernacle, in the *Books of Kings* of the magnificence of the Temple of Solomon, the plan of it drawn in *Ezekiel;* the portrait of the good woman and of her works in *Proverbs . . .* demonstrate that the Jews knew the arts and never neglected their practice." [15]

Rousseau had left his mark on Abbé Bergier's perception of ancient Judaism. True, the Jews had never erected pyramids like the Egyptians, nor did they excel in sciences and pictorial arts like the Greeks or in military arts like the Romans. But what did they lose thereby? It was not buildings or the arts of luxury or military discipline or conquests that rendered a people happy, but peace, agriculture, abundance, reason, virtue. (Though the Church was fighting Voltaire and the Holbachians, many of the gentler ideals of the Enlightenment found a place in prerevolutionary ecclesiastical thinking.) Above all, temporal rewards had nothing to do with the grace of salvation. It might even be that worldly success was an obstacle to beatitude. God did not choose the Egyptians, Greeks, Phoenicians, or Romans as his people, but the insignificant Hebrews.

Bergier stuck to his thesis that the disdain for Jews exhibited by the ancients became widespread only when they were dispersed and their religion was contaminated, when their commonwealth had lost its pristine character. In the turbulent times after the coming of Christ, the obduracy of the Jews contributed to this aversion. That the Jews reciprocated the hatred of the pagan nations was comprehensible enough after the persecutions they suffered, but hostility was ingrained neither in their essential esprit (in Montesquieu's sense) nor in their original state of mind. "To confound the last centuries of their history with the first, modern manners with the ancient ones, the old age of a people with its finest years, as the disbelievers do, is to confuse everything and to be irrational beneath a false show of erudition."[16]

The Jews were fanatical, intolerant, and unsociable—these were the major charges of the philosophes, for whom tolerance, sociability, and the absence of zealotry were the prime virtues of civilization. But the intolerance of the Jews, Bergier argued in his apology, was directed principally against idolatry and the abominations that accompanied it: prostitution, human sacrifice, divination, magic. Bergier saw no benefit to mankind in countenancing such practices. Moreover, the Jews were intolerant only within their own boundaries and never presumed to extirpate idolatry among their neighbors. Other nations failed to exercise similar restraint as they burned one another's sanctuaries. The Jews never forced conversion on anyone; why should they not be allowed to be exclusive in their own territory? As for their xenophobia, were not most peoples hostile toward one another—the English and the French, for example?

Bergier confronted one last problem, the conclusion of every Christian theological treatment of the Jews: what of their destiny at the end of the days? Bergier's response was not original and seems to be little more than a way of bringing his treatise to a close. It was a widespread belief among Dutch and English Protestant commentators that virtually all the Jews would be converted before the final day of judgment. This was the position taken by Increase Mather, for example. Bergier's view of the future salvation of the Jews was more restricted. In Paul's epistle to the Romans (11:26) the hope expressed was based on a prophecy of Isaiah (59:20), but it was limited to those Jews who would give up their false ways. True, God never repented of his gifts, nor of his original choice of Israel, but those gifts could be made useless by infidelity. In Bergier's interpretation, Paul envisaged not a mass conversion of all Jews, but a gradual conversion. Bergier knew of only three Church Fathers who held fast to the belief in a total conversion of the Jews. He was dubious that, upon the coming of the messiah, the Jews in America would leave their possessions and go to the promised land.

Judaism as a religion and Jews as a people were either idealized or rendered contemptible by the French Enlightenment. Few commentators allowed for a middle ground or a nuanced portrait. Polarized impressions generated stereotypes. A similar tendency can be discerned in the eighteenth-century treatment of the Chinese and the American Indians; but for the black or white portrayal of the Jews there was always a long tradition to latch onto, and the sources and motivating forces of a pejorative or adulatory work can readily be identified. Bergier's disquisition on ancient Judaism was the most detailed, if often long-winded, defense of the religion that the radical French Enlightenment had singled out as its chief target. But there were others, notably that of Abbé Grégoire.

Abbé Grégoire on the Regeneration of the Jews

On August 23, 1788, the Royal Society of Sciences and Arts of Metz awarded a prize to Henri Grégoire, a curate of the local diocese, for his *Essai sur la régénération physique, morale et politique des Juifs.* The victory had been hard to come by; on the first go-round in the competition—to write on the question "Are there ways to render the Jews happier and more useful in France?"—all the essays submitted had either been rejected or sent back to their authors for revision. After some wavering the academy decided to give three prizes, to Grégoire, to Claude Antoine Thiery, a Protestant lawyer, and to Zalkind Hourwitz, a Jewish immigrant from Poland whose essay had at first been ignored.

As a piece of research or rhetoric, Grégoire's treatise even in its revised form leaves much to be desired. Its concrete proposals involved the grant of civil status to the Jews under certain conditions. The initiative had to come from the Christian authorities, who would impose on the rabbis compulsory education in secular subjects, the abolition of usury, encouragement of intermarriage, and the free social intercourse of Christians and Jews. In brief, Grégoire envisioned the end of separatism through assimilation, a presage of the Napoleonic solution. The "revolution"—the word is his—was not to be precipitate; every effort would be made to lead Christians and Jews into their new relationship through persuasion. Grégoire was aware of the resistance that would be offered both by Christians and by pious Jews intent on preserving every last rule of the rabbinic law.

By this time, there were echoes in France of the writings of German scholars and bureaucrats who had begun to discard traditional views of ancient Judaism and to look for a resolution of what had become known in the German principalities as "the Jewish question." Many of their ideas were transmitted in Mirabeau's little book on Moses Mendelssohn. In addition, the survival of German speech in Alsace and Lorraine made German conceptions especially accessible in the region where Abbé Grégoire officiated.

What Grégoire had to say on the nature of historical Judaism was for the most part derivative; he followed Basnage and Michaelis. He deplored the medieval persecutions as contrary to the spirit of Christianity, and for the fall of Jews into the ugly business of usury he blamed Christians, who excluded them from decent occupations. He cited with approval Christian Wilhelm Dohm, the German official who had written a major treatise advocating civil rights for Jews. In general, Grégoire preserved the conventional myth of papal protection of the Jews, and he was critical of the hidebound orthodoxy of the talmudists and the cabbalists. But the rhetorical passion with which he depicted the sufferings of the Jews through the ages and his espousal of equal rights for Jews in the later revolutionary assemblies earned him a place of honor in Jewish historiography as an exemplary Judeophile.

Grégoire wrote with open admiration of Mendelssohn and maintained close relations with Jewish intellectuals and notables in Metz. Though he accepted the deicide thesis and castigated Jewish moneylenders for encouraging young nobles to become profligate and sink hopelessly into debt, he was certain that the moral vices of the Jews could be wiped out if the government implemented his system of regeneration. Since Grégoire was elected bishop of Blois under the revolutionary dispensation, his name became anathema to official Catholicism in the nineteenth century. For later anticlericals, his defense of Jewish and Negro rights made him a symbol of the penetration of Enlightenment ideas into the Church of the late *ancien régime,* though he himself throughout his long life proclaimed an unwavering belief in Christ the Redeemer.

The formal granting of civil rights to Jews during the French Revolution had thus been prepared by the works of a number of Christian publicists: Abbé Gregoire's prize essay at Metz; Mirabeau's eulogy of Moses Mendelssohn, the civilized Jew he had known in Berlin; Abbé Guénée's point-by-point refutation of Voltaire's attack on biblical Israel; and Abbé Bergier's long articles in the *Encyclopédie méthodique,* evidence that in the heart of French Catholicism traditional theological views had been seriously modified. During the heated revolutionary debate on civil rights for Jews, clerical forces organized a stubborn opposition and raised the dread specter of churches transformed into synagogues. But the French Church was not united in this contest, and awareness of the greater threat posed by infidel radicalism brought about, at least for a brief moment, a defense of ancient Israel. This did not remain the official ecclesiastical stance over the next two centuries, when theological hostility to Judaism tended to merge with the new "scientific" and political antisemitism.

The Revolutionary Dispensation

The debates in the revolutionary assemblies that preceded the lifting of legal Jewish disabilities opened up some ancient wounds. The Sephardic Jews of Bordeaux sought priority in the liberation, and their behind-the-scenes intervention often delayed the bestowal of equal rights on Ashkenazic Jews in Alsace and Lorraine. Popular protests against the economic activities of Alsatian Jews had already figured in the *cahiers de doléances,* and during the assembly discussions, tumults in the eastern provinces were reminders that declarations of the rights of man and of the citizen could remain hollow revolutionary rhetoric. Jews served in the national guard and in the army, but inveterate prejudices were not wiped out by the mere promulgation of solemn decrees.

Napoleon in his manner proposed the most radical solution to the Jewish problem in France and in the lands he conquered. The assembly of Jewish representatives he convened at Paris adopted a venerable title, the Sanhedrin, and Jewish delegates wore special costumes that befitted their status. Napoleon's personal attitude toward Jews bore the marks of a vulgar Voltairean. His negotiators forced the Jewish delegates to accept a settlement that mimicked his arrangements with the churches. A consistory was established with broad powers over the internal organization of Jewish communal religious affairs. At the same time, however, the Jews became free citizens of France—as well as the satellite states Napoleon fashioned on the Continent—and they were admitted to secular university establishments. Rabbis wrote hymns that sang Napoleon's praises; in Eastern Europe, Jewish folklore made him a new Cyrus; believers had renewed visions of the Days of the Messiah. Though the Restoration reimposed some disabilities on the Jews, the consistory survived, an agency of emancipation or a body of apostates in the eyes of its differing Jewish constituencies.

Whatever his motives, Napoleon made possible a new life for Jews in France that led them to push in unexpected directions and embark on curious enterprises. The Rodrigueses and the Pereires became founders of the Saint-Simonian movement, and the Ashkenazic Rothschilds and the Sephardic Pereires fought bitterly with each other for the control of French finance in the nineteenth century. The Napoleonic impress on organized French Jewry remained deep, until the great immigration of Jews from North Africa after World War II once again altered the character of formal Judaism in France.

10

The German Janus

THE LUTHERAN GOD'S rage against the Jews did not abate despite the balm of Pietism. Everything in the Old Testament pointed to the coming of Christ, and once the Jews rejected him, they were virtually beyond redemption. Luther had taught that at the end of the days only a handful of Jews, those who converted, might be saved. Jews could not be systematically exterminated, but their houses and synagogues should be burned and they should be driven off into barren lands; the time had come to put an end to their living in luxury on the fruits of Christian labor. Though this harsh judgment was mitigated in the preaching of the pietists, who tried to instill a new temper into a Lutheran establishment that had become prosperous and territorial, the official churches of the German principalities preserved Luther's loathing of Jews and Judaism.

Leipzig remained a center for Judeophobic publications well into the eighteenth century, and residual elements of their spirit survived the introduction into the universities of nationalist and historical-critical researches. Gottfried Wilhelm Leibniz, a native of Leipzig, may have been relatively immune to vulgar Judeophobia, but even "the great European" and preacher of ecumenicalism was not wholly emancipated from the judgment of the Lutheran dispensation into which he was born. His close friendship with individual Jews was accompanied by acceptance of stale formulas on the nature of Judaism. The spirit of Martin Luther's slashing broadside, *The Jews and Their Lies,* was still alive and virulent in the Germanic world two hundred years after its first appearance.

Juden in the Leipzig Lexicon

The fourteenth volume of the *Grosses Vollständiges Universal Lexicon* (Grand Complete Universal Lexicon), published in Leipzig and Halle in 1735, included an article on "Juden, oder Jüden" that in brief compass offered a stereotyped Lutheran view of Judaism. A large part of the article was devoted to the question of whether the term "Juden" applied only to the descendants of the tribes of Judah and Benjamin, who had been allowed by Cyrus to return to Jerusalem after the Babylonian captivity, or whether it referred also to the earlier exiles from the kingdom of Israel. The author concluded that, by the time of the return, "Judah" had come to mean all the tribes and included even those who remained in the Persian kingdom and did not journey back with their brethren. In Christ's day, the tribes were so intermingled that no Jew could know from which one he was descended, making fulfillment of the prophecy that the Jewish messiah would come from the progeny of David difficult to prove. The Jews might once have been God's chosen people, but after their rejection of Christ he cast them aside. Thenceforward they were no longer *Ammi* (my people), but the children of Satan. This orthodox Lutheran doctrine, still being advanced in the eighteenth century, was sharply at variance with the usual Puritan and Anglican positions that God had never departed from his original choice of Israel and the restitution of the Jews was merely delayed because of their sinfulness.

The 1735 article, which used the word "Greuel" (horror) to describe God's feeling toward the Jews, paired them with the abominable pagans. Even though they had the Old Testament, it was a sealed book because one could come to the Father only through the Son, whom they denied. Since the Jews believed that each verse of the Old Testament could be interpreted in 600,000 ways (a hyperbolic statement of some enthusiastic cabbalist pretenders), what could be learned from them about its definitive meaning? This was a reiteration of Luther's reluctance to consult the rabbinic tradition in the elucidation of the Scriptures, despite the presence of such learned Christian Hebraists as Sebastian Münster among his disciples. The Jews exalted the Talmud high above the Bible and believed God himself studied the new commentaries—a deduction from the Lutheran literal reading of midrashic tales that God would expound the hidden meanings of the Torah in heaven. The whole doctrine of the Jews about *their* messiah was so confused that there was no agreement among the various sects. Yet the future advent of a messiah was their central article of belief. The name of Christ was odious to them, and they spat when they uttered it.

The inclusion of this article on "Juden" in the most influential German encyclopedia of its day highlights the distance between Lutheran orthodoxy and a new view of Judaism that isolated Enlightenment figures, such as Lessing and Dohm, were asking their compatriots to consider. There is no counterpart in French or English encyclopedias of the seventeenth and eighteenth centuries to this vituperative passage of the Leipzig *Lexicon:*

> And how often have they slaughtered Christian children, crucified them, battered them to pieces! They are the worst thieves, and betrayal is their distinctive insignia. They are forever swearing falsely, even when they must take the most terrifying oaths. Then they can always be absolved by appearing before a rabbi or three Jews. Yes, God has marked them in their very natures. Clearly, a Jew has something about him that makes him immediately recognizable and distinguishable from other people. They rouse disgust and horror . . . Since they have been rejected for almost 1700 years, they must have committed infinitely graver sins than their forefathers. Verily, they killed the Son of God, and crucified the Lord of Glory, whose blood still weighs upon them, and fulfilled the judgment that they rendered upon themselves. To this day they continue to rage against the Gospel.[1]

The blood-guilt accusation was repeated as demonstrated fact, though reference was made to Wagenseil's denial. This Lutheran view of the Jews held forth little prospect of their conversion. Among thousands who had been baptized into the Christian faith, almost none remained steadfast. The author of the article doubted whether there would be a miraculous mass conversion before judgment day, much as he would have liked to see it come to pass.

This normative view of Jews in the orthodox Lutheran community, enshrined in an official encyclopedia, had hardly budged from Luther's scathing pamphlets of the 1540s. Calvinists and Anglicans in the seventeenth century had found various uses, mostly benign, for rabbinic commentary of all periods. By the eighteenth century, Catholics also turned to rabbinic scholarship to facilitate conversion and fight incredulity. The Lutheran denomination was an exception in its rejection of the worth of the rabbis of the Talmud and the Middle Ages. When Lutherans studied rabbinics it was primarily for polemical purposes, to ridicule superstition. The learned works produced by the outstanding dynasties of Christian Hebraists in Lutheran universities—the Carpzovs of Leipzig, for example—were rarely free of the bitterness and derisive spirit of the founder of their denomination. The pioneering Christian Hebraists of the sixteenth century, Reuchlin and Münster, were forgotten.

In this light, the transformation of attitudes among some Lutheran intellectual luminaries in the second half of the eighteenth century is all the more striking; there is little preparation for the emergence of Lessing or Nicolai or Dohm. For the most part, Luther's judgment of Judaism could not be put aside indifferently even by thinkers who left his theological orthodoxies behind. The Judeophobia he bequeathed assumed many guises, and it survived among Germans into the twentieth century. But two transitional figures, in the world of scholarship Michaelis, of an old Halle family of professors and theologians, and in literary circles the ordained pastor Herder, introduced novelty into the Germanic perception of ancient Israel. Their appreciation of Judaism seemed heterodox, even heretical, to official interpreters, but it was not in fact as sharp a departure from Luther as some imagined. Acceptance of primitive Israel and disdainful rejection of post-biblical rabbinism was a combination that could ultimately be assimilated by the orthodox and the heterodox alike.

Michaelis' Ethnology of the Ancient Hebrews

Johann David Michaelis was born into academic life in Halle in 1717. He was the oldest son of the theologian and orientalist Christian Benedict Michaelis (d. 1764) and grandnephew of the theologian and biblical scholar Johann Heinrich Michaelis (d. 1738). Initiated early into biblical research, Michaelis also studied medicine and the forbidden philosophy of Christian Wolff. He wrote his dissertation on a standby of Lutheran scholarship—a defense of the antiquity of Old Testament accents and points—maintaining the orthodox position of Buxtorf the Elder and of his own father, Christian Michaelis. In 1741 Michaelis took the scholar's counterpart of the aristocratic grand tour and spent a number of years at Oxford, Leiden, and Hamburg. Back in Halle, he taught Semitic languages and lectured on the Bible, natural history, and the Latin classics. In 1745 he abandoned the Lutheran pietists of Halle with whom he had once consorted and found a post in Göttingen, where he emerged from a spiritual crisis to become the leader of the historical-critical school of biblical interpretation.

For nearly half a century, until his death in 1791, Michaelis was a star of the Göttingen university firmament, which included the eminences Albrecht von Haller, Johann Matthias Gesner, and Johann Lorenz Mosheim. He held his professorship in the philosophical faculty, though allowed the privilege of lecturing on dogmatics and morals. His teaching concentrated on Old and New Testament exegesis, Hebrew antiquities, Mosaic law, the Hebrew, Arabic, Aramaic, and Syriac languages. As a teacher he was renowned; students extravagantly claimed that he was the greatest who had ever been and ever would be. His lectures were spiced with wit, graphic illustrations, and sometimes coarse humor; in his later years his asides and digressions outweighed the substance of his presentations. In 1751 he became secretary of the new Göttingen learned society, but left it after disputes with the classicist Heyne. During the military occupation in the Seven Years' War, he succeeded in lightening the burden of the foreign presence on his colleagues through his amicable relations with French and Swedish officers. His sponsorship, from a safe distance, of a famous research expedition to Egypt and Arabia that was financed by Frederick V of Denmark won him a European reputation. Toward the end of his life, honors poured in upon Michaelis from Sweden, France, and Britain. He was said to be arrogant and vain, scornful of other scholars, and resentful of those who presumed to correct his errors.

No one escaped Michaelis' mordant sarcasm, not even Augustine. In a dissertation entitled *The Influence of Opinions on Language and Language on Opinions,* awarded the prize of the Prussian Royal Academy of Sciences and Belles-Lettres in 1759, he charged the bishop of Hippo with gross linguistic ignorance. Punic, a Semitic language cognate to Hebrew, was Augustine's mother tongue, Michaelis recalled; it was the soul of his speech, as Latin was its body. When Augustine resorted to Punic to explain and illuminate passages of the Old Testament, the good bishop spoke Hebrew without knowing it. Had this indolent churchman troubled to study the relationship between Punic and Hebrew, he would have deserved to be called the father of oriental philology. As things stood, Michaelis was plainly reserving that honor for himself.

When Lutherans began to be touched by the Enlightenment, their scholarship underwent renovation. Since an Enlightenment theology could not live comfortably with the crudities of Luther's rantings against the Jews, Lutheran Hebraism took refuge in the historical-critical inquiry into the Bible that diverged from the passionate literalism of Luther and his followers. Enlightenment Lutherans continued to shy away from rabbinism, even though, in the name of the new openness and to fend off critics, they sometimes dipped into the Talmud or the literal rabbinic interpreters of the Middle Ages.

Under the aegis of Michaelis, there was born a Lutheran ethnological reconstruction of Mosaic law as it had been taught by Moses himself, not by the talmudic distorters of the second commonwealth and the confused rabbinic commentators of the diaspora. The Old Testament was to be understood as the work of flesh-and-blood men writing in a given time and place in the Near East. The authors of its different books could be considered divinely inspired, but as men they belonged to specific epochs and could not escape historicity. Since the historical narratives of the Old Testament spoke for themselves and did not require much exegesis, Lutheran interpreters concentrated on the Pentateuch as a code of civil laws or on the books of the Prophets, Psalms, Proverbs, and the Song of Songs as sublime literature, religious poetry, and folk wisdom. The world of ancient Israel was seen through the eyes of either a master of jurisprudence or a literary critic of the noblest poetry composed by mankind. The paths of the interpretations sometimes crossed, for they had in common a quest for the spirit of the Hebrews before the political catastrophes of the second commonwealth, when the original purity of Judaea was totally corrupted by Greek and Roman influences.

The mission of a new-style Lutheran professor of philosophy, theology, or Hebrew—not completely emancipated from the spirit of Martin Luther—was to discover the true Mosaic law, scraped of the encrustations of the benighted rabbis. Michaelis, the outstanding exemplar of this innovative type of Hebraist, was not interested in the Mosaic code for its own sake or for the purpose of displaying erudition and historical-critical method. His goals were universal. Observance of Mosaic laws was no longer obligatory for Christian societies, even though vestiges of those laws remained in modern systems of jurisprudence; but since the Pentateuch was the most ancient embodiment of legislative policy, it was worthy of investigation because it would instruct mankind in the basic principles of the philosophy of law. Mosaic learning was useful for an understanding of the origins and therefore justification of many contemporary legal decisions. In addition, a thorough comprehension of the Mosaic system would help a learned divine refute unbelievers who mocked the books of Moses, by demonstrating that their author was motivated by feelings of humanity, that his edicts were an advance over the barbarous customs prevalent among the ancient heathens.

Between 1770 and 1775 the six parts of Michaelis' *Mosaisches Recht* (Mosaic Law) were published in Frankfurt; a revised edition appeared in 1785; and the work was soon translated into Dutch, Danish, and English. For the less than orthodox and official Lutheran world, Michaelis' was the most recent authoritative presentation of the fundamental laws of Mosaic Judaism, and it earned its author a British knighthood and election to the Royal Society of London. Michaelis' chef d'oeuvre, rendered into English as *Commentaries on the Laws of Moses,* had been many decades in preparation. The title finally chosen by the translator, the Reverend Alexander Smith, was tailored for English readers familiar with Blackstone's commentaries; at one time Smith had contemplated "Spirit of the Mosaic Laws," to highlight the book's affinity to the work of Montesquieu.

While lecturing at Göttingen on oriental philology, Hebrew antiquities, exegetic theology, and other biblical subjects, Michaelis wrote profusely on sundry aspects of the Mosaic polity: marriage laws, the punishment of homicide, the laws of usury, the nomads of Palestine, the Hebrew census, the Hebrew months, the troglodytes of Mount Seir, the oriental mode of sheep breeding, the levirate law, the sabbatical year, the law of polygamy, the value of the shekel, prices prior to the Babylonian captivity, the cherubim, the history of glass among the Hebrews, the nature of the Hebrews, Jewish architecture in the time of Solomon, the Mosaic laws promulgated to tie the Israelites to Palestine, arguments for the immortality of the soul deducible from the Mosaic writings. Dissertations of this sort had been the staple products of Dutch, Swiss, German, and Swedish universities since the seventeenth century, and the giants of Christian Hebraism in England published mammoth treatises on similar subjects, for example, John Selden's *Hebrew Wife.* Learned societies of Europe in the eighteenth century markedly favored Greek over Hebrew studies, but there were enough professorships in Protestant universities on the Continent to keep up a steady flow of doctorates on particulars of the laws and customs of the Hebrews.

What distinguished Michaelis' work was his attempt at a broad synthesis rivaling comprehensive studies in the seventeenth century and, perhaps more significantly, his reliance on European travel literature for information on life in the "oriental" world. Going beyond the philological studies of Near Eastern languages, which had been the standard fare of late-seventeenth-century biblical research, Michaelis explored the customs of the desert Arabs to throw light on the nature of Mosaic laws. He enlisted the ethnology of contemporary Arabs to explain the manners of the pastoral society of the patriarchs and the life and laws of the Hebrews wandering in the desert under Moses. Similarly, the ways of early kings of Judah and Israel were compared with those of pagan kings in the same region.

Michaelis' study had been prompted by a request from Olaus Rabenius, professor of law and syndic of the University of Uppsala, who was residing in Göttingen in 1756, that Michaelis give him a private course on Mosaic jurisprudence. This was no act of mere intellectual curiosity on Rabenius' part. The Swedish professor, who was later entrusted with the task of codifying the laws for his country, told Michaelis that in Sweden the civil law of Moses until recently had been considered a subsidiary law, and he was convinced that traces of its former authority survived even though it was no longer quoted in legal decisions. In his dedicatory epistle to Rabenius when the book was published, Michaelis placed special emphasis on the idea of liberty as the animating force of the Mosaic constitution. The Pentateuch had not committed Israel to an absolute king, nor had it promulgated an immutable constitutional law that would forever fix the structure of the polity. There may have been provision for the appointment of a king at a future period, but not without the establishment of checks on his power. Michaelis held that the Mosaic law allowed for change in the prerogatives of the ruler, their augmentation and diminution with the needs of the times.

Mosaic Law is informed by the philosophical conception of a limited monarchy, for which its author found support both in ancient Mosaic law and in contemporary England, where he had lived for eighteen months as a young man. Christian study of ancient Israel was never solely an exercise in erudition, but rarely was the underlying purpose behind the inquiry more apparent than in Michaelis' voluminous treatise. Viewed historically in terms of the social and economic realities of eighteenth-century Jewish life, the court Jews—army provisioners, moneylenders, tax collectors—who derived their sustenance from the princelets of Germany, were in fact often strengthening the power of petty despots more or less enlightened, at the expense of the traditional rights and privileges of the burghers. In Michaelis' book hatred of court Jews and suspicion of other modern Jews went hand in hand with an anachronistic interpretation of Mosaic law that identified it with a philosophe's idea of political liberty as defined in Montesquieu's theory of the division of powers. There was an implicit contrast between the just Mosaic code of the ancient Jews committed to liberty and the conduct of contemporary Jewish minions of petty autocrats.

Michaelis' reading of the Bible in the light of earlier travel accounts from the east bred in him the grand design of sending a mission of literati to Egypt and Arabia, to collect information *in situ* about the history, languages, nature, geography, and customs of those countries. The ethnographic data would illuminate the Scriptures in a new way. Montesquieu's theory of a dominant spirit among the Hebrews had originally sparked the notion; Herder's conception of the interplay of Genesis and Klima in every Volk later paralleled Michaelis' conviction. The predominant philological and etymological preoccupations of seventeenth-century biblical criticism were being replaced by a growing absorption with lands and customs and age-old cultural determinants. The new literal and historical interpretation of the Bible was becoming less dependent on the meaning of individual words than on the temper of the whole work. And for insight into that temper, one had to turn to the way of life of modern Bedouins. The Mosaic code was still revered as God-given, but since it was born in the desert, the customs of present-day Arabs were the best clues to its comprehension.

There was a fundamental assumption behind the new ethnological theory that the remoteness of desert peoples insulated them from alien influences and that Arab rules of conduct had remained virtually unchanged for thousands of years. To discover a living picture of the society of the patriarchs or the ways of the Israelites before Moses handed down his commandments, one had only to observe contemporary Arabs of the desert. The Mosaic establishment of cities of asylum where an involuntary murderer could take refuge was understandable if one were acquainted with the elaborate rules governing blood revenge among the Bedouins. A multitude of decrees in the Pentateuch that appeared strange and even inhumane would be explained as residual custom, and the wise and benign innovations introduced by Moses, the divine legislator, would be revealed as all the more worthy of respect among enlightened minds. In the eyes of a Michaelis, the mountains of rabbinic rules and the talmudic niceties of urban Jewish moneylenders grew ever more distant from the original intent of Mosaic law. Contemporary Jews were strangers to the values of their own supreme lawgiver. Thus Michaelis could idealize the jurisprudence of the ancient Hebrews and, at the same time, oppose granting citizenship to German Jews whom he chose to regard as morally corrupt.

Michaelis' plan for a scholarly expedition to Arabia had been realized in part when in 1756 he communicated the idea to Count Bernstorff, who in turn convinced King Frederick of Denmark to finance the venture. Michaelis drew up a list of questions to guide the information-gathering enterprise of a heterogeneous group that included a linguist, a botanist, and a surveyor-astronomer. Though all of the squabbling scholar-recruits except Carsten Niebuhr, the surveyor-astronomer, died on the voyage and most of Michaelis' queries remained unanswered, a vast quantity of data was recorded in Captain Niebuhr's *Voyage en Arabie* (1774). The influence of Niebuhr's account is patent in many chapters of Michaelis' work. He profited from extended personal conversations with the lone survivor of the expedition and from his interim reports. The perils and dramatic events of the journey were recounted in the newspapers of Western Europe, and Michaelis gained international renown.

Michaelis saw his treatise as effecting a revolution in the understanding of the Hebrew polity. His follower Johann Gottfried Eichhorn toppled Buxtorf from his throne, spelling out in a memoir what enlightened German scholars conceived to be the upheaval brought about by Michaelis' method and use of sources:

> In all preceding treatises on the subject, everything had been jumbled together in the most heterogeneous manner; ancient laws and institutions, mingled with modern; ordinances truly Mosaic, confounded with those of later times, as introduced, reformed, or, at least, altered, by the Persians, Greeks, or Romans; and the real statutes of Moses exchanged for mere Rabbinical regulations, originating either in excessive scrupulosity, or silly misconception. In this state of things, and while, in their inquiries and speculations, authors on this subject betrayed only their credulity, and ignorance of political science, Michaelis made his appearance.[2]

Michaelis would turn Moses into an enlightened legislator in the Montesquieu mold. Moses had had no intention of abolishing practices that were ingrained among the Israelites, for he knew that revolutionary decrees counter to the spirit of a people were fruitless. He allowed the laws governing marriage to remain largely unaltered and tended to leave existing customs untouched. The polygamous family structure was not disturbed. Where the worship of one God was at stake, however, he did not hesitate to issue strict injunctions. When possible he proposed moderate reforms of an Enlightenment cast, aimed toward leniency of punishment, alleviation of the conditions of slavery, defense of the rights of women, protection of the status of strangers, magnanimity to the conquered. The Mosaic laws were judged by the standards of crime and punishment that Montesquieu and Beccaria were insinuating into western society, and by their criteria many of the Mosaic punishments had to be condemned as barbarous. But in most passages Michaelis was an ardent defender of the Mosaic code, extolling its humanity. The abominations that accompanied the practice of idolatry—the defloration of young women and the sacrifice of children—not merely the worship of false gods, justified the harsh sentences meted out to idolatrous nations and Hebrews who fell into their sins. "Was it then too severe in Moses, to keep the people from a religion so abominable, even by the terrors of capital punishment?"[3]

Voltaire, the English deists, and the Holbachians had ransacked the

Bible to discover crimes against humanity, singling out the wholesale slaughter of enemies, human sacrifices, even anthropophagy. Michaelis, without naming the accusers, either found their reading of the texts distorted or pleaded extenuating circumstances. The debate about the nature of Mosaic Judaism was no longer enveloped in a thick mantle of philological scholarship, as it had been in the seventeenth century. The fundamental question was the general esprit of ancient Israel. Ethnology as well as the study of comparative political systems were introduced into the discussion, not to demonstrate the barbarism and primitivism of the Hebrews but to show their general superiority over their oriental neighbors and in many respects over Greek and Roman legislators.

Michaelis' reconstruction of the gruesome particulars of the Canaanite religion served as a foil for the excellence of the Mosaic code. Laws had to be evaluated according to the specific circumstances of a people. The Voltaireans were drawing from the Bible examples of cruel and inhuman practices and weighing them by the rules of civility that were Enlightenment ideals. Michaelis did not so much excuse monstrous behavior as explain it in terms of political and social necessity or ancient custom. The wholesale massacre of a condemned city, including women and children, was interpreted, with the aid of Luther's translation of the Bible and Arabic philology, as a consecration to Jehovah, like a burnt offering of which nothing remains. Michaelis contended that prior to the Babylonian captivity the Israelites rarely meted out such punishments to captured cities. The Mosaic code encouraged informing against relatives who seduced others into idolatry, a commandment that Montesquieu denounced in the *Spirit of the Laws*. Michaelis did not find in the biblical text any specific reference to informing on a father, mother, or husband, and he therefore challenged at least part of Montesquieu's condemnation. Though Michaelis had abandoned old-fashioned Lutheran orthodoxy, he preserved Luther's meticulous adherence to the text of the Scriptures, and the much-admired Montesquieu was not beyond criticism when he interpreted a verse in the Pentateuch too breezily.

Michaelis even suggested that the modern legislator might well learn from the Mosaic code. Its contemporary relevance had been signaled in the sixteenth century by the Huguenot Bertram, and during the seventeenth century Dutch and English treatises on the republic of the Hebrews cited Israelite laws to bolster the constitutions of their own societies and sustain their legitimacy. But they had emphasized the divine origin of the Hebrew constitution. While Michaelis, a practicing Lutheran, alluded to this sacred character in passing, it was not the cornerstone of his argument. The Mosaic code was exalted not for its divine sanction but because it generally conformed to the humane ideals of the Enlightenment. The laws were on the whole lenient (with allowance for the times) and just. Such absolute decrees as violated eighteenth-century concepts of the laws of nations and humanity were imputed to Jehovah's commands and were not always further explained. While Michaelis lavished praise on the Mosaic code, he made no attempt to hide the fact that the Hebrews under their kings had frequently been enticed into the most barbarous usages of the Canaanites. The Phoenicians sacrificed their children to Moloch, and Michaelis read in a commonsense manner the biblical texts that intimated occasional Hebrew aping of those loathsome crimes. The vindicator of the Mosaic law was no apologist for the transgressions of the Israelites when they violated the commandments of their own supreme legislator.

Michaelis was distinguished from the seventeenth-century giants of Christian Hebraism by his obdurate refusal even to peruse the rabbinic learning accumulated through the centuries for what it might offer to a modern scholar. His peremptory rejection of the rabbinic corpus led him into many philological misinterpretations. Ethnology, which freed him from what he regarded as the quagmire of rabbinism, became a new obsession. Michaelis did not bother to dispute with Jewish rabbis ancient or modern about their interpretations. His *Mosaic Law* includes derogatory asides about the rabbis' distortion of the Mosaic law on oathtaking and mocks their methods for the determination of virginity. Michaelis used the Targum, the Aramaic paraphrase of the Old Testament, but kept his distance from the rabbis. He stuck to his reading and analysis of the text of the Old Testament and drew his summary of the Mosaic law with virtually no reference to rabbinic commentaries of any age (Philo and Josephus are accorded a few stray citations). His verdict on the Talmud was blunt: it was no source of information at all on Mosaic law. Michaelis avoided mention of Maimonides, Rashi, Abraham Ibn Ezra—the most respected commentators in Catholic, Calvinist, and Anglican scholarship. He was a vindicator of Mosaic Israel, not of the religion that had become infected with rabbinism.

Having forsaken the traditional Lutheran position that the accents and vowels of the Hebrew Old Testament were divinely inspired—which he had upheld in his youth—Michaelis in the name of the new historical criticism poked fun at stick-in-the-mud Jews who in theory at least would not deviate from the Massoretic text even when it made no sense. When Michaelis reviewed *Ha-Measef* (The Collector), a Hebrew periodical published in Königsberg in 1784, in his *Neue Orientalische und Exegetische Bibliothek* (Göttingen, 1786), he fell upon a piece dealing with the Massoretes. He concluded that even learned enlightened Jews were still likely to cling obstinately to the authority of the Massoretic version of the biblical text, unlike the great majority of Christians, himself included, who now allowed liberal emendations when the meaning required it. In passing he took the opportunity to note that Moses Mendelssohn himself in his translation of the Psalms into German had to deviate occasionally from the Massoretes. Despite Mendelssohn's many overtures to him, however, the Lutheran professor still refused to engage with Rabbi Moses of Berlin. When Michaelis alluded to Mendelssohn in his journal, his tone was condescending. The chasm between them was too great to be bridged. The more Michaelis glorified the Mosaic code, the less acceptable to him appeared the integration of contemporary Jews into German society.

Michaelis and his followers and adapters abandoned the orthodox school of Lutheran biblical criticism, which had viewed the text of the Old Testament as meaningful only in the light of the New, to arrive at an appreciation of the Mosaic code as a system of jurisprudence meritorious in its own right. Rabbinism remained the great distortion. German university scholars no longer called for the burning of the Talmud as Luther had; they merely pronounced the rabbinic tradition of interpreting Mosaic law to be wrongheaded and irrelevant, not even worthy of refutation. By the end of the eighteenth century, contemporary ethnographers of the Near East replaced the rabbis as the true guides to the meaning of the texts. For a comprehension of difficult images and metaphors, professors of poetry could be called upon as auxiliaries. It is difficult to say whether Martin Luther would have been more outraged by these new commentators or by the accursed Talmudists themselves.

The Spirit of Sacred Hebrew Poetry: Lowth and Herder

In 1753 the Oxford professor of poetry Robert Lowth, later bishop of London, whose Hebrew was in fact rather weak, published his lectures *De sacra poesi hebraeorum* (On the Sacred Poetry of the Hebrews). The young Michaelis in an annotated edition corrected Lowth's errors and perfected his rendering of much of the Bible as poetry. Their common discovery of the sacred poetry of the Hebrews was harmonious with Johann Gottfried von Herder's later definition of the creative core of ancient Judaism as its poetic nature, and in time Herder became the standard-bearer of the new doctrine. Thus an Enlightenment interpretation of the spirit of Judaism alternative to the orthodox Lutheran and vulgar perception was invented by a group of German Protestant literary luminaries. They ended up with an emotionalized and romanticized religion of Israel, which they found in the text of the Old Testament.

The Bible as primitive literature pushed away the centuries-long accumulation of literal, anagogical, and allegorical readings, and a Hebrew Ossian was brought forth. This novel reading also served as a German counterpart to the effusive religiosity of the vicar of Savoy's confession of faith in Rousseau's *Emile.* Herder's exaltation of the primitive Hebrew poetry of the Bible as the most perfect expression of the religious spirit generated a religion of feeling that was related to moral beauty and, in tandem with Rousseau's worship of nature, ultimately deflected traditional western religions from their doctrinal and historical pathways—a change of direction so radical that the whole character of European religious experience was profoundly altered. Herder's heterodox poetizing of Judaism had its roots in the German pietism of Philipp Jakob Spener and made its strongest impact on the Germanic world, where Jewish communities were more numerous than elsewhere in Western Europe. Reform Judaism, which distanced itself from traditional rabbinism, owed something to the Christian idealization of ancient Judaism, the object having molded itself to fit the image in the mind of the beholder.

The essential spirit of Judaism, Herder taught, had been made manifest in the earliest documents of the human race, the Scriptures. Language revealed the secret soul of every religious people, and the poetry of the Bible was the *Geist* of the ancient Hebrews in their very beginnings, their creative moment. Among the early Hebrews poetic language was the natural vehicle for sublime religious feeling. The rationalist theologies of the Judaic and Christian religions were secondary; it was the poetic language of religion in music and in verse that was closest to the divine. When Herder, while remaining a Lutheran pastor, abandoned discussion of Jewish and Christian theology and identified Judaism with the beauties of the Hebrew language, he was shielding the early spirit of Israel from the contempt of the Voltaireans and the Holbachians, and from the vituperation of Martin Luther himself. But, at the same time, he opened the way to aestheticizing religious experience among all peoples, which stealthily robbed the Judaic dispensation of its uniqueness.

Herder began book 12, chapter 3, of his *Ideen zur Philosophie der Geschichte der Menschheit* (Reflections on the Philosophy of the History of Mankind; 1784–1791) with a eulogy of the ancient Hebrews. Though their country was small and they seldom appeared in the role of conquerors—size was never a measure of worth for Herder— through the medium of Christianity and Mohammedanism, they laid the groundwork for the enlightenment of the greater part of the world. But Herder writing in detail on the Jews and Judaism left a heap of contradictory judgments; he viewed them from many different angles as his opinions shifted from one position to another. When he examined the Hebrews as a political entity in the ancient world that ended with the dispersion, he admired their well-preserved histories but found nothing worthy of note in their brief existence as an independent polity. Toward modern Jews he was at best ambivalent, and he harbored many doubts and misgivings about their integration into the culture of German society, a viewpoint he shared with his master Kant and with the Hebraist Michaelis. Herder knew little about rabbinic thought, which did not inhibit him from expressing disdain for it, and he was equally ignorant of medieval Jewish philosophy and poetry. But when he turned to the Bible as the essence of the religious spirit, he waxed grandiloquent. His essay *Vom Geist der Ebräische Poesie* (On the Spirit of Hebrew Poetry; 1782–83) became a challenge to the Holbachian *Spirit of Judaism.*

In evaluating the political history of the Hebrews in the Bible, which they themselves had composed, Herder straddled a fence. He treated the accounts in the Pentateuch, Joshua, Judges, Samuel I and

II, and Kings I and II as straightforward narratives, documents, not divine revelations. The earliest histories of the Hebrews had their origin in family chronicles, whose very simplicity guaranteed their authenticity. Their accuracy was in large part due to the fact that for thousands of years these histories had been preserved by the Jews with reverential scrupulosity as a sacred duty. Like Newton before him, Herder esteemed biblical narratives of events as the most meticulous in the world because their transmission, down to the last diacritical mark, was a religious obligation. Herder knew that there were other early accounts of the Hebrews' origins, in particular the work of Manetho the Egyptian priest, who denigrated them; but on balance he preferred the Hebrew version to the slanders of foreign enemies. In his role as a historian of cultures, Herder accepted the veracity of the Jewish text. But then, as was his wont, he withdrew a pace. He could not wholly reject the statements of the "enemies"; he merely advised that they be read with caution. There were times when he would have his Bible and his Manetho too.

Herder described Abraham, the progenitor of the Hebrews, as the sheik of a wandering horde who led a pastoral life after crossing the Euphrates into Palestine. He credited the biblical story of the descent into Egypt, as he did the maintenance of the tribal purity of the Jews until the emergence of Moses the great legislator, who gave them a constitution and molded them into a nation. The religion and mode of life of their fathers were preserved intact, even though certain Egyptian usages crept in. Herder echoed the school that imputed at least part of the religion of the Jews to its derivation from Egyptian religion. This concession of a measure of foreign influence may appear to be somewhat out of harmony with Herder's general thesis of the unitary origins of a Volk, but the lapse is pardonable because he highlights the Abrahamic covenant in its Mosaic version as the form-giving moment of the Hebrews.

Throughout the eighteenth century, secular commentators committed themselves to a given time when the spirit of Judaism took shape. There were a number of alternative periods from which to choose—that of Adam, Abraham, Moses, David founder of the kingdom of the Jews (after God's unfortunate experience with Saul). Enlightenment philosophers, Herder among them, tended to settle on the figure of Moses, not only as the great legislator of his people but as an active political leader who brought them out of Egypt to the border of Palestine. Moreover, this choice of the Mosaic legislator was in keeping with common conceptions of the founders of the Greek and Roman city-states, all of which were led to maturity by famous lawgivers.

The Mosaic constitution was for Herder a profound system of laws that continued to be wisely developed for decades after the first generation of Hebrews who had fled Egyptian bondage died off. But unfortunately for the Mosaic expectation of founding a nation, the initial division of land among the twelve tribes was inequitable; and many smaller nations remained in Palestine even after their conquest by the Hebrews, confusing their political existence. (Herder appears to countenance the military invasion by the Hebrews, though he is usually outraged by new Volk intrusions into the living-space occupied by others.) There was as a consequence a defect in both the "external and internal compact rotundity"[4] of the Mosaic ideal, and restless times of intermittent warfare followed. The disparate tribal forces were never completely amalgamated into a whole even after the establishment of a Hebrew kingship. The third monarch of the Jews, Solomon, proved to be the last who reigned over all the tribes, before they were torn apart by internecine dissension and the purity of the Israelite religion was diluted with the worship of alien gods.

In the course of time both successor kingdoms, Israel and Judaea, were overwhelmed by great powers. The king of Assyria plundered the realm, and Nebuchadnezzar made its feeble monarchs at first tributaries and then, after they revolted, slaves. Israel was thus not an enduring political body. Herder looked at Palestine's geography in contemporary terms. The land recalled the cantons of Switzerland, capable of supporting a nation of shepherds, transformed under Solomon into an empire subject to pernicious foreign ways that corrupted its ethos. The kings became the effete creatures of priests, and the vigor of the refined nomocracy that Moses had instituted was lost. Even after the end of the Babylonian captivity and the return of the Jews to Palestine under Cyrus, the Mosaic polity was never effectively restored. Herder's description of life under the Second Temple is the summary of a pathetic history, derived from the Christian view propounded in its classical form by Raimundo Martini in the thirteenth century, which admired the original Mosaic law but despised the legalistic accretions of the Talmudists. "Their religion was pharisaical;

their learning, a minute nibbling at syllables, and this confined to a single book; their patriotism, a slavish attachment to ancient laws misunderstood."[5]

But it was Herder writing on the nature of Hebrew poetry, not on the polity of the Jews, who exerted the most profound influence on a new view of Judaism in European society. Pastor Herder continued to read the Bible as a revelation, but also as the oldest historical document of the spirit of the Jewish people. In the seventeenth century Spinoza preceded him with the *Tractatus theologico-politicus,* the fountainhead of modern heresy. The crucial difference between them lay in the nature of the history they discovered in the Bible. Spinoza made of the Old Testament a social and political document that embodied the rational wisdom of the great legislator of the Hebrews. For Herder, the Bible was a projection of the soul of the inspired ancient Hebrews, the first people to portray in poetic language the relations of man and God, of man and nature, a prototype for the mythologies of all the peoples on earth.

The concreteness of biblical imagery, its reflection of the religious spirit in a specific oriental environment, was not a limitation of the sublime. Men had to couch their thoughts and feelings in physical terms. When a theologically minded Newtonian read the word "earth" in the Bible, he thought of the geophysical sphere of the scientist. By contrast, in Herder's commentary "earth" meant the soil of which man's primitive hut was molded and the dirt to which he returned. It had color and texture. The Bible, like all primitive creations, continually evoked the actual experience of men. The darkness of Genesis was a thick reality, not a metaphysical emptiness. "Whoever on the desolate open seas, surrounded by night and the fear of death, has hoped for the dawn, he has felt this tangible blackness."[6]

Vico, Turgot, Hamann, and Herder shared the conviction that language contained within it the true history of mankind's stadial development from primitive times to the Enlightenment. But the accord among them ends there. Vico looked on the Enlightenment movement toward abstract rational speech as an inevitable accompaniment of the humanization process, though he was at once appreciative of the sensate language of early primitives and apprehensive of the refinements of the last stages, with the coming of the hypersophisticated "barbarians of the intellect." Turgot longed for the age when the movement from emotive language to symbolic abstraction would reach its ultimate goal in the creation of a universal mode of scientific notation, from which the obscurities of feeling would be banished forever. In revulsion against this idealization of the mathematical, the Germans Hamann and Herder viewed attempts to introduce general terms into a language as a sign of degeneration, decadence, dehumanization. Progress for them meant restoration of the primitive sensibility and vivid forms of expression that prevailed before their desiccation by metaphysical abstractions.

After Herder had recovered from his youthful flirtation with rationalist philosophy under the tutelage of Kant in Königsberg, his theory of religious origins relied on a mixture of theology and history. Religion was a revelation, a divine intervention in an even more intimate sense than Vico's birth of the gods. The revelation, however, was clothed in a variety of historic forms among different nations, so that it was never divested of naturalistic elements. God revealed himself anew each time a national entity was born. In the Hebrew world his revelation had been most complete. It was emotionally all-embracing because the tongue of the Hebrews chosen by him was a perfect vehicle for the communication of religious truth, and the genius of the place was an ideal background for the enactment of the sacred drama. This Judaic revelation was not a unique occurrence, however; with modifications the performance was repeated again and again in the earliest moments of each Volk existence.

Among the Jews, the Bible was the word of God made flesh; among the gentiles, revelation assumed different forms. Egyptian hieroglyphs and Greek religious mysteries were symbolic divine manifestations of the same order, local variations depending on the physical landscape that had originally shaped the soul of the people. "That the Egyptian hieroglyphs deal with knowledge of the gods and of nature, only a Warburtonian head can deny,"[7] was his swipe at the pompous Anglican bishop who was author of the *Divine Legation of Moses.* Through sinfulness and the vice of sensuality, the divine revelation to the heathens was rendered impure, but in its origins a pagan mystery was an exalted truth wrapped in national costume.

When Hamann and Herder defended the worth of mystery religions, they were at the same time aiming polemical darts at those German contemporaries who interpreted the pagan rituals as prefigurations of Christianity or a stage in the progressive ethicization of man. The mysteries were neither academies of natural religion in the mode of Johann August von Starck, the author of *De Tralatitiis ex gentilismo in religionem christianam* (On the Transmissions from Paganism to the Christian Religion), whose appointment to the faculty of theology at Königsberg had outraged Hamann, nor schools of rational philosophy nor ancient masonic lodges nor a stage in Lessing's *Die Erziehung des Menschengeschlechts* (The Education of the Human Race; 1780). The mystery religion of an ancient people comprehended the whole of divinity, even though the form was flawed; religious truth was not instilled in droplets and was no more subject to rational improvement than was language. Religion in any people was a total, not partial, creation; it might be polluted, but it was not subject to Lockian progression, to development through experience. Judaism was a consummate whole in the Old Testament; later rabbinic accretions could only be corruptions.

In the later 1760s and the 1770s Herder was already attacking the philosophes for their abstract conceptions of the primitive that were presumed to apply equally to all lands of the world, since he had begun to see primitive minds revealed in myths as reflections of particular geographic circumstances. French theorists of primitive religion were merely projecting their rationalist, sophisticated selves into the primitive world, instead of attempting to understand the emotional, sensuous, individual character of early peoples. A primitive Volk was bound to its limited space, and its poetic imagery reflected not universal ideas, but a particular landscape. The monistic theory of Nicolas Boulanger, a member of Holbach's circle, that the origin of all myths was the memory of a universal deluge, was an easy object for Herder's mockery in the *Fragmente zu einer Archäologie des Morgenlandes* (Fragments for an Archaeology of the East; 1769): "The deluge is everywhere that there is water, wherever water is poured, wherever one washes with water."[8] For Herder, the waters of the Egyptian Isis-Osiris myth were not recollections of a universal deluge but evocations of the flooding of a specific river, the Nile. Each primitive poetry had a quality not repeated elsewhere, Herder asserted with the conviction of a man who knew the peasants of the Slavic lands on whose borders he had studied and worked. The gods were symbols of nature, not rationalist allegories. They represented the world of primitive men whose senses were more acute than their reason, who were close to the earth and its creatures, who felt themselves an integral part of organic nature and kindred to all living things. The early religions, like primitive poetry, embodied experience of the immediate physical environment into which men were born. Herder's primitive religions were not products of fear alone or of rational perception. They were epitomes of the whole of early man's universe in a particular Klima.

Since Charles de Brosses, author of *Du culte des dieux fétiches* (On the Worship of Fetish Gods; 1760), had been perplexed by the enigma of Egyptian animal worship, Herder felt obliged to fit its practices into his system. He too was against allegorical interpretations of zoolatry, but while de Brosses could not contemplate this cult without revulsion even when he tried to offer an explanation for it, Herder eulogized it as the adoration of a life force. God created man among animals. The primitive Egyptians lived in close proximity to their beasts, and they knew their spirit and their feelings. "We? What is an animal to us? In our palaces, in our discussion clubs, in our stone edifices remote from everything in nature, what is an animal to us? Who looks upon it except for play or pleasure or for system-making?"[9]

The religion of the Hebrews fit into this schema of the ancient world; though similar in character to other primitive religions, it towered above them as the truest expression of divinity. The question of the diffusion of religious rituals and beliefs was inconsequential. The spirit of Israel was the echo of divinity itself; the ceremonial borrowings of the Jews were mere trivia. Judaism was to be appreciated only in its authentic original form, the Bible, cleansed of later rabbinic accretions.

Herder was aware that critics would relate his work *On the Spirit of Hebrew Poetry* to Bishop Lowth's book, but his purpose in writing the essay was far broader: to reveal the early form-giving spirit of the Hebrews up to the time of their lawgiver Moses, first in the structure of their language, then in their poetic cosmology, and finally in the history of the patriarchs. The poetic narrative of a pastoral people in the first period of its existence as recorded in the Bible was the voice of holiness. Herder's commentary was a counterattack against the deist readings of the Scriptures that demeaned them. In every line of the Old Testament Herder recognized the poetry of a pristine simplicity and the piety of nomads. The bloodthirsty episodes in which the atheists and deists had reveled as illustrations of Hebrew barbarism he justified as the customs of a patriarchal society where absolute paternal authority was natural. Explaining away the cruelty and ritual cursing of enemies and the harsh punishments as common to those remote ages, he celebrated a naively gentle Abraham and his household living in their tents. The image of the noble Arab of the desert had insinuated itself into the European imagination through travel literature; Herder applied the colors of the contemporary nomads of the east to the patriarchal society in the Bible.

The biblical Hebrew society was earthy yet divine, simple yet strong, austere with the law of a barren soil and the necessary life-and-death authority of a father who ruled over a tribe that was his family. True, the Hebrews could be brutal to enemies and had no friendly relations with neighboring peoples. Their one bond was to their God, and the obedience they showed him was their religion. The patriarchs were not wealthy and they often suffered misfortune, but the covenant with God was never broken. Moses the lawgiver writing of these ancient times evoked for the Hebrews the earliest moments of their existence as a nation in a language whose beauty was equaled by that of no other Volk. The idyl of their patriarchs was the creation of the Hebrew people who had no state, a natural people, a people of God.

Corruption had set in with the formation of the political state of Israel and the growth of luxury. The Hebrews were God's people when they were shepherds, wanderers in the desert receiving his law. Once the Solomonic kingdom was established, it was subject to the same vicissitudes as other empires. Finally, the diaspora uprooted the Hebrews from their native soil, and in Herder's philosophy of world history, such exiles inevitably became parasitic. The Jews could not be restored and renewed; at best they might be integrated into European society if they changed their natures. There was no resemblance between the spirit of the ancient Hebrews, a pastoral people, and the urban moneylenders and beggars whom Herder encountered in the German principalities. Abraham, the solitary figure who dedicated himself to God and from whose progeny God built his people, was for Herder the image of total trust, a sharp contrast with the suspicious contemporary Israelites of Western Europe.

The new biblical criticism, the questions of rationalist Christian Hebraist scholarship about precisely who wrote which passages of the Old Testament, left Herder indifferent. For him it was enough that the Bible was imbued with the religious spirit of the ancient Hebrew nation. Learned quibbling over texts interested him no more than the theological structures once erected by rabbinic and Christian apologists to justify the harsh sentences meted out by the patriarchs or to make palatable the resort to subterfuge in order to win parental blessings.

Herder's idealized portrait of ancient Israel had parallels in French literature. But seventeenth-century writers like the Abbé Fleury and eighteenth-century publicists like Senger never became the spiritual mentors of generations of Frenchmen, whereas Herder was the moral and religious guide of a whole sector of the German people. His judgment of ancient Israel took firm hold—but so did his misgivings about Jews who were his contemporaries. Herder and his teacher Kant exemplify the profound ambivalence of the principal moral masters of modern Germany, creators of a Janus-like judge of the Jews and Judaism.

Birth of the Judenfrage

In the decade before the French Revolution, there was a marked rise in the number of writings devoted to what the Germans began to call the *Judenfrage* and the French *la réforme politique des Juifs*. So concentrated a volume of books and articles had not appeared since the British debate over the Naturalization Act of 1753, and the new wave of pamphleteering often took cognizance of the polemical literature that had been published in English. The authors of the 1780s came from a broad social spectrum. Christian Wilhelm Dohm (1751–1820), whose *Über die bürgerliche Verbesserung der Juden* (On the Civil Betterment of the Jews) was published in Berlin in 1781 and 1783 with a royal privilege, though not with the philosophical concurrence of Frederick II, was a highly respected Prussian official in the department of foreign affairs who enjoyed the king's personal favor. In many ways Dohm's two volumes, which were printed by Frederick Nicolai, a close friend of Lessing and Mendelssohn, fixed the terms of the political debate on the civil rights of Jews. Mirabeau, who had been at the Prussian court, considered his own pamphlet of 1787, *Sur Moses Mendelssohn, sur la réforme politique des Juifs* (On Moses Mendelssohn, on the Political Reform of the Jews), a faithful condensation of Dohm's work, which had not been much noticed in France except for Brissot de Warville's brief account in his journal in October 1784.

Two developments brought the Jewish question to the fore at this period, both more relevant to the German than to the French world. One involved bureaucratic discussions on the civil status of the Jews, which had led to Joseph II's grant of a series of restricted rights to the Jewish inhabitants of Austria. The crazy quilt of patents put together by his officials, laws that differed in various parts of the Hapsburg Empire, has helped to create the image of Joseph as the great emancipator of the Jews. In fact, his patents to the Jews were part of an overall policy for dealing with his sizable religious minorities—Calvinists, Lutherans, members of the Greek Orthodox Church—who had been used by foreign powers to foment discontent in the loose-jointed realm. With the acquisition of Bukowina, the clandestine movement of Jews to the west created a vagabond population of about 200,000 paupers, stragglers, and bandits difficult to comprehend within the legal proprieties of an enlightened despotism. Joseph's reforms protected the handful of rich Jewish families in Vienna from the intrusion of other Jews and attempted to push Jews uprooted from his eastern lands into useful agricultural pursuits, tying them to the soil. It was an effort to cope with the Jews less as a religious than as a social problem. Converted Jews like von Sonnenfels, the official in the Hapsburg bureaucracy who had written a book defending his former coreligionists from blood-guilt accusations, had tried to establish the right of the Jews to citizenship in the face of traditional local Catholic opposition. The Catholics' arguments were primarily social and economic, at least on the surface, though the clergy tried to hold out on theological grounds against the grant of civic rights to any of the religious minorities.

In the German principalities and particularly in the kingdom of Prussia, the Jewish question assumed a more philosophical tone, especially after Mendelssohn achieved fame as the most popular philosopher writing in the German language. The intimate friendship of

Mendelssohn with Lessing and Nicolai, who controlled a number of journals, made it difficult for literary lights to continue to look on all Jews as living in fanatical darkness. The rabbis had been disdained as obscurantists, enemies of culture, in popular Christian belief. Now litterateurs were confronted with the anomaly of a Jew from the Dessau community who observed the rituals of his people and yet wrote with admirable clarity on the favorite subjects of contemporary German intellectuals—the nature of the sublime, the characteristics of sentiments, philosophical demonstrations of immortality. The multilingual Mendelssohn reviewed French and English as well as German books and translated parts of the Old Testament from Hebrew into the vernacular. He was a prodigy who, though an autodidact, seemed to free the German language from the ponderousness of the predominant philosophical style. Mendelssohn's *Phaedon,* a dialogue on the immortality of the soul, put into the mouth of Socrates arguments of the Leibnizian and Wolffian schools in a manner that was comprehensible to an educated German burgher and in translation won the plaudits of French, English, Dutch, and Danish readers. Among middle-class literary people Moses Mendelssohn, the German Jewish philosopher who in writing for Europeans had been able to substitute citations from the rabbis with an appeal to plain and simple Enlightenment reason, transformed the stereotype of the Jew. His thinking was so lucid that a new Judaism appeared to be in the making, which on most abstract religious and intellectual matters abolished the distinction between an enlightened Jew and an enlightened Christian.

Mendelssohn's manner was gentle in writing and in personal conversation. He was the incarnation of Lessing's Nathan the Wise, and the leaders of the Berlin Jewish community basked in his reflected glory. When summoned by the chief rabbi of Berlin to explicate Jewish laws on marriage and property for the benefit of the Prussian authorities, he made of Judaism a rational civil religion. His most controversial work remained *Jerusalem, oder über religiöse Macht und Judenthum* (Jerusalem, or on Ecclesiastical Authority and Judaism; 1783), in which he advocated a complete separation of political power from all matters of religion and, with the exclusion of atheists, absolute religious toleration. In his elucidation of the nature of Judaism, there was an assumption that Judaism did not depend on miracles (as some unmentioned religions did) and was in its essence a body of

moral and philosophical principles. One branch of the German Enlightenment was in accord with this position, and Frenchmen like the
young Count de Mirabeau failed to see anything in it that contradicted their beliefs.

In the Germanic world, contemporary Judaism came to be embodied in two polar types, the profligate court Jew Süss Oppenheimer,
who was executed in Stuttgart, and the virtuous philosopher of Berlin, Moses Mendelssohn. Public opinion articulated by the literate
classes leaned toward the generalization of one or the other of these
images. The court Jew was arrogant, an active agent in the extension
of the power of his master at the expense of the burghers, ostentatious
in the display of his wealth and his Christian mistresses. Jud Süss got
his just deserts once his princely protector died. The good philosopher Mendelssohn was the countertype, a sage who filled an intellectual vacuum in German thought between the schools of Leibniz-Wolff
and Kant. His writings on subjects that interested German burghers
with intellectual pretensions and Germans who exercised the liberal
professions made him a normal, sensible German cleansed of the ugly
attributes commonly associated with Jews.

Dohm's Final Solution

While Herder's *On the Spirit of Hebrew Poetry* was in many ways the
most novel perception of ancient Judaism introduced into the late
Enlightenment, other documents published in the German world en-
deavored to find a place in Christendom for contemporary Judaism.
One was dramatic, the fable of *Nathan der Weise* (Nathan the Wise)
presented by Gotthold Ephraim Lessing, the playwright and critic
who dabbled in theology and philosophical history. Another was juridical, the treatise by Christian Wilhelm Dohm that was an incisive
analysis of the Judenfrage by an educated Prussian official endowed
with a broad historical and theological understanding. A third was
the apology written by Moses Mendelssohn.

Of the three, Dohm's book was by far the most adventurous. This
was the finest flower of the enlightened Prussian bureaucracy, which
had set as its purpose the rationalization of the state, making of all
nationals productive, useful, and therefore happier members of civil
society ("bürgerliche Gesellschaft"). Utility for the state, happiness

for individuals, and a consciousness that all men had a common humanity were united. The tone was neither prophetic nor dogmatic; Dohm raised the question of the Jews because their legal disabilities in civilized countries hindered them from contributing their part to the general well-being of the state and of mankind. In the best spirit of the Enlightenment—which like all movements of thought often failed to live up to its principles—Dohm inquired into the origins of the Jews' disabilities, as Rousseau had inquired into the origins of inequality and Hume into the beginnings of religion.

Did the Jews suffer because of their ancestry, their customs, their particular manner of worshiping God? In order to justify in the eyes of Reason the contemporary denial of full citizenship rights and the bestowal of only some human rights, it would have to be clearly demonstrated that the religion of the Jews was saturated with antisocial principles and that their divine commandments ran counter to the dictates of justice and philanthropy. What was known of the religion of the Jews revealed no such harmful principles, Dohm argued. Only the ignorant common people charged the Jewish religion with enjoining its practitioners to behave treacherously to non-Jews, and only fanatical priests had assembled tales about the prejudices of the Jews. The law of Moses, the fundamental law of the Jews that Christians themselves revered, contained no such teachings.

Dohm was prepared to concede that present-day Jews might be "sittlich verdorbener" (more corrupted in their moral conduct) than other nations, but that was the inevitable consequence of the legal constraints imposed on them for many centuries. Dohm, thinking in terms of a simple social model, attributed Jewish immorality to Christian laws. Any species of mankind subject to such hostile political conditions would have been guilty of the same moral violations. Dohm reasoned in the Montesquieu manner: remove the plainly defined social causes of an evil, and the evil would disappear. While among all Judeophobes and some Judeophiles like Dohm there was a consensus that the Jews, or at least many Jews, were living in a state of social degradation, the question was what should come first: abolition of the restrictive laws that had given rise to their corruption or the "decorrupting" of the Jews prior to their admission into civil society.

Dohm recognized as a historical fact the origin of the mutual hatred of Christians and Jews in the crucifixion of Christ eighteen hundred years before, and deplored it as a preposterous residue. The blame, if any was to be allotted, should be laid at the feet of governments that failed to create a feeling of common citizenship among both Christians and Jews and to mitigate the divisive effect of different principles of religion. Since the governments were Christian, it was Christians who were at fault for the unsocial behavior of both parties. Humane feelings should have been instilled in the Jews by showing them, through example, the humaneness of Christians. It was the doing of the Christians if the Jews were not good citizens devoted to the pursuit of general happiness, if they felt aversion and hatred toward Christians, if they were not bound by the laws of honor. The religion of the Jews in no way mandated such conduct; corruption of morals—Dohm meant shady economic and social practices—was the result of prejudices implanted in the Jews and perpetuated by the erroneous policies of Christian governments, a remnant of the barbarism of bygone centuries, an effect of fanatical religious hatred that enlightenment should long since have extirpated.

Dohm's solution to the Jewish problem was not hemmed in with stipulations. States were obligated to extend their protection impartially to all religions and to free the Jews from civil disabilities. But Dohm was not unaware of social problems related to the occupational shift of Jews from moneylending and trade to more varied pursuits. As for the opening of public offices to Jews, he would delay such a move because of their lack of experience. Dohm would initiate the process of acceptance of the Jews by raising their cultural level and abolishing glaring legal disabilities.

But there were many other Christian literati, among them outstanding figures of German thought, who were not ready to acquiesce in Dohm's open-hearted solution. Their priorities were reversed: first let the Jews transform themselves into sociable creatures, and then open the doors to political equality. There were even major philosophers who doubted whether any such metamorphosis was possible for this alien nation. Unlike the Voltairean Judeophobes, many of the German thinkers respected and even admired the image of ancient Israel. For them it was rabbinic commentators and the ceremonial law of postexilic Judaism that had created a chasm between Christianity and Judaism. As long as Jews continued to be fanatically strict in the observance of their ritual law, especially the dietary rules and their holy days, there could be no free and easy converse between them and their Christian neighbors. Dohm had seen no impediment to civil co-existence in the preservation of Jewish ceremonial laws, and he went further than such observant Jews as Mendelssohn in strengthening the power of the heads of the synagogue in the execution of religious bans and excommunication. Dohm regarded the general supervision of the synagogue over its members as a benign moral influence that was useful to the state.

The Predicament of Moses Mendelssohn

Mendelssohn assumed a position that was not easy to explain to Christians, though he tried time and again in letters and in his pivotal work, *Jerusalem*. He was strict in following the code of rituals in his everyday life, but denied that meticulous observance of Jewish rules in any way interfered with the warm relationship between Christians and Jews. Forty years of unbroken friendship with Lessing and the publisher Nicolai proved that Judaism was no bar to intimate daily intercourse. Mendelssohn's house was filled with Christians who came to pay homage to the sage and to hear his words of wisdom. And his correspondence included the leading literati of many religious per-suasions, even those such as Hamann who were bitterly opposed to his aesthetic and theological views.

In some respects Mendelssohn's religious position was fuzzy around the edges. He set up a doctrine of the absolute separation of church and state, but in asides and footnotes he virtually excluded atheists from the polity, as he dilated upon the dangerous fanaticism of unbelievers and, in a prefiguration of Dostoevsky, warned that those who feared no God were likely to fear no law. Mendelssohn insisted, however, on freedom of conscience and thought the state should prosecute only for acts that threatened the civil order of soci-ety, a rather flexible criterion. He opposed the exercise of ecclesiasti-cal power by religious heads in matters of conscience, even within their own religious communities. Members were not to be ousted from their congregations for deviations from the rule, because it was impossible to know whether their convictions might not later lead them back into the fold.

There were Christian polemists such as the Swiss pastor Johann

Kaspar Lavater who in their zeal for their own faith tried to smoke out Mendelssohn on what he thought about Christianity and Christ. Mendelssohn, wary, took the position that Judaism had never been a proselytizing religion and that its commandments were meant for the Jews alone. He studiously avoided religious controversies. But Lavater, whatever his conscious intent may have been, put Mendelssohn in a bind and provoked a public exchange of letters about Judaism and Christianity that delighted the German literary gossips, who were no less addicted to scandalmongering than the French. Viewed in the light of the age-long defenses of Judaism that had been forced on Jews, this was a relatively benign continuation of the great medieval debates on the Talmud. Mendelssohn and Lavater preserved a superficial tone of enlightened gentility; but the dagger thrusts, even the pinpricks, were obvious to the knowing. Though Mendelssohn, as Kant observed, was by far the more skillful dialectician, the restraints imposed on him wreaked havoc with his nervous system and he never completely recovered from the confrontation. The mutual tolerance of Christians and Jews under the German Enlightenment dispensation was not achieved painlessly.

The initial act of provocation has to be set against the background of Lavater's religious enthusiasm—he was later accused by Mirabeau of being a member of the sect of mystical illuminati—and Mendelssohn's determination to avoid any utterance that could be construed as an insult to Christianity or interpreted as a repudiation of his own Judaism or viewed as an escape into a deism that minimized the significance of positive religion. Without asking Mendelssohn's leave, Lavater dedicated to him a German translation of Charles Bonnet's demonstration of the truth of Christianity, and then suggested that Mendelssohn either refute the arguments of Bonnet or, if he was unable to do so, behave as Socrates would have and become a Christian.

To ignore the challenge might have opened Mendelssohn to the charge of deism or indifference, while to attack Bonnet would have enmeshed him in a debate on the relative merits of Christianity and Judaism. In his reply Mendelssohn insisted that he had never given Lavater the least intimation that he was amenable to conversion; he assured him that he had long since examined all aspects of the religious question and remained faithful to his own belief. His reasons were a matter of inner conviction and he would not debate them publicly. He and his brethren lived in a realm where, albeit with restrictions, they were tolerated, and he had no intention of affronting other religions. (After all, Mendelssohn noted in passing, he was prohibited by law from visiting Lavater's Zurich.) But Mendelssohn did not leave it at that and went on to suggest that Bonnet's arguments were of such a character that they could be adduced in support of any religion, not only Christianity. Lavater responded with an elaborate display of regret that he had importuned Mendelssohn, and then proceeded to press him for a hint about the nature of his objections to Bonnet's apology. The swordplay continued without resolution.

Against his will Mendelssohn had become an official defender of Judaism, and though the letters to Lavater intimated that in the course of time ritual commandments with which he was not necessarily in accord had been added to the religious rules of Judaism, he stood by the whole body of the law. In *Jerusalem,* after a rather long-winded exposition of natural law and the social contract and the history of idolatry as a corruption of hieroglyph reading, he came to the uniqueness of the Judaic religion, which he analyzed under several heads. The first part of Judaism was comprised of those eternal truths about God that were discoverable by natural reason alone and were accessible to all men who sought to know them. The second part consisted of historical truths that had been preserved by Jewish tradition and concerned the early history of mankind, the lives of the patriarchs, the covenant between God and his chosen people, the renewal of the bond on Sinai with the promulgation of the Mosaic law. These historical truths had been confirmed by a multiplicity of testimonies so that the evidence was overwhelming. The law, communicated in writing, was transmitted along with oral interpretations from generation to generation. In the initial period under the law, God had ruled his people directly and there was no distinction between the civil and the religious law. Only under the influence of foreign neighbors did morbidity set in, which pushed the people of Israel to demand a king despite the warnings of the prophet Samuel. From then on, the power of the state and the religious law were separated, and the early wholeness was lost forever. The state could thenceforward prescribe social behavior, but in no circumstances was it allowed to interfere with religious conscience.

Though in conversation with Lavater Mendelssohn gave the appearance—or so Lavater thought—of valuing the moral principles of Jesus, he could by no means condone the abstruse theology with which the teachings of the Christian messiah had become entangled. In matters of religion Mendelssohn would be tolerant of any view except atheism; Spinoza's God was for him no God at all, and the refutation of Spinoza's doctrines was central to his religion and his morality. Individual conduct was the measure of a man, Christian or Jew. The ritual laws of Judaism had a rational foundation that he had learned from his guide Maimonides, and avoidance of religious polemics was the path of prudence. Mendelssohn could not countenance grand historical philosophies about the improvement of the human species, even when propounded by his friend Lessing. An individual might perfect himself, but the species remained more or less the same combination of good and evil in all times and places. Religion represented a personal relationship between man and God. A private tragedy of Mendelssohn's last years, during which he was afflicted with all manner of physical and psychological ailments, was his inability to resolve the nagging question as to whether Lessing had in fact been a crypto-Spinozist who denied this intimate personal relationship with God.

Mendelssohn had a difficult time making his religious position clear to most Christians steeped in an inherited conception of Judaism as intolerant rabbinism. Kant considered *Jerusalem* disingenuous. Not all was smooth sailing for Moses of Berlin when the philosopher Friedrich Heinrich Jacobi, once Lessing was dead, published a purported interview in which Lessing had avowed his Spinozism. The pious Mendelssohn, for whom Spinoza was a bête noire as he was to all religious Jews, vehemently denied that Lessing, the darling of his heart, could have concealed from him for decades so black a reality as adherence to the atheistic beliefs of the renegade philosopher. Jacobi's allegations were no minor blow to the image built up over decades of free intercourse and deep friendship between a Christian and a Jew. Did Lessing keep this most important fact of his life from Mendelssohn? Was Mendelssohn's reply to Jacobi's revelation candid, or did Mendelssohn make an attempt to suppress a 1783 letter of his own indicating that he had some knowledge of Lessing's Spinozism? All this was regurgitated ad nauseam by the literary tongue-waggers and cast a pall on Mendelssohn's last years. Viewed in hindsight, the fracas raises questions about how thoroughly he had thought through the dilemmas of the Judenfrage in the German Enlightenment. The popular philosopher who had won the plaudits of German belles-lettrists when he wrote on aesthetics and other subjects that enjoyed a general consensus could not get away unscathed from a confrontation with atheism in an eighteenth-century polity.

One aspect of Mendelssohn's defense of Judaism was colored by a perception that he communicated to Michaelis and Herder. He hoped that, in an aesthetic appreciation of the religious poetry of the Old Testament, Christians and Jews could be joined by a common experience. They could read the Psalms and prophetic works as poetry, Mendelssohn wrote to Michaelis, without theological glosses and debates over whether or not they foretold the coming of a messiah. They could ignore the exegetical apparatus that discovered prefigurations of Jesus in what were poetic effusions of the Judaic religious soul. In one passage of *Jerusalem* Mendelssohn likened religions to different languages in which the same universal humanity found a variety of voices. Though he continued to observe Jews laws and rituals to the letter, he no longer appeared to hold to their supreme religious importance, regarding them as man-made, like commentaries on texts or theological deductions. Since the moral truths of Judaism were reasonable, the same as those of natural religion without revelation, and since each religion was a divinely inspired language, why should he forsake the religion into which he had been born? Proselytization was presumptuous and conversion idiotic.

The consequences of the romantic transformation of Judaism into a religion of moral beauty were far graver than Mendelssohn foresaw. The emphasis on Judaism as an aesthetic-moral experience inflicted a more serious wound on traditional and historical Judaism in the Germanic world than did the sneering of a Voltaire intent upon its uglification. If Judaism and Christianity were equally appealing to the romantic imagination, why balk at the baptismal font? The conversion of Dorothea Schlegel, née Mendelssohn, was the symbolic outcome of the introduction of a new aesthetic metaphor. The raison d'être for Judaism was being shattered by the celebration of the ancient God of the Jews as an inspirer of sweet and lofty poesy.

In his *Jerusalem* Mendelssohn was outspoken in denying the need for uniformities in a modern state. Many ways could lead to virtue, but the dilemmas of the coexistence of Christians and Jews were not easily resolved. If ethical universals led to identical principles, what conceivable moral use was there for the detailed ceremonials of positive religion, especially the Judaic one? If differences were based on inherited national characteristics, could men of different origins live together in amity? Absolute individualism was almost unthinkable; there had to be some communal form such as religion or language by which the individual was fashioned. Both Lessing and Mendelssohn believed in human attributes that characterized virtue, irrespective of status, religion, or political allegiance, and Lessing's freemasonry was related to these ideas. But the ceremonials of Judaism, which set Jews apart from the rest of mankind, struck a discordant note to most enlightened Christians.

Perhaps nowhere is the distance between Kant's and Lessing's secular Enlightenment and Mendelssohn's Judaism greater than in their divergent attitudes toward the burgeoning idea of progress. Mendelssohn, acting as a spokesman for Judaism, was unable to accept the idea of progress either in Kant's version or in Lessing's hundred theses on the education of mankind. Man's relation to God was personal and individual. After Lessing's death Mendelssohn wrote in *Jerusalem:*

I, for my own part, have no conception of a "training of the whole human race," such as my late friend Lessing himself let some historiographer of mankind put into his head. They imagine to themselves, the thing "human race," as a single individual, and think, Providence has put it here on earth, as it were, in a school, to be trained from an infant to an adult. In the main, the human race (if the metaphor will hold good) is, in almost every age, infant, adult, and greybeard at once, only in different places and regions . . . Progress is for individual man, who is destined by Providence to pass a portion of his eternity here on earth. Everyone goes his own way through life. One's route leads him over flowers and meadows; another's across desert plains, over steep mountains or by the side of dangerous precipices. Yet they all get on with the journey, pursuing the road to happiness, to which they are destined. But that the bulk, or the whole human race here on earth, should be constantly moving forward in progress of time, and perfecting itself, seems to me not to have been the design of Providence. It is, at least, not so decided, not by far so necessary for the vindication of Providence, as some are wont to think.

... Most nations of the earth pass many ages in the same degree of civilization, in the same crepusculous light, which appears much too dim to our spoiled eyes. Now and then, a particle of the grand mass will kindle, become a bright star, and run through an orbit, which, now after a longer, now after a shorter period, brings it back again to its stand still, or sets it down at no great distance from it. Man goes on; but mankind is constantly swinging to and fro, within fixed boundaries; but, considered as a whole, retains at all periods of time, about the same degree of morality, the same quantity of religion and irreligion, of virtue and vice, of happiness and misery.[10]

In his refutation of Mendelssohn, Kant made no grandiloquent affirmations after the manner of Condorcet, but unequivocally declared in works written both before and after Mendelssohn's death that life without faith in progress would be intolerable. His expression of the need for a historical and teleological justification of existence has an almost plaintive tone. Nowhere is the ersatz moral quality of the idea of progress as a substitute for a religious absolute more obvious and more pathetic than in Kant's attack on the cyclical theory of history in *Der Streit der Facultäten* (The Strife of the Faculties; 1798). The conviction that the wicked would be punished in the next world as a consolation to the virtuous for enduring the spectacle of this world was considered unworthy of any conception of a moral providence. Hence man must believe—for there is no alternative—in the continual moral progression of the species to make some sense out of life. Can he prove it beyond all question? No. But then it is up to the disbelievers to disprove it. History can raise many doubts on this score, but men cannot act on the hypothesis of antiprogression because it has not been demonstrated. And Kant maintains that in fact men of good will have always operated on the presupposition of moral progress, as has the respectworthy Moses Mendelssohn. The empirical reflection that in the past things have not improved is not an acceptable pragmatic argument against man's continuing to work for moral betterment. Air balloons had not been proved practicable before they were actually sent aloft.

In the nineteenth century, Reform Judaism, which derived at least in part from Mendelssohn, nevertheless embraced the idea of progress with the same fervor as liberal Protestants; but Mendelssohn himself had been far from either surrendering a conception of the unique destiny of Judaism or amalgamating individual destinies into the fate of all mankind. There were rewards or punishments for individuals consequent on their virtuous or immoral conduct, and there were separate fates for the differentiated religions Judaism and Christianity.

Men like Hamann, for whom a mystical union with Christ was the heart of Christian religious experience, could not tolerate Mendelssohn's rational-ethical religion of Judaism. The mocking magus of the north espoused a passionate religion, not one demonstrable through time-worn, frayed proofs of the existence of God. Reducing the variety of religions to merely another form of human differences, like languages, utterly failed to convince Hamann. Nor were Mendelssohn's aesthetic principles, so readily understandable to others, admissible to Hamann, who was discovering the shattering, soul-searing emotionality of the religion of Christ. The latterday Moses of Berlin, the rationalist Jew, still represented for Hamann the dry letter of the Mosaic law that rejected the lofty spirituality of Christ. Tenacious adherence to that law was a victory of antichrist, a denial of Christ's spiritual triumph with which a Christian could make no peace. The old Christian charge of Jewish corporeality was renewed with vigor. For Hamann the new form of Judaism as it appeared in rationalist Enlightenment guise was satanic; and conversion from Judaism to Christianity was not possible through arguments of reason, for Christ had to be lived.

The Euthanasia of Judaism

By the 1780s neither the French nor the German philosophical thinkers of the religious Enlightenment saw any point to continuing the traditional dispute over whether or not the messiah had come. Both expected him, the Jews for the first time, the Christians for the second; but that difference was not worth the reams of theological argument wasted on it. Yet, at the same time, neither Herder nor Kant was content with an unequivocal acceptance of the Jews into European society in the name of the principles of tolerance and humanity they espoused. They turned their backs on Lessing's literary abstraction of Nathan the Wise and absorbed themselves in the practical problems of Jewish social conduct in everyday life and in the political questions of assimilation and emancipation. They felt constrained to reckon with the historical-economic reality that Jews had been engaged for centuries in degrading occupations and behaved in strange ways that set them apart from their Christian brothers. Contemporary polities had to evaluate the nature of the Jews before receiving them on a basis of equality.

Herder, Michaelis, and many others who admired the beauties of ancient Hebrew poetry or the excellence of Mosaic statecraft, when they turned from the magnificent image of primitive Israel to what they perceived as the sordid reality of Jewish communities divided between court Jews flaunting the appurtenances of wealth and power and Jews living in squalor, became aware that after all they were dealing with an alien people, an "Asiatic" people (Herder's adjective). The idea of the Volksgeist—granted that every collective had an indelible spirit engraved on its primordial nature—made the Jews anthropological freaks in European society. After their original Hebrew spirit had been polluted in the diaspora, they failed to adapt themselves to the territorial cultures of the peoples among whom they dwelled. Herder's enchantment with Hebrew biblical poetry, which delighted Berlin Jews thirsty for recognition from the gentiles, ended up as an illumination that, by contrast, only accentuated the darkness of the low moral estate into which the Jews had fallen. Since the Jews had long been restricted to occupations that were now manifestly injurious to the natives of Europe, it was to be expected that Christians should make demands before welcoming them permanently into their midst and securing their position by law. Herder and Kant did not openly summon the Jews to change their religion, after the manner of Lavater's crude challenge to Mendelssohn, nor did they call on them to adopt new beliefs that violated their consciences. They merely urged them to alter their natures and give up their way of living. In reports of private conversations recently published, Kant voiced opinions that mar the heavily cosmeticized portrait of him as the moralist of the categorical imperative. He said flatly to his friend, the gymnasium inspector Johann Friedrich Abegg: "As long as the Jews are Jews and allow themselves to be circumcised, they never will become more useful than harmful to civil society. They are now vampires of society." [11]

Sometimes Herder couched the requirement that Jews be denatured as a condition precedent to their integration in his characteristic humanitarian rhetoric. It was the noble duty of the Europeans to atone for their previous persecution of Jews, which had corrupted this nation, by raising and educating them to a new sense of honor, a process that had to begin by abjuring all mistreatment of Jews. The ultimate goal was their humanization through exposure to the arts and sciences and through training in devotion to the state. It was clearly the right of the bearers of the German Volk spirit to refashion in the dominant mode outsiders who lived among them, a metamorphosis that could not be achieved without great travail, since in Herder's world view salutary change had to be slow and organic and could not be effected with the mechanical speed that some philosophes thought possible in a clockwork universe. In his philosophy of history Herder had described how long and arduous was the task of assimilating elements from abroad that intruded into the native habitat of a Volk. The integration of the Jews would serve a variety of objectives. Rational enlightened despotism required uniformity in administration and could not countenance Jews' living under their rabbinic statutes. Herder, the true believer in the indivisibility of the Volksgeist, had to encourage the transformation of aliens for a different purpose, to school them in the language of the indigenous culture so that where they lived and worked would eventually become their natural homeland.

Kant, whose historical world view envisaged the rule of universal ideal moral principles for all mankind, was similarly aware of how difficult this process would be for an idiosyncratic nation, bound to a religion burdened with traditional arbitrary commandments for the preservation of order in their society, but lacking a rational ethical core. For Kant, Judaism was a welter of stringent rules never synthesized into a universal absolute that could be defended through the exercise of pure reason. Perhaps a moral essence might be distilled from the Mosaic law, but this would entail the sweeping away of thousands of Jewish rabbinic decrees that had no general applicability.

Kant's reading of Spinoza's interpretation of Judaism as a set of regulations designed for a particular people at a given point in time stripped Judaism of any pretense to universality. The dogged obedience to irrational and adventitious precepts and rules of conduct made of Judaism a religion that ran counter to the stadial development of civil society from a cosmopolitan point of view. By the light of Kant's demonstration of the inevitable ethical progress of mankind, Judaism was a retrograde force. Enlightened despotism, and even the French Revolution with its excesses, could be construed as contributing to the fulfillment of mankind's ethical nature in time. Judaism, frozen in an archaic mold, was only an impediment to human perfectibility. Kant's world-historical judgment of the Jew was accompanied by amicable relations with a few Jewish students and with Mendelssohn; but this did not alter his position that Judaism, with its legalistic rigidity, had to be eradicated, preferably through religious euthanasia. Kant demanded radical transformation, insisting on Jewish commitment to a purified abstraction of the law of Moses or to the teachings of a deistic Christianity, which coincided, mirabile dictu, with the spirit and letter of Kant's metaphysics of morals.

Lessing had not imposed conditions for admission of Jews to Enlightenment society, and neither had Dohm. They were not tied to the dogma that eighteenth-century Judaism was degenerate. Lessing had drawn an idealized portrait of the Jew in his play *Die Juden,* Dohm a historically realistic one in his treatise on the civil betterment of the Jews. But Lessing's *Nathan the Wise,* so dear to nineteenth-century German Jews, had presented a figure who bore no recognizable traits of a rabbinic practicing Jew. He was an honest merchant, moved by benevolence, virtue, the needs of the state—in short, an abstraction, a *schöne Seele* of the Enlightenment, a disembodied noble spirit.

The idealist philosopher Johann Gottlieb Fichte, who like Herder had been Kant's student, bluntly concluded that there was no hope at all of integrating Judaism into European society and that the only solution to the Judenfrage was to ship the Jews off to the holy land. In the 1790s the Jewish apologist Saul Ascher recognized that Fichte's writings had inaugurated a new epoch in the history of Christian animosity toward Jews and Judaism. Virtually all the elements of later German antisemitism, as distinguished from traditional Christian Judeophobia, can be discovered in Fichte's *Beiträge zur Berichtigung der Urtheile des Publicums über die französische Revolution* (Essays for the Correction of Public Judgments on the French Revolution; 1793) and in his more famous *Reden an die deutsche Nation* (Speeches to the German Nation; 1808). The old religious attack on Judaism was displaced by a political accusation that the Jews were a hostile and malignant growth within the state. They were more to be feared by ordinary

Germans than were despotic rulers. Laws gave the German peasant a right to his hut, but he had no recourse against the economic power of the Jews, who could dispossess him. If this was the strength of the disfranchised Jews in present-day Germany, imagine their dominion, Fichte threatened, if they were granted the full rights of citizenship. They would mercilessly crush other citizens underfoot. There was no way to bestow civil rights on the Jews except to cut off their heads in the night and replace them with other heads in which there would not be a single Jewish thought. "In order to protect ourselves from them I see no other course but to seize their beloved land and transport them all there."[12]

A new nationalist anthropology was being framed, a pseudo-science of *Volkerpsychologie* that anticipated myths of racial purity with their jargon of superior and inferior peoples. The Germans, "a people's people," had all the positive attributes, while the Jews were irredeemably degenerate. The age-old Christian theological arguments against Judaism were secularized—those who had been eternally damned were now incurably diseased. The spirit of Luther lived on in Fichte, whom Saul Ascher called Eisenmenger the Second.

Again, the paradox of the Enlightenment's intolerance of Judaism emerged. Whether the doctrine preached was Kant's ethical, rationalist universalism or Herder's divine orchestration of an infinite variety of creative Volk spirits, each wedded to its natural habitat in a mystical union, or Fichte's rabid and exclusive nationalism, traditional Judaism would find no place in Western Europe. Conversion had once been regarded by a small minority of Jews as the sovereign means of escaping from the toils of Judeophobia, though it had not shielded the converts in Spain and Portugal. Neither the moral philosophy of Kant nor the philosophical history of Herder held forth the prospect of any such facile solution to the Judenfrage.

For both the rational systematizer Kant and the protoromantic Herder, rabbinic Judaism was an insurmountable barrier to the integration of the Jews into European society. Kant's antagonism had even deeper roots; there was one possible metaphysic of morals, and the Mosaic law, let alone later commentaries, could not yield a rational system of moral principles. Herder's spirit of biblical Hebrew poetry did not require such ordered propositions, and a romanticized Bible was accessible to the Jews if they freed themselves from the restrictions of rabbinism. Both Kant and Herder agreed that the ritual rabbinic code alienated Jews from their fellows in society and made coexistence unfeasible. Yet, when Solomon Maimon, the refugee from the ghetto whose philosophical acumen Kant esteemed, broke with ritual Judaism, he became so isolated that Kant advised him to return to the fold. Kant had not appreciated the predicament of the Enlightenment Jew when he stated ex cathedra that Judaism in its rabbinic form had to be abandoned; the philosopher of the absolute moral way could envisage no mixed solutions. The loftiest authority of the Germanic world left his fellow citizens and their progeny a poisoned heritage. In rendering their judgments on Judaism, Kant and Voltaire may have infected a continent with a rampant virus that ran out of control for nearly two hundred years.

The Flawed Legacy of the Enlightenment

In the eighteenth century, favorable as well as pejorative diagnoses of the nature of Judaism were becoming more numerous, especially when they dwelt on ancient rather than modern Israel. The Mosaic law as unfolded by Michaelis was a model of rational Enlightenment jurisprudence, if allowance was made for the fact that it was born in a pagan, barbaric world. Though imperfect, Moses the lawgiver, who had to compromise with the inherited iniquities of the age and the demands of geography, set his people on the path to humanity and leniency in the administration of justice. Biblical poetry—as read by Lowth, Michaelis, and Herder—was sublime, the highest praise meted out in the vocabulary of current aesthetic theory. The religion of Judaism was to be judged by the human beings it fashioned; and Lessing summoned onto the German stage virtuous, noble Jews capable of self-sacrifice for others, heroes, wise men unpolluted by fanaticism. Even though the Judaic dispensation was not the loftiest spiritual stage humanity was capable of ultimately attaining, it had in modern times given birth to the beautiful soul of Moses Mendelssohn.

On the other side were aligned the enemies of Judaism—Voltaire, Holbach, illuminated Protestants such as Lavater, deistic Christians such as Woolston, Bolingbroke, Morgan, and Gibbon. Voltaire and the Holbachians milked the Scriptures to conjure up the bloody, vengeful God of Jewish zealots. The tradition of priestly craftiness and the justification of the merciless killings of whole nations had been passed on from Judaism to Christianity, which continued to be possessed by the Judaic spirit. If Jews were slaughtered in the Middle Ages, they were but the victims of the monster God they themselves had created. The radical critics of Christianity led the modern crusade against the survival of Judaism; Judaic origins became the most vulnerable spot in the armor of Christianity, and the dagger of disbelief could be dug into Judaism with impunity. Edward Gibbon in explaining the triumph of Christianity in the Roman world turned to an analysis of the underlying drives, the *ressorts,* the springs of action of the early Christians and then traced back their blind passions for martyrdom and persecution—which were sources of strength in the propagation of the faith—to the Jewish origins of Christianity. Judaism was responsible for the character of a religion that looked to heaven for its rewards and so enfeebled the Roman state that it became easy prey to the barbarian invaders. Deist polemists, among them the Christian Hebraist Thomas Woolston and the moral philosopher Thomas Morgan, distinguished between the teachings of a gentle Christ and the savage remnants of Judaism imbedded in Christian doctrines and practices. The deist purification of Christianity meant ridding it of Jewish elements. Woolston had an advantage over many English publicists in his knowledge of rabbinic commentaries, which when read selectively splashed the image of Israel with gore and set it in a frame of fanaticism and superstition.

Though there has never been a uniform perception of Israel in the Christian world, what distinguished the Enlightenment thinkers was the sheer multiplication and variety of their portrayals. Perhaps the only intellectual dogma uniting so diverse an assemblage was Montesquieu's idea that every collective had a dominant esprit. Traditional interpretations of Judaism continued to be produced by the different churches. Numerically, orthodox readings would probably outstrip the innovations, though the pervasive assumptions of the new age touched all of them to some degree. Hundreds of volumes still debated the fundamental distinctions between Judaism and Christianity with the same rhetoric and biblical proof-texts that had been rehearsed in the writings of the early Church Fathers, in the disputations between friars and rabbis in the thirteenth century, in the Lutheran diatribes. Compendia of Latin versions of rabbinic writings were being published in multivolume collections; and dissertations on every aspect of ancient Judaism kept flowing from the theological faculties of the Protestant universities.

And then, at the very moment when the storehouses of learning were bursting with information about Judaism in all ages, the question was raised as to whether the contemporary religious community of Jews had a raison d'être within the boundaries of Christendom. During the Enlightenment, the Christian sects varied in their acceptance of the Jewish presence, but at best it was received with a measure of grudging forbearance and tolerance. In the west—west of Poland, the heartland of traditional orthodox Judaism—Jewish communities set about reforming themselves to fit what they imagined were the new requirements of Enlightenment Christendom. But the place of Judaism remained anomalous in the Christian political world. On the eve of the French Revolution, Christendom left Judaism hanging. It was no longer tied to Christianity by the apostolic bond: the conversion of the Jews was not a necessary part of the drama of world salvation at the end of the days.

Nineteenth-century Western European society was bequeathed the Jewish question in a new form, the presence of the Jews as persons, since their beliefs and rituals had become matters of indifference to many Christians. The existence of Jews as an entity within the European state system was a problem of a different nature from the old theological preoccupation with Judaism. Christians became obsessed with the social, economic, and political behavior of individual Jews or Jewish collectives at the same time that they were losing interest in doctrinal commitments. Christians were not moved by the formal conversion of droves of Western European Jews to a belief in Christ, because Christians now paid only nominal attention to the religious test. It was usually a necessary but not a sufficient condition for reception into restricted circles of the Christian world. Judaism was defined in terms of a collective of Jewish bodies, as Germandom was the designation of the collectivity of Germans, without regard to religious practices. The water of the baptismal font had proved to be as ineffectual as the chrism that was poured on the heads of fourteenth- and fifteenth-century Spanish Jews.

11

The Aftermath of Liberation

AFTER THE AGE of the French Revolution, there was a marked decline in Christendom's preoccupation with the truth or falsity of the substance of Judaism as a religion. The focus shifted to Jews as persons and their role as individual citizens or as economic and social collectives exerting power in the new nation-states of Europe. Fitting the Jewish people into the system of exclusive nationalities was as difficult as previously it had been to find a place for them in the web of dynastic states and aristocratic hierarchies. The expanding concept of religious toleration in the European nation-states was quick to encompass the array of Christian denominations, but often slow to lift restrictions against Judaism in its variegated forms.

The process of abolishing legal disabilities affecting Jews was not a uniform progression. As revolution and political reaction alternated in many nation-states, the laws granting to Jews residence, citizenship, and the right to hold office were passed and rescinded depending on the prevailing winds of tolerance. Long after basic civil rights were accorded to Jews, many institutions public and private remained effectively closed to them. Religious tests continued to govern matriculation in English universities until in the twentieth century they finally fell into disuse or were reduced to meaningless formulas. The major Christian denominations went on with their missionary activities among Jews, especially in the slums of cities where large numbers of immigrants from Eastern Europe were living in poverty. The Jews of Whitechapel were not averse to receiving the handouts of societies for the propagation of the Gospel in return for adopting the Christian religion, at least temporarily. Converts without conviction were common in German states: Karl Marx's father, an upwardly mobile lawyer; the philosopher Eduard Gans, an aspiring academic; the composer Gustav Mahler, for whom the directorship of the Vienna Opera represented the public recognition of his genius despite antisemitic mutterings in the wings. Often enough, conversions were not as magical in opening opportunities to new careers as the neophytes had expected. Conversion, what Heinrich Heine called an admission ticket to western culture, did not readily open the door to prized occupations and to social elites. Even after many generations, the stigma of Jewish ancestry lingered on, to be recalled by an enemy.

Judeophobia and Antisemitism: The Dark Backdrop

As secular attitudes took hold in the nineteenth century, there was a drop in the curiosity of literate Europeans about what was going on behind the doors of synagogues, where sharp conflicts divided Orthodox and Reform Jews, or adepts of the Hasidic movement and their adversaries. The civil conduct of emancipated Jews was generally above reproach and they presented no social problems to their host states. The more prosperous, long-settled Jews of Western Europe tried to restrict the number of newcomers from the east, whose manners were unpolished and who might occasion embarrassment; but the floodtide of immigration could not be stemmed. There were sporadic blood-libel accusations in backward areas, though perhaps they were less frequent than in previous centuries—cases in Hungary, Syria, and Russia gained international notoriety. And the charge of treason leveled against the French Jewish officer Alfred Dreyfus had dramatic social and political consequences for western Jews. A neologism, antisemitism, covered a wide spectrum of feelings that persisted among all strata of the Christian population from revolutionary radicals through those classes with aristocratic pretensions. Generally the Christian clergy of Europe sided with conservative elements in erecting barriers against social innovations; this was particularly true in Catholic countries like Austria and the Papal States. Jews engaged in hazardous capitalist ventures or involved in radical revolutionary movements were by definition prominent in espousing change and hence were to be distrusted and feared. The linking of Judaism, free-masonry, and anticlericalism became a stereotype of the Catholic press up to World War II.

Where Luther and Fichte had denounced the Jews as aliens who robbed the German peasant of his patrimony, Oswald Spengler and the Blut und Boden school argued that the Jewish nature was inca-pable of striking root in any soil and was the carrier of decadence; only those with ancient ties to the land they inhabited could nourish a living culture. Judaism had become the plague of the west, and the spread of its influence a symptom of the disintegration of the Euro-pean world. Judaism's cosmopolitanism was contagious, destructive of all values: this was the obverse of the Jewish exclusiveness con-demned in antiquity. Judaism shaped a Levantine personality that could assimilate all cultures but could create nothing of its own. Ju-daism was equivalent to parasitism—a later mainstay of Nazi propa-ganda.

While ancient obsessions with *limpieza* and Jewish corporeality are recognizable in modern Judeophobic doctrines, novelty was intro-duced with the birth of the European ideology of antisemitism, which intermingled religious and pseudo-scientific phraseology. If some of the ideas can be traced back to the Spanish statutes enforcing racial purity, which banned the admission of New Christians to offices in both the church and the state, the virulence of antisemitic propa-ganda and its possession of organized political parties made it a force in the western world that appealed even to elements in the Christian population with few, if any, relations with Jews. The churches of Eu-rope were infiltrated by spurious biological doctrines, and political parties that were under church direction made antisemitism a promi-nent part of their platforms. Except for outbursts of the blood libel in the countryside, often politically manipulated, antisemitism was only secondarily related to Judaism, its beliefs and its rituals. Anti-semitism assumed the form of a personal fixation in many instances, but it was also raised to a philosophical level using rationalist tools and mechanisms of seduction that eventuated in the Holocaust. Vir-tually no Christian country was immune to the antisemitic virus in one of its multiple mutations. The spread of the disease has been chroni-cled before, and there are few clinicians who would presume to assert with finality that it has been eradicated from Christian consciousness, let alone from the dark recesses of the unconscious, its ultimate refuge.

Antisemitism has sometimes spread to countries like Japan, where there is no historical or religious tie to Judaism and its doctrines, even of a tenuous character. The emergence of the state of Israel as a minor world power further complicates the nature of the phobic element in antisemitism; the idea that the existence of an independent state for part of the Jewish people would free western society of this obsession—long a tenet of Zionist political ideology—appears to be illusory. The desire of rogue elements in Christianity to destroy its progenitor, which was acted out through the agency of Nazism—a Christian heresy recognized as such and condemned by some princes of the churches, but not by others—survived the Holocaust. How Christendom will grapple with its own share of guilt in the events of the early 1940s cannot be foretold. Those Jews who escaped the fate of their European brethren have come to realize that they themselves may not have been without sin.

Whatever residue of Christian religious, as distinguished from academic, interest in Judaism remains in the twentieth century has moved away from the forlorn hope of proselytizing the Jews to moral and political issues involving a Jewish presence in the growing urban areas of Western Europe. Judaism itself has in the meantime undergone profound changes. While the holy land as an idea has always occupied a place of significance in diaspora Judaism, since World War II absorption with the political fortunes of the state of Israel has often reduced synagogal observances to the level of cultic practices, bereft of the deep psychic commitment associated with Judaic religion in the past.

The Science of Judaism

To the degree that Christianity's interest in Judaism as a religion persisted in the nineteenth century, it moved into narrow channels; the questions that were raised tended to be academic and historical. Purely theological polemics between Christians and Jews were conspicuously absent or assumed an ultrasophisticated character. In Jewish communities themselves, the nineteenth-century intoxication with history encouraged an extension of studies into the various aspects of Judaism and early Christianity. Hebraic scholarship came to flourish among German Reform Jews, whose communities could support in comfort learned clergymen ready to devote much of their leisure to the intellectual history of their religion. There were also chairs in Jewish theological seminaries occupied by outstanding erudits, who adopted the scientific methodologies of their non-Jewish counterparts in the German state universities. Solomon Maimon, the Jew who left his ghetto to study with Kant in Königsberg, once bemoaned the fact that the only available general history of the Jews from their beginnings through modern times had been written by the Huguenot polymath Jacques Basnage, who published his works in the first years of the eighteenth century. To fill the gap, the German Jewish world of the nineteenth century produced a galaxy of bibliographers, general historians, and specialized scholars who trained themselves in what were touted as the new scientific methods of the German historical school. The Reform rabbis and professors became skilled in the use of linguistic tools essential to the study of Judaism; they were not bound by the religious prohibitions of orthodoxy, and were better prepared than most Christian academics to investigate the vast storehouse of rabbinic commentaries and philosophical texts with scientific objectivity and a modern critical apparatus. Leopold (Yom Tov Lipmann) Zunz published a manifesto setting forth the aims of the newly founded Science of Judaism. Its periodical, *Zeitschrift für die Wissenschaft des Judenthums,* appeared in Berlin in 1822–23, fortuitously while Hegel was delivering his *Lectures on the Philosophy of History* belittling the role of Judaism in world culture.

As far as the German Jewish scholars were concerned, Judaism had run its course and had finally become an enlightened religion fit for emancipated Jews. This was the appropriate time for a rehearsal of the entire history of Judaism in all its circumstances and variations because no further changes were expected in the future. The minimal ceremonials of the German Reform Jews were fixed forever. The study of Judaism was thus essentially a historical inquiry into the works of the past, as a bygone geological epoch or a buried civilization might be explored. The purpose of these historical studies was not to fertilize or revivify contemporary Judaism, but to petrify it. Nothing that was discovered was meant to upset or trouble anybody,

Christian or Jew; the disputations of the past were now dead and gone. Texts would be edited, bibliographies compiled, and monuments raised—acts of piety, perhaps.

The Science of Judaism in its own eyes was distinguished from the study of world religions like Christianity because it was the creation of one people. Through time Judaism had developed a world outlook, but it remained a particular people's expression of the universal. Though Herder was not frequently cited by the scholars who founded the Science, his idea of the Volksgeist dominated their conception. In the formula of Abraham Geiger, an outstanding figure in the movement, the Science embraced three parts: study of the tongues in which Judaism found its unique expression; the literary and cultural history created by Judaism; and finally its philosophical and religious essence. Judaism was the fullness of the voices of its people throughout the ages. The mission of the scholars was to recover these voices and to present them in the format of modern learning, which usually raised no misgivings among erudite Christians. In practice, the scholarly virtuosity of the proponents of the Science of Judaism, for all its vaunted objectivity, did not disguise a marked preference for what was considered the rationalist over the mystical trend in Judaism.

Despite the rather limited goal of the Science of Judaism, there was an extraordinary flowering of scholarship in specialized periodicals, published in German and accessible to educated Christian Europe. Virgin territory was penetrated with new secular techniques. Many of the judgments of the German Jewish scholars, endowed with a passion for objectivity and an antiquarian zeal, are now being revised, but one marvels at the breadth and scope of their achievement, which catapulted Hebraic studies into modern times and made them part of the universal treasury of learning. Old rabbinic manuscripts were published with the meticulous paraphernalia developed in German universities. And, beginning with Heinrich Graetz, there followed a series of voluminous general histories of the Jews. In imitation of Herder and Hegel, a rabbi of Brod, Nachman Krochmal, boldly advanced a philosophy of Jewish history.

French and English Jewish historical societies were founded, and though their outpouring of Hebraic scholarship failed to equal the erudition of the German publications, it was a belated uncovering of other aspects of Jewish learning, often with patriotic overtones intended to illustrate French and English Jewish contributions to their national cultures. The declaration of principles in the first volume of the *Revue des études juives* forthrightly announced its purpose to make known the rich traditions of Judaism in medieval France, demonstrating how strongly French Jewry was bound to the motherland. French Jewish scholars were bent on integrating the works of their ancestors with the main expressions of French national creativity, a viewpoint not always shared by the German practitioners of the Science of Judaism, who often had universalist pretensions. The society that published the *Revue des études juives* counted among its members both Jews and Christians, not least of them Ernest Renan, who wrote for a general literary history of France a volume on medieval Jewish rabbis, many virtually forgotten.

In the twentieth-century efflorescence of Judaica, areas of religious experience, such as the mystical systems of the Cabbala, that had been neglected by the Science of Judaism were analyzed for the first time with the instruments of western scholarship by men of genius. Gershom Scholem's writings revealed faces of Judaism hidden from Christian eyes since the seventeenth century. Under his guidance, complex theologies were made comprehensible to literate Christians who had long since lost touch with the Christian Cabbala that once fascinated Renaissance poets and scholars. Simultaneously, Martin Buber spread knowledge of the folk wisdom of Hasidism, which had its origins in the rural areas of eighteenth-century Eastern Europe. The parables and sayings of hasidic rabbis had a special appeal among sophisticated Jews and Christians when transmitted through Buber's elegant German prose.

In the twentieth century, the United States joined in the worldwide scholarly recovery of Judaism, in which both Christians and Jews participated. Jewish theological seminaries carried on the learned activities of the German institutions to which they owed their inspiration. Hebraica were also cultivated in some of the great universities by Christian scholars: George Foote Moore at Harvard, with his two-volume summation of talmudic Judaism, and William Foxwell Albright of the Johns Hopkins University in his numerous biblical studies. Harry Austryn Wolfson, a Jew born in Eastern Europe, succeeded Moore at Harvard and published a series of major works in the overlapping areas of Judaism, Christianity, and Islam, with novel interpretations of the Church Fathers, Philo, Crescas, Spinoza, the Kalam. Medieval Jewish philosophy, particularly the works of Maimonides, came to occupy a place alongside the western philosophical corpus, as they had in the seventeenth century.

Though there is no sharp differentiation in the perceptions of twentieth-century Jewish and Christian scholars with respect to Hebraic studies—both adhere to the same academic rules of evidence—Christian scholarship has tended to concentrate on the Bible and the Judaic relationship with early Christianity, leaving rabbinic studies, both halachic and cabbalistic, to Jews, who are more likely to be trained from an early age in the Talmud and cognate Hebraic subjects. Christian scholars could not easily rival the outpouring of Jewish learning that was centered on Judaism, but they were able to carve out for themselves aspects of the field in which they could operate independently, sustained by chairs in theological institutes, seminaries, and a growing number of posts in secular universities. In addition to the two primary areas of Christian concern, the Old Testament and the history of Judaean sects in the centuries just before and after Christ, Christian scholars have been enterprising in the study of Near Eastern mythology, and archaeological expeditions sponsored by universities in Europe and America cast light on the early settlement of the Hebrews in Canaan and on the institutions of neighboring lands, even when some members of these exploratory expeditions were suspected of engaging in espionage as a sideline (*vide* the activities of Lawrence of Arabia and the Palestine Exploration Fund).

When the Zionist movement gained strength in the twentieth century and achieved at least part of its goal in the establishment of the state of Israel, historical evocation of the world experience of the Jewish people assumed a place of intellectual primacy in the new society. History and archaeology were recognized as powerful nation-building forces. Recapturing the past was imbued with nationalistic passion, though somehow the stamp of nineteenth-century German historical scholarship has not entirely worn off. Jewish historiography has retained an emphasis on detail, a wariness of generality, a self-centeredness, a dryness, a simple belief that accumulation is sufficient unto itself.

Through the agency of academic scholarship, Christendom became aware, at least in its learned circles, of the complexity of the intellectual experience of Judaism over the past three thousand years. The intricacy of the relationships between Christianity and Judaism through the centuries has now begun to be closely investigated. On both the Jewish and the Christian sides a certain parochialism has tended to prevail since the passing of seventeenth-century Christian Hebraism. It is reasonable to expect that the very recent proliferation of Judaic studies will fill the gaps in the history of connections between Judaism and Christianity, tearing down the cultural barriers that never separated the two religions as totally as official accounts and our ignorance have led us to suppose.

The Higher Criticism

During the first stage of Christendom's rediscovery of Judaism in the sixteenth century, the focal area of inquiry was the Bible. Scholars in Christian universities and monastic orders busily acquired the instruments needed for rummaging about in rabbinic literature, learning Hebrew and Aramaic, studying rabbinic grammarians, accepting some modes of interpretation, rejecting others. This period of exploration reached its climax in the Christian Hebraism of the seventeenth century, leaving behind as a record of its activity multivolume bibliographies, translations into Latin, and editions of the major texts of Judaica and Hebraica accumulated over a thousand years. The Enlightenment brought a marked shift in emphasis, as the Judaic world began to be studied in a "philosophical" spirit. The minutiae of textual interpretation were abandoned, and literary men calling themselves philosophes turned to the identification of the general spirit of Judaism or of the Jews as a people who were part of a secular *esprit des nations,* the subtitle of Voltaire's universal history. The philosophical way was finally enshrined in the 1820s in Hegel's lectures on the philosophy of history delivered at the University of Berlin, where Judaism was denigrated and crammed into an insignificant pigeonhole in the world history of Spirit itself: "On the whole the Jewish history exhibits grand features of character; but it is disfigured by an exclusive bearing (sanctioned in its religion), toward the genius of other nations (the destruction of the inhabitants of Canaan being even commanded)—by want of culture generally, and by the superstition arising from the idea of the high value of their peculiar nationality." [1]

Nineteenth-century scholars in theological and philological faculties of the expanding university systems handled the Scriptures as
secular objects and subjected the texts to all the manipulations to
which books are heir. As a body of literature, the Testaments were
methodically torn apart to lay bare a complex history of composition
and redaction. The time and manner of writing individual books, previously avoided or approached with caution, became principal topics
of inquiry and were treated with the same emendator's license that
humanist scholars had used—and continued to use—on Greek and
Roman texts. The ever more refined study of languages cognate to
Hebrew and Aramaic provided Christendom with sharpened philological instruments. Accounts of land explorations among contemporary Arab peoples were used to frame generalizations about
nomadic societies that were applied to the early Hebrews and pre-
sumably helped Christians to understand the lives of the patriarchs
and the Israelites wandering in the desert. Christian biblical criticism
jumped from the strained scribal hypotheses of Père Richard Simon's
Critical History of the Old Testament to feats of textual dismember-
ment so daring that one could never be sure of counting accurately
the numerous Isaiahs buried in the chapters traditionally bearing the
name of the prophet in the King James version.

As biblical criticism, aided by auxiliary disciplines, became more
sophisticated, and the old theological concerns were largely supplanted by historical, archaeological, ethnological, and linguistic inquiries, the ties between Judaism and Christianity could no longer be
passed over with a parent-child metaphor or denied by contrasting
the esprits of the two religions. Clearly, the relationship between Judaism and primitive Christianity was factual and specific, and further
researches were likely to unearth dramatic evidence of the close connections of persons, beliefs, and rituals of Judaic and early Christian
sects.

The Origins of Christianity

In the nineteenth and twentieth centuries, Christianity, now faced
with historical rather than theological questions about the origins of
its Church, inevitably became entangled with the definition of Judaism during the centuries immediately before and after the birth of

Christ, when relations with Judaism were the most intimate. The stereotyped parent-progeny formulas of the eighteenth-century philosophes were dry bones that had to be infused with a living spirit. Writing a critical history of the early Church presented the same dangers as compiling a narrative history of ancient Israel. As long as Christians had stuck closely to textual commentary on biblical sources, grammar and philology offered a measure of security, and obvious contradictions among the four Gospels, as well as a growing number of discrepancies among recently discovered manuscripts, could be reconciled by an emendator's ad hoc decisions. But once a critic ventured into the open fields and presumed to write a general history of Christianity, grave questions arose. The fundamental relationship between the two religions could no longer be dismissed with Augustine's facile opposition between Jewish corporeality and Christian spirituality.

As texts of the New Testament were set by side of quotations from the talmudic corpus, the evident kinship demanded further minute examination. The idea that the words of Christ might be illuminated by similar phrases that had once been in the mouth of a rabbi recorded in the tractate *Pirke Avot* (Sayings of the Fathers) had been broached in the seventeenth century. But the philosophes raised the more troubling question of the distinctive esprits of the two religions. Verbal parallels were themselves subject to interpretation, since the same words used in a different context may carry with them a fresh meaning. To believers, discovery of examples of talmudic dicta that bore resemblance to Christ's words merely increased the number of the predecessors without in any way diminishing the divine appearance of the true messiah. To the unbeliever, the triumph of Christianity could be conceived as the victory of one sect over rivals, whose teachings were in many respects not dissimilar from Christ's message. Back in the eighteenth century Gibbon left modern skeptics a classical presentation of the "causes" of this triumph of a Judaean sect throughout the Roman Empire, and in one sense his sweeping generalities have only been refurbished ever since. His key to the enigma lay in the spirit of zealotry Christianity inherited from Judaism.

The search for parallel utterances in the Talmud and the New Testament continued until the publication of an exhaustive twentieth-century compendium, but the piling up of passages that resonate to each other has to confront the theoretical issue of what a parallel signifies. Textual similarities became more impressive as they accumulated, but they did not settle the crucial question of the originality of Jesus and his gospel. Was Christianity merely another first-century Judaic sect like the Pharisees, the Sadducees, and the Essenes, one that happened to bear away the laurels of victory? Had Jesus meant to repudiate the Jewish law? Was Jesus himself an invention of a group of religiasts who called themselves Christians? Skeptics who raised doubts about the historicity of Jesus deeply affected Christendom's perception of Judaism. Christians were now openly confronting historical questions about the founder of their religion that Jews, out of caution, had previously either ignored or referred to only in Aesopian language.

In the twentieth century a major archaeological event, the discovery of the Dead Sea scrolls, heightened Christendom's engrossment with Judaism both in the university and among religious leaders of all persuasions. The manuscripts of what was identified as an Essene sect were utilized to reconstruct the early history of the church, and to reaffirm that the filiation between Christianity and Judaism was factual, not only ideational. The Dead Sea scrolls failed to shake the faith of true believers. Christianity had always recognized the existence of a prodromos in John the Baptist, and the addition of other forerunners was not necessarily disconcerting.

Contradictory positions on whether Christ was the true messiah had been the insurmountable theological barrier that divided Judaism and Christianity from the first century onward. Polemical literature had mounted through the ages over the correct reading of verses in Isaiah, Micah, and other books of the Old Testament by which Christians sought to prove that the sacred books of Judaism had themselves foretold Christ's advent and that the events of his birth, teaching, passion, and death transpired precisely as the Old Testament prophesied they would. The Jews had responded by denying the Christian interpretations, arguing that none of the explicit signs of the coming of a messiah provided in the prophetic texts had in fact been fulfilled. The clinching argument among Jews was always Christ's crucifixion. Instead of the messiah appearing in glory, as the Jews read the texts he was seized and executed as a common criminal. The Jews believed that the Gospels depicting his miracles and recording his words were fictions concocted by disciples who were heretics and false prophets condemned to death by Jewish law. False prophecy is a heinous crime, repeatedly denounced in the Torah and dramatized in the contest between true and false prophets in the first book of Kings. To the rabbinic mockery of Christ and the Apostles, repeated through the ages in uncensored passages of the Talmud, there was at some point added a Judaic history of Jesus in Hebrew put together by authors unknown and published by the German Hebraist Wagenseil in the seventeenth century. The complex manuscript traditions of this *History of Jesus* have only recently begun to be disentangled—there are different versions in numerous library depositories throughout Christendom. The printed text was blasphemous enough; but to this day no one has ventured to assemble the oral histories of Jesus popular among Jews, which have had a flourishing covert existence down to our own time.

Paradoxically, Jewish denial of the originality of Jesus was a replay of the deist challenge to the uniqueness of the primitive monotheistic religion of Israel. First, Israelite monotheism was shown by the deists to be far from the pure belief to which its adherents pretended. Second, even if the people of Israel were monotheists, the conception of one god was known earlier and underlay the beliefs of many other primitive peoples; in fact, monotheism was the original religion of mankind. The same arguments were now recast by Jews in a judgment of primitive Christianity. Apparent similitudes fail to address the problem of degree in debating the origins either of Israel's religion or of Christianity. Commentators may draw up circumstantial lists of similarities and differences, but in the end, if one wishes to emphasize originality and uniqueness, similarities can be dismissed as trivial and superficial. The appearance of Jesus can be viewed as the culmination of world history, the intrusion of an exemplar of moral truth by which all successive historical appearances are to be judged; or primitive Christianity can be regarded as merely another episode in world sectarian religious history, or perchance a digression in the history of Judaism. The creation of the just Elohim of the patriarchs, later revived by the prophets (after the unfortunate reign of the cruel Yahweh, the tribal God of Israel), can be solemnized as the axial event in man's moral history or treated as merely another incident in the history of the vicissitudes of mankind's moral nature.

Three nineteenth- and twentieth-century intellectual episodes in the perennial debate over the originality of Christianity and its kinship to Judaism merit special attention because of both the intrinsic worth of the evidence marshaled in the arguments and the widespread diffusion of the ideas generated: the worldwide acclamation of the writings of the French scholar Ernest Renan, the scandal provoked in German theology by David Strauss's life of Jesus, and, after World War II, the revolutionary explorations following the discovery of the Dead Sea scrolls. These three events transformed Christendom's perception of Judaism in so fundamental a manner that the traditional relationship no longer appears viable.

The Semites of Renan and Gobineau

The definition of Judaism in nineteenth-century Christendom was profoundly affected by the spectacular advances of comparative philology, the development of anthropological theories of race, and archeological discoveries in the Near East. Israel became intermingled with other peoples, as a new nomenclature was imposed on language groups and racial designations. "Semites" were originally conceived as a linguistic order by Michaelis' disciple Eichhorn in the eighteenth century; "Aryans" were an invention of early nineteenth-century English philologists led by William Jones, who studied Sanskrit in India, and by the German philologist Franz Bopp. It was Eichhorn who proposed labeling "Semitic" the cognate languages spoken by the Hebrews, Phoenicians, Carthaginians, Syrians, Arabs, and Abyssinians, inexact though the term was. Jones and Bopp recognized that the language of the Brahmins of India, Persian dialects, Armenian, some Caucasus dialects, Greek, Latin, Slavic, German, and Celtic tongues constituted another group they named Indo-Germanic or Indo-European. Language study, fortified by historical and religious inquiries, gave birth to the idea that these groups created literatures embodying different mentalities. Semitic peoples had no epics; Indo-Europeans had no eloquence in the prophetic mode. The science of comparative mythology recognized a set of common polytheistic myths among the Indo-European-speaking peoples. By contrast, Judaism and its offspring Christianity and Islam were religious systems distinguished by an austere monotheism, an absolutism, and a dogmatism that were fundamentally different from the playful mythologies of the Indo-Europeans.

The rediscovery of Judaism in the nineteenth century centered on the nomenclature that, inaccurate as it might have been, enjoyed a prolonged vogue in secular academic circles—the defining of collectives called Semitic and Aryan as races that were the driving forces of history. Though Renan conceived of these entities as linguistic conglomerates not necessarily coterminous with peoples, nations, or races in an anthropological sense, he frequently fell in with the growing fashion when he referred to Semitic races. Joseph Arthur de Gobineau's *Essai sur l'inégalité des races humaines* (Essay on the Inequality of Races; 1853–1855) still used the old-style three-color scheme of white, black, and yellow, and originally included Israel among the whites; but its history, according to Gobineau, had forced it into proximity with the black Chamites, who were inferior and passive, incapable of highly complex civilization. The denigration of Israel in later race theories carried Gobineau's concepts far beyond his own formulations. He had served for many years as French consul in Persia and his work was inspired by the monuments of the area, which he admired as creations of model Aryan empire builders, the Assyrians.

When Israel's history became part of a large linguistic or racial configuration with supposed common characteristics, its uniqueness was muted. In the seventeenth and eighteenth centuries, as information was gathered on all religions in the world, primitive and civilized pagan, the Jewish people's exclusive possession of many beliefs and ceremonials had been denied. In the nineteenth century, Renan set the religion of Israel in a broad frame that embraced many Semitic peoples, but he still esteemed above all other religious experiences the extraordinary performance of the Hebrew prophets in the ninth to eighth centuries B.C. Though there were similarities to the *navi* (prophet) of the Hebrews among other Semites, the power of the moral God in whose name the prophets of Judaea spoke was exalted above the deities of all other religions. For Renan, the appearance of the Hebrew prophets was a turning point in the religious history of mankind; the tidings of Christ were a continuation and in many respects a repetition of what they had taught. Ever since the seventeenth-century studies of Lightfoot, comparisons of strikingly similar verses in the Gospels and in rabbinic teachings had been piling up in the works of Christian Hebraists, and Renan had only to gather previously noted parallels and to adduce some new ones. But by the latter part of the nineteenth century, Lightfoot himself was largely ignored, even though he had been republished in English and German, while Renan became a towering European intellectual figure, widely read and translated. His eight-volume *Histoire des origines du Christianisme* (Origins of Christianity; 1863–1883), which antedated his other chef d'oeuvre, *Histoire du peuple d'Israël* (History of Israel; 1887–1893), placed in a Judaic spiritual landscape the birth of the God most Europeans worshiped.

A key question has remained the same since the first century: how does Christianity define itself with respect to Judaism? Even when nineteenth-century historians, emancipated from the bonds of the religious denomination into which they were baptized, constructed their visionary history of primitive Israel through a free-wheeling interpretation of the Old Testament, constant asides quickly betrayed their central concern: they were writing about themselves and seeking for the essence of the Christian religion. If the neologism "Judeo-Christian tradition" has a spiritual father, he is the Breton scholar Renan, who once studied for the priesthood at Saint-Sulpice in Paris and grew up to be a Christian heretic. With his history of the origins of Christianity and his history of Israel, he established the continuity of the religious beliefs of the west. His colorful style and recollections of his extensive travels in the Near East, which added another dimension to his narrative, made his work a triumph of academic history interwoven with metahistorical flights of fantasy.

Renan located primitive Israel in a constellation of Semitic nomads. The concept of a just El or Elohim, in contrast with the immoral, polytheistic gods of the Aryans, was common to all Semitic peoples, but the *beni-Israel* tribes imbued the idea of one God with overwhelming force when their Elohim assumed definitive shape in the teachings of their prophets of the eighth century B.C. Along with the Greek (Aryan) discovery of reason, the Semitic concept of monotheism was a prime element in the constitution of western civilization. Monotheism was born in the tents of Semitic nomads and was preserved unadorned by their puritanical patriarchal chiefs. Polytheistic religions were the creations of sedentary civilizations living in an imperial hierarchized system.

Gobineau had used similar terminology to differentiate the races, which he established as physical, anthropological categories. Ranging them in an order of excellence, he bestowed supremacy on the Aryans and turne'd the Semites into a collective body lower on the scale. That racial admixture with inferiors doomed the superior race to degeneration was the underlying assumption of Gobineau's anthropological thesis. While Renan placed the Semitic and Aryan races on an equivalent plane as agents in the building of modern civilization, Gobineau highlighted the radical inequality of races, measured by one criterion—the capacity to exercise power. Renan, though stressing the differences between the Aryans and the Semites, rejected a gradation of excellence; each race was exclusive of otherness, but all were equal in the creation of unique human qualities.

Both Gobineau and Renan relied on novel, often fanciful, linguistic analyses and the reading of hitherto undeciphered epigraphy in erecting their grandiose historical structures, intellectual edifices that leave contemporary readers as baffled as they might be by the euhemeristic creations of the seventeenth and eighteenth centuries, with their underbrush of etymologies dependent on mere auditory or visual resemblances among names of gods and kings. After the learned apparatus is stripped away from these racial systems, their assertions stand as bald as anything a euhemerist might have concocted. While operating on different premises, Gobineau and Renan exerted an enormous influence on the appreciation of Judaism in the second half of the nineteenth century. In the end, the most sophisticated interpretations teased out of a biblical text reflect the temper that is projected into them. Renan is now out of date and Gobineau's racial theories are taboo. The present-day emphasis falls on the *functioning* of the state or tribal or class organization of the past because that is the way we look at our own societies. We have ceased to conceive of them as bearers of ideas.

In 1862 Renan wrote of the "deux grandes races," the Aryan and the Semitic, which had become for him two spiritual poles; their mutual antagonism; and their ultimate fusion to create modern western civilization. When he described humanity evolving through a clash of opposites to achieve a synthesis, it appears as if the Hegelian philosophy of history, at least in a popular form, had belatedly begun to touch the French. From time to time, biological terminology contaminated Renan's historical thought. But whenever he resorted to the term "races," he was quick to explain that he was referring to their ideas, their philosophical and religious way of perceiving the world and expressing their inner being, and not to their physiological heritage. The Semites, who included Islam, had nothing in common with the Indo-European Aryan peoples; they represented two separate species, two different ways of thinking and feeling. In the chapbooks Gobineau has been placed among the fathers of modern antisemitism, while Renan enjoys the reputation of a philosemite. But in their writings there are more than occasional affinities.

Semitic peoples contributed nothing to political thought, Gobineau contended; only Indo-Europeans understood the nature of power. Renan glorified the gift of individual liberty as the primary Indo-European contribution to civilization; in Europe under Aryan influence temporary periods of absolutism always brought about reactions of freedom. The Semitic east knew only anarchy or despotism. In his inaugural lecture at the Collège de France, Renan portrayed David as a sort of rough condottiere—this was the king beloved of the Semitic God—and the wise Solomon as an oriental tyrant. "Theocracy, anarchy, despotism, such, gentlemen," Renan announced ex cathedra, "is the summation of Semitic politics. Fortunately it is not ours. The politics drawn from Holy Scripture by Bossuet (and badly drawn at that) is a detestable politics."[2] He then proceeded to demonstrate, with dogmatic assurance, that the high civilization of the contemporary world owed nothing to the Semites in philosophy, art, poetry, or science. Their wisdom consisted of parables and proverbs. Everything that passed for Arabic science was created by Persians and Spaniards, and was merely a poor adaptation of the Greek. The Semites, with Israel as their finest flower, had been appointed to a nobler mission: they were the founders of our morality and our monotheistic conception of God—a contention that Renan's intoxicating prose did much to propagate and that long remained a stereotype of popular universal history.

When Renan delved into the Old Testament as a sourcebook for the history of Israel, he believed that the text had been composed in its final form hundreds of years after the events depicted; everything in Scripture therefore required interpretation in the light of reason, eliminating the miraculous and explaining the behavior of the protagonists in the historical books of the Old Testament by constant reference to what had been learned from other Near Eastern sources. Renan radically modified the heroic temper in which the age of the judges and the early kingship of Israel had traditionally been cast, especially the period when the tribal Yahweh, vengeful and bloodthirsty, held sway—a falling away from the just Elohim, who was the original God of the patriarchs and was restored by the prophets. Renan treated the circumstances of the biblical narrative, particularly the miraculous events related in the Mosaic account, as obfuscatory embellishments of later priestcraft that had created Yahweh, a denial of the pure spirituality of the monotheistic Elohim born in the silence and unvarying sameness of the wilderness.

The patriarchal justice of the family tent reflected the authentic spirit of Israel. The sorcerer tricks of Moses and the political maneuvers of kingship were corruptions. Renan devoted much of the *History of Israel* to the survival of idol worship among the Israelites and the brutalities of the tribes under the sway of Yahweh. His hostility to the power-lusting Hebrew priesthood constantly obtrudes; only the prophets of Elohim were worthy voices of the religious morality that set human consciousness on a new course. The run of Israel's kings are presented as no better and no worse than the lords of the peoples in the surrounding territories the Hebrews conquered.

The just God of the early Hebrews, puritanical, severe, absolutist, was the negation of the licentious, though rationalist, gods of the Greeks. Both elements had been necessary for the development of humanity up to the present time. In the future, science alone would be sufficient to sustain that progress, without the buttress of religion. Indo-European reason would ultimately absorb the moral values of Israel—a process of amalgamation had been going on since the conversion of the Indo-European peoples by Christianity, a Judaized Christianity. Small wonder that Renan called down upon himself the wrath of the Catholic clergy, whose ultimate demise he was prognosticating. Assimilated French Jews, appreciative of his elevation of the role of Israel in molding the moral conscience of mankind, were grateful for his accolade.

The works of Renan and Gobineau provided nineteenth-century Europe with two contrasting overviews of Judaism. Both were heterodox and were colored by a new-fangled racial vocabulary that purported to be scientific. To the hasty observer, Renan presented Judaism as a creative force; Gobineau, as an agent of degeneration.

David Strauss and the Lives of Jesus

New Testament higher criticism had become a major subject in nineteenth-century German theological seminaries. The study of the synoptic Gospels produced scores of books that examined the variant versions of the life of Jesus and probed the historical accuracy of the New Testament accounts of events in Judaea under Pontius Pilate. The heterodox *Das Leben Jesu* by David Strauss (1808–1874), first published in 1835–36, brought the learned disputations to a boil. The historical-critical enterprise, which preoccupied German religious institutions from the beginning of the nineteenth century to the outbreak of World War I, inevitably involved inquiries into the character of the warring Jewish sects. In the rich theological literature, portrayals of Jesus, all based on New Testament exegesis, ranged from Friedrich Schleiermacher's philosophical treatises through outlandish inventions that converted the resurrection of Christ in gospel accounts into a conspiracy of the disciples to get hold of his body and revive it with antidotes to a poison secretly administered before the crucifixion.

Strauss set out to liberate the Christian religion from reliance on the miraculous deeds of Christ by raising and answering the question of what part of the Gospels should be considered legendary. Contrary to the promise of the title, in the first edition of his work he did not reconstruct a narrative of the life of Jesus, but subjected the four Gospels to relentless internal criticism. The fourth edition of Strauss's work openly repudiated the gospel of John as a fabrication. A popular new version in 1864, after the book had achieved European-wide notoriety, turned Strauss into the heresiarch of the Lutheran world. Steeped in Hegel's philosophy, like many German theologians of the mid-nineteenth century, Strauss conceived of myths, pagan and Christian, as among the loftiest manifestations of Spirit in the course of its development through time. The life of Christ and the birth of Christianity, which might be open to doubt as plain narrative history, were transformed into a powerful myth transcending factual accuracy and representing a higher truth. Orthodox Christians of all denominations, resistant to radical Hegelianization, were repelled by this blasphemy. Strauss imagined that his cleansing the Christian myth of spurious details in the Gospels would not further atheism but would exalt the grandeur of the Christian religion. Similarly, he did not consider unveiling the Judaic origins of Christianity a derogation of its religious worth. In the groping of Jewish sects for spiritual renovation, he saw proof that the religion of Christ was the fulfillment of a longing, the final realization that Pharisaic Judaism was inadequate and that spirit had to ascend to a loftier level.

If in our times the discovery of the Dead Sea scrolls has not troubled Christian believers more, perhaps it is because for over a century heterodox Christian scholars like Strauss and Renan had been treating the Essenes as proto-Christians. The favorable descriptions of communities of Essenes in the writings of Philo and Josephus had for ages been accepted among Christian theologians as worthy sources. By the time the scrolls were published to the world, an Essene influence on the spiritual origins of Christianity had been taken for granted by many scholars—though it was one thing to remark on similarities between the doctrines of the Essene sect and the message of Jesus, another to intimate that Christianity lacked originality. If Strauss and Renan are reread today, the scrolls appear as factual confirmation and elaboration of some of their reflections. The scrolls do not really answer the query of how revolutionary was the Christian emergence from the internecine strife of the Judaic sects. Historical studies of the generations of the rabbis were still in their infancy in Strauss's lifetime. Contrary to Lightfoot, he doubted whether the talmudic dicta offered conclusive evidence about the mentality of the Jews around the time of Christ, since the various passages in this corpus of tractates could not be dated with precision.

On the religious and historical problem of Jesus' relation to Judaism, the gauntlet had been flung down before the orthodox by the German theologian Hermann Samuel Reimarus as early as the eighteenth century. Reimarus forthrightly contested the idea that Jesus meant to break with Judaism and the Mosaic law. In manuscripts kept hidden during his lifetime, Reimarus asserted that Jesus had not the slightest intention of doing away with the Jewish religion and putting another in its place. Lessing scandalized the orthodox when he published these treatises, which he found in Wolfenbüttel where he was librarian for a period. The nineteenth-century German historians of the life of Jesus had but to revive Reimarus with the techniques of the much-practiced higher criticism.

Strangely enough, the first edition of Strauss's *Life of Jesus* was not censored by the Prussian government, while the revolutionary writings of Young Germany were. If books are expensive and heavy enough, governments tend to ignore them no matter how blasphemous they may be. The orthodox theologian J. A. W. Neander advised the Prussian government to leave Strauss's book alone; the potency of the poison it secreted was not at first recognized. Before and after Strauss, the rhetoric of studies of Jesus that emanated from German theological faculties, orthodox and heterodox, in the nineteenth century was very different from that of the flashy little works turned out by the English deists and French philosophes of the Enlightenment. The Germans wrote ponderous books, weighted down with footnotes and seemingly composed for professorial consumption.

The German scholars had to dispose of the historical questions related to the origins of Christianity before taking off on the wings of theology with a new freedom and without the burden of meticulous textual criticism of the Old and the New Testaments. During a period of transition, the scholar-theologian constantly hopped between a biblical verse and the pomposities of the German philosophies on which he was relying to make his theology sound modern. If he could dismiss much in the Gospels as folklore, irrational miracles, bad grammar, political or psychological implausibilities, he could then deal with "pure theology" instead of losing himself in the thickets of biblical criticism. In the end, the traditional view of the text as divinely inspired in its entirety was quietly abandoned by the mainstream of German and other major Protestant denominations.

The uneasiness over philological and historical criticism of sacred texts that prevailed in the Catholic Church was finally stilled with the Second Vatican Council's "Constitution on Divine Revelation," where formal approval was bestowed on such learned studies:

> To search out the intention of the sacred writers, attention should be given, among other things, to "literary forms." For truth is set forth and expressed differently in texts which are variously historical, prophetic, poetic, or of other forms of discourse. The interpreter must investigate what meaning the sacred writer intended to express and actually expressed in particular circumstances by using contemporary literary forms in accordance with the situation of his own time and culture.[3]

The truth and holiness of God's word remain intact even when, in marvelous condescension to human nature, it is couched in the speech of a particular time and place.

The Dead Sea Scrolls

Throughout history Christian scholars have turned to different faces of Judaism in their search for forerunners, progenitors, and parallels. Pico della Mirandola illuminated a primitive Cabbala as the soul of true Jewish belief and discerned Christian trinitarian elements in cabbalist manuscripts to which Jewish converts to Christianity had directed him. Lightfoot found parallels to Christian teaching in dicta of rabbis of the Talmud. Renan accepted Christianity's Judaic forebears and then traced the religion of Israel to the Semitic God called Elohim, who was born among nomads of the desert. On the morrow of the Holocaust, Christians were seeking out the beginnings of Christianity in the newly discovered Dead Sea scrolls attributed to the Essenes.

If Renan was no longer consulted as an authority, his philological scholarship considered antiquated by this time, the Dead Sea scrolls resurrected the question of the originality of Christ by dramatically advertising a hitherto neglected Judaean sect, the Essenes. The bond between Judaism and Christianity was reaffirmed, not through the exegesis of prophetic texts in Isaiah but in the interpretation of teachings of the Essenes, recorded in manuscripts that Bedouins found in jars in the Qumram area beginning in 1947. The weight of scholarly opinion now dates these scrolls from the middle of the second century B.C. to the third quarter of the first century A.D. While Christian scholars everywhere quickly recognized the kinship between the message of Christ in the Gospels and these newly discovered writings of the Essene teachers, there were at first marked disagreements among them in evaluating the importance of the striking affinities. The eminent scholar Albright hailed them as heralding a revolution in the appreciation of the beginnings of Christianity. H. H. Rowley, however, stressed that the members of the Judaean sect that wrote the scrolls were far less "dynamic" than the proselytizing apostles of the early Christians in propagating their ideas, and he cautioned against overstating the identification of the two groups. As the number of scholars studying the Dead Sea scrolls multiplied over the decades, these divergent attitudes have been maintained. Deciphering fragments large and minuscule has become a major enterprise, with attendant squabbles and scandals.

As variously nuanced interpretations multiplied in universities and seminaries, the background of the passion of Christ had to be repainted, not merely retouched. The primary analogy between Judaism and the precepts of early Christianity shifted from rabbinical sayings recorded in the Talmud—which Lightfoot had documented—to the teachings of the Essenes. While vague Essene resemblances to Christian precepts and rituals had formerly been based on summaries in secondary sources such as Philo and Josephus, now modern scholars were in possession of a library of the words written by the Essenes themselves and preserved in the Qumram caves. In the scrolls there are allusions to a teacher of righteousness and to his death; and there are many passages in harmony with known examples of Jewish apocalyptic literature and their vision of a final combat between forces of darkness and forces of light.

Archaeological excavations of the site and scientific analyses of the parchment and leather of the scrolls have brought to life the ancient community, with its ceremonial ablutions, sacred meals, scriptoria, and burial ground, adding a new dimension to the perception of their religious world. It had long been believed that Essene communities held property in common, practiced sexual abstinence, and enforced punishments on violators of their rules of conduct. These reports were now confirmed and fleshed out with details in a "Manual of Discipline." The scrolls, containing long passages from Isaiah and fragments from other prophets, bear witness to the remarkable stability of the Old Testament in its Massoretic version—despite minor variants—which has survived in Judaism until today. At the same time, messianic expectations and ritual performances described in the scrolls appeared to prefigure the rites of baptism and sacred meals in early Christian communities. The descriptive documents dealing with cult rules seem to have been written in a form similar to Mishnaic Hebrew, though it is surmised that the spoken language of the sectarians was Aramaic, the common speech of Judaea around the time of Christ. Variants in the fragments of the biblical books preserved at Qumram cast strong light on the linguistic complexities of Judaea around the time of Jesus. Painstaking analysis of the scrolls has uncovered a tapestry of biblical Hebrew, various derivatives of Mishnaic Hebrew, Aramaic, Greek, and Latin, each serving a different religious or literary purpose and sometimes related to social status and geographic area.

Although the particulars of interpretation have continued to be fought over in the scholarly world—the readings and datings sometimes diverge widely, and scholars such as Norman Golb believe that the scrolls did not emanate from the Qumram scriptorium but were written in Jerusalem and transported to the caves—the Christian and Jewish views of the century before the appearance of Christ have been altered, if not revolutionized. Christendom's comprehension of Judaism and Christianity will never be quite the same. Is Christianity a denial, a fulfillment, a reformation, or a corruption of Judaism? Did true Christianity, as old as creation, really antedate Israelite teachings? Five hundred parallels between the New Testament and the Dead Sea scrolls were assembled in a scholarly compilation by Karl Georg Kuhn and Willem Grossouw. Renan had already observed that Christianity began as a sort of Essenism that succeeded on a broad scale. But the character of the new evidence was different from previous hypothetical constructs and had a mightier impact. Popularizations of the content of the scrolls, such as those of the literary critic Edmund Wilson, diffused historical conceptions about the Judaic origins of Christianity that were part of Hebraist learning for three centuries, but had been closed to the uninitiated.

The early excitement of discovery having worn off, professors of Christian and Jewish studies have settled down to their normal inter- and intramural disputes about nuances of meaning and significance, involving archaeologists, philologists, and historians in the debate. The flow of manuscript finds appears to have ceased for the moment, but they have already brought a richer understanding of what to Christians remains the age of Jesus and to Jews is the tumultuous period of the collapse of the second commonwealth. Jewish historiography has been affected as profoundly as Christian, though the orthodox interpreters of both religions offer resistance to the new ideas. The revelations on the way of life and the teachings of the Essene community have once more raised the prickly question of the nature of Judaism in the period when Jews were dispersed throughout the Mediterranean.

Jewish history has traditionally been written from what may be described as a Pharisaic stronghold, and the history of Judaism in the diaspora has been a monument to the victorious outlook embodied in the Talmud, perhaps to the neglect of other parties and beliefs in Judaism that lost out. When the Christian scholar Erwin Goodenough brought forth his magisterial illustrated work on a hellenized Jewry whose settlements dotted the Mediterranean world and the Near East, he received short shrift from the Jewish scholarly establishment. Goodenough was in quest of a solution to the age-old problem of the origins of Christianity and the speed of its diffusion: in his judgment the urban hellenized Jewry of the Roman Empire provided the fertile soil for the growth of Christianity. The rediscovery of the Essene communities further draws attention from the legalist Judaism whose practices are excoriated in the Gospels and serves as another vantage point for criticizing the standard versions of Pharisaical Jewish history. Perhaps the Essenes were more than an outlandish sectarian sport.

The stereotypes of the triplex of Pharisees, Sadducees, and Essenes among the Jews, and the beliefs of early Jewish Christians, have long been the subject of scholarly reexamination. Instead of a simple opposition—the New Testament image of Pharisaical Jews and the Apostles in conflict—the religious world of the age of Jesus grows increasingly complicated in the light of new Christian and Jewish research. A careful study of early Christian heresies is one of the offshoots of the constantly renewed attempt to capture the spirit of the times in which Christianity was born. As the fruits of scholarship are harvested, the strength of the Judaic seed becomes more, rather than less, recognizable, but the seed is far more intricate in its composition than either Christians or Jews once imagined.

Christendom's perceptions of Judaism are today more eclectic and diverse than they have ever been. In the republic of letters there is a wide spectrum of opinion on virtually every aspect of the history of Judaism. Colloquies proceed with a reasonable measure of civility; intramural Jewish differences are often more acerb than those between Christians and Jews. Specialized journals, from *Sepharad* published in Spain to *Zion* in Israel, testify to a worldwide revival of scholarly interest in Judaica. The academic Christian eyes that examine historical Judaism have become too numerous to count. Old cataracts are being removed, new ones are forming.

In Search of a Common Ground

Since World War II, a number of Christian denominations have issued statements of their doctrinal positions with respect to Judaism.

The emphasis has usually been prospective rather than retrospective, though in 1968–1970 a group of Protestant theologians, with the participation of a number of Jewish and Catholic historians, prepared an extensive two-volume compendium, *Kirche und Synagoge,* in which past theological pronouncements by the European churches were summarized and excerpted. Historical in its schema, this formidable work, which has something of the aspect of a confession, had its origins in a proposal of the Evangelical Church of Germany to the Evangelical Center for the Study of World Views in Stuttgart, and was forthright in its avowal of the anti-Jewish consequences of Luther's "radical utterances." The work takes official cognizance of the blunt fact that the majority of those who participated in the crimes of the Holocaust had in one way or another been reared as Christians.

But the document that created the greatest stir in Christendom was the *Declaration on the Relation of the Church to Non-Christian Religions,* proclaimed by Pope Paul VI as "Nostra aetate" on October 28, 1965. Without formally repudiating past positions, the Second Vatican Council outlined the Church's current attitude toward Judaism, a momentous bringing up to date of doctrine as part of a comprehensive *aggiornamento.* Acknowledging "the bond that spiritually ties the people of the New Covenant to Abraham's stock," the pope formulated succinctly the position of the Church toward the Jews. "In her rejection of every persecution against any man, the Church, mindful of the patrimony she shares with the Jews and moved not by political reasons but by the Gospel's spiritual love, decries hatred, persecutions, displays of anti-Semitism, directed against Jews at any time and by anyone." [4] The text provides a commentary on the Gospel version of the Jews' condemnation of Christ that breaks with the traditional interpretation. After stating that the Jewish authorities and those who followed their lead "pressed" for the death of Christ, the pope declared that nevertheless a Christian was obliged to be selective in leveling the accusation of deicide and had to avoid castigation of the entire body of Jews now and in the past: there was no evidence that all the Jews living at the time of Christ were guilty, nor was the charge valid against the Jews of today. The Jews therefore are not collectively accursed forever on the basis of the account in Scripture, and in catechetical teachings the historical distinctions among them must be observed. The declaration repeats the testimony of the consanguinity of the Jewish people with Christ and recollection of the Apostle Paul's words about his kinsmen in Romans 9. Finally, the Church reknits the relationship between the Old Testament and the New, alluding to the mysterious foreshadowing of salvation through the Church in the chosen people's exodus from Egypt.

While eschewing institutional mea culpas for past behavior, the declaration attempted to redefine a relationship that until the very outbreak of World War II, and perhaps throughout that conflict, was marked by ambivalence. In the decades since the Second Vatican Council, the papacy has expressed in symbolic acts a changed spirit in that relationship. Most significant was the visit of John Paul II on April 13, 1986, to the central synagogue in Rome. In his address to the congregation, the pope elucidated passages in "Nostra aetate" that had remained murky, at least to outsiders. His commentary on paragraph four of the proclamation of Pope Paul VI more than twenty years earlier went further than any previous utterance in setting forth the new bond between the Catholic Church and Judaism. "The Jewish religion is not 'extrinsic' to us, but in a certain way is 'intrinsic' to our own religion. With Judaism, therefore, we have a relationship which we do not have with any other religion. You are our dearly beloved brothers, and in a certain way, it could be said that you are our elder brothers."[5] This was an unaccustomed variant on the family metaphors that Christendom has resorted to for so long. More recently, in 1987 the pope went well beyond the Second Vatican Council in reviewing the relations of Judaism and Christianity and asserted that, for any sincere dialogue, it was necessary for each participant to define its role in the light of its own religious experience. And in December 1990 the Vatican branded antisemitism as a sin against God and humanity and called on the Church to repent of the antisemitism that had found a place in past Catholic thought and conduct.

Protestant churches have also experienced difficulties in coming to grips with antisemitism and the Holocaust on a theological level. The political interests of some Protestant denominations with long historical ties to institutions in the Middle East make it hard for them to accept the demands of Jewish leaders for recognition of the unique role of the land of Israel and the city of Jerusalem. Confession of guilt, at least in a measure, for the evil of the Holocaust comes more easily in those denominations that have deep-rooted theological traditions about the wickedness of human nature and the pervasiveness of sin in this world.

In many western countries, the relationship of Christianity and Judaism has acquired a new rhetoric without formal ratification by any particular church body. The language has gradually insinuated itself into ordinary literate speech but its meaning remains vague. In the west, presidents and publicists, perhaps in quest of a phrase to counter the atheist materialism of official communist ideology, embraced the term "Judeo-Christian tradition." As a reflection of historical reality it is hardly authentic; but however late its origins, it has come to be contrasted with communist values in the "battle for men's minds." The Judeo-Christian tradition also betokens a rapprochement between Judaism and Christianity on some undefined level of discourse, though initially the idea was of secondary import. It is now a slogan leading a life of its own, exuding a spirit of amity and good will. Since it is devoid of doctrinal commitment, it can suggest the benign religious virtues shared by the believers of both faiths.

Christendom's rediscovery of Judaism has thus created a hybrid. To an open-eyed historian, the coupling of these ancient enemies as an adjective to modify "tradition" might appear bizarre, but the western mind has accustomed itself to other unlikely unions, for example Plato and the Bible. While the two traditions as they have evolved are different in form and content, they can be homogenized by making both essentially variations of monotheism, amending the role of Christ in Christianity, and presenting Judaism as a revered forerunner. There is no single, unchallenged, normative Christian or Judaic religion—witness the heresies and excommunications that fill to overflowing the annals of both religions. We know more about the bitter, often bloody, internecine wars that tore Christendom apart. The Jewish sectarian conflicts in the diaspora were less like military battles, perhaps because the antagonists were denied the power of the sword; nevertheless, the quarrels were acrimonious even though armies were not arrayed on open fields. Zealotry has been endemic in both Judaism and Christianity.

This historical essay, which began with Raimundo Martini's ominous *Dagger of the Faith,* concludes, in the idiom of Thomas More, with a utopian wish rather than a great expectation. Though historians may be reluctant to impose on the past a rubric such as the Judeo-Christian tradition, we should not foreclose the possibility of a future syncretism despite manifest institutional impediments. The interpretive skills of Christianity and Judaism have not become so dulled that the hybrid cannot be nurtured. Official Christendom is no longer imbued with what the eighteenth-century atheist Nicolas Boulanger called the "apocalyptic spirit," and the major churches do not vibrate with anticipation of the imminent second coming of Christ. Since neither the Old nor the New Testament is read with fervor except among charismatics and fundamentalists, and even they have not featured the deicide passages in the Gospels, in the course of time the Judaic part in the passion of Christ may be mythologized out of existence, even as the Romans were forgiven for the persecution of the Christians and a pagan Vergil came to serve as a guide for Dante. Judaism may be more tenacious than Christianity in the remembrance of things past, but over the ages the image of a crucified Christ may cease to be a hindrance to the fashioning of an ecumenical tradition that glorifies the Sermon on the Mount, the Psalms, the book of Job, and selected prophets who could be transformed into universal moralists preaching the ways of justice, righteousness, mercy, forgiveness. Voltaire in his more lucid moments would not have asked for more.

Illustrations

Notes

Index

Illustrations

1. Conrad Witz, *The Synagogue,* panel from the Heilspiegel Altarpiece (c. 1435). The tablets of the ten commandments, in imaginary script, are held in the right hand of the figure; her left hand grasps a broken staff. Basel, Kunstmuseum

2. Woodcut from Alfonso de Spina, *Fortalitium fidei contra judaeos, saracenos et alios christiane fidei inimicos* (Basel, c. 1475). Three blindfolded figures are identifiable as Jews by their headgear. The Saracen wears a sword and carries a halberd. Another enemy of Christ undermines with a shovel the base of the Fortress of the Faith. Houghton Library, Harvard University

3. Woodcuts from Johann Pfefferkorn's Low German *Jch heysch eyn boichel gyn der ioeden bicht* (Cologne, 1508). Above, ceremony of *kaparot,* a cock substituting for the ancient scapegoat, on the eve of the Day of Atonement (accusation of worship of the cock is implied); below, bathing, preparation of the meal, and eating before the holy-day fast. Houghton Library

4. Woodcuts from Anton Margaritha, *Das Ganz Jüdisch Glaub* (Frankfurt, 1543). The composite of ceremonies is related to the Day of Atonement: a Jew allows himself to be beaten before the holy day as penance for his sins; priests bless the congregation; poor Christians perform menial tasks for the Jews. Houghton Library

5. Paul Weidner von Billeburg, *Loca praecipua fidei christianae collecta et explicata* (Vienna, 1559), frontispiece depicting the author, imperial physician and convert to Christianity, with his family, at the foot of a cross; a passage from Isaiah 33 is quoted in Latin and Hebrew. Houghton Library

6. Rembrandt, *Samuel Manasseh ben Israel,* etching (1636). New York, Pierpont Morgan Library

7. Rembrandt, *Nathan Admonishing a Contrite David,* drawing (c. 1653). The artist's treatment of the subject (common in Mennonite sermons) is characteristic of his idealized representation of Old Testament figures. New York, Metropolitan Museum of Art, H. O. Havemeyer Collection

8. Rembrandt, *Ancient of Days and the Four Beasts from Daniel 7,* etching for original edition of Manasseh ben Israel, *Even Yekara. Piedra gloriosa, O, De la estatua de Nebuchadnesar* (Amsterdam, 1655). Houghton Library, Frances Hofer Collection

9. Johann Buxtorf the Elder, *Synagoga judaica* (Basel, 1661, edition expanded by his son), title page. The vignettes depict an instructor teaching Genesis in Hebrew, and a circumcision. Houghton Library

10. Johann Christoph Wagenseil, Latin translation from the Talmud tractate *Sota.* The subtitle reads: *Hoc est liber mischnicus de uxore adulterii suspecta una cum libri en Jacob excerptis gemarae versione latina* (Nuremberg, 1674), frontispiece. The woman suspected of adultery is led to the ordeal of drinking the bitter waters. Andover-Harvard Theological Library

11. Christian Knorr von Rosenroth, *Kabbala denudata seu doctrina hebraeorum transcendentalis et metaphysica atque theologica,* I (Sulzbach, 1677), frontispiece. The symbolic figure has her eyes on the ten sephirot (*videt alta*) and holds the keys to the Old Testament in Hebrew and the New Testament in Greek as she leads the way to the Palace of Secrets. Houghton Library

12. John Lightfoot, *Horae hebraicae et talmudicae in Evangelistas* (Leipzig, 1677). The frontispiece draws parallels between the Talmud, represented by a rabbi wearing a prayer shawl and phylacteries, and the Gospels of the four Apostles, inspired by the Holy Spirit. Andover-Harvard Theological Library

13. Raimundo Martini, *Pugio fidei adversus mauros et judaeos* (Leipzig, 1687), frontispiece. The Moor is prostrate, the Jew astounded, at the appearance of the "Dagger of the Faith." Andover-Harvard Theological Library

14. Carlo Giuseppe Imbonati, *Bibliotheca latino-hebraica* (Rome, 1694), portrait of the author. His Hebrew motto reads: "A Shield, and a Sword, and War." Houghton Library

15. Willem Surenhuis, Latin translation of *Seder Nezikin* (Fourth Order of the Mishna), frontispiece, in *Mischna sive totius hebraeorum juris, rituum antiquitatum, ac legum oralium systema* (Amsterdam, 1698–1703). The medallions illustrate the tractates of this Order, identified in Hebrew, beginning with the upper left and proceeding clockwise: First Gate, Middle Gate, Final Gate, Stripes, Testimonies, Sayings of the Fathers, Idolatry, Oaths, False Judgments; Sanhedrin is in the center. The word Nezikin, literally "damages," derives from the opening words of the First Gate. Andover-Harvard Theological Library

16. Romeyn de Hooghe, engraving of Micah prophesying the visitation of divine punishment on the sinful people of Israel and at the same time comforting them with a vision of the heavenly city, from Jacques Basnage, *Histoire du Vieux et du Nouveau Testament* (Amsterdam, 1704). Houghton Library

17. Augustin Calmet, *Dictionnaire historique, critique, chronologique et littéral de la Bible* (Paris, 1722), I, frontispiece. A figure symbolizing the Old Testament is in the shadows. The female symbol of Christianity holds a New Testament with the key to the true religion. Scrolls of the five books of Moses (with Genesis written in Hebrew) are strewn about. Houghton Library

18. Bernard Picart, engraving from *Histoire générale des cérémonies, moeurs, et coutumes religieuses de tous les peuples du monde* (Paris, 1741), I. A circumcision according to the Portuguese rite, at which Christian women are present. Houghton Library

19. Picart engraving (see figure 18). The interior of a synagogue on the Day of Atonement according to German Jewish practice (shoes are removed).

20. Blasio Ugolino, *Thesaurus antiquitatum sacrarum,* I (Venice, 1744), frontispiece. A Jewish high priest and a hooded rabbi are directed toward a female figure on a pedestal who represents the true interpretation of sacred history and the rites and laws of the ancient Hebrews. Andover-Harvard Theological Library

Figure 1

Figure 2

Figure 3

Difen langen tag feyzen fie mehr vñ fleiffig er/ den
den Sabbath/darumb fie denn an difem tag / in jh-
rer kirchen/ hiiter haben von einer öberkeit/ das jhn
nichts begegne/ auch ein armen Chriften/ der jhn die
liechter anzünde/ fo fie außlefchen/ vñ auch auffrich-
ten/ wenn fie niderfallen vnd dergleichen/ deñ jhr kei-
ner darff folliche arbeit ann difem tag thun / difer
Chrift hat gemeynklich ein femel/ oder ftuck brot in
der hand vnd jfft/ denn es feind nur arme tropffen die
folchs thünd/ wie oben auch angezeigt et c.   Beten
                                                Darnach

Figure 4

Figure 5

Figure 6

Figure 7

Figure 8

Figure 9

Figure 10

Figure 11

Figure 12

Figure 13

Figure 14

בבא קמא · בבא מציעא · בבא בתרא · הוריות · סנהדרין · מכות · שבועות · עבורה זרה · עדיות · פרקי אבות

Figure 15

J.V.mundorf. ex delin et. Fecit.

Rom. de Hoogc Inventor et. Fecit.

Figure 17

Figure 19

Figure 20

Notes

1. A Gateway to the City of Books

1. Raimundo Martini, *Pugio fidei adversus mauros et judaeos, cum observationibus Josephi de Voisin,* ed. J. B. Carpzov (Leipzig, 1687), prooemium, p. 2; the work was first published by Voisin in 1651. Arthur Lukyn Williams, in his *Adversus judaeos. A Bird's-Eye View of Christian Apologiae until the Renaissance* (Cambridge: Cambridge University Press, 1935), p. 250, n. 1, found that the apothegm is from Boethius, *De consolatione philosophiae* (3.5), who illustrated his point with a reference to the relationship of Nero and Seneca.
2. *Tractate Sanhedrin,* trans. H. Freedman (London: Soncino Press, 1935), II, 665.

3. Rival Interpreters in the Renaissance and Reformation

1. Michel de Montaigne, *The Essays,* trans. E. J. Trechmann (New York: Random House, 1946), p. 41.
2. Jean Bodin, *Colloquium of the Seven about Secrets of the Sublime,* trans. and ed. M. L. D. Kuntz (Princeton: Princeton University Press, 1975), p. 273.
3. Ibid., p. 471.

4. The Flowering of Christian Hebraism

1. Thomas Godwyn, *Moses and Aaron. Civil and Ecclesiastical Rites, used by the Ancient Hebrewes* (London, 1625), dedication.
2. Willem Surenhuis, *Mischna sive totius hebraeorum juris, rituum antiquitatum, ac legum oralium systema,* I (Amsterdam, 1698), dedication.

5. Seventeenth-Century Uses of Historical Judaism

1. Gilbert Burnet, *The Conversion and Persecutions of Eve Cohan, now called Elizabeth Verboon* (London, 1680), preface.

2. Thomas Hobbes, *Leviathan* (1651), ed. C. B. Macpherson (Baltimore: Penguin Books, 1968), pp. 508–509.

3. Pieter van der Cun, *De republica hebraeorum* (1617); quoted from the English translation, *Of the Commonwealth of the Hebrews* (London, 1653), preface.

4. Ibid., p. 172.

5. Ibid., pp. 175–176.

6. Moses Lowman, *A Dissertation on the Civil Government of the Hebrews* (London, 1740), pp. 1–2.

7. John Lightfoot, *Hebrew and Talmudical Exercitations upon the Gospel of Saint Matthew* (1658), ed. John Strype, in *Works* (London, 1694), II, 93–94.

8. Christian Schoettgen, *Horae hebraicae et talmudicae in universum Novum Testamentum*, I (Dresden and Leipzig, 1733), preface.

9. Increase Mather, *The Mystery of Israel's Salvation, Explained and Applyed* (London, 1669), "Author's Preface to the Reader."

10. "The Diary of Cotton Mather," in Massachusetts Historical Society, *Collections*, 7th ser., VII (Boston, 1911), 169–170.

11. Maimonides, *Mishneh Torah;* quoted from the English translation by A. M. Hershman, *Code of Maimonides* (New Haven: Yale University Press, 1949), III (book XIV), 240 ("Laws Concerning Kings and Wars," chap. 12).

12. Robert Fludd, *Philosophia Moysaica,* quoted in Joscelyn Godwin, *Robert Fludd: Hermetic Philosopher and Surveyor of Two Worlds* (London: Thames and Hudson, 1979), p. 17.

13. Johann Andreas Eisenmenger, *The Traditions of the Jews, or The Doctrines and Expositions Contain'd in the Talmud and Other Rabbinical Writings,* trans. and ed. J. P. Stehelin (London, 1742), I, preamble.

14. John Selden, *Table Talk* (London, 1689), p. 23.

15. Blaise Pascal, *Pensées,* in *Oeuvres complètes,* ed. Jacques Chevalier (Paris: Gallimard, Bibliothèque de la Pléiade, 1954), p. 1236.

16. Increase Mather, *Mystery of Israel's Salvation,* p. 64.

17. Ibid., "Preface to the Reader," signed by W. G.

18. Ibid., "To the Reader," signed by W. H.

6. Transition to the Enlightenment

1. Gottfried Wilhelm von Leibniz, *Sämtliche Schriften und Briefe,* ed. Preussische Akademie der Wissenschaften, ser. 1, *Allgemeines politischer und historischer Briefwechsel,* II (Darmstadt: Otto Reichl, 1923), 191–192.

2. Ibid., ser. 2, *Philosophischer Briefwechsel,* I (Darmstadt: Otto Reichl, 1926), 533.

7. Assault of the English Deists

1. Edward Herbert, Lord Herbert of Cherbury, *De religione gentilium* (1663); quoted from the English translation by William Lewis, *The Antient Religion of the Gentiles, and Causes of Their Errors Consider'd* (London, 1705), p. 2.

2. Ibid., pp. 2–5.

3. Ibid., pp. 31–32.

4. John Toland, *Letters to Serena* (London, 1704), p. 130.

5. Anthony Collins, *A Discourse of Free-Thinking* (London, 1713), p. 121.

6. Anthony Collins, *A Discourse on the Grounds and Reasons of the Christian Religion* (London, 1724), pp. 29–31.

7. Collins, *Discourse of Free-Thinking*, p. 114.

8. Henry St. John, First Viscount Bolingbroke, *Essays*, in *Philosophical Works*, V (London, 1777), 274.

9. Ibid., p. 334.

10. Thomas Morgan, *The Moral Philosopher* (1737), 2nd ed., I (London, 1738), 19.

8. The French Philosophes: An Ambiguous Record

1. Voltaire (François Marie Arouet), *Correspondence,* ed. Theodore Besterman, I (Geneva: Institut et Musée Voltaire, 1953), 146, letter 104, Voltaire to Guillaume Dubois, May 28, 1722.

2. Ibid., XCIII (1964), 140, letter 18,819, Voltaire to Nicolas Toussaint Le Moyne dit Des Essarts, February 26, 1776.

3. See "Key to Pseudonyms and Nicknames," in Voltaire, *Complete Works,* ed. Theodore Besterman, CXXXV (Oxford: The Voltaire Foundation at the Taylor Institution, 1977), 985.

4. Voltaire, *Correspondence,* XXXV (1958), 37, letter 7336, Charles Bonnet to Carl de Geer, January 16, 1759.

5. Ibid., LVIII (1960), 8, letter 11,672, Voltaire to Charles Augustin Feriol, Comte d'Argental, and Jeanne Grâce Bosc du Bouchet, Comtesse d'Argental, April 3, 1765.

6. Ibid., LII (1960), 127, letter 10,440, Voltaire to Comte and Comtesse d'Argental, June 10, 1763.

7. Ibid., IL (1959), 132, letter 9791, Voltaire to Isaac de Pinto, July 21, 1762.

8. Voltaire, *Dictionnaire philosophique* (1728), in *Oeuvres complètes,* Kehl ed., XLI (Paris, 1785), 136, article "Juifs."

9. Voltaire, *Notebooks,* ed. Theodore Besterman (Geneva: Institut et Musée Voltaire, 1952), I, 31.

10. Ibid., p. 31.

11. Ibid., p. 215.

12. [Paul Henri Thiry, Baron d'Holbach], *Opinions des anciens sur les juifs. Par feu M. de Mirabaud* (London [France], 1769), p. 2.

13. [Holbach], *L'Esprit du judaïsme* (London, 1770), pp. 171–173.

14. Ibid., p. 169.

15. Ibid., pp. 175–176.

16. Denis Diderot, *Encyclopédie* (Paris, 1751–1765), IX, 25.

17. Ibid., p. 24.

18. Rousseau, "Des juifs," in *Oeuvres complètes,* III (Paris: Gallimard, Bibliothèque de la Pléiade, 1964), 499.

19. Ibid., pp. 499–500.
20. Montesquieu, *L'Esprit des lois,* bk. 25, sec. 13; quoted from the English translation, *The Spirit of the Laws,* trans. Thomas Nugent (New York: Hafner, 1949), pt. 2, pp. 54–55.
21. Senger, *L'Esprit des lois mosaïques* (Bordeaux, 1785), p. v.

9. Catholic Vindications of Israel

1. Francisco de Torrejoncillo, *Centinela contra judios puesta en la torre de la iglesia de Dios* (Madrid, 1736; expansion of a work originally published in 1673), p. 102.
2. Ibid., p. 215.
3. Johann Conrad Hottinger, *Commentarius philologicus de decimis judaeorum, decem exercitationibus absolutus* (Leiden, 1713), "Praefatio ad lectorem."
4. Augustin Calmet, *Dictionnaire historique, critique, chronologique, géographique, et littéral de la Bible* (Paris, 1722), I, preface.
5. Ibid., p. 240.
6. Ibid., p. 242.
7. Antoine Guénée, *Lettres de quelques juifs portugais et allemands,* 3rd ed. (Paris, 1772), II, 44, n. 1.
8. Ibid., p. 66.
9. Isaac de Pinto, *Apologie pour la nation juive, ou Réflexions critiques sur le premier chapitre du VIIe tome des oeuvres de M. de Voltaire au sujet des juifs* (Amsterdam, 1762), p. 4.
10. Ibid., p. 12.
11. Ibid., pp. 13–14.
12. Ibid., p. 25.
13. Nicolas Sylvestre Bergier, *Encyclopédie méthodique: Théologie,* II (Paris, 1789), 363, "Judaïsme."
14. Ibid., p. 365.
15. Ibid., p. 377, "Juifs."
16. Ibid., p. 379.

10. The German Janus

1. *Grosses Vollständiges Universal Lexicon,* XIV (Leipzig and Halle, 1735), 1499–1500.
2. Johann David Michaelis, *Commentaries on the Laws of Moses,* trans. Alexander Smith (London, 1814), I, xix, preface, quoting J. G. Eichhorn.
3. Ibid., IV, p. 14.
4. Johann Gottfried von Herder, *Ideen zur Philosophie der Geschichte der Menschheit;* quoted from *Reflections on the Philosophy of the History of Mankind,* trans. T. O. Churchill (1800), abridged and ed. Frank E. Manuel (Chicago: University of Chicago Press, 1968), p. 137.
5. Ibid., p. 139.

6. Herder, *Aelteste Urkunde des Menschengeschlechts* (1774), in *Sämmtliche Werke,* ed. Bernhard Suphan (Berlin, 1877–1913), VI, 215.

7. Ibid., p. 387.

8. Herder, *Fragmente zu einer Archäologie des Morgenlandes* (1769), in *Sämmtliche Werke,* VI, 113.

9. Herder, *Aelteste Urkunde des Menschengeschlechts,* in *Sämmtliche Werke,* VI, 370.

10. Moses Mendelssohn, *Jerusalem, oder über religiöse Macht und Judentum* (1783); quoted from *Jerusalem: A Treatise on Ecclesiastical Authority,* trans. M. Samuels (London, 1838), II, 99–101.

11. Johann Friedrich Abegg, *Reisetagebuch von 1798,* quoted by Walter Grab, "Deutscher Jakobinismus und jüdische Emanzipation," in *Deutsche Aufklärung und Judenemanzipation,* ed. Walter Grab, International Symposium, December 1979 (Tel Aviv: Tel Aviv University, 1980), p. 270.

12. Johann Gottlieb Fichte, *Beiträge zur Berichtigung der Urtheile des Publicums über die französische Revolution,* quoted by Grab, ibid., p. 271.

11. The Aftermath of Liberation

1. Georg Wilhelm Friedrich Hegel, *The Philosophy of History,* trans. J. Sibree (New York: Dover, 1956), p. 197.

2. Ernest Renan, *De la part des peuples sémitiques dans l'histoire de la civilisation; discours d'ouverture du cours de la langue hébraïque, chaldaïque et syriaque au Collège de France,* 2nd ed. (Paris, 1862), pp. 15–16.

3. [Xavier Rynne, pseud.], *The Fourth Session: The Debates and Decrees of Vatican Council II* (New York: Farrar, Straus and Giroux, 1966), p. 342, "The Constitution on Divine Revelation," promulagated November 18, 1965.

4. Second Vatican Council, *Declaration on the Relation of the Church to Non-Christian Religions* (Boston: Pauline Editions, n.d.), pp. 5, 6–7; see also Rynne, *The Fourth Session,* pp. 335, 336. The "Commentarium officiale" in the *Acta Apostolicae Sedis* (Rome: Typis Polyglottis Vaticanis, 1966), p. 743, reads: "Praeterea, Ecclesia, quae omnes in quosvis homines reprobat, memor communis cum Iudaeis patrimonii, nec rationibus politicis sed religiosa caritate evangelica impulsa, odio, persecutiones, anti-semitismi manifestationes, quovis tempore et a quibusvis in Judaeos habita, deplorat."

5. *New York Times,* April 14, 1986.

Index